Theatre and Performance in Austria

Edited by Ritchie Robertson and Edward Timms
AUSTRIAN STUDIES IV

Theatre and Performance in Austria
From Mozart to Jelinek

Edited by Ritchie Robertson and Edward Timms

AUSTRIAN STUDIES IV

EDINBURGH UNIVERSITY PRESS

© Edinburgh University Press, 1993

Edinburgh University Press Ltd
22 George Square, Edinburgh

Typeset in Linotron Ehrhardt by
Koinonia Ltd, Bury, and
printed in Great Britain by
The University Press, Cambridge

A CIP record for this book is available
from the British Library.

ISBN 0 7486 0436 7

Contents

Preface ix

PART ONE

Peter Branscombe
The Land of the Piano:
Music, Theatre and Performance in Vienna around 1800   3

John Milfull
The Sexual Politics of Mozart's *Magic Flute* and
the Genesis of Viennese 'Charm'   20

Louise Adey Huish
Beating the Bounds: Fantasy and Farce in Nestroy's Comedy   27

Ian Foster
Altenberg's African Spectacle: *Ashantee* in Context   39

Konstanze Fliedl (translated by Ralph Manheim)
Love's Labour's Lost: Translations of Schnitzler's *Reigen*   61

Srdan Bogosavljević
Hofmannsthal's 'Mythological' Opera *Arabella*   73

John Warren
Friedrich Kiesler and Theatrical Modernism in Vienna   81

Klaus-Peter Hinze
Ernst Weiss: The Novelist as Dramatist   93

Simon Ryan
Performance and Provocation in Graz, 1960–1966   102

T. E. Bourke
The Staging of History in Felix Mitterer's *Die Kinder des Teufels*   116

Allyson Fiddler
Jelinek's Ibsen: 'Noras' Past and Present   126

J. P. Stern
Havel's Satirical Theatre   139

PART TWO: REVIEW ARTICLES

Denis McCaldin
Haydn Studies and the Mozart Bicentenary — 153

W. E. Yates
Recent Nestroy Scholarship — 158

Wendelin Schmidt-Dengler
The Ideology of the Salzburg Festival — 171

PART THREE: REVIEWS

Charles Ingrao
Anton Schindling and Walter Ziegler (eds),
Die Kaiser der Neuzeit 1519–1918:
Heiliges Römisches Reich, Österreich, Deutschland — 178

R. J. W. Evans
Waltraud Heindl, *Gehorsame Rebellen:*
Bürokratie und Beamte in Österreich, 1780 bis 1848 — 179

T. C. W. Blanning
Edith Saurer, *Straße, Schmuggel, Lottospiel:*
Materielle Kultur und Staat in Niederösterreich,
Böhmen und Lombardo-Venetien in frühen 19. Jahrhundert — 180

Tim Carter
Peter Branscombe, *W. A. Mozart: 'Die Zauberflöte';*
John A. Rice, *W. A. Mozart: 'La clemenza di Tito'* — 181

Ewan West
Erich Wolfgang Partsch (ed.), *Franz Schubert: Der Fortschrittliche?;*
Elizabeth Norman McKay, *Schubert's Music for the Theatre* — 184

Peter Branscombe
Hugo Aust, Peter Haida and Jürgen Hein, *Volksstück;*
Alfred Ziltener, *Hanswursts lachende Erben* — 186

Jacques Le Rider
Steven Beller, *Herzl* — 188

Leo A. Lensing
Burkhard Spinnen, *Schriftbilder:*
Studien zu einer Geschichte emblematischer Kurzprosa — 189

Konstanze Fliedl
Samuel Fischer and Hedwig Fischer, *Briefwechsel mit Autoren,*
ed. Dierk Rodewald and Corinna Fiedler — 192

Duncan Large
Robert Musil, *Precision and Soul: Essays and Addresses,*
ed. and tr. Burton Pike and David S. Luft; Hannah Hickman (ed.),
Robert Musil and the Literary Landscape of his Time;
Claus Erhart, *Der ästhetische Mensch bei Robert Musil* — 196

Contents

R. S. Furness
Phillip H. Rhein, *The Verbal and Visual Art of Alfred Kubin* 198

Ian Huish
Jura Soyfer, *Sturmzeit: Briefe 1931–1939;*
Gerhard Scheit, *Theater und revolutionärer Humanismus* 199

Jürgen Thöming
Gerald Stieg, *Frucht des Feuers: Canetti, Doderer,
Kraus und der Justizpalastbrand* 201

Tim Kirk
Jill Lewis, *Fascism and the Working Class in Austria 1918–1934* 203

Jill Lewis
Edith Prost (ed.), *'Die Partei hat mich nie enttäuscht ...':
Österreichische Sozialdemokratinnen* 203

J. M. Ritchie
Johann Holzner, Sigurd Paul Scheichl and Wolfgang Wiesmüller (eds),
Eine schwierige Heimkehr. Österreichische Literatur im Exil 1938–1945;
Peter Muhr, Paul Feyerabend and Cornelia Wegeler (eds), *Philosophie,
Psychoanalyse, Emigration* 205

Darius Gray Ornston
Malcolm Pines and Roy Wisbey (eds), *Translation in Transition:
The Question of the 'Standard Edition'* 207

Iain Boyd Whyte
Günther Feuerstein, *Visionäre Architektur: Wien 1958/1988;*
Peter Noever (ed.), *Tradition und Experiment: Das Österreichische
Museum für Angewandte Kunst;*
John Zukowsky and Ian Wardropper, *Austrian Architecture in the
Nineties* 210

Notes on Contributors 215

Austrian Studies 218

Preface

The central significance of the theatre in German cultural life has often been noted. The work of leading dramatists from Lessing to Brecht not only represents an outstanding artistic achievement, but has made a fundamental contribution to debates about German political experience and national identity. Even today the subsidised municipal theatres of the Federal Republic seem closer to Schiller's conception of the theatre as a moral institution than to the entertainment ethos of Broadway and the West End. To do justice to the German theatrical tradition, the British or American reader needs to take account of this didactic and ideological dimension. But the picture is complicated by the position, within the spectrum of German drama, of a distinctive Austrian tradition with its roots in baroque allegory and popular performance.

This volume focuses on essential features of that divergent tradition, emphasising the concept of performance. In late eighteenth-century Austria the key figures were not Lessing and Goethe, but Haydn and Mozart. It was the interaction between 'Music, Theatre and Performance', as Peter Branscombe's introductory article shows, that gave Viennese culture around 1800 its distinctive quality. Musical life in the Habsburg capital was sustained by a network of aristocratic patrons and enthusiastic participants. And music-making, sometimes associated with amateur dramatics, became an essential constituent of cultural identity for the aspiring middle classes. In Vienna the values of the Enlightenment were not debated with Schillerian moral seriousness but explored through the complex musical allegories of *The Magic Flute*, with its perplexing blend of traditional and progressive motifs. That same work reveals the ambiguity of Enlightenment social values, especially of prevailing attitudes towards women. Indeed, the 'Sexual Politics' of *The Magic Flute*, as John Milfull argues in a second article, reveal assumptions about gender roles which were to persist from eighteenth-century Austria through to the patriarchal prejudices of Vienna around 1900.

In the theatre, however, conventional restrictions can be overcome, as Louise Adey Huish argues in an article about the comedies of Nestroy. She argues that his comic situations are constructed on the borderline between the probable and the possible, creating a threshold where conventions are suspended and fantasy can find free play. It is this technique which enables him to explore the paradoxes of social identity with such wit and insight. This imaginative freedom is one of

Preface

the factors which has contributed to Nestroy's growing reputation, reviewed by W. E. Yates in a further article dealing with 'Recent Nestroy Research'. Nestroy was once regarded as the author of light-hearted if rather cynical farces. The scholarly advances associated with the new edition of his plays have enriched our sense both of the complexities of his work and of the cultural context in which his plays were first performed. But the barrier to a wider international recognition of his achievement lies in the lack of adequate translations.

The problems encountered in translating a specifically Austrian dramatic idiom are addressed more directly in Konstanze Fliedl's article on 'Translations of Schnitzler's *Reigen*'. This play is notorious for its transgressions of sexual decorum. Through an analysis of linguistic nuances which have defied the efforts of successive translators, Fliedl shows that Schnitzler's finest effects occur where deviations from the sexual norm converge with infringements of linguistic register. His dialogue reveals how both sex and language become transformed into commodities through the process of barter known as love.

The reduction of female sexuality to a public spectacle is the theme of Ian Foster's article on the ethnographic displays which were such a feature of turn-of-the-century Vienna. The entrepreneur Carl Hagenbeck specialised in bringing to Europe primitive tribes like the African Ashanti and putting them on display. Taking a text by Peter Altenberg as his framework, Foster documents the complex range of reactions to this black community, which raised fundamental questions about nature and civilisation, sexuality, race and gender, both for liberals and for anti-Semites. But where Hagenbeck's displays tended to present the Ashanti as exotic specimens in a human zoo, Altenberg's texts reaffirm their individuality.

Music, performance and spectacle again converge in the work of Hofmannsthal, the poet who became the advocate of a 'conservative revolution'. For Hofmannsthal, even the writing of librettos formed part of a conscious strategy of cultural politics. His mythological opera *Arabella*, analysed by Srdan Bogosavljević, implies that the collapse of the Habsburg Empire might have been avoided through a reconciliation between Germans and Slavs. Hofmannsthal's conception of performance as a key to cultural identity became most explicit after the founding of the Salzburg Festival, the subject of a recent study by Michael Steinberg. In an extended review of Steinberg's book, Wendelin Schmidt-Dengler shows how difficult it is to interpret Hofmannsthal's dramatic allegories and to define precisely the ideological implications of the Festival he created.

A striking contrast to Hofmannsthal's cultural conservatism is provided by Friedrich Kiesler, the exponent of modernism in theatre and performance. The International Exhibition of New Theatrical Techniques, organised by Kiesler in 1924, confronted the Viennese public with revolutionary new developments in stage design. Kiesler argued that the proscenium stage should be replaced by a spatial theatre that is expandable and dynamic. But, as John Warren shows, he failed to overcome the objections of the Viennese towards experimental styles of production. Thus the year 1924 marks the moment when the Austrian theatre missed its assignation with modernism. The resistance of Viennese audiences

Preface

to revolutionary forms of theatre is confirmed from another angle by Klaus-Peter Hinze's article on the plays of the novelist Ernst Weiss. When Weiss's Expressionist political allegory *Tanja* was performed in Prague in October 1919, the response was overwhelmingly favourable. But when it was repeated in Vienna two months later, it was hissed off the stage.

The conservatism of the Viennese public may help to explain why the revival of literary modernism in post-war Austria occurred not in Vienna but in Graz. An article by Simon Ryan shows that the breakthrough achieved by the 'Grazer Gruppe' was due not only to their journal *manuskripte*, but to a conscious strategy of 'Performance and Provocation'. Texts and sound poems were aggressively declaimed in public as part of a strategy of confrontation with the conservative cultural establishment. And literary cabarets were organised to deflate the pretensions of high culture in the name of pop art. The emergence of Peter Handke as a leading figure in modern German writing is closely linked with his apprenticeship in Graz, where the technique of 'abusing the audience' was initiated.

Three further articles deal with the political impact of contemporary dramatists. Felix Mitterer's reconstructions of historical subjects, analysed by Thomas E. Bourke, owe their effect to a documentary technique which confronts the audience with some of the most problematic episodes from Austrian history, notably the seventeenth-century Salzburg witchcraft trials. Elfriede Jelinek's reworking of motifs from Ibsen's *Doll's House*, as Allyson Fiddler shows, owes its impact to a combination of militant feminism and compelling stage technique, particularly the use of music and montage. Finally, the satirical comedies of Vaclav Havel are analysed in an article by the late J. P. Stern, which focuses on the thematisation of language. The application of linguistically sensitive techniques of satirical comedy to the culture of communism transforms Havel's plays into parables about the predicament of human identity in the modern age.

The volume concludes with a series of book reviews, dealing not only with publications on Haydn, Mozart, Schubert and Viennese popular comedy, but also with studies ranging well beyond the theme of theatre and performance. They help to confirm the distinctiveness of Austrian culture, whether the subject is Musil or Soyfer, Canetti or Kubin, Herzl or Freud. Austrian writers, as Hofmannsthal puts it in a letter quoted from his correspondence with the publisher Samuel Fischer, have hesitated to identify with the mainstream of German culture, since they find themselves 'halfway to somewhere else'. Even the final book review, which deals with recent developments in architecture, reinforces this impression of divergence. For in Vienna the characteristic emphasis, from Otto Wagner through to Hundertwasser, has been on fantasy rather than rationality. Architecture, too, becomes a performance. Indeed, in the contemporary cult of 'architectural delight unconstrained by function' the spirit of the baroque is born again.

Part One

The Land of the Piano: Music, Theatre and Performance in Vienna around 1800

Peter Branscombe

Vienna at the end of the eighteenth century witnessed what is generally regarded as the most glorious period in the history of music; it was also a period of lively theatrical and artistic activity. For the historian, the period marks the change from a predominantly feudal society to one in which, although the imperial family and the aristocracy maintained positions of great power, the middle classes had achieved a considerable measure of autonomy, nowhere more marked than in cultural life. The population of the city grew slowly, as the figures from the official censuses make clear: in 1783 the inner city and its suburbs had a population of 207,797. By 1800 the number had risen to 231,049, but in 1812 – doubtless owing to the exigencies of the wars with France – the figure had slipped back to 224,548. Thereafter the population began to rise quite steeply: 260,224 people in 1820, 317,768 in 1830 and, by 1851, 431,147.[1]

The cultural historian will be aware that, though civic pride led to the foundation of Vienna's principal musical institution, the Gesellschaft der Musikfreunde, in 1812, and to the expansion of the Akademie der bildenden Künste in the same year, the number of Vienna's theatres did not increase with the growth in the population. Indeed it may be held to have decreased with the dissolution of the Theater auf der Landstraße in the mid-1790s, even if the replacement of the Theater auf der Wieden by the splendid and considerably larger Theater an der Wien in 1801, and the rebuilding of the Theater in der Leopoldstadt as the Carltheater in 1847, with a capacity of 2,000, as well as modifications to other theatres, did produce some increase in overall capacity. It was 1869 and 1888 respectively before the Kärntnertor-Theater and the old Burgtheater on the Michaelerplatz were replaced by the grandiose, and considerably larger, new buildings of the Hofoper (Staatsoper) and Burgtheater on the Ringstraße. By then, however – to look far beyond the chronological confines of the present study – the native vitality of the popular theatre tradition had ebbed away, to be replaced by the more international genre of operetta, and the impromptu nature of the city's musical life had given way to the more strictly regimented concert series of the Philharmoniker and the vogue for celebrity recitals.

At the turn of the century the spirit of the baroque lingered on. Martin Johann ('Kremser') Schmidt did not die until 1801, and in the opera house a work such as *The Magic Flute* proclaimed its allegiance to the old order in several ways: the central conflict between Good and Evil is a legacy of the baroque; the bold transformation scenes, the use of traps and a flying machine, as well as the numerous sets of considerable complexity and brilliance, hark back to the splendours of the Jesuit theatre and the court opera of a century earlier; and Mozart in his score employs historicising contrapuntal devices such as fugue, fugato and chorale prelude, as well as hymn, in addition to more modern forms from *opera seria* and *opera buffa*, folksong and, especially, of course, Singspiel. Vincenz Sachetti, who was responsible for the designs for the new productions of the opera in the Freihaus-Theater in 1798 and the new Theater an der Wien in 1802, may also have been the artist commissioned by Schikaneder in the latter year to paint the fresco on the ceiling of his little Schloss in Nussdorf, which depicts the Queen of the Night in triumph on a cloud-chariot drawn by night birds, and accompanied by her Three Ladies, Monostatos, bats and two putti.[2]

The range of talents of many of Vienna's artists in the period under review is by modern standards remarkable. Not only were most composers also virtuosi on one or more instruments: some of them were gifted singers or actors as well. Further, there were no rigid barriers preventing performers from distinguishing themselves in both the classical and the popular repertory. Of the singers who took part in the premiere of *The Magic Flute*, for instance, Benedict Schack and Franz Xaver Gerl as well as Schikaneder himself were skilful composers of unassuming theatre music (Schack had also been a fine woodwind player and may have played Tamino's flute as well as singing the part); the first Pamina, Anna Gottlieb, had created the role of Cherubino in *The Marriage of Figaro* at the court opera as a twelve-year-old, and in 1792 was to begin a long second career as comic actress in the Theater in der Leopoldstadt; Joseph Nouseul had been an actor in the court theatre, and was to be one again, after his engagement at the Theater auf der Wieden. Vincenc Tuček, later a successful composer and music director in Vienna and Budapest, came to notice when he sang Tamino in the first Czech production of *The Magic Flute* at Prague in 1794. Ignaz Schuster, one of the finest of the comic actors in the Leopoldstadt Theatre in the second and third decades of the nineteenth century, was a good composer and versatile singer, able in Bäuerle's parody of Rossini's *Tancredi* to do a brilliant and sustained take-off of the distinguished court opera soprano Borgondio, as well as sing bass in the court chapel choir.[3] And a visitor to Vienna, J. W. Fischer, writes of hearing Mass in the Peterskirche on a Sunday morning in July 1802:

> Besonders zog unter den Sängern auf dem Chore ein sehr braver Baß meine Aufmerksamkeit auf sich. Man sagte mir, daß es Herr [Leopold] Pfeiffer vom Leopoldstädter Theater sey. Ich habe nicht bald irgendwo einen braveren Kirchensänger gehört.[4]
>
> [Among the singers in the choir-loft my attention was particularly drawn to a very good bass. I was told it was Herr [Leopold] Pfeiffer of the Leopoldstadt Theatre. I have hardly heard a better church singer anywhere.]

Joseph Drechsler, best remembered as the composer of three of Raimund's plays and as a prolific composer for the Leopoldstadt in the 1820s, started his career on the music staff of the court opera and concluded it as Kapellmeister at St Stephen's Cathedral (from 1844); during his middle years he was concurrently professor of organ, harmony and thoroughbass at the seminary of St Anna, choirmaster of its church, and founder of a music school; Johann Strauss the younger was later one of his pupils; from 1823 Drechsler was choirmaster at the Pfarrkirche am Hof, and Beethoven recommended him to the Archduke Rudolf in that year.

Movement between theatres and genres was not uncommon. J. H. F. Müller, a tower of strength to the emergent Burgtheater company, had begun his career as a disciple of Prehauser and Weiskern in the Hanswurst ensemble.[5] Joseph Weidmann made his career as actor, director and playwright in the Burgtheater, yet he was widely regarded as being stylistically and temperamentally closer to the suburban theatre tradition; indeed, an entry in Wenzel Müller's diary records Weidmann's assumption of a genuine *Volkskomödie* role:

> D. 12te July 1804 wurde das neu=Sontagskind im Theater an der Wien gegeben, H: Weidmann k: k: Hof Schauspieler, spielte den Hausmeister darin.[6]

> [The 12th July 1804 *Das Neusonntagskind* was given in the Theater an der Wien. Herr Weidmann, imperial and royal court actor, played the concierge in it.]

Friedrich Baumann ('Baumann der Jüngere') moved in the opposite direction. From the theatre at Brünn and then the Theater in der Leopoldstadt (where Mozart wrote for his benefit night on 7 March 1788 'Ein deutsches Kriegslied', K539) Baumann progressed to the court theatre and the Theater an der Wien, maintaining his reputation as a talented singer and actor in works like Schenk's *Der Dorfbarbier*, in which a contemporary called him 'die derbe, komische Natur selbst' ('coarse, comic nature personified'),[7] and, as the last exponent in the Burgtheater 'im niedrig komischen Fache' ('in the low comic genre'), making much of roles like Klaus in *Die deutschen Kleinstädter* and Peter Gutschaf in *Die Organe des Gehirns*, both by Kotzebue (Castelli, I, p. 225).

For much of its history Vienna has hardly deserved its reputation as a city in the forefront of artistic development. However, during the 1780s, and perhaps intermittently in the following decades, this cherished belief is rather more than a myth. The theatre as well as music flourished. Apart from the two court theatres, which catered mainly for the aristocracy and the upper middle classes, there were four suburban theatre companies catering for the local communities, though there is abundant evidence that the audiences included aristocrats and burghers from the city. There was also a very large number of amateur or semi-amateur groups performing frequently, mainly in private houses or in small locales. Though one may question the accuracy of the figure, Joseph Sonnleithner states in his introduction to *Die dramatische Unterhaltung unter guten Freunden* that there were no fewer than 84 amateur theatre groups performing operatic as well as dramatic works for select audiences of friends.[8]

The Land of the Piano

Lest the inclusion of amateur performances of opera should appear an unlikely exaggeration, it may be salutary to remind ourselves that on 13 March 1786 Mozart directed a private performance of *Idomeneo* in the Palais Auersperg, which he had revised for the occasion, rewriting the part of Idamante for tenor and adding the duet 'Spiegarti non poss' io' and the aria 'Non temer, amato bene'. Other operatic performances mounted by Prince Johann Adam Auersperg included Righini's *Armida* in July 1782 and, just over a month before the staging of *Idomeneo*, Gluck's *Alceste* under the composer's direction; there was also a performance of Salieri's *Axur* there in January 1788.[9] Further indications of the range and adventurousness of Viennese amateur musical performances are to be found in the pages of the annual *Theater-Kalender* published at Gotha, for instance in the issues for 1793 and 1794 under 'Nachrichten von gesellschaftlichen Bühnen ... Wien'.[10]

Mrs St George, the widow of a British army colonel, mentions in the journal of her visit to Vienna in 1800 that she attended a concert performance of an opera at the house of a 'Dr. Franc' – presumably Dr Johann Peter Frank, father of the Dr Joseph Frank whose memoirs were included in Robert Prutz's and Wilhelm Wolfsohn's *Deutsches Museum*,[11] and who married the well-known singer Christine Gerardi in 1798.

> June 30 [1800]. – Went to a concert at Dr Franc's. He is a physician, who is supposed to have great skill in his profession. His son's wife sings remarkably well, and with some other amateurs performed the opera of *The Horatii and Curiatii* – the words Metastasio's, the music Cimarosa's – the former very poetical and affecting, the latter brilliant, pathetic, and expressive. I find the *noblesse* can sometimes wave etiquette, and sacrifice their dignity to their amusement, for the auditors were chiefly of the first class.[12]

Concert Life in Vienna

There are many lacunae in the documentation for the early history of concert life in Vienna. Even after the foundation of the Gesellschaft der Musikfreunde there was no regularly organised series of concerts, and the Gesellschaft's orchestra was initially amateur (the traditional date of the foundation of the Vienna Philharmonic Orchestra is 1842). Earlier attempts to establish concert series had only limited success. Forty years before the establishment of the Gesellschaft the Tonkünstler-Societät was instigated by Gassmann for charitable purposes, specifically the support of retired musicians and their families. Its first concert (there were normally four each year, two in Advent, two in Lent, with a major choral work repeated in each pair of concerts) took place on 29 March 1772 with Gassmann's oratorio *La Betulia liberata* as the principal item. From the beginning of the new century Haydn's two late oratorios began to dominate the programmes, often producing very substantial sums for the charity. Another institution that favoured sacred choral music was the series of *Concerts spirituels* inaugurated by Franz Xaver Gebauer in the autumn of 1819;

here the normal pattern was a mixture of orchestral music (usually including a symphony by Haydn, Mozart or Beethoven) and choral music – either a complete mass, or movements from choral works. J. S. Bach did not figure in the programmes until 1839, but Handel was regularly performed, though usually with the revised orchestration initially of Mozart, and then of I. F. Mosel.

The cult of Handel in Vienna, and indeed the interest in earlier music, is largely attributable to the efforts of an amateur, Baron Gottfried van Swieten, son of Maria Theresia's court physician, and Prefect of the Imperial Library as well as President of the Court Commission on Education and Censorship. He presumably became acquainted with the music of Bach and Handel during his years as Austrian Ambassador in Berlin (1770–7); soon after his return to Vienna he began a regular series of concerts of old music, held on Sundays at noon in his rooms at the library. Among the most enthusiastic participants was Mozart.

> Ich wollte sie gebeten haben, daß wenn sie mir das Rondeau zurück schicken, sie mir auch möchten die 6 fugen vom händel, und die Toccaten und fugen vom Eberlin schicken. – ich gehe alle Sonntage um 12 uhr zum Baron von Suiten – und da wird nichts gespiellt als Händl und Bach. – ich mach mir eben eine Collection von den Bachischen fugen. – so wohl sebastian als Emanuel und friedeman Bach. – Dann auch von den händlischen.[13]

> [I wanted to ask you, when you send me back the Rondeau, be so kind and send me also the 6 fugues by händel, and the Toccatas and fugues of Eberlin. – I go every Sunday at 12 o'clock to Baron van Swieten – and nothing is played there but Händl and Bach. – I'm busy making myself a Collection of Bach fugues. – sebastian as well as Emanuel and friedeman Bach. – Also of händl's too.]

Apart from directing these informal Sunday concerts, intended for a small circle of interested acquaintances, van Swieten played an important part in the promotion of choral music, most obviously in his encouragement of Haydn to compose *Die Schöpfung (The Creation)* and *Die Jahreszeiten (The Seasons)*, the texts of which he prepared, and for the setting of which he provided numerous suggestions.[14] It is surely no coincidence that in 1779, the year after Swieten took up his new post in Vienna, Handel's name appears for the first time in the annals of the Tonkünstler-Societät, *Judas Maccabaeus* in Starzer's arrangement being given in the Kärntnertor-Theater on 21 and 23 March. In the mid-1780s Swieten was the moving force behind the formation of the Gesellschaft der Associierten, a group of music-loving noblemen who put on performances of oratorios, beginning with *Judas Maccabaeus* in 1786, and reaching their apogee with the first performances of *Die Schöpfung* in 1798 and *Die Jahreszeiten* in 1801. These concerts took place in Prince Schwarzenberg's palace on the Mehlmarkt, or in Count Johann Esterházy's palace; other performances took place in Jahn's Rooms in the Himmelpfortgasse or in the Burgtheater. Mozart's activities with the Associierten included directing the performance of C. P. E. Bach's *Die Auferstehung und Himmelfahrt Christi* in Lent 1788, and orchestration and direction of Handel's *Messiah* (1789), *Alexander's Feast* and the St Cecilia Ode (the revisions were completed in July 1790; it is not known when these works were first performed). Mozart also arranged *Acis and Galatea*, first heard at a concert arranged for his own benefit at Jahn's Rooms in November 1788 and then repeated at the Esterházy Palace on 30 December 1788. The Handel cult in Vienna, which began well after the composer's death and witnessed performances of *Alexander's Feast* in Lent 1771 and 1772,[15] as well as an earlier performance of the St Cecilia Ode,[16] is a striking example of the incipient sclerosis of the musical arteries that later tended to make Vienna not the world's musical capital so much as a museum for the accepted masterpieces of previous generations.

The number and kind, as well as the location, of concerts in Vienna in this period is bewildering. Mary Sue Morrow has produced valuable calendars of the public and private concerts given between 1761 and 1810 that suggest a remarkable variation in the frequency of such events.[17] We must not assume that even her researches have traced every concert, particularly in the private sphere (where problems of definition arise). In the thirty-one years between 1780 and 1810 – roughly the period from Mozart's arrival in Vienna until the death of Haydn – there were 347 private concerts (on average eleven each year, though one was recorded for 1780, and as many as twenty-seven in 1784 and twenty-six in 1809) and 733 public concerts (on average twenty-four each year, with a low figure of two in 1790, and highs of forty-seven in 1785 and forty-one in 1808). Documentation is comparatively full for the 1780s, thanks largely to the intensity of research into Mozart's activities; the decline in musical life during the Turkish War is clear from the figures both for public and private concerts: after three successive years, 1786–8, each with thirteen private events, the number per year falls to four and three in 1789 and 1790, before picking up somewhat with nine, six and sixteen in the years 1791–3. During this period the figures for public concerts are fourteen, twenty-six and twenty-three in 1786–8, ten in 1789, and two in 1790, followed by twenty-five, ten and twenty-six for the years 1791–3. The deaths of two monarchs in three years help to account for the low figures in 1790 and 1792.

A feature of Viennese musical life during this period is the patronage, and in some cases more active participation, of members of the greatest families in the land, from the Habsburgs down. One repeatedly meets the names of the princely families Esterházy, Golitsin (Galitzin), Grassalkovics, Lobkowitz, Lichnowsky, Paar, Palm, Sachsen-Hildburghausen, Schwarzenberg and Trauttmannsdorff, and among the counts' families those of Apponyi, Batthyany, Franz and Johann Esterházy, Fries, Hatzfeld, Kinsky, Razumovsky, Thun-Hohenstein and Zichy. Some of these noblemen kept their own orchestras, or at least wind bands (*Harmonien*); they participated in Vienna's musical life by performing, arranging and promoting concerts, and donating sums for musical purposes such as the performance and publishing of works, as well as, in Beethoven's case, by guaranteeing him an annual income. If Eduard Hanslick is somewhat too tidy in his judgment that this golden age of aristocratic patronage came to an end in 1809,[18] the year of the second French occupation, the foundations for a new musical culture were by then beginning to be established, thanks to to the growing influence of middle-class or recently ennobled families such as the Arnsteins, Greiners, Hochenadels and Sonnleithners.

Early fruits of the increasing influence of the bourgeoisie include the foundation of the Gesellschaft der Musikfreunde in 1812, its object being 'the advancement of music in all its branches', and the establishment of a conservatory in 1817.[19] Other aims of the Gesellschaft, not all of them swiftly achieved, included the performance of grand choral works (starting with Handel's *Timotheus*, as *Alexander's Feast* was then known, in the Winter Riding School in 1812 and 1813) and of more modest orchestral and chamber concerts for members, held in the Redoutensäle of the Hofburg; the encouragement both of individual talent and even more of corporate ensemble playing; and the establishment of a music library (the later Archiv der Musikfreunde). With the publication of the first number of the *Wiener allgemeine musikalische Zeitung* in 1813, re-established by Mosel in 1817, Austria acquired its first regular music periodical.

Despite the wealth of musical life in this period, Vienna was slow to acquire custom-built concert halls. Even after the foundation of the Musikfreunde it was some years before they acquired, rebuilt and opened their hall in the house 'Zum roten Igel' in the Tuchlauben which was in use from 1831 until the Neues Musikvereinsgebäude was completed in January 1870. The principal venues for concerts in the age of Haydn, Mozart and Beethoven were the five permanent theatres, the casino in the Mehlgrube between the Kärntnerstraße and the Neuer Markt, the Redoutensäle of the Hofburg, Ignaz Jahn's Rooms in the Himmelpfortgasse, the Trattnerhof on the Graben, the refreshment pavilion in the Augarten, and various other open-air locations in the summer months. In 1807 and 1808 the Festsaal of the University was the venue for a notable series of concerts, the last of which, the famous performance of *Die Schöpfung* under Salieri's direction in honour of Haydn's 76th birthday, saw the old composer's last public appearance.

Where private concerts are concerned, a bewildering array of locations was used; in many cases one can only guess at the precise location, but numerous musical events were held in the palaces of the Princes Paar and Golitsin, and the town palaces of the Princes Schwarzenberg and Lobkowitz, and of the Counts Esterházy and Fries, to give some prominent examples. Some of these palaces were large enough to accommodate considerable numbers of performers and listeners. The Palais Lobkowitz just off the Augustinerstraße has a special place in the affections of Beethoven's admirers as the site of the first performances of many of his works: the 'Eroica' and Fourth symphonies, the *Coriolan* Overture, the Fourth Piano Concerto and the op. 96 Violin Sonata. After the Congress of Vienna, when the sway of the old aristocratic families was on the decline, an increasing number of minor aristocratic and middle-class apartments gained in importance as venues for private concerts and recitals, among them several that are singled out by Leopold Sonnleithner for particular mention, such as those of Hochenadel, Kiesewetter (who made a speciality of editing and performing old music), Neuling, Zizius and Zmeskall.[20]

Amateur music-making of a less formal kind characterised the activities of the Schubert circle. The famous Schubertiads of the composer's last years took the place of the earlier music-making he took part in, initially with his father and brothers, and then with the orchestra of Otto Hatwig, a former orchestral musician who was the leading spirit behind a mainly amateur orchestra. The Schubertiads were comparatively small gatherings of literary, artistic and of course musical people, mainly young, male, and unbuttoned in their gaiety. The earliest of which a record survives took place at the apartment of Franz von Schober on 26 January 1821, attended by fifteen or sixteen persons. What Franz von Hartmann refers to as a 'große große Schubertiade' took place at Joseph von Spaun's on 15 December 1826; he names twenty-four who were present, including several ladies, though the total number attending was clearly higher.[21] Grillparzer, the painter Leopold Kupelwieser, Schober, Mayrhofer and Bauernfeld were there, and this is probably the occasion immortalised some forty years later in an imaginative reconstruction by Moritz von Schwind, 'Schubert Abend bei Joseph von Spaun', with Johann Michael Vogl singing to Schubert's accompaniment. From other accounts we know that, when women were present, Schubert often provided dance music at the piano, sometimes extemporising waltzes and Ländler that he wrote down later.[22]

Other Forms of Popular Music

A field of musical activity that gained in appeal during this period is dance-music. It is often forgotten that Haydn and Beethoven, as well as Mozart, wrote quantities of music for the carnival balls in the Redoutensäle; Schubert's output of Deutsche, Ländler, Ecossaises, waltzes and minuets is extremely extensive. The most popular tunes from operatic and orchestral music were swiftly arranged for dancing; the initially small ensembles of Michael Pamer, Joseph Lanner and Johann Strauss senior required far more music than they themselves could supply. We read in the *Jahrbuch der Tonkunst von Wien und Prag* (Vienna 1796, p. 100) that persons requiring the services of instrumentalists for private dances could engage players who on Saturday mornings congregated on the Hoher Markt and on other days on the Brandstatt (Brandstätte) opposite St Stephen's; public dances were held in numerous locales, at first in the Mehlgrube and Jahn's Saal, and from 1807 in two spacious new halls, the Apollosaal in the Zieglergasse (jocularly referred to by Apollo in Meisl's mythological caricature *Orpheus und Euridice*, II, i), and 'Zum Sperl' in the Leopoldstadt.

Eye-witness reports suggest that good music could be heard almost anywhere. An anonymous writer in the *Wiener Theater Almanach für das Jahr 1794* expressed his surprise at the choice of music sung by prisoners at the Militär-Stockhaus near the Neues Tor:

> Ich gieng einst an diesem Fenster vorüber, und hörte die Unglücklichen zu meinem grösten Erstaunen das bekannte Duett aus der Cosa rara: *pace caro mio sposo* im Chor anstimmen. Als sie es geendigt hatten, sangen sie das sanfte Liedchen des verstorbenen Herrn von Iacquin: *ich sass im*

Dunklen Buchenhayn. Fürwahr eine glückliche Phantasie, die ihnen ihren finstern Kerker in einen dunklen Buchenhain umwandeln konnte!²³

[I was once going past this window and to my greatest surprise heard the unfortunate wretches strike up the well-known duet from *Cosa rara*, 'Pace, caro mio sposo'. When they had finished it they sang the gentle little song of the late Herr von Jacquin, 'Ich saß im dunklen Buchenhayn'. In truth a fortunate fantasy that could turn their gloomy dungeon into a shady beech-grove!]

And Joseph Richter, in his famous anonymously published *Briefe eines Eipeldauers an seinen Herrn Vetter in Kakran, über d'Wienstadt*,²⁴ indicates the ease with which one could become familiar with the latest musical hits:

Auf der Wiedn habn s' jetzt wieder ein neue Opera, die heißt: der Spiegel von Arkadi, und wenn d' Wienerinnen nur von ein Spiegel hören, so sind s' gleich dabey; d' Opera soll deswegn auch ein rechten Beyfall finden. Aber da brauch ich kein Geld aus z' gebn: denn man hört d' Liedl davon schon jetzt auf allen Strassen, und in ein paar Tägen führn d' Bierhäuslmusikanten den Herrn Vettern schon d' ganze Opera um 1 kr. auf.²⁵

[At the Wieden Theatre they've got a new opera again, called *The Mirror of Arcady*, and when Viennese women so much as hear of a mirror, they're there in a flash; the opera is said to find much applause for that reason. But I don't need to spend any money, for one can hear its songs already in every street now, and in a few days the tavern musicians will perform the entire opera for my cousin for 1 kreuzer.]

The same satirical source points engagingly to the social importance for a girl of having some musical accomplishment:

Oder wenn ein Fräule im Hause ist, so muß s' ein Weil eins aufn Klavier schlagen, und dazu singen, daß den Herrn und Fraun der Schlaf vergeht. Da muß sich der Herr Vetter um 's Klavier herumstellen, und bravo schreyn, wenn d' Fräule gleich oft heult, wie ein kleiner Hund. Das ist wahr, solche Talenti zur Musik trift man in der ganzen Welt nicht an, wie z' Wien. Es giebt kein Fräule, und nicht einmahl mehr ein Burgerstochter, die nicht 's Klavier schlagt und dazu singen kann. D' Wienstadt allein könnt ganz Europi mit Firtosinnen versehn.²⁶

[Or if there's a young lady in the house she must bang away at the piano for a while and sing to her own accompaniment and keep the men and women awake. The cousin has to stand by the piano and shout bravo even if the young lady often howls like a little dog. That's true, such musical talents are not to be found in the whole world as they are in Vienna. There isn't one young lady, not even a burgher's daughter, who can't play the piano and sing. The city of Vienna alone could provide the whole of Europe with female virtuosi.]

The Land of the Piano

Jupiter makes a similar point in Meisl's mythological caricature *Die Entführung der Prinzessin Europa* some twenty years later: 'Die Gitarre- und Klaviermeister bringen zum Segen / Manchem Ehmann und Papa Kopfweh zuwegen.' ('The guitar- and piano-teachers bless many a husband and father with headaches.')[27]

The demand for music-lessons was considerable, and was frequently met, at high cost to their creative activities, by composers from Mozart down. Residents and visitors alike would have had no trouble in securing the services of teachers. Handbooks and guides, as well as newspapers, advertised what was available. *Nützliches Adreß- und Reisebuch oder Archiv der nöthigsten Kenntnisse von Wien fur reisende Fremde und Inländer* ('Useful Address- and Travel-Book or Archive of the most necessary Information about Vienna for Travelling Foreigners and Residents') is one such.[28] Successive numbers and editions of Johann Pezzl's *Skizze* (later *Neue Skizze*) *von Wien* (1786–1812) confirmed the demand for information that was as entertaining as it was useful. J. F. Schönfeld's *Jahrbuch der Tonkunst von Wien und Prag*[29] contained details that a modern reader can hardly help finding amusing: 'Bartenstein, Freiherr v., Reichshofrath, spielt die Violine gut ... Claus, ein junger Mediciner, spielt die Flöte ganz artig und hat einen schönen, klaren Ton.' ('Bartenstein, Baron von, Imperial Councillor, plays the violin well ... Claus, a young medic, plays the flute very charmingly and has a lovely clear tone').[30] The Gerold publication of 1792 (note 28) came out in a revised and extended edition in 1797, under a new title, *Sicheres Addreß- und Kundschaftsbuch für Einheimische und Fremde, welche vorläufige Kenntniß von der Haupt- und Residenzstadt Wien haben wollen* ('Accurate Address- and Information-Book for Natives and Visitors wishing to have Current Information about the Capital City and Residence of Vienna'); this volume contains the names and addresses of the personnel of the theatres, with an extensive section listing the 'dancing-masters, ... musicians, composers and masters of the keyboard', plus, listed as 'Bürgerl[iche] Künstler [civic, or middle-class, artists] in Wien', details of some seventy instrumentalists, including such eminent musicians as 'Hr. Joseph Weigel' among the cellists, the brothers Stadler among the clarinettists, and the Weidingers among trumpeters (pp. 422–6). Other sections cover language-teachers, French polishers and teachers of drawing.

Instrument-makers and Music Publishers

Though instruments of all kinds were produced in Vienna, the city is most famous for its keyboard-makers. The fame of Johann Andreas Stein (who removed from Augsburg to Vienna in 1794 after the marriage of his talented daughter Nannette to Johann Andreas Streicher, thus giving birth to the yet more famous firm of 'Nannette Streicher née Stein') is due among music historians largely to Mozart's praise for his instruments. However, Mozart's later preference was for the fortepianos of Anton Walter. Other distinguished Viennese makers in this period were Schanz, Seidel, Hofmann, Könnicke, Brodmann, Conrad Graf and Wachtl (Bösendorfer began production in 1828). It is impossible to hazard a guess at the total production of pianos, but it is clear that, even among the not especially musical families, a piano was part of the essential furniture of a smart apartment. Even though most of these makers began mass production considerably later, there was reason beyond the need to silence the doubts of his father for Mozart to write home shortly after his final removal to Vienna: '–und mein fach ist zu beliebt hier, als daß ich mich nicht Souteniren sollte. hier ist doch gewis das Clavierland!' ('– and my speciality is too well loved here for me not to be able to Maintain myself. This is very definitely the land of the piano!')[31]

The enormous demand for printed music in Vienna at the end of the eighteenth century and the beginning of the nineteenth can be inferred from the rapid progress from the handwritten copies that were regularly advertised in the *Wiener Zeitung* in the 1780s as being available from agencies such as those of Laurenz Lausch and Johann Traeg, to the mass of printed material brought out by publishers like Artaria, Cappi, Diabelli, Haslinger, Hoffmeister, Mechetti, Mollo, and the Musikalisches Magazin in the Unterbreunerstraße. The supreme achievement of the late Alexander Weinmann is the series of catalogues of Vienna's musical publishing houses, *Beiträge zur Geschichte des Alt-Wiener Musikverlages*, which including revisions runs to some twenty-eight volumes. These catalogues bear witness to the extraordinary productivity of composers during the six or seven decades from Mozart's day on to the middle of the century, reflected in the almost insatiable demand for compositions written for, or arranged for, the pianoforte, with or without voice, and with or without one or more wind or string instruments – editions exist for almost every imaginable combination.

Artaria was one of the most important suppliers from the mid-1770s on, initially with imported printed editions, then with its own imprint. Haydn enters the catalogue in 1780, Mozart in 1781, and Beethoven in 1793. But for the less demanding customers, series like *Raccolta d'arie* (1787–1804) proved very popular, consisting of piano reductions of favourite numbers from current stage works. Diabelli soon gained ground, with successful series of music for guitar and for piano solo and duet. Vocal music was again much in demand: for decades the *Neueste Sammlung komischer Theatergesänge* put the best-loved numbers from operatic and *Volkstheater* works before the public, in neatly arranged and cleanly printed reductions. Details of the consecutive numbering, as of price, were added by hand on the blanket title-page, and the same practice obtained with similar publications from other houses: Diabelli's own *Favoritgesänge*, Steiner's *Sammlung komischer Theater-Gesänge*, and Haslinger's *Theatralisches Panorama. Sammlung der beliebtesten Theater-Gesänge*, to name well-known examples.

We can be certain that by no means everyone who later claimed to have been a pupil of Mozart was actually taught composition or keyboard by him. But the desire for instruction went beyond individual tuition, as is clear from the large number of books of instruction published. An announcement in the *Wiener Zeitung* on 13 April 1796 informed readers that 'a hitherto unknown manuscript Tutor by Mozart for the Learning of Thoroughbass' ('Ein noch unbekanntes geschriebenes Fundament zur Erlernung des General-Basses von Mozart') was available from Joseph Haydenreich's shop in the Schmelzgasse for 4 fl. 30 kr.

(*Dokumente*, p. 418 /p. 480). This is presumably the same *Kurzgefaßte Generalbaßschule* that was advertised by S. A. Steiner & Co. on 22 August 1817 in the Vienna *Allgemeine musikalische Zeitung* (Köchel, 6, p. 911). A further edition appeared in Berlin in 1822, and English and Italian translations were also produced. The fact that grave doubts about the authenticity of this tutor are held is in this context less significant than the fact that there was considerable demand for such books of instruction. To take further examples almost at random, Albrechtsberger's treatises, published between 1790 and 1804, were considered important enough for his pupil Ignaz von Seyfried to publish *J. G. Albrechtsberger's sämmtliche Schriften über Generalbaß, Harmonie-Lehre, und Tonsetzkunst* nearly twenty years after his death.[32] Seyfried was also responsible for the publication of Preindl's *Wiener Tonschule* (1827) and *Ludwig van Beethoven's Studien im Generalbasse, Contrapuncte und in der Compositions-Lehre* (1832). Joseph Drechsler found time among his other activities to write several tutors, including a *Theoretisch-practischer Leitfaden, ohne Kenntniß des Contrapunktes phantasiren oder präludieren zu können* (Vienna, 1835). A predecessor in the sphere of music for the popular comedy, Ferdinand Kauer, published with Artaria tutors for flute, piano, violin and cello, as well as a study of thoroughbass and a singing manual in the late 1780s and early 1790s, and around 1802 Joseph Eder brought out his *Neu verfasste Klavier Schule ... samt einer Anweisung das Forte Piano gut zu stimmen*, doubtless aiming to increase sales by offering practical advice on tuning the pianofortes that were being manufactured in large numbers. Not surprisingly, the most famous teacher of music in Vienna in the first half of the nineteenth century, Simon Sechter, is the author of a series of treatises and practical guides, published between 1819 and 1854.

Amateur Music-making and Theatricals

An invaluable source for information about the less-publicised aspects of musical life in Vienna from the second decade of the nineteenth century until the 1850s is the memoirs of Leopold von Sonnleithner. These 'Musikalische Skizzen aus Alt-Wien' were published by Georg, Prince Czartoryski in the Viennese periodical *Recensionen und Mittheilungen über Theater und Musik* between 1861 and 1863, and were republished in 1961 by Otto Erich Deutsch in three numbers of the *Österreichische Musikzeitschrift*.[33] They provide details about the patrons who arranged concerts in their homes, and about the repertory and the performers, amateur and professional, who took part. They amplify information derived from playbills, programmes and newspapers about the musical life of the city; the thorough coverage makes the more regrettable the lack of similar documentation for the period dominated by Mozart and then by the young Beethoven.

A striking feature of Sonnleithner's sketches is the prominent part played by women in Vienna's amateur musical life. Apart from those who, still often at risk to their social reputation, went on the stage as professional singers or actresses, there were some women talented and intrepid enough to make the grade as instrumentalists – in Mozart's day there were Regina Strinasacchi and Barbara Ployer, as well as the blind virtuosi Maria Theresia Paradis and Marianne Kirchgessner. What is clear from Sonnleithner's records is the very considerable number of highly gifted female musicians, especially pianists, who made a major contribution to the private musical scene. Many of the leading professionals of the day took part in some of the matinées and soirées – familiar names occur like Antonie Campi, Siboni, Saal, Nestroy (in the 1820s) and even Lablache among singers, and Schuppanzigh and his quartet colleagues and Hellmesberger among string players; a whole galaxy of pianists and composers appeared, including Beethoven and Schubert, Moscheles, Mayseder and Czerny.

Some private patrons were ambitious enough to put on performances of *Die Schöpfung* with forces ranging from almost complete orchestral resources to string quintet or one or two pianos, with or without string bass. Beethoven directed an account of *Christus am Ölberge* at the inn 'Zum römischen Kaiser' on 1 March 1814 for the society named 'Reunion'. Naturally, chamber music was the principal diet for the amateur circles, though several included operatic ensembles, even sizable finales, among their programmes. Others included declamations, and at the home of General Georg Schall von Falkenhorst dramatic entertainments were mounted, running even to Grillparzer's *Die Ahnfrau* – Josef, the son of the house, went on to become a professional actor and senior producer at the Theater in der Josefstadt, his name telescoped to Josef Forst.

Not surprisingly, less is known about amateur dramatics and readings in the Vienna of this period than is the case with musical performances, doubtless mainly because of posterity's greater interest in music, and the fact that, more modest resources and skills being required, fewer references to non-musical soirées are to be found. As we have seen, there were many houses in which music was regularly performed for the benefit of family and friends. Where plays are concerned, the most popular authors, among amateurs as well as in the court and suburban theatres, were the prolific, talented but essentially shallow trio of Schröder, Iffland and, especially, Kotzebue. Their work, as evidence from the repertory lists of the principal theatres, surviving records from the smaller ephemeral stages and references in memoirs and letters show, was immensely popular at every level.[34] Lovers of Jane Austen will recall that the company at Mansfield Park, having endlessly debated their choice of play for home theatricals, happily agreed on *Lovers' Vows* (*Das Kind der Liebe*) as the ideal solution to their quandary.[35] Though Kotzebue's best (and certainly his best known) play, the comedy *Die deutschen Kleinstädter*, dates from after his time as court theatre secretary in Vienna (1797–8),[36] its influence in the Austrian capital as the first of the Krähwinkel plays can hardly be overstated. With breathtaking solipsistic enthusiasm Kotzebue has his 'Herr Bau-, Berg- und Weginspektorssubstitut' ('deputy inspector of buildings, mountains and roads') speak admiringly of his own assumption of the role of the young simpleton, Peter, in *Menschenhaß und Reue*, and in the last scene refer with unconscious irony to a notorious quarrel between Kotzebue and Iffland, promising the heroine as an epithalamium 'eine Ehrenpforte' ('a triumphal arch').[37]

The Land of the Piano

Grillparzer gives a lively account of his own youthful home dramatics ('nur Ritterstücke' – 'only plays about knights') in his *Selbstbiographie*:

> Mein Vater nahm scheinbar oder wirklich von unsern Kunstbestrebungen keine Notiz, ja ich erinnere mich nicht, daß er unsern Darstellungen auch nur ein einziges Mal einen Blick gegönnt hätte. Die Mutter wurde dadurch gewonnen, daß unser Klavierlehrer Gallus, der die Sache, wie jede Kinderei, mit Eifer auffaßte, sich bereit erklärte, unsere Produktionen mit Ouvertüre und Zwischenakten in freier Phantasie auszuschmücken. Diese seine Improvisationen, zu denen er, wenn die Handlung bedeutender wurde, sogar melodramatische Begleitungen fügte, verschaffte[n] unsern Absurditäten sogar eine gewisse Zelebrität.[38]

> [My father apparently or really took no notice of our artistic endeavours, indeed I do not remember that he even once honoured our performances with a single glance. But my mother was won over by them to the extent that our piano-teacher Gallus, who responded to the matter, as to every other piece of childishness, with enthusiasm, declared himself ready to embellish our productions with freely extemporised overture and entr'actes. These improvisations, to which, when the dramatic action became more significant, he even added melodramatic accompaniments, even gained for our absurdities a certain celebrity.]

In a culture like that of Vienna, in which music played a dominant part, instrumental accompaniment to the spoken word was understandably a popular device. This is nowhere more apparent than in the vogue for melodrama in the opera house (the best-known instance is the dungeon-scene in *Fidelio*) and the spoken theatre (Beethoven's *Egmont* music contains a magnificent melodramatic setting of the hero's monologue just before he is led out to execution). There are innumerable examples – Schubert wrote melodramas in four of his stage works, starting with two in his gruesome-Gothick setting of Kotzebue's *Des Teufels Lustschloß* (1813–14).[39] He also tried his hand with conspicuous but often underrated success at a piano-accompanied example for a domestic occasion, the birthday of the lawyer Karl Josef von Pratobevera on 17 February 1826. The text begins with the words 'Leb wohl, du schöne Erde', the opening of the last five stanzas of a one-act play, *Der Falke*, by Adolf von Pratobevera, the son of the birthday celebrant. Schubert's setting, D 829, is traditionally known as 'Abschied von der Erde' (as in the Old Complete Edition and first edition of Deutsch's *Thematic Catalogue*); the autograph is untitled but an early manuscript copy has the heading 'Abschied. Melodramatisch'.[40] As the author's sister, Franziska ('Fanni'), was a talented singer it is surprising that Schubert did not set the words as a *Lied*; perhaps she was to be absent from the celebration, and the composer was accordingly asked to set the words as an accompanied speech for the actor taking the role of Hugo, the old knight, whereas in the play the words were originally given to Mechtild, Hugo's daughter-in-law, with an indication that they were to be sung.[41]

A more unusual form of domestic music-making is described by a British visitor to Vienna; what makes this particularly interesting, apart from its unfamiliarity, is the identity of the musician concerned:

> I entered into conversation with the princess, and the intended performances very naturally became the subject of our remarks. She said that although the living pictures were a novel exhibition in Vienna, they were not new to her, for some years previously, she gave a fête at Eisenstadt, one of her country seats, where they were executed for the first time. Her chapel master, Haydn, the celebrated composer, heightened the interest of the exhibition on that occasion, by performing on the organ some extemporaneous music of a strikingly appropriate character.[42]

Internal evidence enables us to identify the princess as Marie Hermenegild, wife of Nikolaus II Esterházy, for whose name-day Haydn composed his late Mass settings. The occasion described in the above passage was a grand assembly at court at which an entertainment of *tableaux vivants* was to be presented.

The range of artistic activity in the Vienna of this period was indeed amazingly broad. If one artist comes closest to conveying the essence of the place and the age – in his love-hate relationship towards it, as idol of society and then as victim of its fickle taste, in his activities as composer, performer, promoter, director, keen amateur dancer, small-time dramatist and doggerel poet, drawer, vivid letter-writer – that artist is, despite his comparatively brief residence in Vienna and his early death, Wolfgang Amadè Mozart. He must have the last word. He told his sister in a letter on 4 July 1781, 'Meine einzige Unterhaltung besteht im Theater' ('My sole entertainment is the theatre').[43] And where his own sphere was concerned, he managed to maintain for ten years the opinion of Vienna that he expressed to his father in the first flush of his enthusiasm at being there, and a free man; he wrote on 4 April 1781: 'P:S: ich versichere sie, daß hier ein Herrlicher ort ist – und fur *mein Metier* der beste ort von der Welt.' ('P.S. I assure you that this is a Splendid place – and for *my metier* the best place in the world.') (*Briefe*, III, p. 102).

Notes

1. *Statistisches Jahrbuch der Stadt Wien für das Jahr 1883*, p. 20; information kindly supplied by the Archivdirektor of the Magistrat der Stadt Wien.
2. The painting is reproduced in black and white as plate 557 in O. E. Deutsch, *Mozart und seine Welt in zeitgenössischen Bildern* (Kassel, etc., 1961), and in colour on the cover of Wolfgang Sawallisch's recording of *Die Zauberflöte*, EMI CDS 7 47827 8.
3. E. von Bauernfeld, *Erinnerungen aus Alt-Wien* (Vienna, 1923), p. 424.
4. *Reisen durch Oesterreich, Ungarn ... in den Jahren 1801 und 1802* (Vienna, 1803), pp. 100–1.
5. J. H. F. Müller, *Abschied von der k.k. Hof- und National-Schaubühne* (Vienna, 1802), p. 46.
6. 'Kaiser-königl priviligirtes Theater in der Leopoldstadt in Wien ... ', MS Wiener Stadt- und Landesbibliothek, shelf-mark 51926 Ib.
7. I. F. Castelli, *Memoiren meines Lebens*, ed. J. Bindtner (2 vols, Munich, [1913]) I, p. 224.

8. *Philipp Hafners gesammelte Schriften*, 3 vols (Vienna, 1812), III, p. 4.
9. O. E. Deutsch, *Mozart. Die Dokumente seines Lebens* (Kassel, etc., 1961), p. 234; English edn, p. 267 (cited in the text as *Dokumente*).
10. *Theater-Kalender* (Gotha, 1793), pp. 71–9 and (1794), pp. 94–100.
11. *Deutsches Museum* (Leipzig, January 1852), II/i, pp. 27–8, 'Aus den ungedruckten Denkwürdigkeiten der Aerzte Peter and Joseph Frank', here cited after Deutsch, *Dokumente*, p. 476, English edn, p. 561.
12. *Journal Kept During a Visit to Germany in 1799, 1800*, edited and privately published by the Dean of Westminster (preface dated 10 June 1861), from the journal of his mother, Mrs St George, p. 55.
13. *Mozart. Briefe und Aufzeichnungen*, ed. W. A. Bauer, O. E. Deutsch and J. H. Eibl (7 vols, Kassel, etc., 1962–75), III, p. 201; see also Mozart's letter to his sister of 20 April 1782, III, p. 202.
14. See Edward Olleson, 'The Origin and Libretto of Haydn's *Creation*', *Haydn Yearbook* 4 (1968), pp. 148–68; *The 'Creation' and the 'Seasons'. The Complete Authentic Sources for the Word-Books*, ed. H. C. Robbins Landon (University College Cardiff Press, 1985).
15. Deutsch, *Dokumente. Addenda und Corrigenda* (Kassel, etc., 1978), p. 63, English edn, p. 370.
16. Information given to Charles Burney by Gluck in 1772; see *An Eighteenth-Century Musical Tour in Central Europe and the Netherlands*, ed. Percy A. Scholes (Oxford, 1959), p. 83.
17. Mary Sue Morrow, *Concert Life in Haydn's Vienna: Aspects of a Developing Musical and Social Institution*, Sociology of Music No. 7 (Stuyvesant, NY, 1989). See here especially pp. 237–364, 365–411.
18. *Geschichte des Concertwesens in Wien* (Vienna, 1869 repr. 1971), p. 52.
19. C. F. Pohl, *Die Gesellschaft der Musikfreunde ... und ihr Conservatorium* (Vienna, 1871).
20. For bibliographical details see note 33.
21. Otto Erich Deutsch, *Schubert. Die Dokumente seines Lebens* (Kassel, etc., 1964), p. 115 and pp. 388–9; English edn, p. 162 and pp. 571–2.
22. See for example Leopold von Sonnleithner's reminiscences of Schubert in O. E. Deutsch, *Schubert. Die Erinnerungen seiner Freunde* (Leipzig, 1957), p. 141; English edn, p. 121.
23. Pp. 175–6; the references are to Martín y Soler's successful opera of 1786 *Una cosa rara*, and to Mozart's talented friend Gottfried von Jacquin, whose song referred to is no. 2 in a set of six that included two 'borrowed' from Mozart; see Köchel 6, p. 602 (K 530).
24. The series continued for many years under various titles. Quotations are from the selection in two volumes edited by Eugen von Paunel, *Josef Richter. Die Eipeldauer Briefe 1785–1797*, and ditto, *1799–1813* (Munich, 1917–18).
25. I, p. 248 = 15tes Heft (1794), Vierter Brief; the reference here is to the Schikaneder/Süssmayr opera *Der Spiegel von Arkadien*, first performed on 14 November 1794.
26. I, p. 66 = Viertes Heft (1794), Vierter Brief.
27. Karl Meisl, *Die Entführung der Prinzessin Europa, oder So geht es im Olymp zu!* (I, 2; 1816); cited from Karl Meisl, *Ausgewählte Werke*, II = Alt-Wiener Volkstheater, vol. 4, ed. Otto Rommel (Vienna, etc., n.d.), pp. 10–11.
28. (Vienna: Gerold, 1792).
29. (Vienna, 1796).
30. Cited from Hanslick, *Concertwesen*, p. 68.
31. *Briefe* (see note 13), III (1963), pp. 124–5, letter of 2 June 1781.
32. (Vienna, 1826); a second edition followed in 1837, reprinted in 1975; and there were early editions in French and English.

33. *ÖMZ* 16/ii (February 1961), pp. 49–62; 16/iii (March 1961), pp. 97–110; 16/iv (April 1961), pp. 145–57.
34. G. Gugitz and E. K. Blümml, *Alt-Wiener Thespiskarren* (Vienna, 1925).
35. Jane Austen, *Mansfield Park*, vol. I, chapter 14 et seq.
36. After his resignation in December 1798 he was granted a pension of 1,000 gulden a year (as 'Dichter des Hoftheaters') against submission of all his new plays, 45 of which were staged in twelve years. See E. Wlassack, *Chronik des k. k. Hof-Burgtheaters* (Vienna, [1875]), pp. 88–91.
37. See *Die deutschen Kleinstädter*, II, 2 and IV, 12.
38. F. Grillparzer, *Selbsbiographie*, cited from *Sämtliche Werke*, ed. Peter Frank and Karl Pörnbacher (4 vols, Munich, 1965), IV, p. 29.
39. See P. Branscombe, 'Schubert and the Melodrama', in *Schubert Studies. Problems of Style and Chronology*, ed. E. Badura-Skoda and P. Branscombe (Cambridge, 1982), pp. 105–41 (pp. 139–40).
40. Witteczek–Spaun Collection; see the revised edition of Deutsch's *Thematic Catalogue, Franz Schubert. Thematisches Verzeichnis seiner Werke in chronologischer Folge*, ed. the editorial board of the *NGA* and Werner Aderhold (Kassel, etc., 1978), p. 523.
41. See Clemens Höslinger, 'Aus den Aufzeichnungen des Freiherrn von Pratobevera', in *Schubert-Studien. Festgabe der Österreichischen Akademie der Wissenschaften zum Schubert-Jahr 1978*, ed. Franz Grasberger and Othmar Wessely (Vienna, 1978), pp. 119–29 (p. 126).
42. *Journal of a Nobleman; comprising an account of his travels, and a narrative of his residence at Vienna, during the Congress*, published anonymously (2 vols, London, 1831), II, p. 105–6; see P. Branscombe, 'Hanswurst Redivivus: Haydn's Connexions with the "Volkstheater" Tradition', in *Joseph Haydn. Bericht über den Internationalen Joseph Haydn Kongress Wien ...1982*, ed. E. Badura-Skoda (Munich, 1986), pp. 369–75 (p. 372).
43. *Briefe*, III, p. 138; Mozart used almost the same words in talking of the theatre to his father in the letter of 26 May 1781 (III, p. 121) and to his wife on 3 October 1790 (IV, p. 116).

The Sexual Politics of Mozart's *Magic Flute* and the Genesis of Viennese 'Charm'

John Milfull

Und nun gar Wien! Es wurde gerettet. Allerdings. Aber wozu? [...] Etwas vom Islam ist bei diesen Hahndel- und Fasandelmännern immer zu Hause gewesen, und Europa hätt ein bißchen mehr von Serail- oder Haremswirtschaft ohne großen Schaden ertragen [...][1]

[And then there's Vienna! it was saved [i.e. from the Turkish siege of 1683]. Certainly. But for what purpose? These men with their love of chicken and pheasant have always had something of Islam, and Europe could have stood a bit more of the seraglio or the harem without suffering much harm.]

The slightly disreputable Bülow may not be one of Fontane's favourite characters, but these comments from *Schach von Wuthenow* seem to reflect a widely shared perception of the 'immortality' of Vienna, which was to be strongly reinforced by the reception of Austrian literature of the *fin de siècle*. The *Reigen* of Austrian sexuality, exposed in the works of such diverse talents as Schnitzler, Freud and Sacher-Masoch, was easily transformed into the cliché of Viennese 'charm' – for all the occasional scandals, little remained of Schnitzler's ambivalence towards his protagonists but their slightly guilty declaration of love for the Austrian *dolce vita*. The 'seraglio' of the Habsburg capital seemed the ultimate expression of a male-chauvinist social order in which women were degraded to the status of throw-away containers.

It may be productive to trace this development back to the most popular work of the Austrian Enlightenment, Mozart's *Magic Flute*, not only because its misogynistic tendencies seem farcical and outdated, but because they are 'philosophically' founded in a way which can tell us much about the darker side of the Austrian Enlightenment. Perhaps we may find in the idiocies of the *Magic Flute* on the relations between women and men some of the reasons for the failure of this rather timid reform movement, or even the origins of that gentler 'Austrian' form of brutality which tried to set itself up in opposition to the 'dry' Prussian variety after the triumph of the reaction. The motto of this investigation might well be *cherchez l'homme*.

As Alfred Einstein writes,[2] there is no real proof for the popular theory that Mozart and his librettist Schikaneder 'changed direction' in the plot of the *Magic Flute*; I have always been puzzled by the insistence on the 'internal contradictions' of the libretto, which seem to arise from one of the best-known didactic structures of the Enlightenment, the revelation that the exotic or strange is not less, but more, humane than the Europeans who approach it with such prejudice. The classic presentation of this thesis in German is, of course, Goethe's *Iphigenie auf Tauris*,[3] but it had a host of precursors, and indeed, Mozart's first successful 'Singspiel', *Die Entführung aus dem Serail*, is based on a fairly run-of-the-mill variant. Before his true motives are revealed, the Bassa Selim is no less threatening a figure than Sarastro, and the Thoas-like gesture with which he frees the lovers in the name of a higher humanity anticipates, in its turn, Sarastro's role in the 'fulfilment' of Pamina and Tamino. Why then the litany of complaint?

On closer investigation, it is not Sarastro's transformation (however unsatisfactory in current terms) from evil tyrant to enlightened despot that provokes this reaction but the corresponding transformation that has always been assumed in the Queen of the Night and her followers, and the persistence of elements from her sphere in the lovers' progress to 'Enlightenment' (the magic instruments, the three boys). These assumptions seemed to be based on 'readings' which often have little to do with the text: just as there is no real difference between the musical 'registers' of the Queen's arias in Acts I and II, both firmly grounded in the *opera seria* tradition Mozart so obviously identified with the world of the court and the aristocracy, she is presented from the first as a 'star-flaming' figure of fear, *sternflammend* visually and vocally, and her empire, complete with barren mountains and mythic snakes, is scarcely the Good Place. Nor does the function of the 'comic' elements of Tamino's rescue by the Three Ladies seem to have been adequately assessed; it is unusual, to say the least, to begin an opera of such serious intent with a scene in which the hero faints in the face of danger and has to be rescued by three court ladies with silver spears. And even odder to make such goings-on the prelude to heroic coloraturas of maternal grief.

Only odd, however, if we assume the intention to enlist our sympathy for the Queen, her Ladies and other collectors of caged birds. As we shall see, there are good reasons for seeking the source of their presentation rather in the bourgeois critique of aristocratic immorality, and the mixture of fear and titillation its high priestesses invoked in fainting bourgeois heroes exposed to their dangerous charms. It is not the necessity to revise its view of Sarastro at which the audience baulks, but the quite unexpected need to reject or criticise elements of 'female' behaviour (mother-love, flirtatiousness) which have since been idealised or trivialised into axioms. Most of the answers to the apparent 'contradictions' of *The Magic Flute* can be found in the original text itself,[4] only too often truncated in performance; the real 'contradictions' lead outside the opera, to the conflict between feudal and bourgeois moral norms in the transitional society of the Austrian Enlightenment.

Only a man of 'firm mind', a 'sage', knows how to deal properly with women. On his deathbed, Pamina's father feels obliged to warn his Queen, whom he addresses as 'Weib' (woman), of the need for such male supervision. He has passed on the sevenfold sun emblem to Sarastro, '[der] ihn so männlich verwalten [wird] wie ich bisher' (who will wield it in as manly a fashion as I have done hitherto). He continues: 'forsche nicht nach Wesen, die dem weiblichen

Geist unbegreiflich sind. Deine Pflicht ist, dich und deine Tochter der Führung weiser Männer zu überlassen' (do not seek to know about beings that the female mind cannot grasp. It is your duty to surrender yourself and your daughter to the guidance of wise men).[5] The star-flaming Queen has clearly rejected this duty (who could blame her?); it is only her daughter who will succeed in banning such deeply subversive feminity to the abyss where it belongs, by combining her own 'first duty', to respond to the 'sweet urges' of Tamino, the wandering Prince and future Sarastro student, with this older obligation. Only thus can the Empire of the Sun be saved from the devilish revenge of women and blacks; they are driven from the stage with thunder, storm and lightning, and plunged into 'eternal night', while the new royal pair, reuniting the male and female principles, Osiris and Isis, takes up its inheritance. Pamina has shown herself worthy of this honour by learning to respect her fiancé's silence and braving the ordeal of fire and water hand in hand with him, without so much as a question; the terrors of marriage clearly pale in comparison.

Yet it is surprising that the sex roles are reversed with the 'minor' characters, whose search for happiness mirrors and parodies that of their 'superiors'. Papagena very much retains the upper hand in her dealings with Papageno, who gains our eternal sympathy by failing every assignment; she leads him surely and unswervingly to the paradise of eating and breeding. Obviously, women are harmless as long as they remain within the bounds of their allotted domesticity; independence leads inevitably to lust for murder and revenge, and thinks nothing of allying itself with the rape fantasies of the comic-gruesome Moor, even if they are directed against one's own daughter. The three court Ladies in their aristocratic-wanton squabbling over the sleeping prince, the Queen with her weakness for swords and daggers, the 'evil Moor' Monostatos, the black slave who dreams of groping the Princess: they all have their origin in the 'seraglio' of the Habsburg aristocracy, which threatens the 'wisdom' of the bourgeois Enlighteners. Their own women, their 'schönes Eigentum' (fair property), had better stay safely at home, or at least entrust themselves to the counsel of the wise men they call husbands.[6] And the husbands had best restrict themselves to these sanctioned charms – the fate of those who allow themselves to be led astray by 'Weibertücken' (women's wiles) is far too frightening:

> Verlassen sah er sich am Ende,
> Vergolten seine Treu' mit Hohn!
> Vergebens rang er seine Hände,
> Tod und Verzweiflung war sein Lohn.[7]

[At last he saw himself abandoned, his loyalty requited with scorn! In vain he wrung his hands: death and despair were his reward.]

The 'gentle booty' has obviously taken off of her own accord, in the unfair manner to which perfidious female aristocrats are obviously so prone. These 'star-flaming' ladies in their glittering jewels have given the virtuous representatives of the new humanity such a fright that they seek refuge in a 'humanitarian' paternalism which locks itself off from such dangers. Sadly, not all humans are to become brothers, as Schiller instructed Beethoven, but only male humans of the right class. Tamino is quick to learn his lesson:

> Ein Weiser prüft und achtet nicht,
> Was der gemeine Pöbel spricht...[8]

[A wise man examines and disregards what the common rabble says.]

He knows how to protect himself against the 'chatter' of women and (other?) 'hypocrites'. But Papageno cannot resist the lure of women's chatter, he even responds to Tamino's heroic admonition 'Papageno, be a man' with the extraordinary heresy: 'I wish I were a girl!' This disgraceful statement is of course met immediately by a 'very loud' peal of thunder; Old Nobodaddy is not amused.[9] Nevertheless, one can wink at such frailties in the common people, unforgivable as they might be among the elect. Yet again, it is no accident that Papagena and Papageno, not Tamino and Pamina, have the last word: they only admit openly what the others conceal, that the 'heavenly joys' of the bourgeois love ethic presuppose the safety of the domestic shrine, and might otherwise be put to flight by the 'night' of an uncontrolled sexuality.

The boundaries of humanity are charted by Sarastro's congregation with some asperity: a human being may be more than a prince, but anyone who is not instantly grabbed by the teachings of the Elect 'does not deserve to be human' ('verdienet nicht, ein Mensch zu sein'). The freemasons' lodges gave the new middle class the opportunity to fraternise with 'enlightened' aristocrats,[10] but excluded inferior elements such as women, the mob and the 'lesser races'; here the much-vaunted humanism of the *Magic Flute* falls well behind the Early Enlightenment tolerance of *Die Entführung aus dem Serail*, where at least one 'noble Moor', the Bassa Selim, is permitted to instruct the whites in morality, and Constanze and Blonde show a good deal more positive 'spirit'. Even the comic villan Osmin, the harem's Cerberus, comes close to upstaging the rest in a way denied to his slightly sinister echo, Monostatos. The 'Enlightenment from above' of Josephinism does not reach very deep; for a time, it enables a new élite, in which money and talent can assert themselves alongside birth and privilege, but essentially as a counter-revolutionary strategy based in concern at the consequences of a genuine democratisation. After the Leopold interlude, this false 'dawn' soon gives way to the darkness of reaction; the victory goes not to bourgeois virtue, but to feudal whim.[11] Sarastro's realm, which for all its appeals to Isis, Osiris and humanity excluded more humans than it included, did not herald the millennium; even alchemy, on whose symbolic language the Masons drew so heavily, had recognised that the *magnum opus* can only succeed in the union of sun and moon, the male and the female principles. The subordination of woman is the symptom of an ideal of humanity which has got stuck half-way, which is not prepared to surrender the urge to dominate, but merely redefines the objects of domination. The clear-voiced fanfares of Mozart's finale still await their political fulfilment.

The international success of Milos Forman's film *Amadeus* and the play by Peter Shaffer on which it is based has little to do with any genuine insight into

Mozart's sexual psychology, or indeed, into the strange combination of licence and propriety which characterised feudal etiquette.[12] The juxtaposition of bourgeois sentimentality and plebeian crudity which strikes us constantly in Mozart's letters arises from his unusual social situation.[13] Archbishop Colloredo's court musician, who sat at table with the footmen, never really succeeds in attaining the bourgeois independence his talent and self-esteem demand; even the far more bullish Beethoven has to remain dependent on aristocratic patrons. The scatological smut of the servants coexists oddly with the high emotions and the pet names of the new ideology of love; the dream of a great romantic love remains as unattainable as independence. For the most part it expresses itself in the language of the courtly *opera seria*, in Italian; the Fiordiligis of this world may be capable of such a love, but they are out of the reach of a middle-class composer, however talented he may be, and are merely betrayed by their own cavaliers. Aloysia Weber could at least impersonate such wondrous women on stage, but Wolfgang has to make do with her sister and pretend to the 'wunderbare Harmonie' of a bourgeois marriage which his revered older colleague, Franz Joseph Haydn, endures with such irony and bravery. For all their individual disappointments and their suppressed envy of the 'seraglio' of their rulers, they are nevertheless finally at one with Schiller's cellist, Miller from *Kabale und Liebe*, in feeling that bourgeois virtue must resist such 'temptations'; Constanze, too, must be taught how a proper wife should behave. Despite all ambivalences, Don Giovanni's punishment is inwardly affirmed; one must condemn in others what one is not permitted oneself. Wilhelm Meister experiences a similar trauma as actor; on stage, he can assimilate his own bourgeois manners to those of the court, but fate intervenes with almost occult urgency as soon as the Countess attempts to bridge the gulf with an embrace – the taboo is too powerful.

There is no easy way out of this impasse, no victory for the bourgeoisie, or for the bourgeois ideal of marriage. That hangover from feudalism, the officer caste, maintains the tradition of Donjuanism. The *jus primae noctis* may be suspended, but there are many other nights for these quasi-military operations. In the tired embrace of nineteenth-century compromise, the Emperor may seem to become a bourgeois father himself, but it takes only the scandal of Mayerling to reveal the sexual chaos beneath this surface calm. Of course, the harem is no longer so exclusive; even a lieutenant is now admitted. Bourgeois morality is internalised by the men as a permanent bad conscience, yet serves simultaneously as a useful means of keeping women 'in their place'. The sexual liberties of the aristocracy are now restricted to *men* from the 'better circles'; marriage retains its feudal function of consolidating status, career and wealth, and demands at the very least the successful public pretence of wifely virtue. The roles of the houris in this new 'harem' are played almost exclusively by women from the lower classes; the servant-girl of day-time is metamorphosed into Queen of the Night.

Surprisingly, it is once again the 'Prussian' novelist Fontane who provides the most acute analysis of these developments, in the tragicomic *Magic Flute* parody of *Stine*.[14] A piece of 'Austrian' immorality is being acted out in Berlin's

Invalidenstrasse: Count von Haldern, alias 'Sarastro', has set up a modest harem with the help of his faithful confidant Baron Papageno, in which the widow Pauline Pittelkow must serve him as 'Queen of the Night'[15] to keep herself and her family. Sarastro's realm undergoes an almost Brechtian alienation, returning to the harem from which it evolved; not only has Papageno's baritonal *Schmelz* grown 'schadhaft' (defective), his aria on the 'first duty of women' reveals, in its multiple irony, the true character of this duty to share the 'sweet urges' of a male;[16] the lower-class widow has had to entrust herself to the direction of this 'wise man' for financial reasons, to escape from the grinding poverty and exploitation of her youth in the country. The sickly Tamino of the story, the young Count Waldemar (a well-intentioned 'fainter' like his predecessor), encounters a surprising set-back in courting Pauline's virtuous sister Stine, whom she is determined to protect from her own fate. An offer of marriage is no solution; the barriers of class operate in reverse. Stine rejects the ordeal by fire and water of a *mésalliance* with the mixture of pride in her class, resignation and realism characteristic of Fontane's petit bourgeois heroines. Waldemar's ensuing suicide points the author's bitter critique of an aristocracy which no longer honours the frugal virtues of old Prussia, yet lacks the courage to recognise the consequences of its own actions. Baron Papageno, a bird fancier like his predecessor, has seen the light: the chirpy sparrows are the true Prussians in the world history of birds, he says; compared with them, the aristocratic rooster is 'doch eigentlich nur ein Geck' (really only a fop).[17] Yet *Count* Papageno sees no way out, neither for himself nor for Waldemar; as an elderly bachelor (clearly Fontane's preferred 'male fantasy'!), he has the bird's freedom to speak 'wie [ihm] der *Schnabel* gewachsen ist' [my italics];[18] and to be glad when someone has the courage to 'break through' social conventions, but in the last resort he too lacks the 'courage on which success depends' as surely as Waldemar.

The delicate political and aesthetic balance of Fontane's work forbids him the direct question as to why an outmoded moral code cannot be 'broken through'. Arthur Schnitzler, himself a participant in the joys of the 'seraglio' and clearly immune to Fontane's Protestant-masochist views on marriage, is perhaps a more eloquent witness. He too discovered the ethical quality in the sufferings of the 'süße Mädels' who have to put up with his weak-minded Anatols; but equally he describes with all due clarity the advantages of such a system to its beneficiaries, the members of a 'male club' who are not more likely to surrender their sexual privileges than the capitalists to hand over the means of production to the workers of their own free will. Viennese 'charm' had become the advertising slogan of men who had skilfully managed to turn the contradiction between the 'seraglio' of Habsburgia and a bourgeois morality which had never really attained dominance to their own considerable advantage. The ambivalence of society towards these Don Juaninos, the mixture of admiration, envy and modified outrage with which their affairs were recorded, ensured the persistence of a male myth in whose genesis the wise Sarastro and the 'naive' Papageno are by no means uninvolved. For all Goethe's and Hofmannsthal's attempts to 'complete' Mozart's opera, there would still seem room for a *third* part to the

The Sexual Politics of Mozart's Magic Flute

Magic Flute in which Pamina frees Tamino from the decaying masonry of Sarastro's men's group, reinstates her mother and finally breaks the tyranny of the 'wise men'. A triple fanfare might be reserved for the observation: 'Er ist ein Mann. / Mehr, er ist ein Mensch' (He is a man. More, he is a human being).

Notes

1. Theodor Fontane, *Schach von Wuthenow*, Nymphenburger Taschenbuch-Ausgabe (Munich, 1969), vol. 5, p. 10.
2. Quoted by Helmuth Karasek in 'Sarastros totalitärer Sonnenstaat', *Der Spiegel*, 27 (1985), pp. 145–8, a useful review of Ivan Nagel's study *Autonomie und Gnade. Über Mozarts Opern* (Munich, 1985).
3. See Robert R. Heitner, 'The Iphigenia in Tauris Theme in Drama of the Eighteenth Century', *Comparative Literature*, 16 (1964), pp. 289–309.
4. Quoted from the Reclam edition: W. A. Mozart, *Die Zauberflöte* (Stuttgart, 1971).
5. *Die Zauberflöte*, pp. 46–7 (Act II, scene 8)
6. See Barbara Duden's path-breaking article, 'Das schöne Eigentum. Zur Herausbildung des bürgerlichen Frauenbildes an der Wende vom 18. zum 19. Jahrhundert', *Kursbuch*, 44 (1978), pp. 125–40.
7. *Die Zauberflöte*, pp. 41–2 (Act II, scene 3).
8. Ibid., p. 43 (Act II, scene 5).
9. Ibid., p. 40 (Act II, scene 2).
10. See Eva Balazs *et al.* (eds), *Beförderer der Aufklärung in Mittel- und Osteuropa. Freimaurer, Gesellschaften, Clubs* (Berlin, 1979); Paul Nettl, *Mozart and Masonry* (New York, 1970).
11. See Walter Grab, *Ein Volk muß seine Freiheit selbst erobern. Zur Geschichte der deutschen Jakobiner* (Frankfurt, 1984), pp. 401ff.; Leslie Bodi, *Tauwetter in Wien. Zur Prosa der österreichischen Aufklärung* (Frankfurt, 1977). My colleague Ephraim Nimni has drawn my attention to an intriguing, if far-fetched, contemporary interpretation of the Magic Flute as an allegory of the Revolution: see J. Gräffer (ed.), *Josephinische Curiosa* (Vienna, 1848), vol. 3, pp. 174–87. Even more far-fetched, in my view, is Jacques Chailley's attempt to turn Pamina into a Pankhurst of female Masonry in *Musique et ésotérisme: La flûte enchantée, opéra maçonnique* (Paris, 1968).
12. These remarks, I fear, apply equally to Charles Ford's book *Cosi? Sexual Politics in Mozart's Operas* (Manchester, 1991).
13. See *Mozart's Letters*, ed. Eric Blom (Harmondsworth, 1956).
14. See Günter H. Hertling, *Theodor Fontanes 'Stine': eine entzauberte 'Zauberflöte'? Zum Humanitätsgedanken am Ausklang zweier Jahrhunderte* (Berne, 1982).
15. Fontane, *Irrungen Wirrungen. Stine*, Nymphenburger Taschenbuch-Ausgabe, vol. 9, p. 188.
16. Ibid., pp. 196–7.
17. Ibid., p. 217.
18. Ibid., p. 224: 'to speak in his natural voice [untranslatable pun on 'Schnabel' beak]'.

Beating the Bounds: Fantasy and Farce in Nestroy's Comedy

Louise Adey Huish

'Beating the bounds' is a curious Oxford ceremony in which parish boundaries are marked out by beating them with bushes, perhaps to keep out the devil. A second meaning of beating, namely triumphing over, going beyond, allows us by a quibble to glimpse a characteristic paradox of Nestroy's plays, which, in my opinion, are about boundaries in both senses. Interesting though it is to observe how often the word 'Grenze' comes up in the plays, and how often eloping couples and unmasked criminals escape 'über die Grenze', to concentrate exclusively on this concrete use of the term would be of only limited interest. What I am concerned with here is the way in which Nestroy explores and establishes the limits of the possible, beating the bounds in my first sense, and then uses fantasy to go beyond them, to a place where the exuberance of what Ludwig Tieck calls 'comedy without a content' is possible,[1] beating the bounds this time by overstepping them.

The experience of laughing, not at something, but for the sheer pleasure it brings, is one I have always been aware of when reading Nestroy, and for a long time I supposed that it was caused by Nestroy's word-play. More recently I have come to think that that is only part of the story, a hunch reinforced by Hillach's excellent monograph on Nestroy, which puts forward the suggestion that language is at all times bound up with situation, and that the two cannot be considered separately.[2] I had been moving towards a similar conclusion when thinking about what we might call hypothetical language in Nestroy, constructions which evoked what a character *might* say, were he a different person or in a different situation. This kind of language points to an imagined freedom from constraints which has its parallel in many of Nestroy's comic situations, most obviously, perhaps, in those which exist on the borderline between the probable and the possible. In order to find out where this borderline lies, it is necessary to explore where reality ends and fantasy begins.

The form of Nestroy's plays is curiously appropriate to his 'Weltanschauung'. Audiences who wished to be reassured that God was in his heaven and all right with the world obliged him to write comedies,[3] so he subverted their expectations with bleak farces which reflect firstly the supremacy of chance, as opposed to the harmonious world order we associate with the so-called 'Volkstheater', and secondly the pessimism, even cynicism, of his outlook. The happy ending, when it comes, is forced and artificial, emphasising the fact that things do not actually work out for the best in the real world.[4] For this reason, Preisner's notion of the 'tragische Posse' (tragic farce) seems at first sight appropriate: he suggests that Nestroy's plays show us a world in which there is no reliable escape from the bleakness of the human condition.[5] He attributes this to the alienation which comes with capitalism and urban industrialism, and claims that for the most part, Nestroy's characters are part of a marionette theatre in which there are only two options: puppet or puppet-master. The kind of laughter I experience when reading Nestroy convinces me, however, that even at his most cynical, he is more life-affirming than this.[6] If cynicism is the property of the failed idealist, then perhaps we should look for the frustrated idealism in the plays, and find it not in their content, but in their energy, in the movement towards escape, fantasy and freedom.[7]

I shall concentrate on five plays which seem in different ways to illustrate this movement into fantasy. Three of them – *Der Färber und sein Zwillingsbruder, Der Talisman* and *Einen Jux will er sich machen* – demonstrate a certain basic pattern, which is present in modified form in two others, *Liebesgeschichten und Heurathssachen* and *Gegen Thorheit giebt es kein Mittel*.[8] All five were written fairly close together, spanning the years from 1838 to 1843 (the three 'core' plays were written between 1840 and 1842). They thus belong in what was arguably Nestroy's most uncompromisingly realist period, after he had moved away from the 'Zauberstück', and before he adopted the extreme stylisation of the later plays; perhaps, then, he compensated for the eradication of the magic world as the location of fantasy by increasing the elasticity of the real world. The pattern might be described as follows: each play focuses on what we might call *thresholds*, moments of transition when a character is moving from one set of conventions to another, and there is a momentary space where fantasy can break in. The idea of a threshold encompasses both aspects of my theme, in that it shows clearly where the limits of a particular situation lie, but implies by definition the possibility of going beyond them. Going beyond the limits in fantasy enables a character to come to terms with what they mean in reality and he is then able to make conscious choices which would not otherwise have been possible. In *Der Färber und sein Zwillingsbruder* the threshold is that of marriage, in *Einen Jux* it is that of promotion, and in *Der Talisman* it is that of social integration. In each case, a context is established, which is characterised by restriction and closure; then the transitional situation is introduced and the real world put on hold, so to speak. An opening is created which leads into the world of fantasy, with its potential for creativity and change. Eventually the character is returned to the real world, but the changes which have taken place in the fantasy world, in the sphere of alternative reality, persist even after the real world has reasserted its supremacy, and become changes in reality as well.

Der Färber und sein Zwillingsbruder focuses on Kilian Blau, a dyer, and to a lesser extent on his twin brother Hermann, a swashbuckling soldier; the fact that Nestroy played both reinforces the notion that Hermann is Kilian's *alter ego*. Kilian, timid and conformist, is about to get married, while Hermann abhors the very idea. Kilian is forced to impersonate Hermann to save him from a court martial when he goes absent without leave, and in the process of doing things 'as his brother would have done them', he discovers a boldness and sense of initiative he never dreamed he possessed. At the same time, he engineers a marriage for his brother as well, which Herman eventually accepts with good grace; thus he is brought into the social fold as Kilian comes to glimpse a world beyond.

The play opens with a scene between Hermann and his fellow soldiers, who are, significantly, acting as border guards. Quizzed about his daredevil lifestyle, Hermann voices the conviction that happiness is closely bound up with the consciousness of danger, danger which lies literally over the border. 'Nur bei der Linie der Gefahr kommt man hinaus ins Freie des Vergnügens' ('The only way out into the open spaces of pleasure is by crossing the boundary-line of danger'), he remarks, and goes on: 'Wer sich scheut, diese Linie zu passieren, der bleibt ewig in der staubigen Vorstadt der Langweiligkeit hocken.' ('Anyone who is afraid to cross that line will be stuck for ever in the dusty suburb of boredom.') He compares his attitude to that of his brother, who has chosen the safe profession of dyer, and is all set to '[vervegetieren] im viereckigsten Zirkel der Spießbürgerlichkeit' ('vegetate away in the squarest circle of bourgeois philistinism') [1.3]. This image, evoking all that is circumscribed and constricted, provides the perspective from which we first see Kilian Blau, who bewails in his 'Auftrittsmonolog' the difficulty he has in expressing his feelings, and goes on to prove it by proposing to the girl of his choice by pointing at her. Pusillanimous, unromantic and obsessed with security, he does indeed appear to exemplify the lifestyle his brother abhors. But the situation is not as straightforward as it seems, as is evident from that opening monologue, where Kilian describes the problem of being tongue-tied with the most astonishing loquacity. Even in conversation with Roserl he alternates between awkward monosyllables and verbal floods which recall the heady volubility of his brother, suggesting that the potential for fantasy is latent in his personality too. Hermann, on the other hand, disappears and does not appear again until the end of the play, when it turns out that he has been forced to spend the duration of the action locked in his mistress's wardrobe, surely the 'viereckigster Zirkel' of them all. It does not surprise us, therefore, when Kilian is seduced by his kind heart into covering up for his brother's absence by impersonating him at the garrison, for the brothers clearly have more in common than one might think.

The empty space in which Kilian acts out his fantasies is created not merely by his brother's forcible removal from the scene, but also by the fact of his betrothal. At first his intention is for marriage to follow as hard on the heels of betrothal as is physically and legally possible – avoiding that creative gap between love and marriage which is the focus of the later play *Liebesgeschichten und Heurathssachen* – but the urgency of the situation means that the wedding celebrations are put on hold. From this point on he acquires a different persona and a different set of priorities, which he is only able to assume at first with the greatest of difficulty, but with which he becomes increasingly at ease. Much of the play's comedy derives, of course, from the discrepancy between what

Hermann would do or say and Kilian's own reaction in the same circumstances; but equally and more joyfully comic is our pleasure in watching Kilian throw off the restrictions of his own personality and discover for himself that happiness is closely related to risk. The turning-point comes when he is forced to go into battle to save his brother's honour; although on his return it transpires that a heroic rush into the thick of the fighting was his horse's decision rather than his own, the appearance of bravery is half way to bravery itself, and Kilian earns promotion for his brother before embarking on another dizzy series of adventures which culminate in a love scene with Cordelia, in which he is forced to behave 'as his brother would have done'. He finds himself betrothed to Cordelia on Hermann's behalf, and only his brother's fortunate reappearance saves him from a complicated dual existence. Herman, after his lengthy sojourn in the wardrobe, is inexplicably chastened and decides it is time to become a solid citizen, so that the play closes on the celebration of his marriage to Cordelia, which becomes fused in the final chorus with the suspended celebration of Kilian's marriage to Roserl.

The confusion of identity and the merging of fact and fantasy are sustained thematically in the play by a number of episodes in which characters act out scenes which might take place or have already taken place. The conviction with which they do so creates uncertainty in the audience as to what is true and contributes to the blurring of boundaries. Linguistically, confusion is sustained by the use of fantastic similes, and by other devices which serve to reinterpret the plain facts of everyday language, such as synonyms, and restatings like this one from near the end of Act I:

> KILIAN: Wie weit haben wir in die Löwenschlucht?
> STURM: Zwei Stunden.
> KILIAN: Das fahren meine Pferd' in hundertzwanzig Minuten. [I. 16]

> [KILIAN: How long does it take to get to the Löwenschlucht?
> STURM: Two hours.
> KILIAN: That'll take *my* horses a hundred and twenty minutes.]

Even the central characters' names underline Nestroy's intentions. Dictionary definitions of the word *blau* include 'Blau als Farbe der unbestimmten Ferne – ins Blaue hinein. Blau als Farbe der Täuschung, Verstellung und Lüge: "das Blau vom Himmel herunterlügen", d. h. Unwahrheiten erzählen'. ('Blue, colour of the hazy distance: into the blue. Blue, colour of lies and deceit: 'to charm the blue down out of the sky', i.e. to tell stories.') Given the widespread use of *sprechende Namen* in Nestroy, this is surely no coincidence.

Einen Jux will er sich machen, like *Der Färber und sein Zwillingsbruder*, suggests that the escape into fantasy is not unlike walking along a tightrope. The play centres on the clerk Weinberl's longing to look back on just one day when he behaved like 'ein verfluchter Kerl' ('a devil of a chap') [I. 13]. When he learns that he has been promoted he takes a holiday and goes off in search of adventure; he has no idea of how to find it, but eventually it finds him, and the vertiginous experience brings him a wife, a business partnership and a new outlook on life. Nestroy opens with a series of scenes which convey the suffocating dullness of small-town life. Marie, thwarted in her love for Sonders, is to be kept a virtual prisoner; Zangler finds himself stifled in a new dinner jacket which allows no room for his dinner; and the new valet Melchior is locked inside his limited vocabulary. Weinberl's 'Auftrittsmonolog' sets the tone for what is to come: he contrasts real life, sordid and prosaic, with the fantasy world of shops, where delicacy and imagination are still possible. His eloquence suggests that he is already excited at the prospect of promotion, but the knowledge that he is to be made 'Associé' knocks him sideways. When he learns that his promotion will only date from after his boss's short holiday, he conceives the idea of going off on the razzle himself, sowing his wild oats, as it were, before settling down to remorseless respectability. Here too, then, a threshold is reached, and the real world is put on hold for a brief spell. Weinberl himself sees his promotion as the crossing of a boundary: 'Grad jetzt auf der Gränze zwischen Knechtschaft und Herrschaft, mach ich mir einen Jux' ('I'll have my high jinks right here on the borderline between serf and master'); Christopherl sees his corresponding promotion as an escape into freedom: 'Ich bin heut frey gsprochen worden, kann man die Freyheit schöner als durch ein Jux celebrieren?' ('Today I've been set free: is there any better way to celebrate freedom than with high jinks?') [I. 13] Here too disguise is the necessary accompaniment of the shift into fantasy: even before they leave for the big city the confusion created by Weinberl's impersonation of Zangler gives them a 'Vorgeschmak von Jux' ('a foretaste of high jinks') [I. 21].

By the beginning of Act II, Weinberl and Christopherl have already begun to tire of the city. They are kicking their heels in a back street, wondering whether to go home, when adventure strikes. Significantly, it is adumbrated in story-book form, as Weinberl turns their situation into the clichés of 'das Abentheuerliche' [II. 1]; although the clichés are immediately subverted, this shift into fantasy mode is the start of their headlong adventure. From the moment when Weinberl starts to exercise a little initiative, he acquires a new identity as 'Herr von Geist' [II. 5], an identity which is recalled at the end of the play when Weinberl and Christopherl return, thoroughly disillusioned with adventure, to find thieves in the shop. As Weinberl goes in to outwit the thieves, a commentary is provided by Melchior's well-known musings as to whether the sinister noises he can hear are made by 'Menschen' or 'Geister', virtually all of which can be read as if 'Geist' meant 'wit' and not 'ghost' [III.21–2]. Weinberl's wit enables the thieves to be caught and Zangler appeased, so that Herr von Geist does become the husband of Frau von Fischer after all: the new persona Weinberl acquires in the fantasy world is sustained even after he has returned to the real world.

In the course of their adventures, Christopherl and Weinberl significantly lose the key to the 'Gewölb', and it is only the episode in which they catch the robbers that opens up the shop again, restores them to the security they crave, and sets reality back in motion. Weinberl's tangled fantasy existence as a 'verfluchter Kerl' almost prevents him from crossing the threshold into the respectable world of promotion, but once he recognises, like Hermann Blau, that 'Gefahr' is indeed the source of 'Glück', once he starts to take risks in the real world, he finds both material success and, one can only suppose, true love.

The rich chaos of fantasy is sustained thematically, and indeed linguistically, by multiple disguises and confusions of identity: even the wax copy which the robbers make of the key to the shop is a case of false identity. Synonym and restatement are used to fragment identity as in this speech of Melchior's: 'Nicht eigentliche Damen, sondern nur was man so sagt [.] Dieser Herr (Zu WEINBERL.) schämen Sie sich, (Zu FRÄULEIN BLUMENBLATT.) war in einem Garten mit zwey Frauenzimmern, die ich Anfangs für Weibsbilder gehalten hab, wo sich's aber nacher gezeigt hat daß es Wittwen waren.' ('Not exactly ladies, that's a manner of speaking. This gentleman – shame on you! – was in an outdoor restaurant with two females, whom I took at first for women, but then it turned out that they were really widows.') [III. 5] A further device which Nestroy uses frequently in this play is to offer a kind of narrative gloss on reality, which turns actual events into fiction: examples include the Gothick clichés of 'das Abentheuerliche', already mentioned, the ladder in III.12 apparently conjured up by Weinberl's description of it, and the newspaper headline 'Verwegner Kleiderdiebstahl durch einen jungen Purschen' ('Young fellow in daring clothes theft'), read out by Zangler as Christopherl escapes past him dressed in Frau von Fischer's hat and shawl [II. 18]. As in *Der Färber und sein Zwillingsbruder*, we find alternative realities acted out, a notable example being Weinberl's virtuoso description of a busy moment in the store [I. 11]. While the relative absence of exuberant imagery in this play is appropriate, given that even fantasy keeps driving the characters into tight corners, *Der Talisman* offers us a work in which fantasy and language alike are more like a house of cards, precariously balanced but nevertheless reaching for the sky.

Titus Feuerfuchs, the hero of *Der Talisman*, is rejected by society because of his red hair. Circumstance brings him into brief possession of a series of coloured wigs, each of which takes him to a further stage in his quest for a wife and a fortune. He creates a new persona for each wig, and achieves dizzy heights before he is decisively unmasked – or unwigged – and finally opts for his true identity, and the love of a red-haired goose-girl. Once again, the opening of the play focuses on restriction and closure through the character of Salome Pockerl. She is the female counterpart of Titus Feuerfuchs, who turns up shortly afterwards jobless and friendless; but even he rejects her, probably because she confronts him with the image of his own physical and emotional poverty. Stripped of everything he has, he nevertheless describes himself in optimistic terms as standing 'in den Hemdärmeln der Freiheit da' ('in the shirt-sleeves of freedom') [I. 8]. He is not yet prepared to settle for a bare minimum, and chance is prepared for the time being to abet him. The stage set mirrors the situation showing 'eine Gartenmauer mit einer kleinen offenstehenden Tür, welche in den Herrschaftsgarten führt' ('A garden wall with a small door leading to the garden of the estate; the door is ajar'). A high wall and an open door; poverty, prejudice and the chance gift of a wig. 'Meine Karriere geht an, die Glücksfpforte öffnet sich' ('My career is taking off, the portal of good fortune is opening') [I. 13]: transformed by a head of black curls, Titus will try his luck in the big house, but Salome warns him right from the beginning, 'Sie geh'n so stolz bei der Tür hinein, daß ich immer glaub', ich werd's noch sehn, wie s' Ihnen bei der nämlichen Tür hinauswerfen wer'n.' ('You're going through that door so proudly that I can't help thinking I'll be there to see it when they throw you back out through that same door.') [I. 14] Both figuratively and metaphorically Titus crosses a threshold, for at the beginning of the play he is a social outcast, and by the end he has acquired a wife and a position in society; walking through the door into the estate he enters the world of fantasy and hypothetical possibility, and from the experience he learns what he does not want as well as what he does. He is indeed thrown out of the door, as Salome predicts, but the end of the play sees him leave the big house voluntarily to take up the threads of real life again.

The events of *Der Talisman* are far more stylised than in either of the plays we have so far considered. The pattern of repetitions generates its own momentum, so that in structural terms the fiction overrides any sense of reality. Black wig gives way to blonde wig and finally to grey wig; the gardener's widow gives way to the lady's maid and then to the lady of the house; each languishing widow invites Titus to step into her dead husband's clothes. The quasi-allegorical names of the characters reinforce this sense of stylisation, as does the fact that Titus's imagery varies according to the woman he is trying to woo. His extravagant volubility foregrounds the notion of language-as-game, as well as language-as-mask. Salome is the only woman who recognises that Titus's linguistic flourishes constitute ornament rather than communication: 'Ich versteh' Ihnen nit, aber Sie reden so schön daher' ('I don't understand a word you're saying, but you talk so nice') [I.8].

In *Der Talisman* confusion of identity is again central to the plot, but in this case, it is Titus's identity alone that is in flux as each step up the ladder presents him with yet another potential identity to try out. The fact that the personality of the other characters is merely a pose, so that they appear to us as cardboard cut-outs rather than people, reinforces our sense that Titus is taking up a series of positions rather than living through real experiences. The most sinister poseur in the play is undoubtedly the hairdresser, Marquis, whose name, like his profession, is the epitome of fraudulent disguise. He is also the embodiment of chance in the play, for his first appearance is an accident, in both senses of the word, as a result of which Titus acquires his talisman, the black wig. Marquis then appears again in the big house, where he revenges himself for Titus's interest in Constantia by taking the wig away again, but not before he has provided the blonde wig which Titus then dons *in extremis*. The fact that Titus is able to carry off a dramatic change of hair colour not once, but twice (the second occasion is when, wearing a grey wig, he convinces Spund that he has turned grey overnight) demonstrates the power of Titus's fantasy, which even the interventions of chance cannot shake.

The narcissistic power of fantasy is also conveyed by Titus's ability to cast off each set of experiences without regard for the consequences. This suggests that other people have no real existence for him, so that they can be put aside at will. Resentment against this high-handedness reaches its high-point when Titus, now private secretary to Frau von Cypressenburg, arranges to have Flora, Plutzerkern and Constantia dismissed in order to protect his new, blonde, identity: it is as if the fantasy of omnipotence created here then calls forth an equivalent counter-wave of reality. Thus Titus's punishment, when it comes, is much more drastic than anything meted out to Kilian Blau or Weinberl: he is literally thrown out, and not allowed to keep even the clothes he stands up in. Perhaps this opens his eyes to the precarious nature of success, even though the call back to the big house promises to set the vertiginous process in motion all over again.

The second fantasy which Titus is invited to pursue is that of money: perhaps Fortuna will prove a stronger lure than Amor, as she does in *Lumpacivagabundus*. Spund, the wealthy relative who would have made Titus his 'Universalerbe' (sole heir) if only he did not have red hair, is introduced only after Titus's first house of cards has collapsed. Inheritance is as arbitrary a form of luck as winning a fortune in a lottery, as is made ironically clear when Spund refers to his immense cleverness in finding himself heir to innumerable friends and relatives, yet for all Titus's scepticism, he allows himself to be seduced by the transformatory power of wealth into physical and linguistic dissembling once again. This time the knife-edge between fantasy and reality is even more acute. The prize is greater than ever before, since Spund's 'Universalerbe' will come into millions; the deceit, too, is more outrageous than ever, and is reflected in the stage business, where a hand proffering a pair of scissors appears, as it were, form nowhere to cut off Titus's tell-tale queue.

Over and over again in the play we are shown both the power and the fragility of Titus's fantasy, doubtless the source of our fascination and thus of the dramatic tension. The sustained punning and far-fetched metaphors – almost all of which belong to Titus – have a brittle quality which reinforces the artifice of the plot; Titus's breathtaking impudence has us constantly anticipating his unmasking, but the presence of mind which he sees as essential to real good fortune seems to thrive on danger. Perhaps Titus would even have managed to talk himself out of the tangle with Spund but the fact is that he no longer wants to. However, even the unexpected sentiment of the ending, in which Titus rewards Salome for her unselfish affection by marrying her, is made more credible by the artificiality of his reasoning: the more red-haired people there are, the less likely they are to encounter prejudice, so that he is indirectly serving his own ends by producing red-haired offspring. What Titus describes at the beginning of the play as a 'Nolens-volens Leidenschaft' ('a willy-nilly affair') [I. 14] thus becomes a matter of reasoned choice, and the fantasy interlude at the big house an experimentation with alternative forms of reality.

I shall now consider briefly two other plays which have a bearing on my theme, *Liebesgeschichten und Heurathssachen* and *Gegen Thorheit giebt es kein Mittel*. *Gegen Thorheit* predates the other plays, having been written in 1838; *Liebesgeschichten und Heurathssachen*, written in 1843, comes at the end of the chronological sequence. There is a kind of logic in their progression in that *Gegen*

Thorheit demonstrates the negative power of fantasy, while *Liebesgeschichten und Heurathssachen*, although it still deals with fantasy's creative potential, does so in a much less clear-cut way.

Gegen Thorheit giebt es kein Mittel tells the story of Simplicius Berg, who, as his name suggests, is the archetypal dupe. The younger son of a rich family, he has enough money to indulge his fantasies, but no requirement to shoulder the responsibilities which ought to go with wealth. His elder brother Richard functions as a kind of secularised 'Zauberkönig', who repeatedly bales Simplicius out when disaster strikes. As in *Der Talisman*, Nestroy creates a highly stylised structure where repetition creates its own momentum, but this time offers us a fantasy interlude without any framework of reality. The threshold has been crossed before the play begins, as Simplicius has already come into his fortune; and the never-ending supply of money, the 'Tischlein-deck-dich' of the modern world, ensures that he need never emerge from the world of fantasy. It is as if Titus Feuerfuchs were assured of an endless succession of wigs, though money is of course, as we have seen, a much more potent kind of wig, since whoever possesses it will never be thought ill-favoured. The artificial plot, with its succession of stock situations, its inevitable intrigues and unmaskings, points again to a brittle and unreal situation.

Preisner sees Simplicius as the pure fool, a positive counter-pole to the appalling Herr G. whom he extrapolates from Nestroy's Gundlhuber to present as the brutish forerunner of Nazi attitudes (Preisner, pp. 21–5 and 87–90). In my opinion, this is a complete misreading of the character. Certainly Simplicius's gullibility is exploited in the play by those who wish to take advantage of his money or even of his kind heart; he is probably even exploited by his own brother, who grows in self-righteousness as Simplicius expands in stupidity. We feel no real sympathy for him, however, partly because of his incorrigible foolishness, but more importantly because his stupidity takes on active force when it affects the lives of others.[9] It ceases to be a ludicrous but harmless complacency, and becomes a rather terrifying narcissistic fantasy.

This is made apparent from the outset by Simplicius's inability to listen to what others say. He cannot conceive of the possibility that anyone might not find him irresistible (his money is actually only a metaphor for this sense of self-importance), and he is unable to concede that other people have desires and inclinations which have nothing to do with him. Nestroy provides a telling foil for Simplicius in the character of Anselm, his manservant, who, with the cheerful stupidity of the typical Scholz-Rolle, interprets every sign of rejection when he is in love as merely an obstacle to be overcome. In this play Nestroy abandons the typical counterpoint of the Nestroy- and Scholz-Rollen; here they work together to create an intensified sense of a world in which external reality counts for nothing, where the creative possibilities of 'Einbildungskraft' (imagination) have been replaced by the rigidity of 'Einbildung' (conceit). Here, fantasy has nothing to do with risk, nothing to do with experimentation (disguise and confusion of identity is at a minimum in the play), and everything to do with getting one's own way at any price.

The language of the play reflects this, for there is little of that linguistic exuberance we associate with Nestroy, and comedy derives mostly from situation. The only point at which Simplicius does assume another persona is when he dresses up as a clown in III. 11, and interestingly this is the moment when we feel greatest sympathy for him (perhaps this is why Preisner accords the scene such importance). It is stunningly good theatre, a quick-change performance requiring extraordinary sureness of touch as Simplicius puts on his clown's make-up without a mirror. But the melancholy smile of the clown would not catch at our heart if it did not reflect our sympathy for the man behind the mask, who seems to have accepted poverty and lovelessness and to have found a satisfaction of sorts in serving others. Our disappointment and indignation are thus all the stronger when we find that actually nothing has changed: when Simplicius comes into money again the clown's smile is wiped off, the absurd costume exchanged for the dandyism of wealth and kindness of heart replaced by indulgence and selfishness. Perhaps this does beg political interpretation as the evils of capitalism, but more compelling is the notion of money as fairy-tale empowerment: Nestroy's narrative has more to do with Midas than with Croesus.

In *Liebesgeschichten und Heurathssachen*, the last of the plays in our sequence, Nestroy exhausts the possibilities of this fantasy theme. It does not conform to quite the same pattern, although it still deals with a kind of threshold: the one which divides 'Liebesgeschichten' from 'Heurathssachen'. Whether the first becomes the second is principally a matter of money, as we see in the play from the two serious love affairs, Alfred–Ulrike and Fanny–Buchner. The conventional melodrama scenario is turned upside down by the aptly-named Nebel, who functions as a kind of Lord of Misrule, stage-managing events and fostering confusion. The structure of the play is similar to that of *Der Talisman*: Nebel appears inviolable as one situation after another appears to confirm the supremacy of his fantasy; finally, however, he goes too far and tumbles all the way back down the beanstalk. The part of Nebel is like those of Kilian Blau, Weinberl, Titus and Simplicius, a role Nestroy wrote for himself, but in this instance it is not on his experiences alone that the play turns. He is, it is true, in love with the wealthy but ugly Lucia Distel, and he is as poor as a church mouse. His position ought, then, to parallel that of Buchner, but he assumes a false identity as Baron von Nebelstern, and, by a fortunate coincidence, is taken to be the disguised son of Baron Vincelli, so that his identity becomes confused with that of Alfred. As the two serious male characters become associated with Nebel, the fantasy on which he thrives spreads out to encompass them all, and a state of flux ensues, in which no one is quite sure any longer of anyone else's identity, fortune, or intentions. Nebel's fantasy sustains the dramatic action for most of the play, but at the end he is unmasked and sent away penniless and partnerless; unlike Titus Feuerfuchs, however, Nebel does not learn his lesson, but goes off unrepentant, presumably to spread confusion elsewhere. Thus the empty space created by the threshold between love and marriage is not experienced by one person alone, but becomes a more generalised state of being; the fantasy, on the other hand, is generated by a single character, that of Nebel.

Perhaps, then, we should let Nebel have the last word, as – albeit ironically – he sums up here the creative energy of the imagination which can conjure up something from nothing:

> Der Fortuna als Mittelding zwischen Bettler und Guerilla entgegentreten, das Maximum von ihr begehren, wenn man auch gar keine Ansprüche darauf hat, das is die wahre Anspruchslosigkeit, das zeigt von edler Souffisance, von fabelhaftem Selbstgefühl, mit Einem Wort, es ist ein schönes Streben. [I. 5]

> [To step out to meet one's fortune as something between a beggar and a guerrilla, to demand the maximum, even when one has no right to it whatsoever, that is real modesty, it demonstrates noble self-sufficiency, a fabulous confidence in one's own abilities; in short, it is a fine endeavour.]

'Ein schönes Streben' indeed, to struggle beyond the farcical bleakness which dominates Nestroy's universe towards something which promises release. The mistake which critics have made up to now, it seems to me, is to assume that reparation is always a matter of content, that Nestroy only manages to go beyond the 'tragische Posse' when his heroes are convinced of the values of humanity. All the plays I have dealt with here have endings which might raise a wry smile at best, but this is no reason to relegate them to the marionette theatre. They do offer a kind of release in their form, a holiday from the dull restraints of everyday living. By acknowledging those restraints and then going beyond them – turning aside from the straight and narrow road to do a little dance by the wayside – Nestroy shows us that there are two sides to the boundaries of life, that there is beating the bounds, and *beating* the bounds. And even if, in the end, we have to return to the greyness and the routine, surely we all feel better for a holiday?

Notes

1. For a discussion of the term, see Helen Louise Adey, 'The Shakespearean Criticism of Ludwig Tieck: Conception and Creation', unpublished doctoral dissertation (Cambridge, 1987).
2. Ansgar Hillach, *Die Dramatisierung des komischen Dialogs: Figur und Rolle bei Nestroy* (Munich, 1967). Jürgen Hein, *Spiel und Satire in der Komödie Johann Nestroys*, Ars Poetica: Studien 11 (Bad Homburg v.d.H., Berlin, Zurich, 1970) incorporates Hillach's insights into his study of 'play' in Nestroy, but does not deal with fantasy in the specific sense intended in this essay.
3. For a qualification of this view, see Johann Hüttner, 'Der ernste Nestroy', in W. E. Yates and John R. P. McKenzie (eds), *Viennese Popular Theatre: A Symposium* (Exeter, 1985), pp. 67–80.
4. On Nestroy's happy endings, see W. E. Yates, '"Die Sache hat bereits ein fröhliches Ende erreicht!": Nestroy und das Happy-End', in Jean-Marie Valentin (ed.), *Das österreichische Volkstheater im europäischen Zusammenhang 1830–1880* (Berne, 1988), pp. 71–86.

5. Rio Preisner, *Johann Nepomuk Nestroy: Der Schöpfer der tragischen Posse* (Munich, 1968).
6. For a more radical view of laughter as a life-affirming quality of Nestroy's work, see Rudolf Münz, 'Nestroy und die Tradition des Volkstheaters', *Impulse*, 11 (1988), pp. 192–254, esp. pp. 242–54.
7. Peter K. Jansen, 'Johann Nepomuk Nestroys skeptische Utopie: Märchen und Wirklichkeit in *Der Talisman*', *Jahrbuch der deutschen Schiller-Gesellschaft* (1980), pp. 247–82, argues that the fairy-tale provides an alternative to the disenchantments of reality. Jürgen Hein, 'Der utopische Nestroy', *Nestroyana*, 6 (1985), pp. 13–23, sees the interplay of satirical and utopian elements as a distinctive feature of Nestroy's theatre. W. E. Yates, 'Nestroy', in *Literaturlexikon. Autoren und Werke deutscher Sprache*, vol. 8 (Gütersloh, Munich, 1990), pp. 351–5, sees escape as a key to the comic structure of Nestroy's plays.
8. Where possible, references and quotations are taken from the new edition of Nestroy's works, Johann Nestroy, *Sämtliche Werke, Historisch-kritische Ausgabe*, ed. Jürgen Hein and Johann Hüttner (Vienna, Munich, 1977–) (*Einen Jux will er sich machen*, vol. 18/1, ed. W. E. Yates; *Liebesgeschichten und Heurathssachen*, vol. 19, ed. Jürgen Hein; *Gegen Thorheit giebt es kein Mittel*, vol. 15, ed. Louise Adey Huish (forthcoming). All other references and quotations are taken from Johann Nestroy, *Sämtliche Werke, Historisch-kritische Gesamtausgabe*, ed. Fritz Brukner and Otto Rommel, 15 vols (Vienna, 1924–30) (*Der Färber und sein Zwillingsbruder*, *Der Talisman*, vol. 10).
9. See Louise Adey Huish, 'A Source for Nestroy's *Gegen Thorheit giebt es kein Mittel*', *Modern Language Review*, 87 (1992), pp. 616–25 for a discussion of the way in which Nestroy's adaptation of his source deliberately diminishes the sympathy we feel for the central character.

Altenberg's African Spectacle: *Ashantee* in Context

Ian Foster

On the first page of Peter Altenberg's *Ashantee*, below the main title, are the words: 'Im Wiener Thiergarten bei den Negern der Goldküste, Westküste.'[1] For the uninitiated this is puzzling, not to say shocking. Negroes from the Gold Coast in a Viennese zoo? How did they get there and what were they doing?

For the Viennese, the 1890s offered a host of sorely needed attractions and distractions. Thanks largely to immigration, the city's population had more than doubled in the previous twenty years, reaching nearly 1.8 million by the turn of the century. There was a chronic housing shortage that led to overcrowding and aggravated the already inadequate sanitation. Long-term dissatisfaction brought Karl Lueger's Christian Social Party to power in Vienna under the twin banners of anti-Semitism and anti-liberalism. Yet for the masses there were less controversial pastimes. The summer of 1896 presented a particularly rich and diverse programme. As well as the formal theatre and opera, which closed for July and reopened in August, there was a wealth of entertainment on offer at variety theatres around the city. Ronacher's 'Etablissement', for example, offered Bernardi the 'human chameleon', Diamantine Vernici, 'Verwandlungs- und Serpentinentänzerin' ('serpentine transformation dancer'), a concert singer, and the 'athletic feats' of Miss Katy Dare. No fewer than fourteen 'sensational acts' were on the programme at Danzer's Orpheum. There was also cinema. In the Kärntnerstrasse, the Lumière brothers were showing 'living photographs' only one year after their first performance in Paris. Beyond mere amusements, the weather and state occasions could drive politics from the front pages. August began with an unseasonably violent storm and ended with the Schwarzenbergplatz decked out in bright colours and rows of oriental towers for the visit of the Russian Tsar. In the popular press, the continuing search for a bomber in Leopoldstadt, whose attack on the workshop of one Markus Basch had cost the life of an apprentice, still occupied the headlines.

The Prater

And then there was the Prater. The layout and significance of Vienna's pleasure park had been reshaped by the World Exhibition of 1873 and the regulation of the Danube in 1875. The World Exhibition, held on land adjacent to the Volksprater, had been a financial failure, but it had bequeathed a new landmark to the city in the shape of the giant circular building known as the Rotunde. While the rest of the exhibition halls were pulled down, the Rotunde survived and was used for a variety of purposes – everything from circuses to trade fairs – until its destruction by fire in 1937. The Prater's other great landmark, the giant wheel built by the English engineer Bassett, was begun in 1896 and completed in the following year.[2] A shorter-lived attraction, opened in 1895, was the extensive mock-up of Venetian waterways and palazzi known as 'Venedig in Wien', also situated at the Prater's northern end. Real gondoliers, wrestlers and an Italian restaurant were imported to add an authentic flavour to this ancestor of the modern theme park. The park areas of the Prater and its main avenues were also somewhat livelier than in their present incarnation. The famous three coffee-houses were then intact and open for business. At the same time, the Prater was a centre of prostitution and all kinds of criminality.

The Volksprater itself, the city's fun-fair, suffered from its proximity to 'Venice in Vienna' and the mixed delights on offer at the Rotunde and in the surrounding park. The 1890s were, in fact, the beginning of a long-term decline. In 1896, however, Calafatti's famous roundabout and Kratky-Baschik's Magic Theatre were still drawing crowds, though nowadays only street signs remind pleasure seekers of a more expansive past. Also commemorated by a street sign in the Prater is a vivarium. And it was near the present-day Vivariumstrasse that the Wiener Thiergarten Altenberg refers to on the title page of *Ashantee* was situated.

The 'Wiener Thiergarten am Schüttel', to give it its full name, had a somewhat mixed history. Founded in 1863 as a menagerie with some two hundred mammal specimens, nearly a thousand birds and fourteen reptiles, the establishment had become insolvent in 1866 and had been forced to sell its collection and premises.[3] There were repeated attempts to revive the zoo over the following decades, none of them successful enough to compete with the more colourful Prater attractions next door. In 1893, the premises of the nearby vivarium (founded in 1888) were acquired by a 'Wiener Thiergartengesellschaft'. This society was then responsible for reopening the zoo in the following year. However, despite the society's name, the zoo's major attractions from 1895 until its closure in 1901 were not animals, but people. More accurately, non-European people. Hans Pemmer, in his history of the Prater, gives an intriguing list: 'In this way, Zulus and Matabele came in 1895, *Ashanti* in 1896 and 1897, Indian Fakirs and Senegambians in 1898, Peshwaris, Siamese, Japanese and Berbers in 1899, Dervishes, Bedouins, Boers and Kaffirs in 1900.'[4] Lest the reader gain the impression that this paradoxical phenomenon was confined to a five-year period in Vienna, one should immediately add that Pemmer's list represents a perfunctory survey and no more. In order to grasp the full implications of the Prater displays, one must take into account the activities of the pioneer of the human zoo, Carl Hagenbeck.

Hagenbeck's 'Völkerschaustellungen'

Hagenbeck, born in Hamburg in 1844, was the son of a fish merchant who sometimes displayed exotic animals to bolster the family income.[5] This activity had grown out of occasional purchases of live seals caught accidentally in fishing nets. Hagenbeck senior also bought animals from homecoming mariners and occasionally resorted to forgeries. At first, the Hagenbecks acted mainly as traders, showing most animals only until a permanent home was found for them in a menagerie or circus.

By 1859, Carl Hagenbeck had left school to join a flourishing family business, and in the following decade the firm traded all over Europe, even competing with the major animal suppliers in London. Hagenbeck's autobiographical account of the development of a trade in live exotic animals is infused with the spirit of a 'Gründerzeit' pioneer. By the 1870s, as growth in the animal trade began to slacken, Hagenbeck looked around for further areas in which the business could expand. It was at this crucial moment that an animal painter, Heinrich Leutemann, described by Hagenbeck as an old friend, made a suggestion that was to determine the direction of the family busines for the next thirty years.

In 1874, Hagenbeck was asked to import a herd of reindeer for sale to various zoos. Leutemann wrote suggesting that a family of Lapps should be brought along to tend the animals. The family, including a mother and two young children, arrived in Hamburg along with the reindeer in mid-September 1874, and attracted a crowd of thousands. Soon the public's enthusiasm for such displays knew no bounds. These early versions of what later became elaborate 'Völkerschaustellungen' are described by Hagenbeck as 'anthropological and zoological exhibitions', emphasising their close connection with the animal trade. In fact, as the exhibitions grew, zoological gardens began to take a commercial interest in them and were keen to arrange with Hagenbeck for such events to be staged on their premises. Just how seriously Hagenbeck took their scientific value, despite his frequent assertions that they served an educational purpose, may be gauged from his description of preparations for an expanded 'Ceylon' exhibition in 1884: 'This time it was not just a matter of elephants and their mahouts but of an exhibition of peoples in the grand style with all the necessary ethnological and zoological bits and bobs [mit dem nötigen ethnographischen und zoologischen Drum und Dran].'[6] A born showman, Hagenbeck had seized on the notion of displaying 'exotic' peoples as a spectacle that needed to be staged with sufficient pseudo-scientific gloss to make it palatable not only to the voyeuristic masses, whose tastes he knew well enough, but also to a more selective bourgeois audience, and ultimately to the ruling classes. He notes proudly in his autobiography that the Emperors of Austria-Hungary and Germany, together with sundry titled heads of Europe, took a keen interest in the exhibitions. The moment at which the upper classes began to arrange special visits to the 'Völkerschaustellungen' set a seal of social respectability on the whole venture.[7]

By the late 1870s, the animal trade had declined to the point where the Hagenbeck family firm was barely able to continue profitably. The 'Völkerschaustellungen' actually kept the entire business afloat for a number of years until demand picked up again. The arrival of each troupe of 'exotic' peoples became a carefully staged publicity stunt. They would be ferried through each new city in open carriages or marched through the streets in a procession with animals. Some of the Hagenbeck exhibits made grand tours of European capitals. The Ceylon exhibition of 1884, which Hagenbeck describes as a 'giant Ceylon caravan', toured major European cities from April onwards, arriving in Vienna in late summer. The site of the exhibition was the Rotunde in the Prater. So great was the number of customers that Hagenbeck's management introduced special 'people's prices' and cheap matinée shows for children (a calculated move to gain even more publicity). Within the first week the event received a visit from the Emperor Franz Joseph.[8] Greater things were yet to come. In the following two years the Ceylon exhibition toured the rest of Europe, finishing its run in Paris in 1886, where Hagenbeck was able to claim that a million people had visited the display in two-and-a-half months.

As Germany began to stake its claim alongside other European powers to territories in Africa and elsewhere, the 'Völkerschaustellungen' became an exercise not only in pseudo-anthropological education but also in propaganda designed to convince the public that expenditure on colonial ventures was worthwhile. The rise of Hagenbeck's displays coincided with the birth and nurture of German Imperial ambitions. What the spectators were seeing were captive peoples, paraded like enslaved warriors through the streets of Rome.[9] Yet while this aspect must remain uppermost in one's mind in considering German responses to Hagenbeck's spectacles, the case of Austria-Hungary was rather different. Habsburg colonial ambitions were confined, by and large, to the Balkans, where the Empire succeeded Turkey as controlling power in the 1870s and went on to annex Bosnia-Hercegovina in 1908. To be sure, there may well have been a degree of vicarious Imperial pride (the superiority of Europeans in 'civilising' distant corners of the globe), but there was also a specifically Austro-Hungarian, indeed Viennese component in the cultural impact of the arrival of groups of exotic peoples around 1900, and this local component will form the main subject of the following sections.

By the first decade of the twentieth century, the 'Völkerschaustellungen' were such an integral part of Hagenbeck's activities that he constructed a permanent site for the displays when he expanded his own zoo in Hamburg-Stellingen in 1908. Within months an 'Ethiopian village' was installed. Given the scale of such exhibitions and their enormous popularity, their relevance to an examination of the literary portrayal of 'exotic' peoples and the wider themes of colonialism and exoticism in European literature need scarcely be stressed. However, much of the available secondary literature has been written without reference to this context.[10]

The Ashanti in Vienna

The arrival of the Ashanti in Vienna in 1896 was carefully orchestrated in the classic Hagenbeck manner, though it is not entirely clear from contemporary accounts whether Hagenbeck was directly involved. The route taken by the party was circuitous in the extreme, leading through the whole first district of the city and calculated to gain maximum attention. On 10 July, the *Wiener Allgemeine Zeitung* announced:

Tomorrow (Friday), a most curious theatrical pageant will be offered to passers-by in the most populous parts of town. According to our reports, almost the entire population of an Ashanti village – around 70 black men, women and children – will land with the Budapest post boat at Weissgärber quay and travel in a long column of 15 carriages via the Ring, Kohlmarkt, Graben, Rothenthurmstrasse and Praterstrasse to the villa colony which has been built for them in the Wiener Thiergarten.

A few days later, on 14 July, advertisements began to appear announcing a 'grand ethnological display'. The attraction was well timed, since the school holidays began on 17 July. By the end of the first week, the management were laying on special direct buses and installing extra cash registers to cope with the flood of visitors. By the end of August, nearly 300,000 had passed through the turnstiles of the Wiener Thiergarten (*Wiener Allgemeine Zeitung*, 9 August and 5 September 1896). The seventy inhabitants of the Ashanti village were then joined by a further twenty-five Ashanti from a touring group, thus allowing the management to advertise, somewhat disingenuously, '100 natives'. Between the Africans' arrival in July and their departure on 16 October nearly half a million sightseers visited the village – that is, between five and six thousand a day.

Before going on to describe the cultural impact of the presence of 100 Africans – of which Altenberg's text represents an important part – it is worth looking more closely at what the Ashanti village offered its public. Firstly, it is important to observe that, as with all Hagenbeck-style people exhibitions, we are in no way dealing with an attempt to re-create an African village. Not only is it impossible to speak of authenticity, simply because the Ashanti and other similar groups were being treated as exhibits, and the presence of an observer inevitably affects what is being observed; even the basic premises of authentic re-creation were falsified. For example, the huts that composed the Ashanti village were built before the arrival of the 'natives' and according to European expectations. None the less, some features of the village were an effort at re-creation. As with all Hagenbeck-style shows, the main attraction was intended to be the people themselves and their way of life, however distorted by the presence of watching crowds. The first advertisement for the village in July 1896 used the following words: 'Ashanti village. 70 native men, women and children. Industry, school, national games, war-dances and combats.' While the 'industry', which seems mainly to have involved the fabrication of 'native' artefacts for sale to the public, and the 'school' might be described as authentic, the last three elements were clearly designed for mere entertainment.

One can also observe a process of accommodation to the expectations of the paying public, probably under the influence of a profit-hungry management. (Some press reports suggest that the Thiergarten was already in financial difficulties.) Accounts of Ashanti in Vienna reveal two examples. In the first, a religious ceremony welcoming a new child into the community was promoted in lurid, voyeuristic tones: 'Although the celebration is in fact an intimate one, put on by the blacks for the blacks, there will nevertheless be no lack of interesting things for the visitors to see' (*Wiener Allgemeine Zeitung*, 1 September

1896). From then on, African religious ceremonies, usually described as 'Fetischtanz', were a regular part of the programme. The use of the term 'fetish' is in fact peculiarly appropriate, since it derives from the Portuguese *feticeiro* and rests on a European misunderstanding of West African religious practices.[11] The second case concerns artefacts made by the Ashanti. In 1896, the sale of souvenirs went unmentioned in the publicity for the village, though it evidently represented a source of extra income. Shortly before the departure of the Ashanti, 200 such ethnographic items were disposed of in a raffle. In the following season, in April 1897, a group of 120 Africans, among them some who had participated in the previous year, arrived for a display entitled 'Africa's Gold Coast and its Inhabitants'. This time, however, the presence of a full complement of goldsmiths, gunsmiths, potters and bronzeworkers was advertised from the start, and a full African bazaar was planned as part of the attraction.

The process of accommodation to the expectations of the public did not stop at mere shifts in emphasis like these. The presence of the Ashanti provided the impetus for exotic spectacles. Following the arrival of a party of 37 Javanese in June 1897 – who in due course set up their own 'authentic' village and coffee-house, where visitors could be served by 'native women' – the management of the Thiergarten planned an 'Ausstattungs-Pantomime' involving all its 'exotic' specimens, human and animal. This was entitled 'The Sacrificial Feast of the Javanese or the Kidnapping of the Plantation Daughter' and involved a cast of 150 people, Javanese and Ashantis, together with horses, elephants and cattle. The body of the spectacle was composed of 'scenes from plantation life', punctuated by comic 'Intermezzis' (*sic*) performed by clowns and Ashanti children.

Such displays were frequently presented in circus arenas or in association with large exhibitions. Similar performances were often titled 'Spektakelstücke'. Indeed, the dividing lines between circus, zoo and exhibition and theatre were not at all clear. Often, animal acts we would now more readily associate with the circus would form part of a zoo's attractions. Exhibitions with pseudo-historical or scientific-sounding titles (like 'Life in Ancient Rome', 'The Queen of Abyssinia's Feast', 'To Siberia' or 'The Death of Zriny') could easily involve what were essentially circus acts dressed up in historical costume. Hagenbeck and his imitators discovered that supposedly serious science could be dressed up as entertainment.

Over the period of the Ashantis' two seasons in Vienna, as the local public became familiar with their presence, the presentation shifted from the original pseudo-scientific framework – what Hagenbeck calls the natives' life and activities – to a more openly theatrical terminology. One description of the 'Pantomime', for example, referred to the skill of the Ashantis in playing their role.[12]

The Cultural Impact

For two short seasons Vienna was struck by an African fever. Not only were the Ashantis themselves the subject of a flood of press reports, detailing, among other things, their visits to the city sights and their shopping trips, but, more importantly, the figure of the African entered the city's cultural discourse in an unprecedented way. The Ashantis were, of course, by no means the first blacks to visit Vienna. Street names in the city again give us clues to this submerged portion of history. There is, for example, an Afrikanergasse in the Leopoldstadt, whose name derives from an eighteenth-century official delegation from Morocco.[13] The Mohrengasse presumably has a similar background. Around 1800, the Viennese Natural History Museum boasted a number of stuffed black Africans among its prize exhibits, two of whom had been exotic servants to Central European royalty.[14] There are also numerous examples of non-European peoples being displayed to a paying public. In the early nineteenth century, two Brazilian Indians were displayed at the Schönbrunn Zoo; in the 1840s, four blacks featured in the de Bach circus. Africans, then, were not a new sight. Perhaps the only novelty in the 1890s lay in sheer numbers. Yet numbers alone cannot explain why the figure of the African came to play such a striking role. By the late summer of 1896, the Royal and Imperial Court Opera was performing a German version of a five-act opera by Meyerbeer and Scribe, entitled *Die Afrikanerin*. For those seeking more durable mementos, Viennese manufacturers were soon producing 'delightful little Ashanti groups with brown complexions and curly hair'.[15] Soon there were Ashanti jokes and Ashanti cartoons in the humorous papers.

One principal source of the fascination that the Ashanti exerted on the Viennese imagination was blatantly sexual. Scanty clothing (the women were usually topless, the men in loincloths) was deemed a sign of their naturalness. Africans displayed in Europe from the end of the eighteenth century onwards were conventionally presented in thin, revealing garments.[16] These were noble savages who had no need of the sartorial trappings of civilised Europeans. This rhetoric of naturalness disguised a prurient voyeurism. Yet while voyeurism may account for the kind of crowds that flocked to see the Ashanti, the resonance of the African spectacle should not be explained away by reference to the European fetish for visual titillation.

There is another theme in the Viennese press reports of the time and – in so far as it is realistic to reconstruct it from what such reports have to tell us – in the cultural discourse of the city. This theme can best be seen in the shifting terminology used to describe the Ashanti. This consisted of a series of terms that could be applied both to the Ashanti and to the Viennese. For example, the Ashanti were frequently referred to as 'our black guests', which would cast the Viennese in the role of 'hosts'. When the Viennese public visited the Thiergarten village, they became the 'guests' of the Ashanti. Other terms were similarly reversible: in their village the Ashanti were 'natives' ('Eingeborene' or 'Einheimische'), where the Viennese, otherwise 'natives', could become 'strangers' or 'visitors' – the last two names then being applicable to the Ashanti in the appropriate context. One finds, in fact, a whole rhetoric constructed around the poles of familiarity and otherness. For example, Viennese newcomers to the Ashanti village might, it was often suggested, find themselves in need of a 'cicerone' or guide and would find one among the village's 'habitués' – not the Ashanti, but those who had already explored this foreign territory. Altenberg casts himself in this role in a letter to Hugo Salus where he describes five hours as 'Führer durch Aschantee von einer ganzen Anzahl von Damen'[17] (guide through Ashanti for a large number of ladies).

The significance of this rhetoric of difference – of belonging and not belonging – in a city where over half of the population had been born elsewhere and where virulent anti-Semitism was in the process of celebrating its political triumph is plain. Within a few weeks of arrival in Vienna, the Ashanti entered a highly differentiated language of racial/ethnic difference. According to one interpretation, political anti-Semitism was successful in Vienna precisely because it was the one shared language in a polyglot city of immigrants.[18] It provided the decisive catalyst for Vienna's African fever of 1896.

Local anti-Semitic rhetoric cast the Jews in the role of the eternal outsider. Recent immigrants from Galicia were termed ignoble savages fresh from 'Halb-Asien'. The Ashanti, as black Africans and symbolic absolute Other, offered the perfect foil for the anti-Semites. The anti-Semitic *Kikeriki* published the following poem:

Der Fetisch-Tanz

Die Fetisch-Tänze der Aschanti-Wilden,
Die jetzt für Wien die great attraction bilden,
Nennt unsere Judenpress 'unvergleichlich',
Wir aber finden, wie auch leicht aufzeiglich,
In nächster Nähe ein Vergleichsobjekt.
Seht doch nur, wie 'so schein wie kaner'
Im Kaftan der Galizianer
Die Beine schlendert und sie wieder streckt
Im tollen Tanze um ein Fetisch-Tier
Das goldene Kalb, den alten Apis-Stier!

(8 October 1896)

[The fetish dance of the Ashanti savages which now form Vienna's great attraction are called incomparable by our Jewish press. We, however, find it easy to point to a nearby object of comparison. Just look at how 'the most handsome of them all' in Galician caftan glides and stretches his legs in the mad dance about a fetish animal, the golden calf, the old Apis bull.]

Contempt for liberal support for the Habsburg state thus voiced itself in an anti-Semitic rhetoric that pictured all Jews as caftan-wearing Galician aliens. In this chain of thought the Ashanti formed a vital link.

At the same time, the Ashanti offered a vehicle not only for anti-Semites to make comparisons but also for the liberals themselves. The liberal view of the Ashanti sought to outflank the 'otherness' foisted on the Jews by espousing a humane cultural relativism. The liberal press couched its reports in a would-be scientific phraseology, displaying an enlightened ethnological curiosity. A good example may be found in the *Neue Freie Presse* of 6 October 1896. After a 28-year-old Ashanti gunsmith named John Ahadji died of pneumonia, the reporter observed the villagers' reactions to the sad news: 'The whole tribe performed a mourning rite, which, despite its peculiar and noisy form, did not fail to have a moving effect on the European observers of these scenes.' This is the authentic liberal view of the Ashanti: that these were, despite superficial differences, fellow human beings whose customs and habits, however strange they seemed to the average Central European, could engage the interest and sympathy of the observer. Inevitably, however, the liberal enlightened view of noble savages who were part of the great family of humanity tended to aestheticise and idealise the Ashanti. A little later in the same article we read: 'A curious picture was presented by the black women as they continually pressed blossom-white handkerchiefs to their eyes.' The opportunity to present the reader with a striking image undermines the sympathy appropriate to a funeral.

Ashantee

Altenberg's sketches on the Ashanti are conventionally described as the response of an aesthete to the natural innocence and spontaneity of the Africans exhibited in the park.[19] The unreflected racist assumptions behind such descriptions require no further comment, but even the notion that the text is primarily 'Altenberg's response' is problematic. Most, but not all, of the short prose passages are concerned with encounters between the narrator figure, variously styled Peter A. or Sir Peter, and the Ashanti. Originally, the sequence consisted of thirty-three sections.[20] Twenty-three of the original sketches plus a further five new texts were incorporated into the fourth edition of *Wie ich es sehe* in 1904 under the title 'Ashantee'. The following texts were added after 'Der Automat': 'Ehebruch', 'Prügel', 'Mitgift', 'Erbfolge'. After a slightly altered version of 'Ritterlichkeit', a new sketch entitled 'Mütterlichkeit' was added. The rest remained in the original order, despite the omission of several substantial texts, including 'Gespräch', 'Die Hütten (Abends)', 'Ein Brief aus Wien', 'Le Coeur' and 'Conclusion', and the shorter pieces 'Einmaleins', 'Akolé' and 'Le départ pour l'Afrique'. In both versions the text is dedicated to 'Meinen schwarzen Freundinnen, den unvergeßlichen "Paradieses-Menschen" Akolé, Akóshia, Tioko, Djojo, Nah-Baduh' ('To my black women friends, the unforgettable people from paradise'...). These names and the events mentioned in the text, like the storm referred to in 'Akolés Gesang. Akolés süßes Lied' (*Ashantee*, p. 39), also appear in the press reports of 1896. To a certain extent, therefore, the text describes the exhibition of 1896 (the book appeared in the spring of 1897). In a letter to Schnitzler, Altenberg even refers to the Ashanti woman Nah-Baduh by name as the 'letzten Wahnsinn meiner Seele'[21] ('last madness of my soul').

The first section of *Ashantee* purports to be a quotation from *Meyers Conversations-Lexikon*, a popular encyclopedia. The source Altenberg gives for the text (volume one, page 900) corresponds to the fourth edition of Meyer's encyclopedia.[22] However, the encyclopedia entry is some 1,500 words in length and Altenberg's 'quotation' less than 150. All the elements in Altenberg's text appear in the same order as in the encyclopedia article, with a few important exceptions. Rereading the Altenberg text after looking up the reference given, it becomes obvious that the former was intended to offer 'notes' on the latter.

The number of elliptical sentences bears out this interpretation. But these are notes of a particular kind.

What does Altenberg's abbreviated version of the encyclopedia article contain? The reader is informed that 'Ashantee' is a 'Negro kingdom' in West Africa partly conquered by the English, a fertile country with a moderate climate, whose palm and rubber trees are 'nutzbar' ('useful' – presumably for European industries). The main food crop is yams. Altenberg's version adds a comment here that the yam is 'eine unserer Kartoffel ähnliche Pflanze' ('a plant similar to our potato'). The inhabitants of Ashantiland are 'true, woolly-haired negroes', who speak Oji and are known for their skill in weaving and goldwork. They are polygamous. Where Meyer's encyclopedia refers to 'customary polygamy', Altenberg's version laconically notes 'Es herrscht Vielweiberei' ('Polygamy prevails'). Furthermore, the Ashanti practise a 'fetishist' religion. Here again Altenberg adds details not in the original. Where the encyclopedia mentions evil spirits which the priests of the Ashanti have the power to placate through mysterious means, Altenberg's elliptical version names these means explicitly as 'geheimnisvolle Ceremonien und hysterische Tänze' ('mysterious ceremonies and hysterical dances'). The Altenberg text continues with General Wolseley's defeat of the Ashanti king in 1874 and the subsequent forbidding of human sacrifices. It ends with references to works by Brackenbury and Stanley on the history of the conquest and colonisation of West Africa. Meyer's encyclopedia gives no fewer than nine references.

Altenberg's condensed version contains, in fact, the entire repertoire of colonialist clichés about Africa. Ashantiland is a potentially profitable place inhabited by uncivilised negroes. The additional mention of hysterical dances and the way the notion of African polygamy is introduced overtly signal the image of the African as sexually voracious and beyond the bounds of supposed European restraint. The reference to human sacrifice ('Der König [...] gelobte Abschaffung der Menschenopfer', p. 4; 'The king vowed to abolish human sacrifice') clearly implies that such sacrifices still take place. And where the idea of human sacrifice is mentioned, another colonialist cliché, the native as cannibal, cannot be far away. The chocolate confectionery known as 'Mohrenkopf' or 'Negerkuss', still widely available under these names in the German-speaking countries, is a modern echo of this idea. By consuming the Moor's head one is forcibly reminded of a cannibalistic rite in 'darkest Africa'. Similarly, one flavour of ice cream that can be bought in present-day Vienna has the name 'Aschantis'. The dark pieces of nut in the lighter ice cream supposedly represent the heads of the Ashanti in a white crowd.

Altenberg's possible reasons for placing a text like this at the beginning of the sequence have not been adequately explained by previous commentators. Sander Gilman sees it as part of an overtly ideological frame, whose main function is to 'counter or undermine the popular tone of the Prater's exhibition of the black' by setting the Ashanti in the context of the 'textual ethnological museum' of scientific discourse.[23] Though this is not his main point and he is more concerned with what he calls coded references to black sexuality, Gilman's account is rather misleading. The 'quotation' is not intended chiefly to condemn the populism of the Prater, but is in fact part of a critique of liberal notions of 'Bildung' and, indeed, culture. Its reduction of the original lengthy article to a brief series of lurid details about fetishism, hysterical dances and human sacrifices, framed by remarks about climate and potential profitability, satirises the hypocrisy of the liberal interest in science.

Liberal conceptions of a cultivated, scientific view were openly mocked by the anti-Semitic press of the period. In its pages, the Ashanti were implicitly and explicitly compared with the Jews – to the detriment of both. For example, the weekly *Wiener Neueste Nachrichten* published a *feuilleton* entitled 'Aus dem Thiergarten im Prater' by one Robert Horn on 14 September 1896. This text quotes extensively from the fifth edition of *Meyers Konversations-Lexikon* of 1895, adding the comments of its author:

> The Ashanti are genuine negroes who speak Oji. I must confess to my shame that I can hardly speak Oji at all [...]. Ashantiland is in fact the gold-producing country of Guinea and gold is the only currency. Here Nature rather than Rothschild seems to have taken care of the regulation of value.

The mocking tone in which information is given here signals contempt for the 'Bildungsgut' on display. Each item in the encyclopedia entry is linked to some manifestation of Viennese life, frequently to something Horn sees as the fault of the Jews. Towards the end, a caricature Jewish 'Schornalist' accompanies the narrator around the zoo.

Altenberg, of course, does not gloss his chosen text. His technique is more subtle, but both he and Horn have a similar target. One might draw a parallel here with Karl Kraus, whose declared enemy was not the anti-Semitic press, but the leading liberal newspaper, the *Neue Freie Presse*. Seen in the context of the whole sequence of sketches on the Ashanti, Altenberg's version of the encyclopedia text forms one half of a framing device. The second half is the penultimate text, the address to the Ashanti woman Nah-Baduh. The reader thus progresses from an encyclopedia entry on the Ashanti, a laconic sequence of 'Bildungsklischees', to personal contact, almost an invitation to begin a correspondence.

Critics have disagreed about whether the sketches on the Ashanti have a plot. Camillo Schaefer argues that there is no continuous action. Sander Gilman, on the other hand, insists that they have an 'overall literary structure lacking in [Altenberg's] other works'.[24] It might be argued that the movement from a taxonomic 'they' to a vocative 'you' constitutes a kind of plot, but there is also a plot of a more straightforward kind. The story, which will be dealt with in greater detail below, concerns the relationships between the narrator and two young Ashanti women. At first, it is Tíoko who interests him and, apparently, responds to his advances, though he appears equally fascinated by Akolé. The arrival of Nah-Baduh from Budapest precipitates a crisis in the existing relationship, with the narrator now unable to avoid hurting Tíoko's feelings because of his adoration of Nah-Baduh. In this instance, however, the text makes it plain that the narrator's love is unrequited, or at least not greeted with an equal response. There is also a further complication, since one of the Ashanti men,

Altenberg's African Spectacle, Ashantee

Noe Salomon Dowoonah, is also in love with Nah-Baduh. Along the way, other relationships among the Africans and between them and the Viennese are described, but the main thread binding the texts together when they are read in sequence is the narrator's involvement first with Tioko, then with Nah-Baduh, and the emotions evoked within this central triangle. Four of the seven substantial texts in the first edition which do not appear in the 1904 revision refer to Tioko and Nah-Baduh. Altenberg's revision, which is much more widely known than the first edition, therefore makes the Peter A.–Tioko–Nah-Baduh triangle less obvious. The five new texts in the second version are all of a more general kind.

The main theme of *Ashantee* is not, therefore, as its author's contemporary Max Messer argued, the problematic nature of Western culture and the destruction of the equation of culture with humanity.[25] Nor is it, as Camillo Schaefer puts it, 'glorification of freedom', although both of these are major themes. The main theme is articulated by the movement from third to second person, by which Altenberg's text goes beyond liberal ideology and offers the idea that what really counts in the end is not some notion of enlightened tolerance, but the ability to build a personal relationship with someone of a different culture and ethnic origin. Only through such a relationship can the gulf that separates the Viennese voyeurs from the inhabitants of a Hagenbeck display be transcended.

Altenberg's critique of the attitudes and presuppositions of the abbreviated encyclopedia entry at the beginning of Ashantee is a revision of liberal ideology, not a rejection of it. That this is indeed the case is illustrated by the second text in the collection, entitled 'Der Hofmeister'. At eight and a half pages, this is the longest text in the collection. Despite this, it has received only the most cursory treatment. The private tutor of the title leads his two charges, the girl Fortunatina and the boy Oscar, into the Thiergarten display. First, they arrive at the cage of two pampas hares, where the tutor deplores the ignorance of the masses who throw sugar and bread to the animals. On a pedantic note, he asks Fortunatina to remind him to refer to a standard work by Brehm when they return. They then move on to the bear cage, where again the tutor demonstrates his superior knowledge of animal behaviour by succeeding in tempting one of the animals into the water.

Up to this point, the tutor appears to be a parody of the liberal, cultivated 'Bürger', eagerly displaying his 'Bildungsgut' and involuntarily exposing his intellectual conceit. He may even be a self-parody by Altenberg, as the description of his clothing and appearance suggests (in particular the pince-nez!). However, the text is more complex than a simple parody, and the perspective of the narrator less easily defined. The section begins with a description of the ticket kiosk at the entrance to the zoo, where the ticket-seller sits eating a pear (foreshadowing the peach given to the pampas hares by the tutor). The ticket-seller says: 'Les enfans [*sic*] ne comptent pas' [...] wie wenn man sagt 'Marsch, verschwindet, Ihr habt wenig Bedeutung –' ('Children don't count' [...] as though saying 'Go on, get lost, you are insignificant') (p. 5). The point of Altenberg's text is precisely the opposite. Children do count, and their views are given equal weight by Altenberg's narrator.

The next cage visited is that of a lioness. Fortunatina is fascinated, but Oscar is unimpressed. The narrator verbalises his thoughts for the reader 'Eine Löwin, was sieht man?! Eingesperrt ist sie –' ('A lioness, what can one see? She is in a cage –') (p. 6). The tutor is absorbed in his own reverie on Fortunatina and the lioness and reflects that there is no shame in dreaming of oneself as a wild animal. The verbal phrase 'sich in Thiere hineinträumen' expresses a wished-for identity of human being and animal, 'Fortunatina und die Löwin'. Fortunatina herself daydreams about an African night: 'Man hat Beispiele, dass – Afrika. Afrika. Kaltblutigkeit, Entschlossenheit haben oft im letzten Momente den kühnen Jäger –' ('There are examples of – Africa. Africa. Coolness and determination have often rescued the bold hunter at the last moment.') (p. 7). She pictures the tutor in the yellow leather clothes and boots of the colonial hunter-explorer. As well as explicitly announcing the African theme, this passage illustrates the subtle shifts of perspective characteristic of Altenberg's writing. Whose view are we to take seriously here? That of the boy, who thinks a caged lioness a dull attraction? Or the tutor, who contemplates the caged beast and its human observer as an aesthetic phenomenon? Or the girl, who dreams of a wild Africa as the setting for heroic adventures?

This problem grows still more acute when one considers the scenes which follow. Now that the word 'Africa' has been uttered, the stage is set for the Ashanti to appear, dancing to their syncopated rhythms (as the tutor pedantically observes). Fortunatina compares the rhythm to the sound of a train and suggests 'real' music could be written to accompany it. Oscar is again unimpressed and comments: 'Für Die ist es jedenfalls Musik' ('They think it's music, at any rate'). At this point the main theme is sounded again. The tutor says:

> Mache nur nicht gleich solche Abgründe zwischen Uns und Ihnen. Für Die, für Die. Was bedeutet es?! Glaubst Du, weil das dumme Volk sich über sie stellt, sie behandelt wie exotische Thiere?! Warum?! Weil ihre Epidermis dunkle Pigment-Zellen enthält?! (p. 9)
>
> [Don't create such gulfs between us and them. For them, for them. What does that mean?! Do you think because the stupid masses place themselves above them and treat them like exotic animals?! Why?! Because their epidermis contains dark pigment cells?!]

The pretentious reference to 'pigment cells' and the bourgeois arrogance towards the stupidity of the masses indicate again that the tutor is a parodic figure whose words are not to be taken too seriously. But at the same time, the insistence that the Ashanti be encountered as people, as individuals first and foremost, encapsulates the whole movement of Altenberg's text.

Tíoko

Exactly at this point the first personal encounter takes place. The tutor gives the Ashanti girl Tíoko a necklace of glass beads. Again, this action is presented from various points of view. The tutor is inspired by the spontaneity of Tioko's response to the gift and admires her beauty. Fortunatina reflects on the gentleness of the scene: 'Wie im Paradiese ist es eigentlich, wo Menschen und wilde Thiere –' (It's just like paradise, where people and wild animals –'). Her uncompleted thought is immediately undercut by Oscar's cynicism. He asks how much the beads cost and why the tutor should have them with him, and questions Tioko's motives. Presenting beads to the natives may also have unfortunate associations in the mind of modern readers, though these are not necessarily in the foreground here. Leaving the zoo behind, they sit for a while on a bench. The tutor presents Fortunatina with a necklace similar to that he had given to Tioko, an action which embarrasses Oscar, since it suggests that the tutor's motives in making the first gift were not an attempt to buy Tioko's time and interest. The tutor explains in response to Fortunatina's question that Tioko spends the evenings doing domestic chores for the ticket-seller, to which she responds: 'Ich hielt sie für die Tochter des Königs!' (I took her for the king's daughter!) (p. 12). The constant interplay between the three characters, now aestheticising and idealising, now hard-headed and cynical, is rather like the switch of perspective in Kafka's short story 'Auf der Galerie', where a woman riding bareback in a circus act creates an illusion of grace and beauty that prevents the observer in the gallery from intervening in what he knows to be merely a gaudy show.

Throughout *Ashantee* aestheticising tendencies are repeatedly set against a sympathetic portrait of the discomforts and indignities suffered by the human exhibits. Towards the end of 'Der Hofmeister', the narrator describes Tioko:

> Tioko, im Garten, bebt, legt den dünnen heliotropfarbenen Kattun über ihre wunderbaren hellbraunen Brüste, welche sonst in Freiheit und Schönheit lebten, wie Gott sie geschaffen, dem edlen Männer-Auge ein Bild der Weltvollkommenheiten gebend, ein Ideal an Kraft und Blüthe. (p. 12)

> [In the garden, Tioko shivers, places the thin heliotrope coloured calico dress over her wonderful light-brown breasts, which otherwise live in beauty and freedom, as God created them, to present the noble male gaze with an image of perfection in this world, an ideal of vigour and fruitfulness.]

This passage is followed by 'Gespräch', in which the narrator encounters Tioko in person. She complains of having to go about half-naked for the entertainment of the visitors:

> Wilde müssen wir vorstellen, Herr, Afrikaner. Ganz närrisch ist es. In Afrika könnten wir nicht so sein. Alle würden lachen. [...] Der Clark sagt: 'He, solche wie in Europa gibt es genug. Wozu braucht man Euch?! Nackt müsst Ihr sein natürlich.' (p. 14)

> [Sir, we must play the part of savages, Africans. It is quite silly. We could not behave like this in Africa. Everyone would laugh. The clerk says: 'Bah,

there are enough people like those in Europe already. Why should we need you? You must be naked, naturally.']

God may well have intended Tíoko's breasts to be exposed for noble-minded male onlookers, but the proprietors of the zoo know all too well that they are appealing to far less noble-minded European tastes for erotic display in an exotic setting. This constant undercutting of notions of a pure, aesthetic interest in the Ashanti has the effect of colouring the whole aesthetic vocabulary at Altenberg's disposal. When the narrator uses words like 'ideal', 'rein', 'zart' ('pure', 'delicate') and so on, they automatically evoke an erotic subtext.

The question of the exposed breasts of the Ashanti women as symbols of their naturalness or as an erotic focus for the voyeuristic fantasies of European males is again addressed in the ninth sketch, 'Cultur'. A young Ashanti woman, 'big Akolé', and a seven-year-old girl, 'bibi Akolé', are invited to dinner with Frau H. After the meal both are given a beautiful French doll, 'zum Spass' (for fun), as the narrator puts it. Both sing their dolls to sleep, and then 'big Akolé' uncovers her breast to feed her doll. Little Akolé is said to be in despair, for she cannot feed her doll in this way. The reactions of the dinner guests are as follows:

> Frau H. sagte ihren Gästen, es wäre der heiligste Augenblick ihres Lebens. Die Gäste fanden Ähnliches, wenn auch nicht so bombastisch. Selbst monsieur R. de B. lächelte, wie man eigentlich nicht lächelt, wenn man lächelt – (p. 29)

> [Frau H. said to her guests that it was the holiest moment of her life. The guests were of a similar opinion, if not quite as bombastic about it. Even Monsieur R. de B. smiled in a way one really ought not to smile when one smiles.]

The ambiguous smile of Monsieur R. de B. is the sign of his erotic interest in the supposedly natural display. Altenberg is documenting a significant cultural moment in the evolution of Western mores: the point at which the female breast has become so overloaded with erotic significance that even its exposure for the fulfilment of its biological purpose becomes taboo. If one reflects for a moment on typical attitudes towards ethnological films, for example, where shots of women breastfeeding their babies seem to be almost *de rigueur*, as contrasted with cases where women in Western countries have actually been arrested for feeding their babies in public, then the subtlety of Altenberg's ambivalent account of the Ashanti's nudity can be readily appreciated.

At this level, the meaning of Peter A.'s outburst in the same sketch, 'Neger sind Kinder' (negroes are children) (p. 28), also takes on further meaning. This is plainly not meant as a reflection of that nineteenth-century cliché that black Africans somehow represented a more primitive childlike stage of cultural development. For Peter A. children and blacks are linked because they are 'Etwas [...], was uns zum Tönen bringt' (something that makes us resonate) (p. 29). Children and blacks are potent figures in our imaginations, figures on to whom we project our fantasies: 'Sie selbst spielen kein Instrument, sie dirigiren unsere Seele' (they themselves play no instruments; they conduct our soul). And that imagination, in Altenberg's terms, cannot but conceive of the child – as well as the black – in erotic terms.

At this point, it is wise to reflect on the socio-cultural context of Altenberg's literary predilection for pre-pubescent girls. (The 'ideal' Ashanti women are referred to as 'Mädchen' on several occasions.) Prostitution, and in particular child prostitution, was rife in Vienna in the late nineteenth century. The eroticisation of children was therefore no mere aesthetic phenomenon. Yet while it is difficult to read *Ashantee*, or any of Altenberg's other collections for that matter, without becoming aware of the implications of this fixation, it is also important to note that Altenberg's texts are always 'self-undermining artefacts'. For example, the narrator's attraction to Tíoko, referred to above, is not simply the record of an erotic dalliance but respects the integrity of its subject by stating the terms within which the fantasy has been constructed. Tíoko appears both as object of the narrator's fantasy and as victim of the zoo-keeper's exploitative practices. Forced to pin down exactly where the sympathies of the narrator lie, one cannot but conclude that he is on the side of the oppressed, though this passionate sympathy may at times be overlaid with a more dubious erotic interest. It is striking, for example, that the Africans and children in the text are all referred to by their first names. The adult Europeans remain nameless; at most the reader learns their professional title ('der Clark', 'der Thiergarten-Direktor') or perhaps an initial (Fräulein D., Frau H.).[26] Moreover, the narrator's portrayal of the relationships between the Ashanti is a differentiated one. In 'Die Hütten (Abends)', the hut of the young men is empty – as males they have the freedom of the city. The unmarried young women, on the other hand, are forced to stay behind. In 'Ritterlichkeit', the Ashanti chief Bodjé tells Peter A. how he has beaten Nah-Baduh for refusing to dance: 'Wofür zahlen die weißen Menschen?! Es ist unsere Pflicht' (what are the white people paying for? It is our duty) (p. 59). Peter A. plainly does not approve and is troubled by the beating; in response to his silence Bodjé asks "Was hast du, Herr–?!' (What is wrong, sir?). In the first version, the sketch ends with Peter A.'s reply 'Nichts, Bodjé–' (Nothing, Bodjé). In the 1904 revision, Altenberg adds a final sentence from Bodjé: 'Nun, Herr, ich werde sie von nun an träumen lassen in ihrer Hütte'[27] (Now, sir, I will leave her to dream in her hut from now on). This addition accentuates Peter A.'s role in acting on behalf of the Ashanti women, but the substance of the text remains the same: that the Ashanti men are equally capable of exploiting the women in the group when commercial interests are at stake.

The relationship between the narrator and Tíoko develops in the ninth, tenth and eleventh sketches, 'Paradies', 'Der Abend' and 'Ein Brief aus Accra'. In the first of these, the narrator asks Tíoko what she would like most to be given. She replies that she would like green and pink glass beads. In the second, he kisses her for the first time. In the third, the narrator is attracted to Akolé, who tells him firmly 'Go to Tíoko' (p. 34). The context of this instruction is particularly important. One of the women, Monambo, asks Peter A. to buy a 'piss-pot' (the English term is used) for herself and the other two women present, since the nights are cold and they have to leave the hut to urinate. As in the case of the Ashanti women's exposure of their breasts, the text crosses here into a territory shaped by sexual taboos. Witnessing or, in this case, talking about how a woman performs a bodily function amounts to intrusion into the private sphere. When Monambo says that Peter A. would readily give Tíoko a piss-pot as a present, she alludes to a sexual relationship between them. The vulnerability of the Ashanti women left alone in the evenings is also powerfully evoked by the image of a woman squatting to urinate outside the hut. After the discussion with Monambo, the narrator kisses the hand of each of the three women:

> Akolé war zu schön! Ich kniete mich nieder, küßte sie auf die Stirne, die Augen, den Mund –
> 'Go to Tíoko – ' sagte sie sanft.
> Monambo, Akóschia verkrochen sich in ihren Kattunen. (p. 35)

> [Akolé was too beautiful! I knelt down, kissed her forehead, her eyes, her mouth –
> 'Go to Tíoko – ' she said gently.
> Monambo and Akóschia retreated in their calico dresses.]
> (At this point the 1904 version adds a third 'Go to Tíoko'.)

Since the paragraph which then closes the sketch describes the narrator leaving the hut at daybreak, suggesting the figure of a lover, it is evident that the repeated instruction has not been followed and the narrator has spent the night with Akolé. This interpretation can be substantiated by the fact that three of the following four sketches, ('Akolé', 'Akolé's Gesang. Akolé's süßes Lied' and 'Complications') all concern Akolé and not Tíoko. Tíoko does not, however, vanish from the text completely, and there is more to be said about her.

Nah-Baduh

The nineteenth sketch is in the form of a letter in Altenberg's rather shaky English to the Ashanti woman Monambo. A translation of the letter forms the twentieth sketch. The repetition stresses again the theme of communication despite a limited vocabulary, and the letter form suggests the overall movement of the text. Peter A. writes to Monambo in English because he cannot address himself directly to Nah-Baduh. As he admits, he only knows one word in Ashanti ('misumo' – 'I love you') and that word is insufficient to describe the complexity of his feelings. Nah-Baduh's spontaneous gesture (she lays her head on his shoulder) has captivated him. At the same time, he knows that he is not alone in her affections, and there is another whose presence concerns Nah-Baduh more: 'I suppose, the reason of all this will be the joung "Black-man" Noe Salomon Dowoonah' [sic] (p. 47).

In the following sketch, 'Prinzessin in Grün', he lists the presents 'Sir Peter' has made to Nah-Baduh. In 'L'homme médiocre', the theme raised by the first present-giving to Tíoko is sounded again. If the Ashanti women accept gifts from admirers, does this make them venal? For the mediocre man, the association between gifts and women of easy virtue is unavoidable: 'Ich hörte aber, man könne junge schwarze Mädchen kaufen?!' (But I heard that one can buy young black women) (p. 53). Peter A. insists that this is only true '[u]nter den Bedingungen der Liebe' (on condition of love) and that once 'bought' in this way the woman will remain with a man only as long as love endures. With this idealised version of Ashanti marriage Altenberg's text is playing on a literary topos that reaches back to the beginnings of exoticism in European literature. The morality of the natives the traveller finds in a distant land is always more practical, more sensible than that of the stuffy Europeans.[28] Here the distant land has itself apparently come to visit. Altenberg's sketches on the Ashanti represent a development of the two main strands in the satirical use of exoticism: the distant land as comparison for a depraved and corrupt Europe, and the naive eye of the traveller who arrives from overseas and is shocked by the behaviour of his hosts.[29] In *Ashantee* Africa quite literally comes to Europe; the naive eye and the distant land are both present.

In the twenty-seventh through to the thirty-second sketches, the relationships between the narrator and Tíoko and Nah-Baduh are resolved. In 'Le Coeur', Tíoko expresses her feelings of worthlessness now that she knows that Sir Peter loves Nah-Baduh. The scene is the hut of the young women on a cold September evening. The narrator quotes ironically from the local newspapers: 'Unsere schwarzen Fremdlinge im Thiergarten haben Nichts von ihrer Laune eingebüßt' (The good mood of our black foreigners in the Thiergarten has not suffered) (p. 60). The Ashanti women attempt to comfort Tíoko in her despair. She insists: 'Tíoko finish', which the narrator 'translates' as 'mit T. ist es aus' (It is over for T.). She goes on to say that Noe Salomon Dowoonah loves Nah-Baduh, yet Nah-Baduh does not love him. Therefore, they will both be sad when they return to Africa. She believes Nah-Baduh should remain in Vienna with Sir Peter, an idea taken up by her companions. The sketch ends with Tíoko leaving the hut and not responding to calls for her to return, despite the cold outside.

The following piece, 'Conclusion', begins with a description of Nah-Baduh resting her head on Herr Peter's shoulder 'Wie damals', a repetition of the scene that had inspired the narrator's affection for her. It continues with an incident late in the evening when Noe Salomon, the young man who also loves Nah-Baduh, approaches Herr Peter. The narrator exclaims: 'Was gibt es –?! Wir haben nichts mit einander zu schaffen – ?!' (What is it? We have no quarrel with each other) (p. 63). Does he fear his rival perhaps? But Noe Salomon merely asks for an old overcoat. Herr Peter gives him his own new coat and leaves with the remark that he finds the evening warm, like a spring night.

In 'Palawer (Rath der Männer)', the men of the village decide to give Tíoko to the zoo-director as a leaving present. Tíoko accepts this decision, but asks whether Sir Peter knows of it. The chief Bodjé replies that it is none of Sir Peter's business. The scene then switches to the zoo-director telling a group of people how he had refused this offer. They are surprised at what they consider his lack of romantic feeling. He responds:

> Nichts Romantisches würde es sein. Die Welt ist leer. Eine verfehmte Magd würde sie bald bei uns. Ich habe diese schwarzen Menschen dennoch lieb gewonnen. Gegen mich selbst. (p. 66)
>
> [It would not be romantic. The world is empty. She would soon be a figure of scorn if she remained among us. But I have learnt to like these black people. Despite myself.]

This also helps to explain why Peter A. is then reported to have said that the zoo-director should have accepted the offer, as he would have got on well with Tíoko. For what the director admits, in fact, is that despite his prejudices he has learned to see the Ashanti as individual human beings and not as examples of 'true woolly-haired negroes'. He refuses because he knows that Tíoko's life in Europe would not be 'like a chapter of Victor Hugo or Dumas amid the confinements of barrack-room life'.

In 'Der Tag des Abschiedes' a postscript is added to the narrator's relationship with Tíoko when Tíoko's mother gives Peter A. a small, wooden African stool on which Tíoko used to sit and cry. The present is to serve as a reminder that Peter A. once loved her. There follows a short conversation between Nah-Baduh and the narrator. First, Nah-Baduh asks what Peter A. will give her as a goodbye present. He offers eight yards of silk and thirty shillings. She concludes: 'Poor ...no Afrika!' Rich ...Afrika!' (p. 69), which the narrator interprets to mean that she knows that Peter A. would come with her to Africa if he had the money, a knowledge that makes her powerful in the narrator's eyes. In 'Le départ pour l'Afrique', a few final words are exchanged between Peter A. and Nah-Baduh on the station platform as her train is about to leave. There is a farewell embrace, indicated by two lines of dashes following the statement which offers the view of a third person narrator: 'Sie steigt langsam herab auf den Perron zu ihm' (She steps slowly down on to the platform beside him) (p. 70).

The penultimate text 'Ihre Addresse' closes the sequence on Nah-Baduh by suggesting a future to the relationship, albeit an open-ended one. The last text, 'Spätherbst-Abend', is a conversation between the zoo's watchman Joseph and its director. Joseph says that a man was asking for the director. The man (obviously the figure of Peter A. is intended) went into one of the huts and left a quarter of an hour later. The director remarks:

> Schon gut, Joseph. Übrigens, die Hütten werden morgen abgebrochen – Wir brauchen Platz für die Seiltänzergesellschaft und den Ballon captif. (p. 72)
>
> [All right, Joseph. Anyway, the huts will be pulled down tomorrow – we need room for the tightrope act and the captive balloon.]

In the final brief text, therefore, two possible relationships with the Ashanti are outlined: that of the empathetic observer Peter A., who lingers over the sadness of their departure; and that of the spectacle-seeking audience, for whom the zoo director is keen to provide new and different attractions.

Conclusion

Altenberg's complex literary portrayal of the Ashanti in the Prater needs to be seen in the context of the political and social forces that were attaining their definitive form in the late 1890s. For the liberals, the Ashanti became an emblem of cultural difference that was used quite consciously to relativise internal tensions within the Habsburg state, particularly the rise of political anti-Semitism and its view of the Jews as aliens who had insinuated themselves into Austrian society.

By avoiding the kind of enlightened relativism proposed in many liberal accounts of the Ashanti exhibition, Altenberg's sketches reject the implicit colonialist view of Meyer's lexicon, a view which distinguishes between 'Kultur-' and 'Naturvölker' and considers the latter only to be a suitable subject for an ethnological display to enlighten the former as to their supposed origins and their actual superiority. Altenberg's text involves the reader intimately in the lives of the individual African characters, but at the same time never loses sight of the problematic relationship the inhabitants of a Hagenbeck-style display must have had with the surrounding society. As such, the attempt to close the gap between the Ashanti and the Viennese, or avoid it opening in the first place – a theme announced by the tutor in 'Der Hofmeister' – may ultimately lay itself open to that eternal response of the anti-Semite, 'some of my best friends...'. Readers engaged by Altenberg's text, moved by the relationships between the narrator and Tioko and Nah-Baduh, may in the end conclude that these Africans are perhaps 'some of one's best friends', but that does not change the view of Africa on the whole as a dark continent peopled by uncivilised savages. The problem of prejudice remains. As one liberal Viennese satirist put it: 'The Ashanti have gone. Unfortunately our own blacks are staying.'[30]

Notes

1. Peter Altenberg, *Ashantee* (Berlin, 1897). The sketches on the Ashanti are accompanied by nine further sequences of sketches on other subjects. The modern edition can be found in Altenberg, *Gesammelte Werke in 5 Bänden*, ed. Werner Schweiger (Vienna and Frankfurt, 1987), Vol. I, pp. 231–70.
2. See Bertrand Michael Buchmann, *Der Prater. Die Geschichte des unteren Werd* (Vienna, 1979), pp. 71–5, 80–1.
3. See Hans Pemmer and Nini Lackner, *Der Prater von den Anfängen bis zur Gegenwart*, revised by Günter Dünigl and Ludwig Schmauer (Munich, 1974), p. 113; Gustav Jäger, *Kurzer Führer durch den neueröffneten Wiener Thiergarten am Schüttel* (Vienna, 1863).
4. Pemmer and Lackner, *Der Prater*, p. 113. All translations are my own.
5. See Carl Hagenbeck, *Von Tieren und Menschen. Erlebnisse und Erfahrungen* (Berlin, 1909); also *Neue Deutsche Biographie* (Berlin, 1965), Vol. VII, pp. 487–8.
6. Hagenbeck, *Von Tieren und Menschen*, p. 94.
7. I am grateful to Jacob Langford (Ithaca) for drawing my attention to the significance of social status in Hagenbeck displays.
8. Hagenbeck, *Von Tieren und Menschen*, p. 415.

9. See Stefan Goldmann, 'Wilde in Europa. Aspekte und Orte ihrer Zurschaustellung', in Thomas Theye (ed.), *Wir und die Wilden. Einblicke in eine kannibalische Beziehung* (Reinbek, 1985), pp. 243–69; 'Zur Rezeption der Völkerausstellungen um 1900', in Hermann Pollig *et al.* (eds), *Exotische Welten. Europäische Phantasien* (Stuttgart, 1987), pp. 88–95.
10. See Sander L. Gilman, *On Blackness without Blacks: Essays on the Image of the Black in Germany* (Boston, 1982), and *Difference and Pathology: Stereotypes of Sexuality, Race and Madness* (Ithaca, 1985).
11. See Edris Makward, 'Two African Travellers from Germany: Leo Frobenius and Janheinz Jahn', in Reinhold Grimm and Jost Hermand (eds), *Blacks and German Culture* (Madison, WI, 1986), pp. 54–64 (p. 58).
12. Hagenbeck, *Von Tieren und Menschen*, p. 457; *Wiener Allgemeine Zeitung*, 25 August 1897.
13. Christine Klusacek and Kurt Stimmer, *Leopoldstadt* (Vienna, 1978), p. 249.
14. See Goldmann, 'Wilde in Europa', p. 248. This practice has not entirely vanished: the Museum of Natural History at Banyoles, near Barcelona, contains the preserved body of an African Bushman, stolen from his grave and stuffed in 1916. The display caused great offence to African participants in the 1992 Olympics (report in the *Observer*, 8 March 1992).
15. *Wiener Allgemeine Zeitung*, 22 September 1896.
16. Gilman, *Difference and Pathology*, p. 112.
17. Quoted in Hans Christian Kosler, *Peter Altenberg. Leben und Werk in Texten und Bildern* (Munich, 1981), pp. 78, 80. The only date indicated is the year 1897.
18. See Steven Beller, *Vienna and the Jews, 1867–1938: A Cultural History* (Cambridge, 1989), pp. 193–7.
19. For example: 'Altenbergs Hinwendung zum noch Unverbildeten und Natürlichen zeigt sich auch in anderer Ausprägung: in seiner Begeisterung für die Aschanti, einen westafrikanischen Negerstamm, der als Attraktion für langere Zeit im Wiener Tiergarten ein authentisch aufgebautes Dorf bewohnte. Das alltägliche Leben dieses Volkes, vor allem das der Frauen und Kinder hat Altenberg in seinem Zyklus *Ashantee* bewundernd abgebildet', Irene Köwer, *Peter Altenberg als Autor der literarischen Kleinform* (Frankfurt, 1987), p. 49.
20. See Altenberg, *Gesammelte Werke*, ed. Schweiger, Vol. I, p. 359. Schweiger's edition thus represents a synthesis of the 1897 and 1904 versions. While the republication of all the texts is welcome, the considerable discrepancies between Altenberg's own editions should not be glossed over.
21. Camillo Schaefer, *Peter Altenberg. Ein biographischer Essay* (Vienna, 1980), p. 40.
22. *Meyers Konversations-Lexikon. Eine Encyklopädie des allgemeinen Wissens*, 4th edn (Leipzig and Vienna, 1890), Vol. I, pp. 900–1.
23. Gilman, *Difference and Pathology*. pp. 111–12.
24. Compare Schaefer, *Altenberg*, p. 40, with Gilman, *Difference and Pathology*, p. 111.
25. Reprinted in Kosler, *Altenberg*, pp. 80, 82.
26. A recent example of this technique can be found in Nadine Gordimer's short story 'A Soldier's Embrace', where only the African characters are given names, while the white South African figures are identified only by their generic titles: the wife, the lawyer, the butcher, etc. See Gordimer, *A Soldier's Embrace* (London, 1980).
27. Altenberg, *Wie ich es sehe*, 5th edn (Berlin, 1910), p. 327. This edition and all subsequent ones are identical with the fourth.
28. The best-known example is Diderot's *Supplément au voyage de Bougainville* (1772), where the discrepancy between European marriage laws and sexual morality is exposed through a dialogue between a native chief and a missionary priest, who is trying to persuade the Tahitians of the virtues of Christian civilisation.
29. The figure of Pedro in Hofmannsthal's play *Cristinas Heimreise* (1909) offers a more

conventional example of the naive eye of the foreign traveller, though Hofmannsthal makes the satirical comparison less obvious to the audience, since Pedro initially appears to be merely a figure of fun.
30. *Die Bombe*, 25 October 1896. Black was the political colour of the Christian Social Party.

Love's Labour's Lost: Translations of Schnitzler's *Reigen*

Konstanze Fliedl
(translated by Ralph Manheim)

The earliest known translation of a work by Arthur Schnitzler is the French version of *Sterben* (1895), which appeared that same year in the French periodical *La Semaine littéraire*, and a year later in book form.[1] While on a visit to Paris in 1897, Schnitzler wrote a letter to Richard Beer-Hofmann in which he spoke enthusiastically of the bookstalls on the banks of the Seine: 'As you will soon see, every imaginable book is available there; for the thrill of it, I haggled with one of the booksellers for a copy of *Mourir* – the woman let me have it for sixty centimes...'[2]

That was not the end of Schnitzler's 'haggling' over his literary output. During his lifetime, he was translated not only into all Western European and Scandinavian languages, but also into Hungarian, Romanian, Czech, Polish, Russian, Yiddish and Japanese. Unauthorised translations and unpaid royalties became a serious problem, especially in the years between the World Wars, when transfers of hard currency made up a significant part of his income. For the first American translation of *Reigen* in 1920, he received $50, which at the time came to 9,090 Austrian crowns (two years later, another transfer of $50 brought him 3,500,000 Austrian crowns).[3]

Thus *Hands Around*[4] was hardly big business; it was published by subscription in an edition of 1,475 copies. Nevertheless, though belatedly, it played a part in the '*Reigen* scandal' that erupted in 1921 in Vienna and Berlin, and culminated in 1922 in the Berlin prosecution of the producers of the play at the Kleines Schauspielhaus. When in March 1922 *Reigen* was to open at the Green Room Club in New York, the Society for the Prevention of Vice stepped in and a public reading had to be substituted for the theatrical performance. The play was not produced in New York until October 1926. This performance at the Triangle Theater, restricted to male subscribers, was allowed to proceed without interference.[5]

In 1929 a bookseller was indicted for stocking the German text of the play, but the case was dropped. In the following year legal action was taken against a bookshop employee who 'unlawfully possessed a book called *Hands Around*, with intent to sell and show the same, and which was a lewd, lascivious, obscene and disgusting book'. In a first trial judgment was suspended. Proceedings were resumed at the Court of Special Sessions where three judges (against two) agreed that 'a book of this kind must properly be held to be disgusting, indecent and obscene'.[6] The case then went on to the Court of Appeals where the defence attorney, Morris L. Ernst, submitted a memorandum, reviewing the reception of *Reigen* in German-speaking countries, citing the trial of the Berlin actors, quoting from the affidavits of experts presented at the Berlin trial, and stressing Schnitzler's worldwide reputation.[7] As a result, the ban on the book was lifted.

To us this trial is of interest because it parallels the history of *Reigen's* reception in Europe.[8] By citing the affidavits of the European experts, Morris L. Ernst perpetuated an interpretation of the play that was to dominate subsequent *Reigen* criticism. For example, Ludwig Fulda, rather surprisingly identified as 'the outstanding German dramatist of the present day', is quoted as saying: 'I consider the great ethical value of this play to be its inexorable truthfulness and its exposure of the merely sexual passion which is devoid of all other qualities.'[9] The Leipzig professor Albert Koester contributed the following:

> This drama has been called erotic. I believe that no word could be less appropriate. What we have in these ten scenes is not eroticism but mere sexuality. According to my opinion it is an eloquent outburst on the part of the author, who holds up a mirror to the world and says, 'You see that what you consider love is mere sexuality. There is a curse on the communion of bodies if it is not also a communion of souls.'[10]

What is here transmitted is not only the tenor of the Berlin judicial proceedings as recorded by Wolfgang Heine in his book *Der Kampf um den Reigen*,[11] but also an interpretation of the play which, though it led in Berlin to an acquittal and in New York to the lifting of the ban on the book, is, as Ludwig Marcuse has pointed out, highly problematic. Schnitzler's play, he writes, is defended as 'a work of art', which by definition cannot be immoral. One might speak of immunisation by tautology. Both in Berlin and New York, eminently respectable authorities were cited in defence of *Reigen*. Parallels were drawn between Schnitzler's text and hallowed examples from world literature, such as Shakespeare's *Romeo and Juliet* or Wagner's *Die Walküre*, where the curtain rises or falls before or after coitus. The classical-liberal definition of art upheld by these authorities could not do justice to Schnitzler's innovation.

> They [the 'experts' who testified for the defence at the Berlin trial] said hardly anything which could have convinced even the most willing. They sat in a citadel of works of art and shot with dead arguments. They were alienated from the people; not because they were of a different class, but because they did not exist in the present. They were well informed about the past, gentle and well-meaning and without a future. They did not suspect that this trial compromised them more than it did the petty bourgeois on the other side, who had gone mad.[12]

Against the radical anti-Semitism of the other side, which went hand in hand with hostility to art, such arguments could accomplish nothing, even if they led to acquittal: for 'these triumphs belong to that class of victories which are defeats. An obscene work was acquitted by means of arguments which left the old sexual morality of the world of imagination only more soundly established.'[13] Through the Memorandum, this approach to the play was exported. If a translation is merely the expression of a particular reading, if it embodies nothing more than one of a number of readings,[14] then this episode in the history of *Reigen* is of paradigmatic importance in so far as it throws light on the central problems concerned in translations of *Reigen*.

With *Reigen* we discover paradoxically that an extremely 'simple' text is virtually untranslatable. If it is assumed that the surface structure of an original cannot be preserved in translation, then its 'eternal relevance' becomes all-important. The form of the original becomes contingent; a nucleus of meaning is peeled out and transposed into the target language. The moralising interpretation of *Reigen* is consonant with this conception. If our sole concern is with the 'anthropological constants' in Schnitzler's cycle, the depiction of crude instinctual behaviour that has not been culturally moulded, cultural differences between the languages of the original and of the translation are of no importance. Schnitzler is then regarded as a critic of all-too-human weaknesses and a defender of eternally human values. Comparison of *Reigen* with the medieval Dance of Death[15] lends further support to this conception by bridging historical distance. Viewed as a treatise of this sort, the play should be easy to translate. The numerous American and English translators of *Reigen*[16] may originally have been beguiled by the possibility of translating in this way. In the praxis of translation, however, this interpretation of *Reigen* soon proved inappropriate. Precisely the untranslatable elements of the original lend striking confirmation to the subsequent reservations of the critics about reading *Reigen* as a moralising dance-of-death allegory.[17] The basic problem of translation, the problem of communicating a foreign mode of discourse and hence a foreign mode of thought, is not so easily solved; nor can the content of a work be separated from its form. Already the translator of the first American version deplores the loss of linguistic nuance: 'Any attempt to turn dialogue so full of delicate shadows as this of Schnitzler into a language like English, whose genius tends rather to a graphic concreteness and realism, is full of pitfalls and difficulties.'[18] Later interpretations concentrated on Schnitzler's linguistic characterisation of social realities. *Reigen* is wholly situated in Viennese turn-of-the-century society, and portrays this society in its language. The colloquial Viennese of the characters embodies the basic linguistic markers that reflect the norms and conventions of *fin-de-siècle* Vienna. Any attempt at translation runs the risk of losing these distinctions, which are embedded in the original language. In her preface to the first English translation of Frank and Jacqueline Marcus (1953), Ilsa Barea explains these distinctions to the reader, while deploring the fact that Schnitzler requires such an elaborate explanation:

> [...] the atmosphere of language is so characteristic of that bygone Viennese society, and at the same time so impossible to transmit into another language with an entirely different social tradition behind it, that it would be an even greater pity to ignore it [...]
> What is lost in translation, inevitably, is the subtle shading of the

language. [...] In *Merry-go-round*, the pompous Husband, the Actress and the Poet all use the savourless equivalent of the King's English while they are self-conscious, only to drop into the friendly Viennese when they are natural; the Young Married Woman and the Young Gentleman speak stilted 'book' German while they deliberately play at making love in the grand style. Schnitzler used the shades of inflection with an easy mastery, neatly characterising the social position and range of education of each person by sets of untranslatable little words.[19]

Nevertheless, Ilsa Barea still sees an opposition between these distinctions and the universally human background of the play: 'these words also serve to show the sameness of the whole human procedure, whether the play of the pursuit of "love" – the inverted commas are essential – is acted out between the Chambermaid and the uncouth conscripted Soldier, or between the Count and the celebrated Actress.'[20]

Against this view it must be argued that *Reigen* demonstrates the inseparability of dialogue and 'action', manner of speaking and manner of making love. The 'love play' of the characters is socio-culturally differentiated by means of language. For this, too, the target language has a different 'register'. Indeed, it has been observed that English is ill-suited to the translation of 'pornographic subjects, metaphorical argot and low life', that a 'middle language' adapted to these purposes is 'mostly unavailable': 'We have either the very coarse or the very clinical.'[21] Linguistic 'no-go areas' seem to have entirely different boundaries.

The only way of dealing with these difficulties seemed to be 'free translation'; Edwards and Glaser, for example, set out to translate the 'spirit' rather than the 'letter'.[22] Still, their text and those of Marcus and of Eric Bentley, which first appeared in 1954,[23] are relatively faithful. The English translations of *Reigen* are not such '*belles infidèles*' as some of the French versions of Schnitzler, which, as Elsbeth Dangel has shown, are true neither to the letter nor to the spirit.[24] Between the two basic types of translation, the 'word-for-word' and the 'free', the relative merits of which have been under discussion for centuries, the translator of *Reigen* is hardly at liberty to choose. The colloquial speech of the characters, so rich in nuances of meaning and so simple in syntax, as well as the strictly conventionalised discourse, forces his hand.

In other respects as well, *Reigen* and its translations offer a classic example of the precarious dialectic between original text and translation. It has been said that every translation magnifies a text;[25] if it is also true that a translation must inevitably diminish a text, this dialectic represents a special danger to a work like *Reigen*, the profundity of which is situated in its untranslatable surface. Schnitzler raised this very objection to an early translation: 'Read the English *Reigen* through. A really amusing piece of work with some delightful passages – and yet it could be better; in some spots it could have reached higher and wider.'[26] For it has long been recognised that the hallmark of Schnitzler's plays is their 'superficial' conversational tone and that Schnitzler's critique of language and society is expressed through conventional rhetoric. Translators are faced with the dilemma: how can they do justice to an original whose most distinctive feature they are condemned to lose?

All these facets of the problem of translation – the relationship between 'content' and 'form', between 'fidelity' and 'freedom', between the effectiveness of the original and the reception of the foreign-language version – recur in connection with the new translations that burgeoned in 1982 when the copyright expired. Frank and Jacqueline Marcus did a new version for the BBC;[27] John Barton adapted a translation by Sue Davies for a production by the Royal Shakespeare Company;[28] and *Reigen* was produced by the Royal Exchange Theatre Company in Manchester in a version by Charles Osborne.[29]

Charles Osborne had deplored the 'Stoppardisation' of Schnitzler and saw no justification for the extreme freedom with which Stoppard had translated *Das weite Land* (*Undiscovered Country*).[30] He himself was determined to keep closer to the original and wrote: 'To try to reproduce the original essence seems to me something well worth doing.'[31] Paradoxically, Osborne's text, as produced at the Royal Exchange, was updated to a time somewhere 'between the Beatles and Bob Marley'. One critic found this updating 'staggeringly pointless'; the fascination of the play, wrote the *Guardian* reviewer, lay precisely 'in its portrait of *fin-de-siècle* Vienna. If there is a parallel with our own society, surely we can make it for ourselves.'[32] *The Sunday Times* reacted in similar terms: 'The transposition in time does terrible things to the text. If these *are* the swinging sixties, then the social intercourse [...] would not have taken place in the terms used.'[33] In other words, an English-language production should not blur the foreignness of the original. But the evidently more authentic Royal Shakespeare production of Barton's adaptation met with a divided reception. The text itself, it was remarked, is not materially different from Osborne's version: 'Barton maintains this is because many of the lines are in such simple German that it is difficult to translate in any other way.'[34] This fidelity to the text, reflecting the simplicity of the original, met with some approval: '*La Ronde* as it should be played'.[35] Other reviewers claimed that neither translation nor production could hold a candle to Max Ophuls's film version (1950), but ultimately put the blame on the play itself. Thanks to scandals and lawsuits 'the play has been elevated to a position that it hardly merits'.[36] *The Sunday Times* concluded: 'The production as a whole was a mess', as was the play, 'an aimless piece'. 'Schnitzler comes across as a shallow critic of shallowness.'[37]

Thus the recent translations and productions of *Reigen* have in many respects posed the question of *Reigen's* translatability in a new way. The difficult balance between fidelity and freedom, between 'dated' and 'updated', seems to throw the play itself out of kilter. The question now becomes: Is the play *worth* translating? Either the translations bring out the shallowness of *Reigen* or they fail to convey its depth.

Comparison of the translations shows that they differ most widely among themselves and encounter the greatest difficulties in their treatment of the trifling details characteristic of the linguistic, social and physical topology of the late Habsburg monarchy. When the Count, for example, says that things are no different in Vienna than 'in die Nester' where he was garrisoned,[38] one translation transforms the typically Viennese confusion of dative and accusative into an original contribution to Hungarian geography, by writing: 'in the Nestar, where I was stationed'.[39] Conversely, details are lost which in the original add up to the author's sharply delineated portrait of his milieu. Furthermore, Schnitzler's dialogues take place in a setting which physically reflects the double moral standard of the society of his place and time. The juxtaposition of social supervision and libertinage has its places, corridors and nooks, among them the notorious *'chambre séparée'*. The Vienna apartment block had in its stairwell a place of casual 'encounters',[40] but comings and goings could be observed by the 'Hausmeister' through the 'Guckerl'. For example, when the Young Woman arrives at the Young Gentleman's trysting room:

> DIE JUNGE FRAU: Wo bin ich denn eigentlich?
> DER JUNGE HERR: Bei mir.
> DIE JUNGE FRAU: Dieses Haus ist schrecklich, Alfred.
> DER JUNGE HERR: Warum denn? Es ist ein sehr vornehmes Haus.
> DIE JUNGE FRAU: Ich bin zwei Herren auf der Stiege begegnet. (338)

Ignoring the fact that this takes place in a 'house of assignation', Marcus (1953/19) and Bentley (1954/18) render 'bei mir' as 'in my house'; which makes the Young Woman's line about meeting two gentlemen (who may have recognised her) on the stairs meaningless.

The 'Guckerl' through which the Chambermaid in the third scene is told to look (336) also gives rise to problems. Edwards/Glaser (1920/52) translate rather helplessly 'peek through the curtains'; Osborne (1928/14): 'Just have a peep'; Marcus (1982/12): 'through the keyhole'. Other translations have 'peephole'. It is true that American or English doors are rarely equipped with peepholes. Such xenophobic protection of intimacy is in keeping neither with English stand-offishness nor with America openness.

Another Viennese speciality is the 'Hausmeister'. The American translations call him 'janitor'; the English 'doorkeeper', 'landlord' or 'porter'. The last three have a very different function, while the janitor is utterly lacking in the terribleness of the Viennese 'Hausmeister', whose menacing presence is so palpably delineated in Schnitzler's *Der Weg ins Freie*.[41]

Furthermore, Schnitzler's characters are presented with unmistakable marks of their class. These, too, are culturally conditioned and cannot simply be transposed into a similar system of social stratification. For example, the Husband – who in the Royal Shakespeare production was reportedly 'a little too much of a bedroom Polonius'[42] – identifies himself as a 'Bildungsphilister' by quoting from the classics to justify his sexual abstinence in the marriage bed: 'Man ist nicht immer der liebende Mann, man muß auch zuweilen hinaus ins feindliche Leben, muß kämpfen und streben!' (353) The quotation from Schiller's *Das Lied von der Glocke* (ll. 106–8), which indeed refers to the division of tasks in bourgeois marriage and here becomes a satirical comment on the extra-conjugal activities of husband (and wife), goes unrecognised in most translations; only Marcus (1953/40) renders it in rhyme, 'go forth into hostile life, to battle and strife', while Bentley (1959/81) calls attention to Schiller in a footnote.[43]

The Austrian fixation on academic titles is notorious; they are worn almost as decorations. When the poet wants to play the piano for the 'Süsses Mädel', she says: 'Ich habe geglaubt, Robert, du bist ein Doktor', because 'die Schriftsteller sind doch alle Dokters' (365). She draws a distinction between writer/Doktor and musician/Künstler. This distinction cannot be carried over into societies where the title 'doctor' is largely confined to medical men and little used in other contexts. Edwards/Glaser (1920/143) simply make the 'doctor' a 'professor'; in Marcus (1953/55) the writer has to admit: 'I [...] haven't got a degree.' Bentley (1954/51) has the girl enquire: 'of philosophy?' The confusion is considerable.

The Viennese took a keen interest in the theatre and in stage stars, which often extended to the most intimate details of their idols' private lives. It seems quite natural that the Young Woman should observe in passing that even Odilon did not wear a corset (342). This mention of a local celebrity (Helene Odilon née Petermann, 1864–1939, was an actress at the Deutsches Volkstheater in Vienna and Alexander Girardi's first wife) was bound to give translators trouble; not all, however, stick their necks out as far as Edwards/Glaser (1920/73), who identify Odilon as 'a Parisian dancer, famous in the nineties'.

The Actress embodies the theatricality and sexual libertinage which public opinion attributed (approvingly for the most part) to members of this idolised profession. At the very start she adopts a pious pose:

SCHAUSPIELERIN [*empört*]: Siehst du nicht, daß ich bete?
DICHTER: Glaubst du an Gott?
SCHAUSPIELERIN: Gewiß, ich bin ja kein blasser Schurke. (371)

The translations of the 'blasser Schurke' are quite amazing. Again it is Marcus (1953/65) who comes closest with 'pale villain', which he provides with inverted commas to make it look like a quotation. Edwards/Glaser (1920/166) have 'fool', Osborne (1982/57) 'monster', Barton/Davies (1982/47) 'atheist', while Bentley (1954/59) goes a step further with 'anarchist'. Marcus (1982/57) has the most colourless solution, 'I'm devoutly religious' – with which the speech loses its specifically theatrical character.

The complex character of the Actress also provokes the only out-and-out translation mistake. She tells the Count how on seeing him sitting in the first row at the theatre 'sie sei so geflogen' (381). Since Edwards/Glaser (1920/197) this has been rendered metaphorically – 'as on wings', 'as though walking on clouds'. But 'fliegen', and not only in Austria, also carries the meaning of 'trembling (like a leaf)'; thus her reaction was not one of exaltation.

The soldier represents a Viennese subspecies whose mentality is typified by his 'mir sein mir' (330). To the credit of the Anglo-American language, it contains no such locution. As was to be expected, it gives the translators a hard time: Edwards/Glaser (1920/32) have: 'I can take care of myself'; Marcus (1953/6), 'You don't have to worry about me'; and Bentley (1954/8), 'Just leave it to uncle'. Nor is there any equivalent in English for the soldier's mixture of bestiality and resignation during coitus:

> STUBENMÄDCHEN: Ich kann dein G'sicht gar nicht sehen.
> SOLDAT: A was – G'sicht... (331)

Glaser/Edwards (1920/36) translate: 'Don't matter – my face...' Marcus (1953/8), 'Who cares about my face'; Bentley (1954/10), 'My face? ... Hell!' Osborne (1982/8), 'Never mind my – face'; Barton/Davies (1982/6), 'What's my face got to do with it?' None of these astonishing variants catches the profound obscenity of this 'speech', bordering on speechlessness, which throws a blinding light on the brutal anonymity of the body treated as object.

Because *Reigen*'s social critique is embodied in numerous untranslatable details, the translators seem to have been obliged to concentrate on its 'universally human' content. But in this cycle there is something that transcends its social and historical setting, something that may well be translatable and worth translating, namely, the rhetoric of 'love'. Obviously the love discourse of the individual characters cannot be divorced from their discourse in general, but *Reigen* lays bare the economy of love discourse, which thus disclosed might survive translation. The ideal love discourse is always a summit meeting between two systems that are intrinsically isomorphic:

> Eros and language mesh at every point. Intercourse and discourse, copula and copulation, are subclasses of the dominant fact of communication. They arise from the life-need of an ego to reach out and comprehend, in the two vital senses of 'understanding' and 'containment', another human being. Sex is a profoundly semantic act. Like language, it is subject to the shaping force of social convention, rules of proceeding, and accumulated precedent. To speak and to make love is to enact a twofold universality: both forms of communication are universals of human physiology as well as of human evolution. It is likely that human sexuality and speech developed in close-knit reciprocity. Together they generate the history of self-consciousness, the process, presumably millenary and marked by innumerable regressions, whereby we hammered out the notion of self and otherness.[44]

On the other hand, both are impaired by the crisis of individual subjectivity. At the turn of the century, in the work of Karl Kraus, for example, the critique of language coincides with a critique of the sexual double standard. Similarly, *Reigen* draws a parallel between language and sexuality; it shows 'the degradation of language, which both implies and partakes of the degradation of the actual experience with which it is concerned'.[45] Both modes of communication become alienated when both language and sex are treated as commodities. What Schnitzler demonstrates in his 'light' dialogue is a series of barter transactions that call themselves love. Love is a transaction, marriage a business. Each of these ten scenes identifies a particular sort of profit aimed at, and their wit – for *Reigen* is not a dreary play – consists in contrasting the naked truth with the rhetorical veils thrown over it. What is laid bare is not bodies, but the way in which they are commodified. Where the rules of the market are not observed, one party is always the loser. In the first scene, it is the Prostitute who breaks the rules by giving herself 'free of charge'. Rather than money, she wants an emotional bonus, and that the Soldier is not prepared to give her.

Thus cheated, she wants at least to be paid at the usual rate, but this, too, is denied her. Contrariwise, in the last scene, the Count wants to make it appear that he has given something for nothing, but this lavish gift becomes the Prostitute's normal fee. In the second scene Marie comes off the loser. Still, the Soldier's love discourse has somewhat improved. From here to the end of the dialogues, amounts of love are appraised and negotiated – from the untranslatable 'ich hab dich lieb' to 'ich bete dich an' – a rhetorical inflation.

In some respects, the translations done over a period of years reflect changes in English usage. 'Geliebter', for example, starts out as 'sweetheart' (Glaser/Edwards 1920/25), progresses to 'friend' (Marcus 1953/3) or 'boyfriend' (Bentley 1954/7), and ends up as 'lover' (Barton/Davies 1982/2). The magic formula 'ich liebe dich' does not occur in *Reigen*; this paradoxically is the decency-barrier imposed on the characters of *Reigen*, the dividing line beyond which the prostitution and trivialisation of language may not go. 'I love you' seems unavoidable in translation. 'Ich hab dich lieb' is heightened or attenuated; 'daß du mich lieb hast' (351) is rendered in Barton/Davies (1982/37, 32) by 'that you are fond of me' and 'weil ich dich lieb hab' (356) becomes 'because I love you'. The love discourse in *Reigen* is a special variant of Schnitzler's 'Konversationssprache', which is effective precisely because of what it does not say. Here something more than concealment is meant. Such silence is a lie in the same sense as are those words of which it is said elsewhere in Schnitzler 'that we have nothing else'.[46] The language of Schnitzler's characters is marked by secondary meanings but also by meanings the words do not carry – a fact that makes exorbitant demands on the translator: 'Unfortunately for the translator, the dictionary can say only what words mean, not what they do *not* mean.'[47] Here once again the problem of translation intersects with Schnitzler's characters' communication problem. What words do not say demands almost superhuman restraint on the part of the translator. From this point of view the 'Stoppardisation' of Schnitzler is indeed a problem. What the characters in *Das weite Land* say means more in Stoppard's version than in the original. A minor character observes that the voice of a loved one can readily be distinguished from among many distant voices: 'Wenn dann plötzlich unter all diesen Stimmen eine heraufklingt, die man kennt [...] da kann man plötzlich auch die Worte verstehn.'[48] Not content to make one of his witty puns out of this instant perception of words made intelligible by love, Stoppard repeats the same turn of phrase in the passage where Friedrich Hofreiter hears the voice of the actress Frau Meinhold-Aigner: 'A familiar voice floats up to me.'[49] The German text does not have this repetition. The hearer of the English text is obliged to believe in an earlier affair between Friedrich and his friend's wife – not at all what was intended in the text.

Osborne's 'faithful' translation of *Reigen* also says more than the original. At

Translations of Schnitzler's Reigen

the end of the scene between the Young Woman and the Husband, we read:

DIE JUNGE FRAU: So lieb hast du mich heut.
DER GATTE: Ja, so lieb. (353)

This exchange is an allusion to the love-rhythm that the husband had proclaimed at the start: now, after a period of abstinence, a honeymoon was in order. Johanna Bossinade has commented as follows on this economy of conjugal love: 'The husband has just explained his sexual restraint in a crudely materialistic argument as a profitable curtailment of production.'[50] The 'heut' refers precisely to this dating of the love conjuncture. Osborne (1982/34) drops this dating and, perhaps worse, transforms the husband's reply into the declaration that has been avoided as taboo throughout this play:

YOUNG MARRIED WOMAN: Tonight you made love to me just like the first time.
HUSBAND: Yes – I love you so much.

With such overproduction the translators sell *Reigen* short. For this they are not entirely to blame. The business of translation must take 'loss' into account; but sometimes it is this depreciation that first throws light on the value of the original: 'The failings of the translator [...] localise, they project as on to a screen the resistant vitalities, the opaque centres of specific genius in the original.'[51]

Notes

1. (Paris, 1895), tr. Gaspard Valette.
2. Letter to Richard Beer-Hofmann, 20 May 1897, in Arthur Schnitzler, *Briefe 1875–1912*, ed. Therese Nickl and Heinrich Schnitzler (Frankfurt, 1981), pp. 322–3.
3. Cf. Auslandsabrechnungen, Nachlass, Mappe 237, University Library, Cambridge.
4. Arthur Schnitzler, *Hands Around: A Cycle of Ten Dialogues* (tr. L. D. Edwards and F. L. Glaser), (New York, 1920).
5. Cf. Gerd K. Schneider, 'The reception of Arthur Schnitzler's *Reigen* in the Old Country and the New World: a study in cultural differences', *MAL* 19 (1986), 3/4, pp. 75–89 (p. 80).
6. *New York Law Journal*, 15. 7. 1930.
7. Morris L. Ernst, *Memorandum* (New York, 1930).
8. Ibid., p. 6. The translation was provided by the Translation Bureau of the Bar Association of the City of New York.
9. Ibid., p. 15.
10. Ibid.
11. Wolfgang Heine, *Der Kampf um den Reigen: Vollständiger Bericht über die sechstägige Verhandlung gegen Direktion und Darsteller des Kleinen Schauspielhauses Berlin* (Berlin, 1922).
12. Ludwig Marcuse, *Obscene: the History of an Indignation*, tr. Karen Gershon (London, 1965), p. 198.
13. Ibid., p. 213.
14. Cf. Ralph-Rainer Wuthenow, *Das fremde Kunstwerk: Aspekte der literarischen Übersetzung* (Göttingen, 1969), esp. p. 9.

15. Cf. Richard Alewyn, 'Zweimal Liebe: Schnitzlers *Liebelei* und *Reigen*' [1960] in his *Probleme und Gestalten: Essays* (Frankfurt, 1974), pp. 299–304 (pp. 302–3); Heinz Politzer, 'Arthur Schnitzler: The Poetry of Psychology', *MLN* 78 (1963), pp. 353–72 (pp. 359–60); more recently Helga Schiffer, 'Arthur Schnitzler's *Reigen*', *Text & Kontext*, 11, 1 (1983), pp. 7–34.
16. Richard H. Allen's Schnitzler bibliography lists, up to 1965, eleven different editions in seven translations; since then five more editions, some being new translations, have appeared.
17. Among others Hartmut Scheible, *Arthur Schnitzler in Selbstzeugnissen und Bilddokumenten* (Reinbek, 1976), p. 65; Rolf-Peter Janz and Klaus Laermann, *Arthur Schnitzler: Zur Diagnose des Wiener Bürgertums im Fin de siècle* (Stuttgart, 1977), p. 56.
18. *Hands Around*, p. XIII.
19. Ilsa Barea, Introduction to A[rthur] S[chnitzler], *Merry-Go-Round (Reigen)*, (tr. Frank and Jacqueline Marcus), (London 1953), pp. vii–x (pp. ix–x).
20. Ibid., p. ix.
21. Richard Howard, 'A Professional Translator's Trade Alphabet', in William Arrowsmith and Roger Shattuck (eds), *The Craft and Context of Translation: A Symposium* (Austin, 1961), pp. 163–171 (p. 166).
22. *Hands Around*, p. XIII.
23. Eric Bentley's translation was available to me in two slightly different editions: A. S., *La Ronde: Ten Dialogues* (New York, 1954); and A. S., *La Ronde*, in A. S., *Plays and Stories*, ed. Egon Schwarz, The German Library, Vol. 55 (New York, 1982), pp. 53–116 (this last is a reprint from *The Classic Theatre*, ed. Eric Bentley [New York, 1959]). Further editions appeared in 1955 and 1973.
24. Cf. Elsbeth Dangel, 'Das Elend der Übersetzung: Bemerkungen zu Dominique Auclères Schnitzlerübersetzungen', *MAL* 17 (1984), 1, pp. 49–57. On Auclère's French translation of *Reigen* and Paolo Chiarini's Italian translation, see the comprehensive linguistic study by Gudrun Held, 'Hofmannsthals *Rosenkavalier* and Schnitzlers *Reigen*: Zwei Beispiele zur Übersetzung der Wiener Gesellschaftskomödie des Fin de siècle', in Wolfgang Pöckl (ed.), *Österreichische Literatur in Übersetzungen: Salzburger linguistische Analysen* (Vienna, 1983), 169–274. Aware of the hidden depths of Schnitzler's language, which expresses through conversation the impossibility of communication, Held analyses the translations of 'conversational and contact words' like 'geh', 'na','ja' and 'so'. Her findings show that by dispensing with these elements, the translations also forfeit their value as metalinguistic signals.
25. 'To class a source-text as worth translating is to dignify it immediately and to involve it in a dynamic of magnification'; George Steiner, *After Babel: Aspects of Language and Translation* (London, 1975).
26. Diary, entry for 2 November 1920 (unpublished).
27. A. S., *La Ronde*, (tr. Frank and Jacqueline Marcus) (London, 1982).
28. A. S., *La Ronde (Reigen)* (Harmondsworth, 1982) (adapted by John Barton from a translation by Sue Davies for the Royal Shakespeare Company).
29. A. S., *The Round Dance and Other Plays* (tr. with an introduction by Charles Osborne) (Manchester, 1982).
30. A. S., *Undiscovered Country (Das weite Land)* (London, 1980) (in an English version by Tom Stoppard).
31. Hugh Herbert, 'Dancing to the Tunes of Vienna', *Guardian*, 2 January 1982, p. 10.
32. Michael Billington, *'The Round Dance'*, *Guardian*, 6 January 1982, p. 9.
33. Robert Hewison, 'Ten characters in search of Dr Schnitzler', *Sunday Times*, 10 January 1982, p. 39.
34. Hugh Herbert, 'Dancing to the Tunes of Vienna'.

35. Michael Billington, 'La Ronde', Guardian, 21 January 1982, p. 9.
36. Francis King, 'Clumsy Encounters', Sunday Telegraph, 17 January 1982, p. 14.
37. James Fenton, 'Tales from the Vienna Woods: J. F. on the Problems of Sex and Schnitzler', Sunday Times, 17 January 1982, p. 40.
38. A. S., Reigen, in A. S., Die Dramatischen Werke (2 vols, Frankfurt, 1962), vol. 2, pp. 327–90 (p. 379), henceforth referred to by page numbers.
39. Marcus 1982, p. 68. In the following the tanslations are cited by names and publication dates.
40. On Schnitzler's novel Therese, see Elsbeth Dangel, 'Vergeblichkeit und Zweideutigkeit: Therese, Chronik eines Frauenlebens', in Hartmut Scheible (ed.), Arthur Schnitzler in neuer Sicht (Munich, 1981), pp. 164–87.
41. A. S., Der Weg ins Freie: Roman, in A. S., Die Erzählenden Schriften (2 vols, Frankfurt, 1961), vol. 1, pp. 635–958, p. 763. As recently as in Doderer the characters were required to behave like 'real Hausmeisters'; H. von Doderer, Die Strudlhofstiege oder Melzer und die Tiefe der Jahre: Roman (Munich, 1951), p. 589.
42. Billington, 'La Ronde'.
43. The classical English translation of these lines runs:'The Husband must enter/The hostile life/With struggle and strife.' The Poems and Ballads of Schiller (tr. Edward Bulwer Lytton), (Edinburgh 1852), p. 199.
44. Steiner, After Babel, p. 38.
45. Martin Swales, Arthur Schnitzler: A Critical Study (Oxford, 1971), p. 234.
46. Cf. Christiaan L. Hart Nibbrig, Rhetorik des Schweigens: Versuch über den Schatten literarischer Rede (Frankfurt, 1981), pp. 163–7.
47. Alan Duff, The Third Language: Recurrent Problems of Translation into English (Oxford, 1981), p. 88.
48. A. S., Das weite Land, in A. S., Die Dramatischen Werke, vol. 2, pp. 217–310 (p. 254).
49. Stoppard, Undiscovered Country, pp. 38–9 (p. 42).
50. Johanna Bossinade, '"Wenn es aber ... bei mir anders wäre." Die Frage der Geschlechterbeziehungen in Arthur Schnitzlers Reigen', in Gerhard Kluge (ed.), Aufsätze zur Literatur und Kunst der Jahrhundertwende (Amsterdam, 1984), pp. 273–328 (p. 313).
51. Steiner, After Babel, p. 301.

Hofmannsthal's 'Mythological' Opera *Arabella*

Srdan Bogosavljević

On completing his work on *Die ägyptische Helena* in the autumn of 1927, Richard Strauss asked his librettist, Hugo von Hofmannsthal, for a new subject, suggesting that a possible source might be found in the milieu of Wagner's *Die Meistersinger*. Hofmannsthal, however, rejected the suggestion, mainly because he was attracted by a world that was closer in time: 'My imagination', he replied, 'would be more inclined towards an atmosphere of comedy, dating from a much more recent period – about 1840 or 1850.'[1] What the poet had in mind was a 'farcical modern comedy' in a vaudeville style (H/S, p. 566) on which he had started work in 1924: *Der Fiaker als Graf* ('The Coachman as Count'). He wrote to Strauss on 1 October 1927:

> Two years ago I spent some time on a comedy, made notes, sketched out a series of scenes, and then put the work aside again. It was called *Der Fiaker als Graf* [...] The subject was delightful, but in the end it proved unsuitable for *present-day costume*. The state of affairs in it was still true in my youth (*as long as the court and the aristocracy were all-important in Vienna*) – today it would need to be set in an earlier epoch. (H/S, p. 587; my emphases)

A month later the plan assumed a more definite shape, as the *Fiaker* material fused with another fragment, the story *Lucidor: Figuren zu einer ungeschriebenen Komödie* ('Lucidor: Characters for an Unwritten Comedy'). The end product was none other than Hofmannsthal's last libretto, *Arabella*. The basic situation in the story resembles that of the libretto, but at the same time there are several important differences between the two works: for example, while Arabella's prospective husband in *Lucidor* comes from the Tyrol, in *Arabella* the titular figure marries a land-owner from Croatia called Mandryka, with whom she falls in love at first sight; and the fragment is set 'at the end of the seventies',[2] whereas the historical setting of the libretto is the period between 1860 and 1866.[3]

This difference in period is highly significant. The 1860s are divided from the 1870s by a number of decisive historical events, of which only a few can be mentioned here. In 1873 the *laissez-faire* economic policies and the uncontrolled speculations of the 'Gründerzeit' resulted in the disastrous Stock Exchange collapse which inaugurated a depression lasting until 1896. In 1866 Austria was expelled from the German Confederation and thus compelled to agree to the (fatal) constitutional compromise with Hungary and to seek a new sphere of influence in the Balkans.[4] The 1870s also saw a sharp increase in nationalism, especially among the Czech lower middle classes. By contrast, the Croats still seemed to be the most docile nation, because of their alleged loyalty to the Emperor. Hence it is no accident that the Slav in *Arabella* is not Czech, not a Pole, but a Croat.

All these historical processes are reflected in Hofmannsthal's libretto. Since, however, reflections of historical events in a work of art do not correspond directly to extra-literary facts, there is some danger that in treating a work as the reflection of history one may violate its aesthetic structure.[5] While Hofmannsthal's libretto is not a mere reflection of history, it is, as I hope to show, an ideologically questionable attempt to elevate history into an almost mythological scheme. In order to gain insight into the ideological premises of this scheme, one must dismantle the mythopoeic framework and thus do a certain amount of violence to the work's structure. By exposing this framework, however, I have no wish to belittle the work on ideological grounds, still less to question its author's greatness; for even his ideological aberrations are justified by the work.

The collapse of the Dual Monarchy and the aristocracy put an end to the world into which Hofmannsthal was born and whose beliefs he shared, albeit with reservations. 'What a world we have blundered into', he wrote in a letter to Carl J. Burckhardt. 'The bare timber-work is visible, trembling right down to the foundations. Will anyone still study history? Will anyone need history?'[6] For Hofmannsthal the dissolution of old Austria represented a trauma that had a lasting influence on his literary work: 'I realise quite well', he writes on 15 July 1927, just before starting work on *Arabella*, 'what guides my pen in such dark moments: it is old Austria, which was forced out of existence but somewhere wants to return to life.'[7] Thus old Austria was for Hofmannsthal an unresolved problem that repeatedly had to be 'resolved', for: 'Everything that ever existed is still present; nothing is settled, nothing is completely disposed of, all that has been done must be done again; old life returns, gently transformed, to the circle of life.'[8] This last implies a conception of history as an ongoing cyclical process. And Hofmannsthal, after all, saw the present as the ghostly return of a decisive historical moment: 'The situation,' he writes in 1928, 'is assuming, with mysterious necessity, a rigid death-mask, as before 1859, as before 1866.'[9] This remark makes it clear why Hofmannsthal chose the period before 1866 for 'present-day costume'.

One of the problems that Hofmannsthal wanted to 'resolve' in *Arabella* on the mythopoeic plane was the nationality problem and in particular the Slav problem which finally brought about the downfall of Austria-Hungary. Before the war Hofmannsthal had virtually disregarded this problem, taking the existence of the 'marginal nations' in Austria-Hungary for granted and treating them with paternalist condescension as 'our Slavs'. If he introduced a Slav as a literary character, as he did with Frau Vuic in *Reitergeschichte* ('A Tale of the Cavalry', 1899), his characterisation scarcely went beyond the traditional demonic portrayal. It was the war that forced Hofmannsthal to confront the complexity of the problem. He began to propagate the myth of Austria as a 'true organism', an organic unity of diverse ethnic components, held together by the 'Austrian idea' which could only be grasped by 'an act of faith and will'. In his speech 'The Austrian Idea' (1917) the poet declared:

> Narrow partisan and ideological considerations – which are wrongly considered the sole forms of political expression – are far weaker than the destiny that for us means comprehending European consciousness within the German character and striking a compromise between this German character, divested of its sharply national features, and the Slav character (RA II 457).

In Hofmannsthal's ideological scheme, Austria became the quintessence of European consciousness and its imbrication with the Oriental Slav character.

After the war, Hofmannsthal's attitude to the Slavs underwent a lasting change.[10] On the one hand, he tried for the first time to understand the distinctive identity of the Slav nations; on the other, the Slav no longer appears in his work merely as a quasi-demonic figure on the hero's journey into horror, but as the creator of order. In *Der Unbestechliche* ('The Incorruptible', 1922), for example, the loyal but ambitious and envious Ruthenian Theodor establishes order among the members of an aristocratic Austrian family who are at the mercy of their own frivolity. The Slav is no longer merely the passive object of paternalist treatment, but an active subject playing an important part in the life of the Austrian family.[11]

The second problem that the figure of the Slav was intended to resolve in *Arabella* is that of liberalism as the cause of Austria's collapse. Hofmannsthal's critical rejection of liberalism first assumed sharp outlines during the war. When the poet discovers in the Austrian people 'a mute resistance [...] to the liberalism of the sixties' (RA II 17), when he plays off 'the idea of order against the idea of freedom' (RA II 30), when, in his speech on Beethoven, he wishes to relieve the 'limited individual [...] of his excess of freedom' (RA II 80), he is propagating a 'conservative revolution' whose purpose is to restore the validity and dignity of the old social and political bonds that are said to have been undermined by liberalism. As the speech 'Das Schrifttum als geistiger Raum der Nation' ('Literature as the Nation's Spiritual Space', 1927) indicates, this revolution is to reverse the disastrous consequences arising from the Renaissance.

In *Arabella* Hofmannsthal 'shows' that even at its height in the 1860s liberalism was gradually leading to an economic and political catastrophe. The action of the libretto takes place on the last day of Fasching (Carnival), just before the fasting and penitence required by Lent. Yet the world of *Arabella* foresees no such change; its awareness of life is confined to the frivolous atmosphere of Fasching and the waltz, which, as the bourgeois dance *par excellence* in contrast to the dignified aristocratic minuet, serves to legitimate the unbridled sensual celebrations. Behind this carefree façade, however, a malevolent process is under way, which is already affecting the Viennese nobility. Not only are such bourgeois customs as the waltz infiltrating what used to be tightly-sealed aristocratic circles; the nobility's entire 'credit' is 'tottering'. Arabella's father,

Count Waldner, is wholly devoted to card-playing (probably to be understood as a symbol of the frantic speculation of the 'Gründerjahre') although his family is virtually bankrupt. Waldner has lost his last penny, and his remaining possessions belong in reality to his creditors, the representatives of the liberal bourgeoisie. The Waldners (an ironic name, since 'Wald' means forest!) are living in a hotel; they are homeless, mere noble beggars, living from hand to mouth while awaiting the death of a rich and miserly aunt.

Since the family's financial situation permits it to keep only one daughter in a style befitting her station, the younger daughter, Zdenka, has to be disguised as a boy. Although she is sensitive and loving, free from doubt and calculation, her true nature is doomed to frustration. As Zdenka is a Slav name, her character contains Slav as well as Austrian features. Arabella's name, on the other hand, may allude to the Italian element in the Austrian heritage.[12] Described by her younger sister as 'proud and coquettish and cold',[13] Arabella seems at ease in the frivolous liberal atmosphere of carnival. Three empty-headed counts, interested only in horses and dancing, strive for her favour; one of them, the Hungarian Elemer, attracts her by his masculine manner, but even he cannot bind her affections.[14] However, Arabella's inability to commit herself and find fulfilment, her state of unattached freedom, are painful for her; she longs for the right man and for genuine love, perceiving intuitively that the meaning of life consists (to borrow Hofmannsthal's words) not in an excess of freedom but in valid social bonds. Arabella's nature, too, is still frustrated.

In order to repair her family's financial situation, Arabella is to be married off as quickly as possible. In the first version of Act I she is prepared to marry an Austrian builder. In the end, however, she marries a wealthy Slavonian magnate who has come to Vienna in search of the beautiful woman whose picture Waldner sent to his old army comrade, Mandryka's (now deceased) uncle. This ingenious move, intended to attract a source of wealth, sets in motion the action of the libretto, which develops almost along the lines of the fairy-tale.[15]

Mandryka[16] comes 'from a half-alien world (Croatia), half a buffoon, yet also a fine fellow, capable of deep emotions, wild and gentle – almost demonic' (H/S, p. 602). Yet all these qualities, seen by Hofmannsthal as typically Slav,[17] would not enable him to gain Arabella's hand if he were not also very rich. On deciding to go to Vienna, he simply sells an entire forest, together with all the people and animals living in it, since he knows that in the capital every step costs money, and he is averse to penny-pinching. The transformation of a forest into money, however, presents not the slightest problem. In contrast to Hofmannsthal's *Jedermann* ('Everyman'), who represents the modern world, money is for Mandryka not an end in itself. He does not need it in his village, only in a world that is itself dominated by money. But even his use of money in the city is justified by the sublime purpose for which he uses it: that of removing the obstacles between himself and his beloved. As in Hofmannsthal's *Danae*, money is sublimated by serving a spiritual force.[18]

Unlike the Viennese nobility, Mandryka is untouched by the economic consequences of liberal ideology. He is not enslaved to creditors and other representatives of liberalism; when he needs money, he simply calls, like a king, upon the Jew of Sissek (Sisak). Nor has Mandryka been affected by ethical and psychological liberalism. While the urban nobility is homeless, Mandryka lives in a village surrounded by virgin forests. While the Viennese nobility conceals its lack of integrity behind a series of masks, Mandryka is a whole man. The Viennese nobility tries to suppress its awareness of the meaninglessness of its existence in a frivolous party atmosphere; Mandryka's existence is embedded in the succession of generations and in an awareness of the whole of life. Finally, while the informal relation between the Viennese nobility and ordinary people is no more than a Carnival fiction, Mandryka's relationship with his subordinates is genuine: he is above them, yet also one of them.[19]

Mandryka embodies Hofmannsthal's 'dream of society as an organic formation which has grown up naturally'.[20] As Claudio Magris has said, he 'expresses the poet's yearning for the world of feudalism'.[21] But this figure also points to the possibility of restoring the old order by uniting the Austrian and the Slav characters. Before such a union can occur, however, each must be transformed.

Although Arabella's proud, coquettish character is changed by love at first sight, her love must first pass the test of withstanding a social intrigue. The intrigue originates from Zdenka's concealed affection for Matteo, a poor middle-class officer, who has been rejected by Arabella. Fearing that this rejection may drive the weak and self-pitying Matteo to suicide, Zdenka gives him a letter containing a key, supposedly the key of Arabella's bedroom. Mandryka accidentally overhears the conversation between Matteo and Zdenka and jumps to the conclusion that Arabella has deceived him. His trust in her, already shaken, is further reduced when he and Waldner catch Matteo and Arabella in conversation at night. Just when the relationship between Mandryka and Arabella seems to have been finally destroyed, Zdenka, no longer dressed as a boy, appears on the stairs and confesses her 'sin'. Mandryka successfully persuades Matteo to marry her. This marriage, however, does not restore the trust between Mandryka and Arabella, until the latter, following Zdenka's example of loving self-sacrifice, resolves to forgive Mandryka. Finally Arabella hands Mandryka a glass of water, as the customs of his village require, and the union between the Austrian beauty and the Slav is sealed for all eternity.

> ARABELLA: And we are betrothed and joined for sorrow and joy, for hurting and forgiving!
> MANDRYKA: For ever, my angel, and for everything that is to come!
> ARABELLA: And you'll believe – ?
> MANDRYKA: You'll stay as you are?
> ARABELLA: I can't change, take me as I am!
>
> (D V 578)

Intended to marry for money, they actually marry for love; degrading dependence on money is turned into an alliance sanctified by higher necessity or destiny. Nothing hinders this alliance except the Viennese fondness for intrigue and the fact that the true Austrian character is not yet a reality; and this very fact is what puts at risk the union between Arabella and Mandryka.

By helping Matteo to gain Zdenka's hand, Mandryka enables Zdenka to become what she is; by binding Arabella to himself, he helps her to fulfil her destiny. The Slav therefore has no need for enlightenment from above or paternalistic supervision; he is an agent in his own right, guaranteeing the eventual emergence of the true Austrian character, apparently a mixture of half-Slav inwardness and half-Italian grace. Translated from the symbolic structure of the libretto into the language of politics, this scheme suggests both a wish-fulfilment fantasy and a rebuke to the Slavs of the former Dual Monarchy for betraying their historic mission.

Waldner – that is, old Austria, undermined by liberalism, financially and spiritually bankrupt – goes on gambling, like a senile old man trying to fill up the last days of his life. He will again lose every penny, for the Slav cannot continue financing his addiction for ever. Yet the alliance will endure. The future of Austria rests on this emotional symbiosis, just as in *Der Rosenkavalier* the future of the nobility is guaranteed by Octavian, its young and fresh element. Both Austria and the nobility have a future.

How could anyone indulge in such fantasies ten years after both the Dual Monarchy and its nobility had been condemned to death by history? Was not *Arabella* written against the grain of history? Is it not a 'sterile polemic against history'?[22] In order to express his concealed 'thesis' that the collapse of the monarchy was not historically necessary, Hofmannsthal is returning to a decisive moment and trying to show how things could have turned out differently. This possibility is hinted at symbolically by the prophecy at the beginning of the libretto. The fortune-teller correctly foresees the family's future, but her latest prophecy is different from the preceding one: 'The cards fall better than last time'[23] (D V 515). Within the symbolic structure of the libretto, this implies that history is, so to speak, being give a chance to correct itself. And indeed the entire work is a magical invocation of history in order to transform it on a higher, mythopoeic plane.

Arabella is a myth of conservative restoration, intended to instil meaning into a political life that has been rendered meaningless. Like *Die ägyptische Helena*, *Arabella* is a mythological opera, but to an even greater degree; for the myth on which Hofmannsthal's last libretto is based was more alive and had a more important function.

Notes

1. Richard Strauss, Hugo von Hofmannsthal, *Briefwechsel*, ed. Willi Schuh (4th edn, Zurich, 1970), p. 578. Henceforth cited in the text as H/S and page number.
2. Hugo von Hofmannsthal, *Gesammelte Werke*, ed. Bernd Schoeller, 10 vols (Frankfurt, 1979): *Erzählungen, Gespräche und Briefe, Reisen*, p. 173.
3. Hofmannsthal vacillated between 1860 (H/S, p. 612f.) and the 1860s (H/S, p. 638). Finally he set the action in the year 1866 (H/S, p. 645).
4. The 'Ausgleich' (compromise) between Austria and Hungary in 1867 represents the beginning of the Dual Monarchy as a unitary state. The 'Ausgleich' complicated Austria's policy towards the South Slav peoples under the brutal and chauvinistic rule of the Hungarian magnates. The Slav population of Hungary held the government in

Vienna responsible for their maltreatment, and in 1905 they paradoxically asked their actual oppressors, the Hungarian nobility, for help against Austria.
5. Thus Tumler writes: 'Mehr noch als fur den *Rosenkavalier* gilt für *Arabella* der Unterschied: wenn in einer Dichtung etwas gespielt wird, heißt das nicht, daß es in der Geschichte schlechthin Deckung hat.' Franz Tumler, '*Rosenkavalier* und *Arabella*', Neue Deutsche Hefte, 3 (1956), p. 371. While Tumler's dictum applies to *Arabella* without qualification, it must be said that in many ways his interpretation also presupposes an ideological critique.
6. Hugo von Hofmannsthal, Carl J. Burckhardt, *Briefwechsel*, ed. Carl J. Burckhardt (Frankfurt, 1956), p. 14.
7. Ibid., p. 246.
8. Hofmannsthal, *Reden und Aufsätze* II (in *Gesammelte Werke*, ed. Schoeller), p. 392. Henceforth cited in the text as RA II and page number.
9. Hugo von Hofmannsthal, Josef Redlich, *Briefwechsel*, ed. Helga Fussgänger (Frankfurt, 1971), p. 97.
10. This change in Hofmannsthal's attitude to the Slavs was first apparent when he considered editing an anthology of nineteenth-century Czech poets as part of his planned 'Austrian Library'. In 1922 he wanted to edit a 'Czech Library' as a counterpart, and wrote the preface to a translation of Czech and Slovak folk-songs. In the 1920s he also studied South Slav customs and folk-epics.
11. J. B. Bednall, 'The Slav Symbol in Hofmannsthal's Post-war Comedies', *German Life and Letters*, 14, i/ii (1960), pp. 34-44, draws attention to the presence of Slav figures in the post-war comedies but does not elucidate their symbolic function.
12. Hofmannsthal, *Dramen* V (in *Gesammelte Werke*, ed. Schoeller), p. 523. Henceforth cited as D V and page number.
13. Hofmannsthal, whose maternal grandmother was Italian, drew attention to the Italian element in the Austrian character in his reply to d'Annunzio's 'Neunte Canzone' (RA I, pp. 625-9).
14. The ideological implications of the grouping Elemer/Arabella/Mandryka are clear: Arabella is attracted by the Hungarian, but her destiny is only fulfilled by her compromise with the Slav character.
15. Rudolf H. Schäfer, *Hugo von Hofmannsthals 'Arabella'* (Zurich, 1967), p. 248, shows conclusively that *Arabella* contains elements of fairy-tale.
16. Richard Exner, in 'Arabella: Verkauft, verlobt, verwandelt?', *Hofmannsthal-Forschungen*, 8 (1985), p. 74, finds that 'Mandryka' in Russian means something like 'vagabond'. The name, however, does not occur in the Serbo-Croatian area.
17. Hofmannsthal describes Grillparzer's Ottokar as representing 'das glänzende, dämonisch kraftvolle, aber unsichere slawische Seelengebilde' (RA II, p. 410).
18. Exner misunderstands these connections when, in the article cited above (pp. 70-4), he casts doubt on the love between Mandryka and Arabella because of its supposedly mercenary nature and describes the Croat as 'besitzbesessen'.
19. Mandryka was thus conceived as a thoroughgoing contrast to the Viennese nobility, as the following statement from one of Hofmannsthal's letters confirms: 'Den drei leichtfertig nach Frauen und Mädchen jagenden Grafen, dem ganzen zweifelhaften Milieu dieses kassierten Rittmeisters Waldner haftet etwas Ordinäres an, ein etwas ordinäres und gefährliches Wien umgibt diese Figuren [...] vor allem aber ist dieses vergnügungssüchtig-frivole, schuldenmachende Wien die Folie für Mandryka – ihn umgibt die Reinheit seiner Dörfer, seiner nie von der Axt berührten Eichenwälder, seiner alten Volkslieder – hier tritt die *Weite* des großen halb-slawischen Österreich herein in eine Wienerische Komödie und läßt eine ganz andere Luft einströmen' (H/ S, p. 639).
20. Schäfer, *Hofmannsthals 'Arabella'*, p. 158.
21. Claudio Magris, *Der habsburgische Mythos in der österreichischen Literatur* (Salzburg,

1966), p. 228.
22. Ibid., p. 222.
23. 'Die Kartenaufschlägerin entwickelt alle Figuren u. das ganze Stück.' Hofmannsthal, *Sämtliche Werke*, Kritische Ausgabe, Vol. XXVI: *Operndichtungen* IV, ed. Hans-Albrecht Koch (Frankfurt, 1976), p. 245.

Friedrich Kiesler and Theatrical Modernism in Vienna

John Warren

It is no secret that Austrian theatre (which effectively means Viennese theatre), although occupying a major position in German drama, has hardly been in the vanguard of either dramatic or theatrical experimentation. In 1928, Max Reinhardt explained why he had opened a drama school in Vienna by saying: 'weil hier die große Vergangenheit des Theaters in gewissen unverlierbaren Traditionen noch lebendig aufzuspüren ist' (because the great theatrical past still lives on here, indestructible and absolute).[1] Certainly tradition is what we associate with Vienna's theatre, although before the First World War Koloman Moser and others associated with the 'Wiener Werkstätte' had made some interesting attempts to bring Viennese theatre into line with developments in the fine and applied arts.[2] Kokoschka's early dramatic attempts (rooted in student theatre and associated by most critics with Expressionism) stand out as the exception, and he found a more congenial home in Berlin, in the group surrounding Herwarth Walden's journal *Der Sturm*. After the war, Hans Kaltnecker, who showed some promise as an Expressionist, died before his talents could be tested, and Arnolt Bronnen and Ferdinand Bruckner (Theodor Tagger) both made their names in Berlin.

In the early 1920s we look almost in vain for a Viennese contribution to what Fiebach terms 'Abstract and Total Theatre'.[3] But let us be clear about what we are seeking, for 'theatrical modernism' is no easier a term to define than 'modernism' itself: do we mean modernist *drama*, avant-garde theatre, or experimental theatre? In this short contribution, by 'modernism' I mean the theatrical equivalent of that move to abstract or non-figurative art which had taken place in the fine arts before 1914. In Munich there were Kandinsky's experiments;[4] elsewhere in Germany modernism produced the work of Schwitters, Schreyer, Schlemmer, Wauer and many more. France, Italy and above all Russia made major contributions to the search for new directions in the performing arts. Among the theatrical modernists only one Austrian made a major contribution to the ferment of constructivist, kinetic and machine art. This was Friedrich Kiesler, whose mechanical-kinetic sets for Čapek's *R.U.R.* (staged in Berlin in 1922) were the first expression of what John Willett calls the 'two-pronged impact of Constructivism'.[5]

Kiesler, who in later life termed himself an 'avantgardiste', was born in Czernowitz in 1890. He studied in Vienna, both at the Technische Hochschule and the Kunstakademie, taking a degree at neither institution but winning *two* prizes. Relatively little is known about his formative years in Vienna, where his major contribution was to mount the exhibition of modern theatre technique in

1924. The following year he designed the Austrian Pavilion at the World Fair in Paris and in 1926 he left Europe for the United States where he took American citizenship and changed his first name to Frederick. There have been two exhibitions of his work in Vienna (in 1975 and 1988) but there is, as yet, no monograph on his life and work.[6]

Where did Vienna stand in relation to the modernist movement of the early 1920s? Had Modernism vanished with the Empire, the 'emigrations' to Berlin, and with the series of deaths that struck down so many leading figures in 1918 and 1919 (Koloman Moser, Otto Wagner and Heinrich Lefler, to name just those involved in theatrical experiment)? Kiesler was friendly with Adolf Loos and with the 'neue Bewegung' (men such as Cary Hauser, artist and stage designer, Johannes Itten, soon to move to the 'Bauhaus', and the artist Erich Heckel). These embattled survivors should in theory have been strengthened by the many Hungarians who arrived in Vienna after the failure of Béla Kun's Communist revolution in 1919. But, as Lee Congdon has shown, few Viennese took any interest in the Hungarians.[7] Some moved on to Berlin immediately (Moholy-Nagy); others when they could (Béla Balasz in 1926); one or two, notably the leader of the MA group Lajos Kassak, stayed until return to their homeland was possible. In the first few years after the war Vienna was still in a state of shock, and it was easier to cling to past values than to pioneer the new. It was a city where inflation and political unrest created financial rather than artistic speculators and where philistinism was rife.

Although encouraged by Loos, Kiesler, like most Viennese of the 1920s, made his name in Berlin. He went there in 1921 to make contact with Hans Richter, then editor of the modernist art journal *G*, and it was probably there that he came under the influence of Russian constructivism. In 1922 he was asked to design Čapek's futuristic 'robot' play *R.U.R.*, which, when staged in December 1922, placed him immediately in the forefront of the avant-garde. Theo van Doesburg, El Lissitzky, Schwitters, Moholy-Nagy and Richter came to the second performance and were so impressed with his mechanistic-kinetic designs that he was accepted as a member of van Doesberg's *De Stijl* group. They were impressed by the first film projections in the German theatre, the use of synchronised music, and a small television-type screen which by means of an apparatus of mirrors produced reflections of the off-stage actors. In the spring of 1923 Kiesler took part in the meetings in Vienna which helped bring about Hans Tietze's 'Gesellschaft zur Förderung moderner Kunst' ('Society for the Promotion of Modern Art') and this contact gained him the post of chief architect and designer to the 1924 exhibition which was in part promoted by the society.

Even earlier, Kiesler's ideas on theatre design had been extended by the sets he designed for Berthold Viertel's production of Eugene O'Neill's *The Emperor Jones* in Berlin. Viertel was then directing 'Die Truppe' with Ernst Aufricht. In his autobiography the latter tells how Viertel, needing an 'attraction' to sell his production, fetched Kiesler back from Vienna. Kiesler recounted that instead of using the normal term 'Bühnenbild' (stage design) in the programme, he invented the term 'Raumbühne', an expression for which the critic Alfred Kerr immediately took him to task. This controversy produced Kiesler's concept of the 'Raumtheater' and his attack on the limitations of the proscenium stage ('Guckkastenbühne').[8] Viertel's production of *The Emperor Jones* used a highly raked open stage, with automatic scene change, the action being accompanied by constantly changing lighting and acoustic effects. These innovations may have been an exciting contribution to modernist theatre but they were, so Aufricht tells us, a disaster for that particular production.[9]

The next stage of Kiesler's meteoric European career was his appointment as 'designer and architect' of the 'Internationale Ausstellung neuer Theatertechnik' (International Exhibition of New Theatrical Techniques) which was one of many exhibitions to accompany the second Festival of Music and Theatre in Vienna in the autumn of 1924. Not only did he mount the exhibition, edit, design and contribute to the catalogue (a strikingly handsome document, owing much in graphic design to *De Stijl*), but he also designed and built a 'constructivist' stage in the Konzerthaus where modern theatre techniques and exhibitions of lighting were demonstrated and where readings and even a play were mounted.

Before we examine Kiesler's achievements and the Viennese response to them, it is worth noting the scope of this festival. When we see what was being performed (in the opera house as well as on the stage) the contrast with the revolutionary ideas contained in the exhibition and programme, as well as with Kiesler's constructivist 'Raumbühne', becomes apparent.

On 14 September 1924, the festival was opened by Karl Seitz, the Mayor of Vienna, to the sounds of a special fanfare donated by Richard Strauss. It was to last until 19 October. The opening ceremony over, Seitz led the guests of honour into the Rathaus to view the exhibition of 'Modern Viennese music from Bruckner to the present' and the second, greatly extended Viennese festival was under way. Like its precursor, which had been held in 1920 and devoted solely to music, this festival was organised by Dr David Josef Bach, editor of the *feuilleton* section of the *Arbeiter-Zeitung* and leader of the Social Democratic 'Kunststelle'. With a credit of 100,000 Schillings from the city's reorganised funds, Bach was determined to show that Vienna could mount a major arts festival. The motivation was as much political as artistic.[10] Reading today the list of performances in the opera, concert-house and theatre one can only marvel at the strength of Vienna's cultural resources despite the city's appalling post-war situation. Certainly 1924 was a promising year for the socialist administration of the city. Under Hugo Breitner's dynamic financial leadership the administration had turned its huge deficit round and was about to embark on the ambitious programme of public housing that was to make it the envy of Europe. Austria's inflation was over and the country was enjoying a brief period of political calm.

A series of major exhibitions on theatre, art and music provided the background to an outstanding programme of premières and performances. At the opera Strauss conducted a performance of his own *Salome* with Jeritza in the title-role, and two days later, on 20 September, he conducted a première of Gluck's *Don Juan*. The following night Jeritza sang the role of Marietta in Erich Korngold's *Die tote Stadt* with Franz Schalk conducting, and Richard Tauber as Paul. Lotte Lehmann and Alfred Piccaver starred in *La Bohème*, and in the Redoutensaal Schalk conducted a performance of *Figaro* with Elisabeth

Schumann and Richard Mayr. Julius Bittner's *Rosengärtlein*, with Alfred Jerger, was the fourth operatic première of the festival. The Rosé quartet gave recitals and the series of concerts of modern music was inaugurated by a concert on 17 September which included works by Josef Hauer, Franz Schreker and Arnold Schoenberg. A landmark for Schoenberg and modernist opera was the first performance at the Volksoper of his *Die glückliche Hand*. The two muses were joined in Hofmannsthal's adaptation of Molière's *Der Bürger als Edelmann* with music by Richard Strauss, conducted by the composer in the Redoutensaal. This major event was accorded a double review by the *Neue Freie Presse*, Raoul Auernheimer reviewing the comedy and Julius Korngold, the composer's father, reviewing the music.

Theatrical offerings were wide-ranging and had special appeal to connoisseurs of Austrian theatre. Among over thirty productions, the Austrian classics – Grillparzer, Raimund, Nestroy and Anzengruber – were prominent, great interest being shown in a guest performance by Alexander Moissi as Alfons in *Die Jüdin von Toledo* (and Montezuma in Hauptmann's *Der weiße Heiland*). The Burgtheater produced Richard Beer-Hofman's *Jaakobs Traum* and, as standard repertoire works, plays by Shakespeare and Schiller and Goethe's *Iphigenie auf Tauris* with Hedwig Bleibtreu and Raoul Aslan. Hermann Bahr's *Der Franzl* was premièred during the festival, and his *Das Tschapperl* and *Josephine* (with Leopoldine Konstantin) revived. Other Austrian premières included Max Mell's *Apostelspiel* in the Josefstadt (with Helene Thimig and Oskar Homolka) and Schnitzler's *Komödie der Verführung*. The Director of the Burgtheater, Franz Herterich, put on works by two young Austrian dramatists; Ernst Fischer's *Das Schwert von Attila* and Walter Eidlitz's *Der Kaiser im Wald*. Richard Billinger's *Der Knecht* also received its first performance during the festival.

German drama was represented by an outstanding production of Ernst Barlach's *Der tote Tag*, the Viennese première of Georg Kaiser's *Kolportage* and Hans-José Rehfisch's play *Wer weint um Juckenack*. The latter was hardly to Viennese tastes, being described by Felix Salten in the *Neue Freie Presse* of 26 September as being 'unattractive in a north German sense, as sandy and barren as a Berlin building-site'. Berlin theatre was better represented by a guest performance of the Russian cabaret theatre, 'Der blaue Vogel' (reviewed by Ernst Lothar in a *feuilleton* of the *Neue Freie Presse* on 7 October). As I have indicated elsewhere,[11] post-war Viennese attempts to create a modern theatre had not been a success, and, although impressive in scope, the plays performed during the festival (Barlach's *Der tote Tag* apart) must be described as routine traditional theatre. Kiesler's exhibition and catalogue were designed to show the Viennese that the other cultural centres of continental Europe (there were no contributions from the United Kingdom) could display a whole range of exciting modernist theatrical experiment.

The musical and theatrical performances of the festival were matched by many exhibitions, of which the most important for the theatre was the International Exhibition of New Theatre Techniques, held in the Konzerthaus, and devised and mounted by Friedrich Kiesler. He also designed and edited the 'Katalog Programm Almanach' which provided a series of key articles on modern theatre as well as listing the ninety-five groups of work exhibited. The catalogue was designed in a striking and modern layout, so modern, with articles set both vertically and horizontally, as to be at times a little difficult to read.

Some idea of the lack of Austrian interest in avant-garde theatre may be gained from the limited number of Austrians among the contributors to both the articles and the exhibits. The articles (mostly short) present a conspectus of contemporary ideas on avant-garde and experimental theatre. It was a remarkable achievement for Kiesler to have assembled such a distinguished list of European contributors.

Before surveying the content of the articles, I shall give a brief outline of the major exhibits and exhibitors. These include examples of the work of the leading theatre designers of contemporary Europe. Sketches, figurines, manuscripts, models and photographs gave an impressive overview of avant-garde developments from Russia through to Italy. I shall mention only the most famous. Germany was represented by George Grosz (his designs for Goll's *Methusalem*, and for *Androcles and the Lion* and *Caesar and Cleopatra*), by Oskar Schlemmer (designs and figurines for *Das Nusch-nuschi*, the *Triadische Ballett* and Kokoschka's *Mörder, Hoffnung der Frauen*), by Moholy-Nagy, El Lissitzky, Cesar Klein, Rochus Gliese, Lothar Schreyer, Alfred Kunz (including seven superb designs for Kaiser's *Gilles und Jeanne*) and by a complicated set of designs, figures and machinery for a 'Mechanisches Ballett' by Kurt Schmidt. The French contribution included notable examples of the work of Fernand Léger and Georges Braque: by Léger designs and figurines for 'La Création du Monde' and for 'Skating Rink', and by Braque the designs and figurines for *Les Fâcheux*. Léger's 'Ballet mécanique' was screened in the 'Raumbühne' during the festival. Russia, which provided inspiration for so many theatrical modernists, was strongly represented. George Jakulov's model and figurines for Tairov's production of *Giroflé Girofla* (which was to come on tour to Vienna in 1925) and Alexander Vesnin's constructivist model and ten sketches for *Der Mann der Donnerstag war* were the most important exhibits of the seven Russian contributors. The futurist Enrico Prampolini, author of *Manifesto dell'Atmosfera Scenica* (1924), was perhaps the most important of Italy's twenty exhibitors. There were masks from Japan, Java, New Caledonia and Ceylon, a dance costume from Brazil, musical scores and instruments, photographs of Polish theatre and contributors from the Netherlands and Scandinavia. Among this feast of theatrical modernism Austrians would have been pleased to note work by Hans Poelzig (seven plans for the Salzburg 'Festspielhaus' project), by Harry Täuber (including the designs and figurines for the 1922 Burgtheater production of Franz Werfel's *Spiegelmensch*), by Hans Fritz (designs and sets utilising his 'Würfelbühne'), by Oskar Laske (including the figurines for Reinhardt's production of *Der Diener zweier Herrn*), by Oskar Strnad (his model for a 'Ringbühne' and his designs for *Hamlet, Dantons Tod* and *Der weiße Heiland*) and by Cary Hauser (preliminary sketches for Csokor's *Die rote Straße*).

The exhibits provided a colourful, varied and, for the Viennese public, no doubt somewhat weird insight into the world of theatrical modernism. The programme supplied within its eighty or so pages a stimulating statement of a truly modernist approach to theatre. Still of interest today as a source document on stage design and theatrical development, it must have been almost incomprehensible to the Viennese public of 1924. For a city which had just taken Max Reinhardt's 'Theater in der Josefstadt' to its heart, the range of modernist ideas must have conjured up an alien and possibly hostile world. A quick survey of the major articles will demonstrate that Kiesler had managed to include most aspects of theatrical modernism.

Kiesler's five contributions to the catalogue start with his statement on 'Das Railway-Theater' in which he visualises a central spherical stage ('Bühnenkern') around which the auditorium will move. Today's theatre, he argues, has much in common with the sports arena. Speed is essential. The individualistic actor, like the 'wings' (Kulissen), will disappear, and film will be used to create the suggestion of milieu. Poetry will be neither formal verse nor extemporisation, and the author will be replaced by the engineer who, with the greatest mathematical precision, will create what Kiesler terms an 'optophonetische Spielsymphonie'. There follows a ten-line call to action, 'Abrüstung der Kunst' ('Remove art's protective scaffolding'), which urges young theorists to 'quitter les mansardes sacerdotales!', and abandon the pedestals of the various artistic 'isms'. 'Enough of projects', he cries, 'we want realities.' The answer is 'to Live!'

Kiesler's third and fourth contributions provide a description of the mechanistic-kinetic stage designs for Čapek's *R.U.R* (with two illustrations) and an example of the mechanically projected set, a forty-five minute sequence with six projections (illustrated). From the description and photographs one gains some idea of the amazing effects created by Kiesler in 1922.

His final contribution, 'Débâcle des Theaters – Die Gesetze der G.-K.-Bühne' ('Theatrical debacle – the rules of the proscenium stage', pp. 43–58), is his attack on the proscenium stage, which he developed during the altercation with Alfred Kerr. Attacking traditional theatre, he argues that the old slavery of actors to the text must be broken. The present form of theatre is artificial, outdated and traditional ('Barockokotheater'), and also largely social. Calling for a radical revision of theatrical convention he argues that sight-lines should be clear from every part of the auditorium. Actors must learn to use the whole stage area and be allowed to develop what he terms an 'elemental intensity'. The relationship between art and nature must be rethought and traditional stage scenery replaced by the use of colour and film projections. The important elements of the play are sound, the actor, stage properties, stage machinery, and light. All these have to be welded into a unity. He ends his arcane and complicated observations with a twelve-point attack on the proscenium stage (including, as point 9, a complicated algebraic formula), calling for its replacement by the spherical 'Raumbühne'. The stage, he argues, must not be a box with a curtain as cover but an 'expandable space'. Vitality and dynamism are vital for the modern stage and are not helped by painted stage sets; only when the stage has ceased to be a static, box-like picture will it be possible to develop a more organic and flexible form of theatre.

Many of the points made by Kiesler in this comprehensive assessment of the weaknesses (as he saw them) of traditional theatre are developed by other contributors to the exhibition catalogue. Fernand Léger in his essay 'Das Schauspiel: Licht/Farbe/Film' ('The Play: Light, Colour, Film') pleads for new forms of 'Schauspiel'; forms which would surprise, which would be fast (he calls for 'units' of fifteen to twenty minutes), and would use light, colour and movement, which would abandon the cult of the 'star actor' and turn to acrobats, to team work and 'to all the new theatrical means which seemed to have remained in the shadows'. Léger also contributes (in French) a description of his 'ballet mécanique' (film de Fernand Léger et Dudley Murphy, synchronisme musical de Georges Antheil), and this film was screened during the exhibition.

The attack on actors (somewhat out of place perhaps in a city which, as Max Reinhardt remarked, prided itself on its acting traditions) is also taken up by Herwarth Walden who commented in his short piece 'Theater' on the megalomania of self-styled artists. It is, he argues, a sickness which seems to affect actors more than others. For Walden sound, colour and form are more important than words, and theatre should return to what he terms the 'primal artistic awareness': only then can theatre become a work of art.

William Wauer, in his short contribution 'Der Schauspieler', attacks contemporary styles of acting but is rather more positive about the actor. It is the actor who creates 'life' within the play, for the author has only recounted it and the producer only arranged it. Wauer also makes the important point that the actor can choose an 'optical' or an 'acoustic' method of presentation or a combination of the two. The question of speech is addressed by Rudolf Blümner, who asks whether theatre is 'Schau-Spiel-Kunst oder Hör-Spiel-Kunst?' (primarily a 'visual' or an 'aural' performance). Examining both types of stage language (declamation and the attempt at naturalism) he deduces that it is impossible to achieve the real rhythms of everyday speech and turns his arguments against actors, claiming that 'they do not possess the souls of real humans and are in fact dead'. Thus Blümner's contribution unites the attack on the actor with the analysis of the problematic nature of dramatic language.

The obsession with language is present in even stranger form in B. F. Dolbin's contribution, 'Die Technifizierung der Verständigung' ('the technification of understanding'), which warns against Zamenhof's artificial language, Esperanto, claiming that if it were used to present works of literature, it would annihilate their metaphysical dimension. More helpful, and still in the 'acoustic sphere', is Luigi Russolo's short piece, 'Die Kunst der Geräusche' ('The Art of Sounds'), in which he urges that, having learnt to see with 'futuristic eyes', we should now learn to listen with 'futuristic ears', and that the stage should capture the sounds of our motor cars and of our industrial cities.

There were two other contributions from Italian futurists, from Enrico Prampolini and Filippo Marinetti. Prampolini (writing in Italian) in his 'L'Atmosfera Scenica' seems to be not very far from Kiesler when he talks of the 'magic triangle' of 'synthesis, dynamism and plasticity'. Marinetti's 'Wir erfinden das Anti-Psychologische, Abstrakte Theater' ('We are discovering the anti-psychological and abstract theatre') is a thoroughgoing attack on the various forms of psychological drama which he denounces as boring, monotonous, non-lyrical and 'anti-Italian'. He prides himself on having developed the 'theatre of surprises' (teatro della sorpresa), which appears in two new forms (tested in a tour of eighteen Italian cities): the abstract anti-logical and anti-psychological theatre and a theatre based on a synthesis of muscle, sport and mechanics.

Two shorter pieces consider differing theatrical elements. The first, close to the central theme of theatrical modernism, is Hans Fritz's 'Würfelbühne' (a stage of cubes), in which he describes his simple system for set construction based on a set of 'cubes', which, he argues, once purchased, could free a theatre from naturalistic and historical stage sets as well as the recurrent heavy costs of such designs, while allowing for ever new creations. The second, 'Theaterprojekt' by Wilhelm Treichlinger and Fritz Rosenbaum, argues the importance of the actor in creating a 'rhythmical' work of art, and suggests a method (a form of apron stage with spot lighting) whereby the actor becomes the focal point. Their formal plans seem nearer to Greek theatre than to Kiesler's concept of the spherical 'Raum-Bühne'.

Distant too from Kiesler's mechanistic-kinetic theatre are the arguments in Lothar Schreyer's 'Die Bühne des Menschen' ('the Human Stage'). Schreyer, who had been active in Walden's Berlin 'Sturmbühne' before founding his own 'Kampfbühne' in Hamburg, argues here, cogently and persuasively, for a 'human stage', since the theatre 'reflects man's spiritual condition' and 'like every art is a human act of purification'. Today, he feels, we are nearing a 'theatre of machines', but although agreeing that a mechanically constructed composition is possible, he sees such theatre as the antithesis of the human stage. For Schreyer, the highest form of theatrical art is the freeing of the human spirit through the disciplining of the body.

There are three more important contributions on aspects of contemporary theatre which must be mentioned before we can try to assess the reception of the exhibition and its catalogue. One is by the Berlin writer of proletarian drama K. A. Wittfogel, who outlines the 'Grenzen und Aufgaben der revolutionären Bühnenkunst' ('Limits and tasks of revolutionary theatre'). Although he implicitly attacks Vienna for failing to provide the workers with a revolutionary theatre, Wittfogel turns his main attack on bourgeois theatre at a time, as he sees it, of decadence. One strategy of attack, he suggests, would be to parody and mock the standard bourgeois repertoire; Goethe, Ibsen and Strindberg, as well as Sternheim, Unruh and Kaiser, should be 'destroyed' to make way for a truly socialist theatre. (Again we note these are sentiments hardly likely to win favour in Vienna.) Secondly, from Iwan Goll (the author of the anti-bourgeois grotesque *Methusalem oder der ewige Bürger*) comes a witty demand for a drama which, using the whole range of modern techniques (including gramophone electronic display and loudspeaker), will create a most improbable reality – the 'superdrama' ('Überdrama'). As Goll expresses it, 'art is not there to make the fat "Burger" feel comfortable, so that he shakes his head and says "yes, that's the way it is. Let's go to the buffet now!" Art, insofar as it will educate, improve or make an impact, must strike the ordinary man, terrify him as a mask does a child, as Euripides terrified the Athenians...' Thirdly, there is a contribution from René Fülöp-Miller on 'Die neue russische Bühne' ('The new Russian Stage'), in which he explains the latest developments in Russian theatre with particular reference to Meyerhold and Tairov. This straightforward informative account was reinforced by Fülöp-Miller's *feuilleton* article on Meyerhold in the *Neue Freie Presse* of 24 September.

The catalogue also contained an example of Walter Mehring's 'Dadaist' humour (a short sketch about a modern 'Pied Piper', a bus driver who drives his passengers via the lunatic asylum and the morgue to hell-fire) and, from the Hanover avant-gardiste Kurt Schwitters, a sketch in which a philistine public pours scorn on Schwitters's demands for the establishment of the 'Merz-Bühne'.

When the catalogue is considered alongside actual exhibits, it can be argued that Kiesler and his colleagues had managed to cover all major innovations in contemporary European stage techniques. Those Viennese who saw the exhibition and read the catalogue cannot have been in any doubt as to the position of Viennese theatre compared to the rest of Europe. Kiesler's constructivist stage in the Konzerthaus (three levels, joined by a spiral ramp) was used for dramatic readings, the performance of Léger's 'ballet mécanique', theatre performance (on 4 October a performance of Paul Frischauer's *Im Dunkel*) and also displays of lighting technique by Ludwig Hirschfeld-Mack. This completed a stimulating month of avant-garde theatrical activity of which Kiesler said in recollection, 'it was as if utopia had become reality'.

We do not know what the public made of it (although the exhibition made a deficit), but the press response ranged from the earnest and fairly positive articles which appeared in the *Neue Freie Presse* (praise for Kiesler's efforts in a review on 24 September, for example) and the *Neues Wiener Journal* (an interesting article, praising the positive method of exhibiting, by Theo van Doesburg on 31 October 1924) to the satirical accounts provided by the popular press.[12]

Karl Kraus responded in typical manner to the theatre festival. In a short article, 'Um Nestroy', he congratulated himself on persuading Josef Jarno to stage Nestroy's *Eine Wohnung ist zu vermieten* and took the opportunity of attacking the Burgtheater production of *Einen Jux will er sich machen*. He also gave two lectures (published, along with the article, in *Die Fackel*).[13] The first lecture, 'Klarstellung', given on 5 October, is an impassioned attack on efforts to create a modern stage ('with fancy lighting, bridges over the orchestra pit, flights of steps, all the inflated impotence of cubism, all the fussiness of an all-powerful and usurping producer, all the madness of trying to "suggest" scenic reality through coarse nonsense...'). The following day Karlheinz Martin, the Berlin producer who worked closely with Rudolf Beer in Vienna, defended the idea of the 'Raumbühne' and attacked the traditional theatre in an article in the *Neue Freie Presse*. This occasioned Kraus's second lecture, given on 9 November, 'Das Mangobaumwunder' ('the miracle of the mango-tree'). Its title derived from Martin's comments that scenery was not needed ('It is like the miracle of the mango-tree: one only needs believers, the tree grows by itself and the court theatre stage designer only has to paint it for the stupid bourgeois...'). Kraus used this opportunity to attack those modern practitioners of the theatre whose roots were not in drama or literary theatre, the use of revolutionary Russian theatre as a defence of 'Berliner Humbug', Berlin Shakespeare productions, the decline in acting standards, and Martin's own *Weber* production. When Kraus writes on modern theatre it is often difficult to separate reason from obsession, but at least he saw clearly the conflict which existed between the dramatic and the theatrical. His arguments here, trenchantly and wittily presented, must have done much to confirm the Viennese in their hostility towards experimental theatre. He was to return to the attack on Karlheinz Martin in the next issue of *Die Fackel* where, in the article 'Nestroy and das Burgtheater', he refers to Martin's production of Wedekind's *Franziska* is scathing terms.[14] His contempt for the concept of the 'Raumbühne' rumbles on in various couplets he wrote for his own Nestroy 'performances'.[15]

Another critic worth quoting is the level-headed Oskar Maurus Fontana, who reviewed three productions which had been specially mounted for the 'Theaterwochen' (Barlach's *Der tote Tag*, Billinger's *Der Knecht* and Mell's *Apostelspiel*) under the title 'Die drei Dichter des Wienertheaterfestes' (*Berliner Börsen-Courier*, 28 October 1924). More important than his favourable review of the works performed are his comments on the festival in general. He found that the ideas of the radically new constructivist theatre had been brought down to the level of 'Dada' by what he termed 'die unsagbare Leichtfertigkeit leider auch der Ausstellungsleitung (Maler Friedrich Riesler [*sic*]) ('the unspeakable frivolity, unfortunately, of the exhibition organiser, the painter Friedrich Riesler'). As Fontana saw it, this 'Unernst' ('lack of seriousness') and 'lack of direction' of the would-be theatre reformers meant that theatrical life in Vienna would continue as before and stage sets would continue to be, as he phrased it, 'der alte Kohl der Ansichtskartenpanoramen' ('the old picture-postcard rubbish').

Not only does Fontana himself show a lack of 'seriousness' in not ascertaining the correct name of the artistic director, but when 'modernism' in Vienna is presented with a certain lightness of touch (there is surely often an element of 'épater le bourgeois' in avant-garde art?) he equates it with 'Dadaism'. If one of the festival's most positive critics could make such comments, what hope was there for an acceptance of theatrical modernism in Vienna? We can see the same rejection of the unusual, of the 'new', that had been witnessed in reactions to Schoenberg and his followers before the First World War.

There was, as far as I can see, only one attempt in Vienna to profit from the examples and demonstrations of modern theatre technique given during the festival, and that came from the Berlin producer Karlheinz Martin, who worked in Vienna during the 1920s for Rudolf Beer. His production of Wedekind's *Franziska* used Kiesler's 'Raumbühne', and was the only modernist production to be transferred from Vienna to Berlin. This powerful production, complete with half-naked dancers, jazz-band on stage and constructivist raked set equipped with spiral staircase, must have realized Kraus's worst fears. Fontana, in his review of 3 January 1925 (*Berliner Börsen-Courier*) entitled 'Entfesseltes Theater in Wien' (a reference to the Russian Tairov), commented very favourably on Martin's treatment of the 'modern mystery play' and on the use for the first time in Vienna of the constructivist stage.

Fontana paid tribute to Kiesler (getting his name right) for having introduced the concept of the modern stage to Vienna. 'Kiesler', wrote Fontana, 'was the first to show Vienna what there was, and what was to be fought for... conservative intellectuals may have mocked but in the end the idea triumphed.' He ended his review (which also dealt with Hansi Niese in a typical Viennese comedy) by remarking that Vienna had managed to combine an example of the old type of theatre which the city always protected and 'das neue entfesselte Theater, dem es sich erst nach Zögern ergab' ('the new liberated theatre which it adopted only after some hesitation') and asking which would prove the stronger: the radicalism of the new style or the 'sanft-zähe Konservatismus Wiens' ('the soft but dogged conservatism of Vienna').[16]

The answer, I am afraid, was the latter. Despite the efforts of Rudolf Beer, whose two theatres, the Raimund Theater and Deutsches Volkstheater, regularly staged guest performances of the latest word from Berlin,[17] and the performance of Brecht's *Baal*, with Hofmannsthal's prologue, at the Theater in der Josefstadt, Vienna never showed any enthusiasm for modernist productions, not even for the Tairov touring company in 1925.[18] The Kiesler exhibition during those autumn weeks of 1924 (together with the catalogue) had offered Vienna a chance to take stock of theatrical modernism but the chance was rejected. Why? Perhaps we had better let Karl Kraus have the last word, for he once said that Berlin would adapt to tradition before Vienna would accept the machine. Vienna's theatrical history certainly proves him right.

Notes

1. *Max Reinhardt; Ich bin nichts als Theatermann*, ed. Hugo Fetting (Berlin, 1989), p. 428.
2. For a thorough account of theatrical experimentation in Vienna before the First World War, see Gertrud Pott, *Die Spiegelung des Sezessionismus im österreichischen Theater* (Vienna, 1975).
3. Joachim Fiebach, *Von Craig bis Brecht: Studien zu Künstlertheorien in der ersten Hälfte des 20. Jahrhunderts* (Berlin 1975), pp. 157–66. For excellent overviews of experimental and avant-garde theatre, with sections on all major figures cited in this article, see Paul Pörtner, *Experiment Theater* (Zurich, 1960) and Manfred Brauneck, *Theater im 20. Jahrhundert: Programmschriften, Stilperioden, Reformmodelle* (Reinbek bei Hamburg, 1982).
4. For a stimulating account of theatrical modernism in Munich (albeit with a far broader remit and rather too generalised cross-referencing to Vienna) see Peter Jelavich, *Munich and Theatrical Modernism: Politics, Playwriting and Performance, 1890–1914* (Cambridge, MA, 1985). For his comments on Kandinsky see pp. 217–34.
5. See John Willett, *The Theatre of the Weimar Republic* (New York, 1988), p. 81, and for a broader view of the modernist movement in Central Europe, John Willett, *The New Sobriety: Art and Politics in the Weimar Period, 1917–33* (London, 1978).
6. Details of his work can be gained from R. Held, *Endless Innovations. The Theories and Scenic Design of Frederick Kiesler* (unpublished Ph.D. thesis, Bowling Green State University, 1977); Pörtner, *Experiment Theater*, pp. 66–9 and 138–40 (although there are one or two minor factual inaccuracies there is a good survey of Kiesler's work on pp. 167–8); Brauneck, *Theater im 20. Jahrhundert*, pp. 132–7, 221–5, 505–6; Hans Curjel, 'Frederick Kiesler'; *Bauen und Wohnen*, No. 11 (Zurich, 1951); C. Goodman, 'The Current of Contemporary History: Frederick Kiesler's Endless Search', *Arts Magazine*, September 1979, pp. 118–23; Thomas Weingraber, 'Über den Mann, der

Utopia Realität werden ließ', *Parnassus*, March/April 1988; and the exhibition catalogues *Internationale Ausstellung neuer Theatertechnik: Katalog Programm Almanach*, ed. Friedrich Kiesler (Vienna, 1924; reprinted by Löcker und Wögenstein, Vienna 1975) and those published by the 'Galerie nächst St Stephan' (Vienna, 1975) and the 'Museum des 20. Jahrhunderts' (Vienna, 1988).

7. See Lee Congdon, *Exile and Social Thought: Hungarian Intellectuals in Germany and Austria 1919–1933* (Princeton, 1991), especially ch. 3, 'Lajos Kassak: the MA Circle'.
8. See Pörtner, *Experiment Theater*, p. 66.
9. For a description of Kiesler's set see Ernst Josef Aufricht, *Erzähle damit du dein Recht erweist* (Berlin, 1966), pp. 56–7. This was the actor Oskar Homolka's first appearance in Berlin, and Aufricht claims that only 'die Kiesslersche [*sic*] Raumbühne' ruined the evening.
10. A short account of Bach's involvement in the festival is provided by Henriette Kotlan-Werner, *Kunst und Volk: Das Leben Dr David Josef Bachs (1874–1947) und sein Wirken in der Sozialdemokratischen Partei Österreichs* (Vienna, 1977). For details of Bach's role as artistic adviser to the Social Democratic administration see Helmut Gruber, *Red Vienna: Experiment in Working-Class Culture 1919–1934* (New York, 1991), pp. 96–113.
11. See my articles 'The Viennese Theatre of the First Republic', *Scottish Papers in German Studies*, 1 (1981), pp. 56–73 and 'Max Reinhardt and the Viennese Theatre of the Inter-War Years', *Maske und Kothurn*, 29 (1983), pp. 123–36.
12. For example, the front page of the *Kronenzeitung*, 25 September, and the articles in the *Volkszeitung*, 27 September, and *Der Tag*, 4 October. Naturally enough, the satirical weekly *Der Götz von Berlichingen*, 3 October, commented on the exhibition with gusto.
13. *Die Fackel*, 1924, 668–75.
14. *Die Fackel*, 676–8 (Vienna, 1925); see especially pp. 33–40.
15. See *Die Fackel, ibid.*, pp. 42–3. The couplets of Nestroy's *Der konfuse Zauberer* were rewritten by Kraus for a performance given on 13 January 1925.
16. Both Fontana's reviews are printed in Oskar Maurus Fontana, *Das große Welttheater: Theaterkritiken 1909–1967* (Vienna, 1976), pp. 82–6 and 86–90.
17. Beer was described by Hofmannsthal as 'der jüngste, tätigste und wohl auch begabteste Theaterdirektor Wiens', but there is as yet no monograph on this talented and progressive director, whose career, paradoxically, was ruined by his being appointed (jointly with Karlheinz Martin) to take control of Max Reinhardt's Berlin theatres in 1932. For a short account of his Viennese achievements see Warren, 'Viennese Theatre of the First Republic', pp. 64–7.
18. Fontana, *Das große Welttheater*, pp. 98–102, review 'Tairoff und Wir', *Berliner Börsen-Courier*, 10 July 1925.

Ernst Weiss:
The Novelist as Dramatist

Klaus-Peter Hinze

After decades of undeserved silence about the Austrian Jewish writer and physician Ernst Weiss (1882–1940), once considered a novelist ranked with Joseph Roth, Franz Kafka or Alfred Döblin, he finally came into his own with the centennial publication of his collected works in sixteen volumes.[1] This anniversary edition created a wave of academic research on his novels, short stories and philosophical essays. Unfortunately, his dramas and his poetry were not included in the collected works; indeed, it is hardly known that the novelist wrote for the stage. Had the timing, location and presentation of his dramatic productions been different, Ernst Weiss would also have a reputation as a dramatist.

By 1919, the year of the first performance of a Weiss drama, he was already a highly acclaimed novelist with works such as *Die Galeere* (The Galley, 1913), *Der Kampf* (The Struggle), 1916, later known as *Franziska, Tiere in Ketten* (Animals in Chains, 1918), and *Mensch gegen Mensch* (Man Against Man, 1919). His reasons for writing a play were external and rather personal. In 1913 he had fallen in love with the eighteen-year-old Johanna Bleschke. She was beautiful, charming, intelligent, ambitious, and talented. Weiss gave her the stage name of Sanzara (in Sanskrit 'Samsara' means the constant cycle of reincarnations). Under the name of Rahel Sanzara she eventually became known as a dancer, a film and stage actress, and, finally, an accomplished novelist. In June 1914, Weiss, Sanzara and their friend Franz Kafka were spending some holidays at the Danish seaside resort Marielyst when the war broke out. Weiss saw immediately, he writes, 'daß man jetzt keine Dichter, sondern Ärzte brauchte. Ich hatte die Möglichkeit, nach Dänemark zu fliehen, blieb aber und meldete mich sofort bei meinem Regiment in Linz. Ich machte den ganzen Krieg mit' (... that medical doctors were needed, not poets. I had the chance to escape to Denmark. I remained, however, and reported to my regiment in Linz. I was on active duty the entire war).[2] He spent the next four years at the Eastern Front. Rahel Sanzara wanted a career of her own. She took acting and dancing lessons, gave performances in Berlin, Vienna, Prague and Budapest in the flashy dance show *Die weiße Sklavin*[3] (The White Slave), and tried to begin a film career by acting in some detective stories. She found little success, however, and was reduced to typing Weiss's manuscripts, which he sent her from the Front. She also took care of his business with publishers. Forced to live on the money that he sent her, she was deeply depressed that she had failed to establish herself on the stage or in film. To cheer her, Weiss wrote to her in February 1917: 'Aus "Tiere in Ketten" mache ich im Sommer ein Theaterstück und Du mußt die Olga spielen, [...] ich denke es mir gut.'[4] (This summer I will make a play out of 'Animals in Chains' and you should play Olga, [...] I think it will do well.) She must have answered too enthusiastically, because a few weeks later Weiss retracted his promise, writing, 'Ich bin unbedingt für Deine künstlerische Existenz, doch die Rolle der Olga, wenn etwas aus dem Stück würde (von hier aus ganz unmöglich) erfordert Dialekt und wahnsinnige Kunststückchen. Aber die Idee Theater an sich, könnte Dich reizen.'[5] (I am decidedly in favour of your artistic existence. But the role of Olga – if anything were to come of the play (from here quite impossible) would demand a special dialect and outrageous performance tricks! But the idea of theatre *per se* could be attractive to you.)

The 'Olga drama' project took another six years to finish, but in 1919, while working in a Prague hospital, Weiss completed another play, *Tanja*,[6] a drama in three acts with a dreamlike epilogue. The work combines the drama of the Bolshevik revolution with the tragedy of prostitution. Above all, it represents the struggle and ultimate destruction of a man and a woman who love and hate each other. The theme is typical of Weiss's pessimistic outlook and recurs in most of his early works; he one described this idea to a friend as 'you cut yourself and I bleed'.[7] Love in this context is nothing but an aggressive egotism, the wish to possess, hurt, and subdue the partner. The interhuman relationship reflects the eternal combat between good and evil, or, in Weiss's terms, between God and Anti-God, in which it seems that the good will always be defeated. The yearning for fulfilled love, brotherhood and humanity remains alive, but can never be satisfied. This pessimistic philosophy was reinforced by his devastating experiences during the war, and it also influenced his poetic style. Weiss became one of the 'sprachgewaltigste Expressionisten' (linguistically most powerful expressionists), in Walter Sokel's judgment.[8] Weiss later explained his turn to expressionism: 'In diesem unbeschreiblichen Grauen des Krieges verbrüderten sich die Herzen. In einer Art fruchtbarer Panik waren wir besessen von einem Bedürfnis nach Herzlichkeit, stammelten Umarmungen und Küsse, denn wir fühlten uns unfähig, diese Umwälzungen in vorgeschriebenen und gemessenen Worten wie zuvor zu beschreiben.'[9] (During this indescribable horror of the war, our hearts united. In a sort of fearful panic we were possessed with the need for kindness. We stumbled through embraces and kisses and we felt unable to describe this revolution in prescribed and measured words as before.)

The historical background to *Tanja* is the beginning of the Bolshevik revolution in Moscow, which Weiss had followed with fascination and scepticism while stationed on the Russian front. Tanja, a young prostitute and spy for the police, meets her first lover Vladimir again after eight years. He does not remember or recognise her. From the single night they spent together eight years ago, Tanja had a son, Ilja, whom she came to hate as she did his father. She kept the child in a wooden cage, tortured him and allowed him to die. Vladimir, a leader of the revolutionary troops, has just assassinated a Tsarist general and is seeking refuge. By pure chance he comes into Tanja's room. However, since her love has turned to such extreme hated, she betrays him to the Moscow secret police. Thwarting her plan, however, the police capture them both and throw them into prison. In a touching love scene, when Vladimir finally recognises Tanja, she persuades him to commit suicide before the executioner comes. He swallows poison and is dying in her arms when revolutionary troops come storming into the prison to free him. Tortured by feelings of pain and guilt, Tanja despairs so deeply that she becomes insane. She is taken to a mental hospital, where an unexpected transformation takes place within her. In spite of all the hatred which has ruled her life and actions, goodness has not completely died in her. As Weiss later explained in a newspaper interview, only in the state of insanity does Tanja encounter the value of life.[10] Recognising her own failure, she jumps out of the window.

The plot is very simple: a mother brutally kills her little boy, drives her lover to commit suicide, becomes insane, and kills herself. The extremely shocking effects and strong dramatic tension could have been too much to digest for any audience if the work had not been raised to a level between realism and stylised allegory. The language becomes music, everyday actions become dance movements, and objective words achieve a mystical dimension. The spectator (or reader) suspects a deeper message and in the epilogue experiences a surrealistic, dreamlike scene: in a blazing white, sunlit 'Andalusian' street café, one sees the dead Tanja, next to her Lada, a good-hearted whore who had loved the dead child Ilja, and an old peasant woman; the music of a waltz is constantly repeated, and behind a large transparent screen appears the funeral train of Tanja's son, led by a group of young boys dressed in white. Tanja recognises her inner self and her senseless life; feeling that she has been forgotten by God and yearning for love, she is finally capable of shedding tears. Simultaneously, the audience sees Tanja dying, surrounded by a doctor, a nurse and a priest. The doctor pronounces her dead and the priest declares: 'Gott hat Tanja zu sich genommen.' (p. 115) (God took Tanja to himself.)

In a newspaper interview during the same year, Weiss explained the ending: 'Ich meine [...] daß Gottes Hand auch noch in der Hölle fühlbar wäre.'[11] (I mean to say that the touch of God's hand can be experienced even in hell.) It was exactly this message, given in the epilogue, that had a deep effect on Kafka, who had seen one of the first performances. He reportedly said to his young friend Gustav Janouch, 'Am schönsten ist die Traumszene mit Tanjas Kind. Das Theater wirkt am schönsten, wenn es unwirkliche Dinge wirklich macht. Dann wird die Bühne zum Seelenperiskop, das die Wirklichkeit von innen beleuchtet.'[12] (The dream scene with Tanja's child is the most beautiful. It is theatre at its best when it turns the unreal into the real. Then the stage illuminates the soul and clarifies inner reality.)

On October 1919 *Tanja* had its première at the Kammerspiele in Prague, with Rahel Sanzara playing the title role and the young Hans Demetz directing. The reaction of the public and the critics was overwhelmingly favourable: 'Ein großes dramatisches Talent hat sich zum erstenmal [...] offenbart'[13] (A great dramatic talent has revealed itself for the first time), said one reviewer, who even argued: 'In diesem Drama liegt Größe und, wenn nicht alles trügt, erstand da ein neuer Schiller mit seiner allumfassenden Menschenliebe und der gottgegebenen Sprache des gewaltigen Pathos.'[14] (There is greatness in this drama and, if I am not mistaken, a new Schiller has arisen with his all-encompassing love for humanity and his God-given talent for emotional language.) The success of the

Ernst Weiss: Novelist as Dramatist

play was a triumph not only for the author but also for Sanzara, whose career as a great stage performer began with this production. She became the prototypical actress of female roles in the expressionist theater. Demetz, who had had his doubts about this inexperienced young woman playing a leading part, explained her appeal: 'Mit ihren tänzerischen Bewegungen und ihrer abgerissenen Sprechweise konnte die Sanzara den inneren Aufruhr der Tanja sehr gut wiedergeben. Über Nacht wurde sie zum Liebling des Prager Publikums. Alle jungen Damen ließen sich wie sie einen Bubikopf schneiden.'[15] (With her dancelike movements and staccato recitation and speech, Sanzara was capable of expressing the inner turmoil Tanja experiences. Immediately she became the favourite star of Prague audiences. All the young ladies imitated her bobbed hair.) Demetz stressed the tremendous effect of the play's political implications and revolutionary background, although these aspects are quite superficial in the work itself: 'Immer wenn die Revolutionstruppen mit ihren roten Fahnen das Gefängnis stürmten, konnten wir auch mit stürmischem Applaus auf freier Bühne rechnen.'[16] (Every time the revolutionary troops with their red flags were storming the prison, we could count on roaring applause to interrupt the performance.)

After her success in Prague, Sanzara received an enviable contract from the Darmstadt Landestheater, under the directorship of Gustav Hartung, and the novelist Ernst Weiss seemed to have begun a promising career as a dramatist. Theatres in Germany, Switzerland and Austria bought performance rights for *Tanja*. Many years later, when asked which was the happiest day of his life, Weiss replied, 'Der Tag meines einzigen großen Theatererfolgs im alten, unvergessenen Landestheater [sic] in Prag, im Herbst 1920 [sic] [...] Es ist schön, sich einmal im Leben von einer großen Menge unbekannter Menschen geliebt und verstanden zu wissen.'[17] (The day of my single great stage success was in the autumn of 1920 in the unforgettable Landestheater in Prague. It is so wonderful, once in a lifetime to be loved and understood by an anonymous crowd.)

On 23 December 1919, *Tanja* was performed in the Deutsche Volkstheater in Vienna, with Ida Roland, the star of Viennese stages, in the title role. Instead of the expected success, however, the performance was a complete disaster. The author later wrote about this evening:

> [...] damit ich nicht zu stolz werde, wurde das Stück drei Monate später in Wien gespielt und – nach dem Erfolg der ersten zwei Akte – ausgezischt. Ich sah in meiner Blindheit nichts von diesem Theaterskandal und ging am Schluß lächelnd auf die Bühne, um zu danken.
>
> Aber ich wurde ausgepfiffen und ausgezischt. Ich erstarrte, machte kehrt und zeigte den Leuten den Rücken. Die Kritik, die mich in Prag gelobt hatte, schmähte mich in Wien, so daß mir nichts übrig blieb, und ich kam nur mit dem nackten Leben vom Ort meines Unglücks davon.[18]
>
> [To keep me from getting too proud, when the play was performed in Vienna three months later, it was rejected with boos and hisses after the success of the first two acts. I was too blind to see the scandal, went on the stage at the end of the performance to take a smiling bow – and was

hissed and booed. Stiff with shock I turned my back to the audience. The critics who had lauded me in Prague condemned me in Vienna. There was nothing to do but to flee from the place of disaster.]

What had gone wrong? First of all, Weiss had revised his play and taken out all direct political allusions; he had 'die roten Farben weiß entfärbt'[19] (whitewashed the red flags), as his friend Albert Ehrenstein explained. Furthermore, the Viennese theatre audience was not yet ready to accept the new style of expressionist drama, unlike the audience in Prague, where many works of this movement had their first performances. Most significantly, however, Ida Roland was not capable of acting in Sanzara's style or of understanding the new form of drama, as the director Bernhard Reich explains in his memoirs:

> Die Roland hatte als Schauspielerin eine große Karriere gemacht. Sie zeigte auf der Bühne leichtsinnigen, fröhlichen weiblichen Charme und konnte blendend *scène d'affaires* spielen. In Wien war sie Kassenmagnet. Im ganzen war sie jedoch völlig in den Vorstellungen und in der Technik des alten Theaters verwurzelt und konnte auch nur so spielen. In der Aufführung tat sich allerdings eine unheimliche Gegensätzlichkeit zwischen dem Spiel der Roland und dem Spiel des Stückes auf. Groteske Nebenfiguren und der Kontrast zwischen komplizierten Seelen und sturer, tierischer Umgebung schockierten. Das Publikum wurde rabiat, pfiff und zischte sogar seinen Liebling, die Ida Roland nieder.[20]

[Roland was a very successful actress. On stage she showed her gay and frivolous feminine charm and played the *scène d'affaires* brilliantly. In Vienna she was a box-office hit. In general, however, her acting was deeply rooted in the traditional conceptions and techniques and she could not adapt her style. In this performance there was a tremendous gap between the actress's playing and the play itself. Grotesque secondary characters and the contrast between complex souls and the stolid, bestial surroundings were shocking. The audience was infuriated and even hissed and booed their darling Ida Roland.]

This antipathy is clearly apparent in the responses of the reviewers. Besides panning this performance of Weiss's *Tanja*, they took the occasion to attack the whole circle of Prague writers, throwing in several anti-Semitic remarks for good measure:

> Diesen jüdischen Prager Dichtern ist es in unserer Literatur bisher zu zahm zugegangen, sie wollen sie mit Gewalt revolutionieren, und so ist denn die Moldaustadt nachgerade ein Herd der übelsten literarischen Revolution geworden. *Tanja* ist innerlich verwandt mit dem *Golem* Meyrinks. Gift und Bomben wüten, ein Kind wird zu Tode gequält, eine Irrsinnige stürzt sich aus dem Fenster. Sie haben es auf unsere Nerven abgesehen, diese Prager Dichter, nicht auf unser Herz.[21]

[Those Jewish writers from Prague have found our current literature too tame, so now they want to revolt with a vengeance. The city on the Moldau has become the birthplace of a disgusting literary revolt. *Tanja* bears an intimate relationship to Meyrink's *Golem*. Poison and bombs rage, a child is tortured to death, a demented woman hurls herself out of the window. They are after our nerves, those Prague poets, not after our hearts.]

A third performance of *Tanja* was prepared in 1924 by Weiss's friend Theodor Tagger (later known as Ferdinand Bruckner) at the Renaissance-Theater in Berlin. Rahel Sanzara was asked to give a guest performance to assert the expressive quality of Tanja's character. Unfortunately, however, literary taste, at least that of the Berlin theatre audience, had changed. Expressionist drama with its erratic ecstasy, stammering utterances and activism had got a bad name. The beginning of a new movement, the realism of the 'Neue Sachlichkeit', could be felt. Even Tagger's direction and Sanzara's acting could not make this performance a success. The great Berlin critic Herbert Jhering, a friend of Weiss's, wrote, 'Rahel Sanzara spielte die Fehler ihres Dichters. Sie spielte seinen Krampf, nicht seine Befreiung, seine Phraseologie, nicht seine Gestalt, seinen Stil, nicht seinen Ausdruck, seine Hysterie, nicht seine Empfindung.'[22] (Rahel Sanzara portrayed the mistakes of her playwright. She portrayed his convulsions, not his deliverance, his phraseology, not his artistic form, his style, not his expression, his hysteria, not his sentiment.) The other great critic of the period, Alfred Kerr, was even more upset about this 'monstrous' play, 'this undramatic Gothic tale', and he warned playwrights and actors alike, 'die Bühne nicht in den Bereich des Kuriositäten-Kabinetts und der Schreckenskammer zu ziehen'[23] (not to turn the stage into a circus side show or a chamber of horrors).

One year before, in 1923, Weiss had finally presented the 'Olga-Drama' that he had promised to write for Rahel Sanzara. Based on the novel *Tiere in Ketten*, the play, entitled *Olympia*, focuses on four characters. With its five acts and its adherence to the Aristotelian unities of time, place and plot, the play appears to be quite traditional, but in content, message and language it is anything but. All four characters are immediately introduced: Franz Michalek, master of a whorehouse, an alcoholic, formerly an imperial officer who was dishonourably discharged for pandering his teenage girlfriend Olympia to his friends; Olympia herself, who had been in charge of the brothel's daily business and who is driven by her masochistic love for Michalek; Maja, another prostitute who wants to become the mistress of the brothel and eventually Mrs Michalek; and Dr Kühn, a bourgeois lawyer, a customer in the house, who wants to marry Olympia. Since Michalek plans to marry Maja and therefore wants to free himself of Olympia, he sends Olympia away. She obeys him and follows Dr Kühn, who gives her money, jewels and respectability, but is sickly and impotent. Olympia's love for Michalek, like an elemental force, drives her back to him. When she sees him again, he is a broken man, old, fat and dirty, and his business is bankrupt. Yet to her he is still her beloved Lord and Saviour, to whom she offers all her money, her jewels and expensive liquors. Maja and Dr Kühn also arrive in the run-down brothel's salon. Maja, who has become crazed with love, jealousy and desire for sexual satisfaction, finally shoots Dr Kühn and herself.

In comparison with the novel *Tiere in Ketten*, this plot is overly simple and offers very little dramatic tension. The real drama takes place within the character of Olympia. It is, as Robert Browning appropriately called this type of drama, 'Action in Character rather than Character in Action'.[24] Its strength lies in its language and poetic imagery, denoting a union of church and brothel, the divine and the profane. The drama is so removed from the original complex novel that it must be seen as a new work of its own. Herbert Jhering stated: 'dieser Epiker schafft ein Drama, das in sich dramatischer ist als viele Dramen abgestempelter Dramatiker'[25] (this novelist creates a drama which is more dramatic than the dramas of many well-established dramatists). *Olympia* was first performed in the Junge Bühne, an experimental stage of the Renaissance-Theater, in Berlin in March 1923 with an exceptionally good cast: Heinrich George as Michalek and Agnes Straub as Olympia. While the critics had differing opinions, it was still an encouraging success for Weiss. His name was suggested for the prestigious Kleist Prize, but *Olympia* received only honourable mention. The prize itself was awarded to the young Bertolt Brecht (for *Drums in the Night*). Several critics saw a close affinity between Ernst Weiss and Frank Wedekind, George Kaiser and August Strindberg. Weiss's indebtedness to Wedekind is especially obvious when he combines religion and sex as he does in the dream scene in the cathedral. Weiss admired Wedekind in many ways, and in a review of this first performance Alfred Döblin maintains, 'Ich bekenne: Thema und allgemeiner Plan sind stärker als bei Wedekind.'[26] (I maintain: Plot and general plan are stronger than in Wedekind.)

Fifty years after this one performance, the young director Alois Heigl tried a new interpretation of *Olympia* at the Staatstheater in Kassel. He updated the play in the style of the theatre of the absurd; the production was strongly reminiscent of Beckett's *Endgame* and *Waiting for Godot*. The critics agreed, however, that the work was too outdated, and otherwise unsuited for the stage; it had little character development or motivation. One critic expressed the hope that the two shots at the end of the play would also kill the whole drama.[27] This performance did not create any interest in a revival of Ernst Weiss as a dramatist.

When Hans Demetz was writing a history of the German theatre in Prague, he came across another Weiss drama, 'Leonore', which he himself had staged in March 1923 but completely forgotten. While *Tanja* and *Olympia* were published, 'Leonore' existed only in manuscript form and as yet no copy has been found. Nevertheless, we know its content because it was again based on a very strong narrative by Weiss, the novella 'Die Verdorrten'[28] (The Withered Ones). Its main plot deals with the pros and cons of abortion: a man and a woman are deeply in love but they cannot afford to have the child that is on its way. Minutes before the actual abortion takes place, the woman begs her lover to let her keep the child but he does not support her. He fears that a child will hinder his career. After the abortion her love changes to hatred and she plans to ruin the man. She marries his rich friend, a banker. Her lover loses all his money and his promising job. When Leonore finds out that her husband cannot give her a child, she demands the services of her first lover. She again becomes pregnant and her husband, who knows that this cannot be his child, divorces her. She moves back in with her bankrupt lover, who becomes seriously ill. She realises that under the circumstances she again has to have an abortion. Afterwards, her lover regains his health and they live together for many years, although they can never have another child. Their curse is to live to be very old, without love or hatred, without joy, without feelings.

It is hard to imagine how Weiss could have injected this extended time element into the drama, and it can be assumed that this strong message was left out in the dramatic version. Other changes must also have been made, for one critic stressed the extreme deviation of the drama from its novelistic source.[29] Its performance received exceptionally high praise from all the Prague critics. Rahel Sanzara was again playing the main character – and it may well be assumed that she was portraying her own fate as a woman and the fate of her relationship with Ernst Weiss – and for both actress and dramatist it was almost as great a success as the first performance of *Tanja*.

Ernst Weiss did not become 'a new Schiller'. These three are the only dramas he ever wrote, although his interest in the theatre continued and is attested by several of his essays on topics such as Wedekind's dramas,[30] performance techniques in *Macbeth*,[31] and the coexistence of the theatre with recently developed moving pictures.[32]

In his essay 'Anmerkungen zum dramatischen Schaffen'[33] (Notes on Dramatic Creation) of 1924, Ernst Weiss officially bade farewell to the theatre:

> Meine eigenen dramatischen Arbeiten *Tanja*, *Olympia* haben mich davon überzeugt, daß ich kein Dramatiker bin. Trotzdem diese Gestalten von ganz außerordentlich starken Persönlichkeiten auf der Bühne verkörpert worden sind, ist so viel Ungelöstes, Unvollkommenes geblieben, daß ich für meinen Teil dem dramatischen Schaffen Adieu sagen will, mit der festen Überzeugung, daß dabei weder mir noch der Welt Schaden geschieht.[34]

> [Both my dramatic works, *Tanja* and *Olympia*, convinced me that I am not a playwright. Although the characters have been played by exceptionally strong personalities, much remained unsolved and incomplete. So for my part I will say adieu to writing plays, and I believe strongly that neither I nor the world will suffer a great loss.]

Looking back at the performance history of Weiss's dramas, it becomes clear that whether or not a play will be successful often depends on circumstances beyond the playwright's control. We may assume that if the text of 'Leonore' were available, this play, with its strong and timeless message about abortion, could have a successful revival. Nevertheless, Weiss probably made the right decision when turning all his creative energy to the epic genre after 1924. Some of the novels and novellas that he wrote after this date rank among the best that his generation produced.

Notes

1. Ernst Weiss, *Gesammelte Werke*, ed. Peter Engel and Volker Michels (16 vols, Frankfurt, 1982).
2. Eduard Wondrak, *Einiges über den Arzt und Schriftsteller Ernst Weiß* (Munich, 1968), p. 24.
3. Diana Orendi-Hinze, *Rahel Sanzara* (Frankfurt, 1981), pp. 24–32.
4. Unpublished letter of the author dated 10 February 1917 (in Deutsches Literaturarchiv, Marbach).
5. Unpublished letter dated 20 March 1917.
6. Ernst Weiss, *Tanja* (Berlin, 1920).
7. Interview with Ernest Scheuer, New York (September 1975).
8. Walter Sokel, 'Die Prosa des Expressionismus', in Wolfgang Rothe (ed.), *Expressionismus als Literatur* (Berne, 1979), p. 170.
9. Ernst Weiss, 'Notizen über mich selbst' (tr. from the French by Sven Spieker), *Weiß-Blätter*, 4 (1985), p. 6.
10. Ernst Weiss, 'Interview zu seiner *Tanja*', *Wiener Morgenpost*, 233 (23 December 1919), p. 2.
11. Ibid.
12. Gustav Janouch, *Gespräche mit Kafka* (Frankfurt, 1968), p. 239.
13. F., 'Kammerspiele. *Tanja*', *Deutsche Zeitung Bohemia*, 41 (13 December 1919).
14. Ibid.
15. Interview with Hans Demetz, Prague (August 1975).
16. Ibid.
17. Ernst Weiss, 'Rundfrage: Der glücklichste Tag meines Lebens', *Deutsche Zeitung Bohemia* (25 December 1923), pp. 11–12.
18. 'Ernst Weiß über sich selbst', in Wondrak, (p. 26).
19. Albert Ehrenstein, 'Ernst Weiß', *Ostseezeitung*, 395 (1923).
20. Bernhard Reich, *Im Wettlauf mit der Zeit* (Berlin, 1970), p. 75.
21. Hofbieder, 'Wochenschau auf Wiener Bühnen', *Neues Montagsblatt* (29 December 1919), p. 12.
22. Herbert Jhering, *Von Reinhardt bis Brecht* (Berlin, 1961), p. 46.
23. Alfred Kerr, 'Ernst Weiß: "Olympia"', *Berliner Tageblatt* (20 March 1923).
24. Park Honan, *Browning's Characters* (New Haven, 1961), p. 47.
25. Herbert Jhering, *Von Reinhardt bis Brecht*, p. 298.
26. Alfred Döblin, 'Drei Berliner Uraufführungen', *Prager Tagblatt*, 57 (22 March 1923), p. 2.
27. L. O., 'Lulus jüngere Schwester', *Hessische Allgemeine*, 282 (12 December 1976).
28. Ernst Weiss, 'Die Verdorrten', *Der neue Merkur*, 4 (1920–1), pp. 119–39.
29. Ludwig Winder, 'Ernst Weiß: 'Leonore', *Deutsche Zeitung Bohemia* (1 July 1923), p. 6.
30. Ernst Weiß, 'Ein Wort zu Wedekinds *Schloß Wetterstein*', *Berliner Börsen-Courier*, 187 (1924), p. 7.
31. Ernst Weiss, 'Ein Wort zu *Macbeth*', *Prager Tagblatt*, 38 (15 February 1921), p. 1.
32. Ernst Weiss, 'Lebensfragen des Theaters', *Prager Theaterbuch* (1924), pp. 97–100.
33. Ernst Weiss, 'Anmerkungen zum dramatischen Schaffen', *Das dramatische Theater*, 1 (1924).
34. Ibid., p. 67.

Performance and Provocation in Graz 1960–1966

Simon Ryan

Ever since its beginnings in the early 1960s, 'Grazer Literatur' has functioned as a literature of opposition. In its initial phase of development up to the time of Peter Handke's literary début in 1966, the literary activities of the first wave of the young Austrian authors, later referred to somewhat incautiously by some publishers and critics as the 'Grazer Gruppe' – the core group closely associated with Graz's 'Forum Stadtpark' and is house publication, the literary magazine *manuskripte* – involved a distinct element of performance and a considerable degree of provocation. After 1966, as the Graz authors began to be treated by West Germany's literary industry as a promising new Austrian literary phenomenon, the performance element diminished, but provocation has continued to be an essential feature of the oppositional stand consistently adopted by the 'Grazer' in Austrian cultural and political matters over the past three decades.

The extent and duration of the oppositional features evident in the literary productions of the Graz circle highlight some disturbing aspects in the relationship between literary culture and society in the Austrian Second Republic. Alfred Kolleritsch (b. 1931), the editor of *manuskripte*, author and leading organiser of literary activities in Graz for over thirty years, has frequently had occasion in his editorial 'Marginalien' ('Marginalia') to reflect, at times bitterly, on the precarious situation of modern and progressive literary ideas within the cultural life of the Second Republic: 'In Österreich muß immer für die Literatur gekämpft werden' ('Literature must always be fought for in Austria').[1] From the beginning, Kolleritsch has viewed the provincial city of Graz as a 'kleine österreichische Monade' ('small Austrian monad') in which Austria's post-war cultural dilemma is reflected in a concentrated form. Although Graz has been an international centre for avant-garde performances in a wide variety of art forms since the first 'Steirischer Herbst' festival in 1968, the polarisation between progressive cultural forces and the bastions of deeply conservative and restorative ideologies has by no means lessened. Indeed, the conservative tenor of political events in Austria since the mid-1980s would appear to represent a significant deterioration in public and private attitudes towards the development of the Second Republic as a open society. In 1989, nearly three decades after the founding of 'Forum Stadtpark' and *manuskripte* in 1960, Kolleritsch noted, with regard to the role of the Graz authors associated with *manuskripte*, the grim prospect of a future 'die mehr den je die Opposition der Literatur gegen die Wiederkehr der Gleichen im Gesellschaftlich-Politischen braucht' ('which more than ever needs the opposition of literature to the recurrence of the same events in the social and political domain').[2]

The two institutions which provided the initial stimulus and organisational focus in the development of the Graz authors were the younger section of the literary wing of 'Forum Stadtpark', and the publication *manuskripte*. *manuskripte* was originally intended to be a vehicle for all sections of 'Forum Stadtpark', including areas such as music and architecture, but the magazine's editorship was rapidly dominated by Kolleritsch, whose interest lay in promoting awareness of avant-garde approaches to literature. From the outset these institutions were intended to promote positive literary alternatives to the cultural malaise of 'Austrianism', which sought to fix the cultural gaze of the Second Republic in the hypnotic contemplation of a fertile Habsburg myth. At the same time they were to oppose the continuing presence in Styria and elsewhere of National-Socialist and Austro-Fascist sentiments which took literary form in a persistent strain of 'Blut-und-Boden'-orientated 'Heimatliteratur'. The latter was promulgated by figures like the Styrian writer Bruno Brehm, and a former Nazi cultural spokesman for the province, Josef Papesch, whose works 'den Heimatbegriff ungeschichtlich als unverrückbaren Besitz einpfählten und das Lokale als völkische Eigenart zum unveränderlichen Wert stilisierten' ('unhistorically surrounded the concept of "Heimat" with a palisade as an unassailable possession and gave to the local, as a national characteristic, the style of an unalterable value').[3] The strategy of Kolleritsch and those associated with the 'Studio der Jungen' was to bring avant-garde literature to Graz, not only to introduce a breath of modernity into the 'literarische Niemandsland' ('literary no-man's-land')[4] of Syria, but also as a counter to a 'gefährliches Kulturvakuum [...] in das immer mehr braune Luft einströmt' ('dangerous cultural vacuum into which more and more brown air is streaming').[5] Kolleritsch viewed avant-garde literature as a weapon in the campaign against unrepentant former Austrian Nazis and supporters of pan-German aspirations who immediately vilified as 'decadent' any literature remotely associated with Modernism: 'Die experimentelle Literatur, im weitesten Sinne, wurde für uns zum Kampfmittel gegen die verstockten kulturpolitischen Strukturen' ('Experimental literature, in the widest sense, became a weapon for us against unrepentant cultural and political structures').[6]

Performance was an essential part of the alternative literary tradition with which the younger Graz authors wished to establish an active connection as a counter to the prevailing mode of Austrianism or the revival of the German tribal myth. Even before 'Forum Stadtpark' was formally established, members of the 'Wiener Gruppe' had staged readings in Graz in 1959 at the invitation of the Graz 'Sezession'. Gerhard Rühm noted that as a result of their appearance in Graz, 'trotz anonymer drohungen und bezeichnender kritik ('Ent-"artmänner" in der Sezession'), eine feste gemeinde zu bilden begann' ('despite anonymous threats and the expected criticism [untranslatable pun on the name of H.C. Artmann: 'decadent men at the Sezession'] a definite community began to form').[7] The 'Wiener Gruppe' had set out almost a decade earlier to research, apply and extend the literary experiments of the historical avant-garde of Expressionism, Futurism, Constructivism, Dada and Surrealism. As the embodiment of Austria's first small but genuinely active young literary avant-garde movement after 1945, the 'Wiener Gruppe' had a special significance for the early orientation of the young Graz authors. The appearance of members of the 'Wiener Gruppe' at the Graz 'Sezession' in 1959 announced the arrival of this alternative tradition in the Austrian hinterland:

> Als ganz Österreich in den tausendjährigen Schlaf versank und das Erwachen nicht mehr zu den großen Veränderungen in der Kunst zurückfand, verschwand ein ganzes Zeitalter. In Form eines Lernprozesses, dem sich nicht allzuviele anschlossen, tasteten sich einige in die große Tradition der Moderne zurück. Für die Literatur leistete diese Arbeit die Wiener Gruppe. Sie ging die Wege der ästhetischen Revolutionen des Jahrhunderts nach und fand dazu die eigene Stimme, die Rezeption schlug um ins Schöpferische.
>
> Für unsere Anfänge in Graz war die Begegnung und die Freundschaft mit den Wienern das große Aha-Erlebnis.[8]
>
> [When all of Austria sank into the sleep of a thousand years and the awakening no longer found its way back to the great changes in art, a whole age disappeared. In the form of a learning process in which not all that many joined, some groped their way back into the great tradition of Modernism. The 'Wiener Gruppe' carried out this work for literature. They followed the paths of this century's aesthetic revolutions and found their own voice as well: reception turned into creativity.
>
> For our beginnings in Graz, the meeting and friendship with the 'Wiener' was the great moment of recognition.]

The programme of readings and performances first offered by 'Forum Stadtpark', together with the texts published in the early issues of *manuskripte*, demonstrate the firm intention of Kolleritsch and the members of the Forum's 'Studio der Jungen' to foster in Graz the rapid development of what has been described as 'der Mut zur Moderne' ('the courage [to pursue] Modernism').[9] The participants in the informal group of Graz authors closely associated with the 'Studio der Jungen' and Kolleritsch between 1960 and 1966 as a first wave of the 'Grazer Gruppe' were Barbara Frischmuth (b. 1941), Wolfgang Bauer (b. 1941), Gunter Falk (1941–83), Peter Handke (b. 1942) and Michael Scharang (b. 1941).[10] Initially, the literary section of 'Forum Stadtpark' represented the interests of a middle generation of writers as well as the younger authors who were aligned with Kolleritsch and the 'Studio der Jungen'. The programme also featured readings by local writers whose works were by no means progressive. Kolleritsch none the les managed to invite to readings at 'Forum Stadtpark' a range of writers and critics whose works represented a broad cross-section of post-war avant-garde experimentalism in the German-speaking world.

The first of the avant-garde authors invited by Kolleritsch was not, in fact, a member of the 'Wiener Gruppe', but Helmut Heissenbüttel, a practitioner of an experimental approach broadly categorised as 'konkrete Literatur'. Although based on similar hypotheses about language, Heissenbüttel's texts differ in a number of respects from the 'konkrete Poesie' of Franz Mon and Eugen Gomringer. A common interest in following an objectified positivist approach to language and literary experiment had none the less led to a number of contacts between Heissenbüttel, Gomringer, Mon and the 'Wiener Gruppe' since the mid-1950s. Despite the obvious individual traits in their writing, all shared a theoretical approach in which ordinary language became a laboratory for research into language as a conditioned and conditioning form of human behaviour. Of Friedrich Achleitner, Konrad Bayer, Oswald Wiener and himself, Gerhard Rühm noted: 'theoretisch beschäftigten wir uns vor allem mit sprachwissenschaft, denkmethoden, wittgenstein, den neopositivisten, der kybernetik; am eingehendsten wiener, bei dem diese auseinandersetzung sich auch unmittelbar in seinen literarischen texten abspielt' ('with regard to theory we devoted ourselves principally to linguistics, analytical methods, wittgenstein, the neopositivists, cybernetics: in the greatest depth, wiener, for whom this examination takes place directly in his literary texts').[11] The exception to this approach was the remaining member of the 'Wiener Gruppe', Hans Carl Artmann, whose orientation towards a subject-centred, black romanticism and surrealism led him to depart from the group in 1958. Heissenbüttel appeared at 'Forum Stadtpark' on 15 November 1961 and Mon in June 1964. In February 1962, Friedrich Knilli introduced the positivist literary aesthetics of Max Bense and discussed the work of H. G. Helms and Ferdinand Kriwet. Reinhard Döhl and Reinhold Grimm presented an expert critical and theoretical appraisal of these new approaches to literary production on 19 September 1963. Kolleritsch was not personally drawn to the particular form of avant-garde experiment represented at the time by Achleitner, Rühm, Heissenbüttel and other 'konkrete Dichter'. Nevertheless, in keeping with his policy of openness to the new, he felt that their texts and theories should be presented at 'Forum Stadtpark' and in *manuskripte* as a significant development within the alternative literary tradition he wished to introduce to Graz.

The element of performance found in the early work of the Graz authors entered Graz physically in the 'readings' conducted by members of the 'Wiener Gruppe' and by Ernst Jandl, who enjoyed a close association with the group in Vienna. The concept of performance had only recently reached its peak in the work of the 'Wiener Gruppe' itself in the 'Aktionen' (literally: 'actions', the basic units of a performance) of the two group presentations entitled 'Literarisches Cabaret' (Vienna, 6 December 1958 and 15 April 1959). The staging of literature as an event calculated to produce a shock effect had been an essential feature of the work of the historical avant-garde. The 'Wiener Gruppe' developed their own performance skills initially in the presentation of dialect poems, sound poems and other short experimental texts. By the time Rühm, as the first of the 'Wiener Gruppe' to appear at 'Forum Stadtpark', conducted a reading, on 13 March 1962, 'reading' was largely synonymous with 'performance' as far as the group was concerned. Ernst Jandl appeared in 1964, as did the poet Friederike Mayröcker, who was also associated with Jandl and the 'Wiener Gruppe'. Oswald Wiener and Friedrich Achleitner first appeared at 'Forum Stadtpark' on 5/6 March 1965 and 13 September 1965 respectively.

The early readings and other performances of the young 'Grazer' at 'Forum Stadtpark' were in considerable measure a direct response to the stimulus of exposure to the presence of the 'Wiener Gruppe' and other avant-garde experimentalists, whether directly at 'Forum Stadtpark' or through the pages of *manuskripte*. This exposure provided definite impetus and encouragement to Kolleritsch, Frischmuth, Bauer, Falk and Handke, as well as to later Graz authors, such as Klaus Hoffer (b. 1942) and Gerhard Roth (b. 1942), to stage their own experiments in Graz. Although Bauer, for example, attributes the immediate impulse to write his first one-act play, 'Der Schweinetransport', to a production of Ionesco's 'Rhinoceros' on 1 February 1961 at the 'Rittersaal' in Graz,[12] there is no doubt that he was encouraged to proceed by the fact that 'Forum Stadtpark' and *manuskripte* already existed as outlets for the performance and publication of experimental works. 'Der Schweinetransport' and another Bauer one-act play, 'Maler und Farbe', were staged by the 'Studio der jungen Dramatik' on 10 February 1962.

The 'Studio-Abende', presented by the 'Studio der Jungen', initially offered a programme of readings, chiefly of poetry, more unconventional in content than in form, along with live jazz. Reaction in the local press to readings by Kolleritsch, Frischmuth and others was predictably hostile. The accusation in the *Süd-Ost-Tagespost* – 'Das sind lauter Dunkelmänner' ('They are nothing but shady characters') – gave Kolleritsch and others the idea of staging a series of performances under the banner of 'Dunkelkammern' ('darkrooms') as a means of counter-attack.[13] The published works of the Graz authors and *manuskripte* offer little detailed information on their early involvement with 'Forum Stadtpark'. Elizabeth Wiesmayr's *Die Zeitschrift 'manuskripte' 1960–1970* is the most comprehensive and best documented source of information on the readings and performances conducted by the 'Studio der Jungen'.[14] From Wiesmayr's critical reconstruction, which includes otherwise unavailable quotations from Kolleritsch's personal correspondence, it is clear that the early 'Dunkelkammern' were intended to provoke a direct confrontation with the local representatives of prevailing conservative aesthetic values as well as with the defenders of ideologically suspect 'Heimatliteratur'. According to Kolleritsch, the 'Dunkelkammern' were conceived of as 'aggressive Lesungen mit Texten von Forum-Autoren, Lesungen, die vom Pult und der Leserlampe Abschied genommen hatte, also die Aktion auch darstellten' ('aggressive readings with texts by Forum authors, readings which had bid farewell to the lectern and the reading lamp, and presented action').[15]

The first of the 'Dunkelkammern' was staged at 'Forum Stadtpark' on 26 June 1962. Texts by Kolleritsch, Frischmuth and Bauer were presented within the framework of a manifesto drawn up by Kolleritsch. In the manifesto Kolleritsch took issue with the simplistic view of 'good' and 'bad' art which predominated in Graz whereby only negative values were ascribed to modern art:

> Wir wollen nun darauf hinweisen, daß es hier in Graz Menschen gibt, die damit nicht zufrieden sind. Und so werden wir es von nun an nicht unterlassen zu zeigen, daß der purpurne Mantel dieses Kunstrichtertums aus dem ewigen Geist der Kunst nur eine faule Ausrede ist. Es stimmt uns heiter, wenn Erscheinungen der Moderne mit Nihilismus, mit

infantiler Stotterei gleichgesetzt werden, es stimmt uns heiter, wenn sie von Modernismus und modernistischem Epigonentum sprechen. Wir wissen, daß wir für die moderne Kunst nichts mehr leisten können, wir sind aber trotzdem stolz, Epigonen der Zeit zu sein; modernistische Epigonen: die einzig ehrenvolle literarische Kategorie in unseren für die moderne Kunst so traurigen Breiten.[16]

[We want now to point out that there are people here in Graz who are not content with this. So from now on we will not fail to show that the imperial robe of critics who claim to judge art by the eternal spirit of art is just a lazy excuse. We are cheered whenever the manifestations of Modernism are equated with nihilism, with infantile stuttering, we are cheered whenever they speak of Modernism and Modernist imitation. We know that we cannot do anything more for modern art, nonetheless we are proud to be epigones of the period – Modernist epigones: the only honourable literary category in these latitudes which are otherwise so dismal for modern art.]

A small element of performance in this first 'Dunkelkammer', little more than a gag, gave rise to disproportionate outrage. A leg had been sawn off the seat reserved for the reviewer from the *Süd-West-Tagespost* and replaced by a pile of *manuskripte*. Against the background of the evening's general assault on cherished literary values, this act was interpreted as an insult to standards of civilised behaviour. The reaction in the Graz press was a mixture of indignation at the breach of good manners and incomprehension in the face of the new literature. Wolfgang Arnold, the critic concerned, announced that he would boycott any future performances at 'Forum Stadtpark'. Arnold became a sworn opponent of the young 'Grazer'.[17] Looking back on the frequent confrontations unleashed in Graz over new approaches to literature and art generally, Kolleritsch noted in 1988:

Das Programm der ersten Jahre, obwohl fast nur vom Nachholbedarf und von einzuleitenden Lern- und Denkprozessen bestimmt, gab Zündstoff genug, die Katze der Reaktion aus dem Sack zu locken. Heute, 29 Jahre später, wirkt es grotesk, mit welchen Argumenten und Repressionen das in viele Sparten gefächerte Programm des Forum Stadtpark [...] denunziert wurde und noch immer wird. Man ersparte uns damit allerdings die Profilierungsneurose, 'das Neue um des Neuen willen', ästhetische Probleme hatten politische Relevanz: Ohne diesen Widerstand, der das bewirkte, was er abschaffen wollte, hätte es nie die 'Grazer Gruppe' gegeben.[18]

[Although it was determined almost solely by the need to catch up and introduce the required learning and thinking processes, the programme of the first years provided sufficient inflammatory material to lure the cat of reaction out of the bag. Today, 29 years later, the arguments and repressive ideas with which the programme of Forum Stadtpark was (and still is) denounced within its several divisions appear grotesque. We were, of course, spared the anxiety of creating a distinctive image for ourselves, 'innovation for its own sake'; aesthetic problems had political relevance. Without this resistance, which brought into being the very thing it wanted to eliminate, the 'Grazer Gruppe' would never have existed.]

The second 'Dunkelkammer' on 8 June 1963 featured, among other local artists, a presentation by an actor from the 'Grazer Theater', Herman Teusch, of a prose text by Wolfgang Bauer. The title is not mentioned by Wiesmayr. Bauer's early prose texts, '5 Snobisten lernen Lesen und Schreiben' (1962), 'Ohne Titel' (1962) or 'Mein Dreirad' (1963), for example, essentially function a a critique of blindly accepted patterns of behaviour and conformity to the unspoken rules which regulate life in a market-driven technological society. Bauer employs in these prose sketches a narrative technique based on the frequent repetition and variation of key phrases within the structure of an overall metaphor for a behavioural model, like that of 'Putzen' ('cleaning') in 'Ohne Titel'. A strong parallel with the combinatory narrative techniques employed by the 'Wiener Gruppe' suggests itself. The fact that the text was performed as opposed to read would also appear to be a direct response to the example of the 'Wiener Gruppe'. Similarly, Bauer's adoption of a narrative tone of childlike innocence and simplicity has a precedent in texts composed by the 'Wiener Gruppe', as does his use of dialect.

The third 'Dunkelkammer', presented on 21 June 1964, featured texts by Gunter Falk and Peter Handke which were performed by Herman Teusch and Gerburg Dieter, another actor from the 'Grazer Theater', under the title 'Textserie-Sprechtext-Prosa'. Falk's approach to language was closer than that of any other Graz author to the linguistic positivism of Achleitner and Rühm. By this time, both Bauer and Falk had enjoyed considerable contact with the 'Wiener Gruppe'. Kolleritsch confirms this and adds a significant aside: 'Besonders G. Falk und W. Bauer waren dann mit den Wienern eng verbunden und an späteren Aktionen beteiligt. (Liest man aber das Vorwort zur zweiten Auflage des Sammelbandes der Wiener Gruppe von Gerhard Rühm, sieht es allerdings so aus, als hätte es all das nie gegeben)' ('G. Falk and W. Bauer, in particular, were at that time closely associated with the 'Wiener' and were involved in later performances. (To read the foreword to Gerhard Rühm's anthology of the 'Wiener Gruppe', however, it certainly looks as if all that had never existed').)[19] The texts by Handke and Falk were surprisingly well received by local critics and were generally regarded as more constructive than destructive in intent. The following 'Dunkelkammer', 'Mit Überraschung', staged on 23 June 1964 by Falk, Bauer and Hans Nurser, marks the transition of the 'Dunkelkammern' from readings to the style of a happening in which the audience actively participated. In a clear reference to a sketch from the second 'Literarisches Cabaret', in which Achleitner and Rühm rode a motor-scooter up to the stage, Bauer and Falk entered the room on a moped. The event followed a simple aleatory principle. Bauer, Falk and Nurser staged a party, eating, drinking and smoking, while they played records, projected news clippings on to a screen and read randomly from manuscript pages which lay scattered over the floor. The audience also ate, drank and smoked, eagerly interjecting whenever the mood took them. The obvious receptivity of the predominantly young audience to this style of event was in part conditioned by the burgeoning international Pop Culture of the 1960s. A spirit of playfulness predominated, in strong contrast to the radical, sado-erotic aggression of events like those staged around the same time by Viennese 'Aktionisten' ('performance-artists') like Hermann Nitsch, Günter Brus or Otto Mühl. The nature of 'Mit Überraschung' and subsequent performances by Bauer and Falk indicates that a subjective bohemian spirit was developing in Graz as opposed to the objective, at times dehumanising radicalism practised by some of Bauer and Falk's contemporaries in Vienna. Although Bauer's later plays, for example, often deal with erotic, sadistic or destructive behaviour, they are never without a measure of humour which, however black, is also redeeming. The bohemian tendency evident among the Graz authors is attributed by Wendelin Schmidt-Dengler to an underlying anarchic impulse which drove them to break with prevailing literary modes. It is to this and 'die Konzeptlosigkeit, die eben jener Anarchie verpflichtet zu sein scheint' ('the absence of [an overall] concept, which appears to be an obligatory feature of that anarchy') that he attributes the formative influence their work has had on the reception and production of literature in the Second Republic.[20] An anarchic bohemianism aimed at reasserting the autonomy of the aesthetic domain is also in keeping with the anti-ideological, anti-theoretical stance adopted later in the 1960s, when literature in West Germany was becoming heavily politicised, by almost all the Graz authors.

The first 'Dunkelkammer' of 1965 also contained an element of performance. Within the framework of a multi-media presentation, Hans Nurser undertook to demonstrate that the apparent surface coherence of language is the product of 'wilful' acts of association, a normally subconscious process accessible only to 'scientific geniuses and schizophrenics'. Nurser projected slide images and a seemingly unrelated commentary to simulate the dissociation between words as signifiers and the objects they signify. This was an appropriate forerunner to the next 'Dunkelkammer' on 6 June 1965, when Oswald Wiener presented a section of his anarchic assault on the relationship between language and reality, *die verbesserung von mitteleuropa* (1969). Because of an altercation between Kolleritsch and the Forum's first president, Emil Breisach, over Kolleritsch's invitation to Wiener, this event almost failed to take place.[21] The remaining 'Dunkelkammern' – the last took place on 23 October 1965 – contained little that might be categorised as performance.

The further development of the performance element at 'Forum Stadtpark' was carried out by Bauer and Falk, the two Graz authors who were in closest contact with the 'Wiener Gruppe'. Bauer and Falk staged what they called a 'Pop-Lesung' in the student dining hall of Graz's university on 26 November 1965 and a performance-orientated series of events, 'Happy Art and Attitude', at 'Forum Stadtpark' on 15 December 1965. The 'Pop-Lesung' was essentially an early happening with free beer, where, surrounded by icons of the new Pop Culture which included large-scale images from American comics, Bauer and

Falk read their texts amid a celebration of music by the Beatles. As an event with maximum audience participation and glorification of consumable 'low' or 'trivial' art forms, it represented a radical enough departure from the prevailing cultural ethos in Graz. 'Happy Art and Attitude' was a more tightly constructed event, whose performance components were based on a manifesto of the same name that Bauer and Falk had produced for the occasion.[22] 'Happy Art and Attitude' presented with mock-seriousness an ironic blending of banal and trivial elements with the aesthetic earnestness of high art. Falk's interest as a sociologist in the theory of games combined with Bauer's genial fascination with the absurd stimulated them to generate a variety of 'Aktionen' which included card-games, a boxing-match and 'Body-Art', accompanied by readings from great 'forerunners' of the 'movement', not only Schiller and Freud but also Herbert Marcuse, whose work was then barely known in Graz. The seriousness of this otherwise unserious statement lay in the assertion of the human need to (re-)establish art as a form of creative play:

> 2.1.6 HAPPY ART & ATTITUDE wird Kultur, Gesellschaft sowie die Weltorientierung des Einzelnen auf andere Fundamente stellen, auf die Fundamente von Sinnlichkeit und Spiel, das zwischen dieser und Realitätsmeisterung vermitteln wird. Die Kollegen SCHILLER ('Briefe über die ästhetische Erziehung des Menschen') und Herbert MARCUSE ('Triebstruktur und Gesellschaft') haben dies bereits akzeptiert.
>
> [2.1.6. HAPPY ART & ATTITUDE will set culture, society along with the individual's orientation in the world, on other foundations, on the foundations of sensuousness and play, which will mediate between the sensuous experience and the mastering of reality. Our colleagues SCHILLER ('Letters on the Aesthetic Education of Man') and Herbert MARCUSE ('Eros and Civilisation') have already accepted this.]

As a response to the 'AHA-Erlebnis' experienced by the Graz authors when they first encountered the work of the 'Wiener Gruppe', 'Happy Art and Attitude' (HAA) was an appropriate restatement of the 'Sprachspiel' concept adopted earlier as a paradigm by the 'Wiener Gruppe' from the philosophy of Wittgenstein. The idea of the 'language game' operates as an underlying structure in a number of early works by the 'Grazer', nowhere more clearly than in Handke's plays up to 1970 and in his novel *Die Angst des Tormanns beim Elfmeter* (1970). The performance element in the literary activities of the 'Studio der Jungen' hinges on the desire to present an experience of literature not as the worship of the past or as an attempt to gain power over the minds of others, but as a series of creative 'Sprachspiele'.

Handke was certainly aware of the work of the 'Wiener Gruppe' in the context of his early association with 'Forum Stadtpark'. This is evidenced somewhat later in his enthusiastic review of Konrad Bayer's prose work, *Der Kopf des Vitus Bering*, for the ÖRF in Graz on 2 August 1966: 'Hier scheint sich, endlich, eine neue Literatur anzubahnen' ('Here a new literature finally appears to be opening up').[23] In Handke's case, this interest was somewhat overshadowed by his absorption of the increasingly available flow of information in German in the early 1960s about the attack on language and the conventions of traditional realism by French avant-garde authors in the 'nouveau roman', especially Alain Robbe-Grillet. Handke also found technical and thematic inspiration for his early prose works published in the collection *Begrüßung des Aufsichtsrats* (1967) in the work of such varied authors as Faulkner, Kleist, Flaubert, Dostoevsky and Kafka. He was not generally drawn to performances of the kind which predominated in the 'Dunkelkammern' and did not regard them as a suitable vehicle for the serious communication of new prose forms. His reservations about the expectations governing such events and the potential for misinterpretation of aesthetic intent are made clear in his essay 'Straßentheater und Theatertheater' (1968): 'das Theater als Bedeutungsraum ist dermaßen bestimmt, daß alles, was außerhalb des Theaters Ernsthaftigkeit, Anliegen, Eindeutigkeit, Finalität ist, *Spiel* wird – daß also Eindeutigkeit, Engagement etc. auf dem Theater eben durch den fatalen Spiel- und Bedeutungsraum rettungslos verspielt werden – wann wird man es endlich merken?' ('The theatre as a realm of meaning is so determined that everything which outside the theatre is serious, a matter of concern, explicit, final, becomes *play* – so precisely because of this fatal realm of play and meaning in the theatre explicitness, commitment etc. are irretrievably gambled away – when will this finally be noticed?').[24] Handke did not deny that the game element was adequately represented in performances at 'Forum Stadtpark'. Rather, he was still in the process of giving precise form to his own ideas on the aesthetic and political functions of theatre and working out the strategy he would adopt to launch them. Handke appeared only once in person in the context of the 'Dunkelkammern', on 13 July 1965, when texts by regular contributors to *manuskripte* were read.

Handke staged his first 'performance' in 1966 when he appeared at the Princeton Congress of 'Gruppe 47' to challenge prevailing views of a whole generation of German authors about narrative realism and the political relevance of literature. His much-discussed accusation of 'Beschreibungsimpotenz' was not an arrogant snap judgment but the product of several years' reflection in Graz on the nature of narrative and the function of literature. The timing of what was soon recognised as a turning-point in the recent history of German literature was both immaculate and spontaneous, as Handke's plainly ironic letter to *Der Spiegel* of 23 May 1966 confirms: 'Es schien mir eines der erstrebenswertesten Ziele für einen Schriftsteller, im Spiegel erwähnt zu werden. Von diesem Wunsch getrieben, habe ich mich auch bei der Tagung der Gruppe 47 in Princeton 1966 zu Wort gemeldet' ('One of the most worthy goals for an author to pursue seemed to me to be mentioned in *Der Spiegel*. Driven by this desire, I asked to speak at the conference of 'Gruppe 47' in Princeton in 1966.')[25]

Handke's second and most remarkable public 'performance' was the 'Sprechstück' *Publikumsbeschimpfung*, staged under the direction of Claus Peymann in June 1966 as a part of 'Experimenta 1', at the 'Theater am Turm' in Frankfurt. There is a strong parallel between the basic role-reversal of actors and audience in *Publikumsbeschimpfung* and a central idea which took form in the 'Literarisches Cabaret' of the 'Wiener Gruppe'. Handke's views on language and the function of literary conventions were certainly not new, especially when examined in the context of the history of ideas in Austrian literature from Hofmannsthal onwards. What is new is the fact that Handke succeeded in *Publikumsbeschimpfung* and in other works in revealing the workings of 'ordinary language' by embodying these ideas in literary forms which make accessible an understanding of the role of language in the experiences of ordinary people and not just in the specialised artist-figures of the avant-garde repertoire.

Part of the 'programme' of the 'Wiener Gruppe', as set out in Oswald Wiener's 'Coole Manifest' (1954), was to demonstrate in a detached and systematic fashion that events generally held to be 'Wahrnehmungen' ('perceptions') are in fact psychologically concealed 'Handlungen' ('actions'), performed so unconsciously in everyday life that they become automatic. The 'Wiener Gruppe' thereby hoped to demonstrate as a postulate about the workings of language, in both life and literature, the identity of 'Stil' ('style'), as the linguistic realisation of a mode of perception and 'Wirklichkeit' ('reality') as the perceived result of style: 'einer der grundgedanken unserer nunmehr geplanten veranstaltung war also, "wirklichkeit" auszustellen und damit, in konsequenz, abzustellen. ein anderer, das publikum als schauspieltruppe zu betrachten, und uns selber als die zuschauer' ('one of the basic ideas for the occasion we had in mind was to exhibit "reality" and, in so doing, switch it off. another was to view the audience as a troupe of actors and ourselves as the spectators').[26] On the comparatively small scale of the 'Literarisches Cabaret' this stated intention was carried out.

In Handke's *Publikumsbeschimpfung* virtually the same reversal of roles between style and reality, actors and audience, is realised. In this 'Stück gegen das Theater, wie es ist' ('play against the theatre as it is'),[27] Handke single-mindedly negates the sense of reality and conventional theatre-going expectations of the audience, not so that 'the usual audience will make way for another audience', but 'so that the usual audience will become a different audience' ('damit das übliche Publikum ein anderes Publikum wird').[28] The performance element in this play which refuses to be a play is central to Handke's message. Where it departs from the performances of the 'Wiener Gruppe' is that, instead of seeking to annul the barriers between art and life in keeping with the general aim of the historical avant-garde, Handke seeks to shock the audience into an immediate and personal awareness of what he considers the proper subjective dimension of theatre and literature generally, the realm of imagination and aesthetic play: 'es ist ein unmittelbares Theater [...] Es kann ihn aufmerksam, hellhörig, hellsichtig machen, nicht nur als Theaterbesucher' ('it is direct theatre [...] It can make [the audience] alert, keen of hearing, sharp-eyed, not only as theatre-goers').[29]

An early shift in the public reception of the 'Dunkelkammern' away from the angry indignation of the first presentation by the 'Studio der Jungen' might at first appear to indicate that the shock effect rapidly diminished. A more likely explanation for the fact that the second and subsequent 'Dunkelkammern' from June 1963 provoked a less drastic public reaction and even a measure of positive critical response is that many of the more easily offended, heeding the warning signals in the press, simply stayed away: later audiences were already to some extent converted. A further reason is that *manuskripte* was also drawing an increasing amount of critical fire. Older members of 'Forum Stadtpark', including Breisach, already regarded the magazine's contents as unnecessarily provocative in view of the association's sensitive relations with the city. The Forum's committee regarded *manuskripte* as a financial liability and a source of embarrassment. For a number of years they kept secret from the controllers of the cultural budget the fact that the magazine received financial support from 'Forum Stadtpark'. While avant-garde guests were performing at 'Forum Stadtpark', Kolleritsch was pushing *manuskripte* up to the front line of cultural and political opposition. The second issue of the magazine contained, in addition to texts by Kolleritsch and other 'Grazer', a number of texts by Achleitner, Artmann, Bayer and Rühm. The issue of 800 copies was sponsored by a local Styrian savings bank. When the manager read the proof copy, he ordered the name of the bank to be blanked out. *manuskripte* became the first publication routinely to publish texts by the 'Wiener Gruppe' and played a significant role in bringing their work to a wider audience throughout the 1960s. Under the editorship of Kolleritsch, *manuskripte* quickly reached the leading edge of avant-garde publications in German. Of particular moment for the promotion of the alternative Austrian literary tradition was the regular publication in *manuskripte* of texts by the Austrian Dadaist Raoul Hausmann (1886-1971).

manuskripte openly attacked conservative writers. In *manuskripte* 5/1962 an article appeared under the initials P.V. which attacked Bruno Brehm for the Nazi ideology apparent in his work. The article brought an immediate reaction from Brehm's supporters who, in the magazine *Kunst ins Volk*, attacked the scandalous expenditure of public money of 'loyal Styrians' on 'Forum Stadtpark' as an institution which served only to foster 'decadent' art. As a result, the battle lines were firmly drawn between the 'Grazer' and those who did not wish the 'spiritual peace of the Austro-Germans' to be disturbed.

The provocation *manuskripte* offered to the representatives of the 'große Erbe' ('great inheritance') of Austrian cultural tradition reached its peak with publication of extracts from Oswald Wiener's *die verbesserung von mitteleuropa*. In 1966, a case was brought against the editor for allegedly publishing pornography, as a result of which the 'offending' issue (Issue 18, 1966) was seized by the authorities.[30] Although this anonymous attempt at censorship was defeated at a court hearing in Vienna in 1968, when the proceedings were dropped, all manner of moral outrage was directed by the right-wing press against Kolleritsch, especially as he was a secondary-school teacher. As a source of provocation to former NSDAP supporters, the pornography affair was only exceeded by the award of the Peter Rosegger Prize, Styria's official literary accolade, to Wolfgang Bauer in 1970. Previous recipients had included Bruno Brehm (1961) and Josef Papesch (1963).

By the end of 1966, the literary activities of the 'Grazer' had begun to acquire the distinctive profile which became a recognised feature of the German literary scene in the mid 1970s. Within Austria the Graz authors were already established in their role of opposition to outmoded literary and political ideas. As early as

1964, they began to find themselves increasingly besieged on another front by theorists of the avant-garde, less often by practising authors than by their attendant critics. A little later, as the politicisation of literature intensified in West Germany, criticism also began to be directed at the Graz authors by ideologists of the political left who considered their work to be lacking in overt political relevance. The distancing of the 'Grazer' from a politically committed style of literary expression can be seen in the debate between Kolleritsch and Scharang conducted in *manuskripte* in 1969, and in Handke's key essays, 'Die Literatur ist romantisch' (1966) and 'Ich bin ein Bewohner des Elfenbeinturms' (1967). In the mid 1960s, the oppositional function of 'Grazer Literatur' expanded to include resistance to all ideologically motivated attempts to define literature and the nature of 'literariness' ('das Literarische') in advance of the act of writing. Kolleritsch and other Graz authors adopted a position of anarchic independence because they believed that literary freedom and the aesthetic domain were under attack from all sides.

The performance element in the early work of Kolleritsch, Frischmuth, Bauer, Falk and Handke came to an end in 1966 for a number of reasons. The period from 1960 to 1966 was one of relative youthful innocence and enthusiasm in the development of this first wave of Graz authors. The performances staged by the 'Studio der Jungen' allowed them to absorb and experiment with some of the major techniques of avant-garde experimentalism while they worked to define their own future literary orientation. Within the Austrian literary world of the 1960s, the concept of performance had already produced the necessary historical shock effect and was becoming absorbed by the international proliferation of large-scale counter-cultural events culminating in the student uprisings of 1968.

Notes

1. Alfred Kolleritsch, 'Marginalie', *manuskripte*, 110 (1990), p. 4.
2. Kolleritsch, 'Die Anfänge des "Forum Stadtpark"', in *Literatur in Graz seit 1960 – das Forum Stadtpark*, Walter Buchebner Literaturprojekt 2 (Vienna and Cologne, 1989), pp. 9–12 (p. 12).
3. Kolleritsch, 'Die Anfänge des "Forum Stadtpark"', p. 9.
4. In a letter to Alfred Andersch, 3 May 1963, quoted in Elizabeth Wiesmayr, *Die Zeitschrift manuskripte 1960–1970* (Königstein, 1980), p. 30.
5. In a letter to Hans Magnus Enzensberger, 1963, quoted in Wiesmayr, p. 30.
6. Kolleritsch, *manuskripte*, 110 (1990), p. 4.
7. Gerhard Rühm, 'Vorwort', in G. Rühm (ed.), *Die Wiener Gruppe – Artmann Bayer Rühm Wiener: Texte Gemeinschaftsarbeiten Aktionen*, 2nd edn (Reinbek, 1985), p. 26.
8. Kolleritsch, *manuskripte*, 110 (1990), p. 4.
9. Gerhard Roth, a Graz author of the second wave to associate with Kolleritsch, 'Forum Stadtpark' and *manuskripte*, in an interview with the present writer on 11 November 1982. See Simon Ryan, 'Gerhard Roth and the Graz Literary Revival: the Emergence of an Austrian Author' (Ph.D. dissertation, University of Cambridge, 1989), p. 113.
10. The first wave of Graz authors was followed between 1967 and 1970 by a second wave, who were the last to be drawn into the original informal central core around

Kolleritsch, although by no means the last to be associated with 'Forum Stadtpark' or *manuskripte:* Wilhelm Hengstler (b. 1944), Klaus Hoffer (b. 1942), Reinhard P. Gruber (b. 1947), Gerhard Roth (b. 1942), Helmut Eisendle (b. 1939), Harald Sommer (b. 1935), Alfred Paul Schmidt (b. 1941) and Peter Matejka (b. 1949). Gert Jonke (b. 1946), whose early work is often discussed within the context of 'Grazer Literatur', had only a relatively brief association with 'Forum Stadtpark'.

11. Rühm, p. 27.
12. Gerhard Melzer, *Wolfgang Bauer: eine Einführung in das Gesamtwerk* (Königstein, 1981), p. 20.
13. Manfred Mixner, 'Ausbruch aus der Provinz', in Peter Laemmle and Jörg Drews (eds), *Wie die Grazer auszogen, die Literatur zu erobern: Texte, Porträts, Analysen und Dokumente junger österreichischer Literatur*, 2nd edn (Munich, 1979), pp 13–28 (p. 27, note 18).
14. See note 4.
15. In a letter to Peter Jokostra, 7 April 1964, in Wiesmayr, p. 18.
16. Unpublished manuscript, in Wiesmayr, p. 19.
17. In 1975 Arnold successfully pursued a writ of defamation against Gerhard Roth. Roth had published an open letter to Arnold attacking him for his destructive criticism of Bauer's play *Gespenster*.
18. Kolleritsch, 'Die Anfänge des "Forum Stadtpark"', p. 10.
19. Kolleritsch, *manuskripte*, 100 (1988), p. 2.
20. Wendelin Schmidt-Dengler, *Eine Avantgarde aus Graz*, Klagenfurter Universitätsreden, 10 (Klagenfurt, 1979).
21. See Wiesmayr, p. 95 (note 96).
22. Reproduced in full in Wolfgang Bauer, *Werke*, ed. Gerhard Melzer (7 vols, Graz, 1989), VI, pp. 70–3.
23. Alfred Holzinger, 'Peter Handkes literarische Anfänge in Graz', in Laemmle and Drews, pp. 191–204 (p. 202).
24. Peter Handke, 'Straßentheater und Theatertheater', in *Ich bin ein Bewohner des Elfenbeinturms* (Frankfurt, 1972), pp. 51–5 (p. 53).
25. Handke, 'Pantoffeln', *Der Spiegel* (23 May 1966), pp. 11–12 (p. 11).
26. Oswald Wiener, 'das "literarische cabaret" der wiener gruppe', in Rühm, pp. 401–88 (p. 403).
27. Handke, 'Zur Publikumsbeschimpfung', in Handke, *Stücke 1* (Frankfurt, 1972), p. 203.
28. Ibid.
29. Ibid.
30. Mixner, 'Ausbruch aus der Provinz', pp. 21–2.

The Staging of History in Felix Mitterer's *Die Kinder des Teufels*

T. E. Bourke

In his works for the stage, Felix Mitterer has twice ventured into the world of fantasy, first with *Die wilde Frau* ('The Wild Woman'), which is based on Austrian folk myths, and then with the fairy-tale spectacle *Drachendurst oder der rostige Ritter* ('Dragon's Thirst or the Rusty Knight'). His *Ein Jedermann* is a twentieth-century rewriting of the late medieval morality play *Everyman*. Otherwise, the works are firmly grounded in fact. His first drama, *Kein Platz für Idioten* ('No Room for Idiots'), grew out of his sense of outrage at the news that in a Tyrolean holiday resort a mother and her handicapped child had been barred from an inn in case the guests might feel disgusted by the sight of the child. The monodrama *Sibirien* ('Siberia'), extreme though its representation of the treatment of the elderly might seem, draws its observations from a nurse's real-life experiences of Austrian old-age homes.[1] Even the passion play *Stigma* has its roots in reality, although its figures are fictitious and its setting both geographically and historically unspecified. The figure of the visionary farmgirl Moid, her proto-socialist Christian message, her excommunication by the Church and her arrest, 'zumal sie [...] das gemeine Volk gegen Obrigkeit und Kirche aufgehetzt hat' ('especially as she has stirred up the common people to rebel against the authorities and the Church'),[2] all have their precedents in history, as in the case of the pious shepherd of Niklashausen, Hans Böheim, who professed at the beginning of the sixteenth century to have talked to the Virgin Mary. But because he proclaimed to the multitudes who came to hear him that the papacy was corrupt, that tithes and taxes should be abolished, that the land, forest and water owned by the nobility and clergy should be made common property, he was declared a heretic and burnt at the stake.[3]

Those of Mitterer's works which come nearest to being documentary are *Kein schöner Land*, *Verlorene Heimat*, *Die Kinder des Teufels* and *Verkaufte Heimat*. *Verlorene Heimat* ('Last Homeland'), which was played on the market-place of the Tyrolean village of Stumm in 1987 by local amateurs, reconstructs the shameful expulsion of over 400 Protestant peasants from the Zillertal in 1837, 56 years after the Edict of Toleration and in contravention of it, though it was supposed to remain legally binding until the Concordat of 1855. *Verkaufte Heimat* ('Sold Homeland') is a two-part telefilm based on the fate of the peasants of South Tyrol who were used as pawns on the geo-political chessboard of Hitler and Mussolini in 1939, the year of the so-called 'Option'. *Kein schöner Land* ('No Land More Beautiful') was prompted by the actual case of Rudolf Gomperz, a prominent citizen and tireless promoter of skiing in and around St Anton in Tyrol, who, after the Annexation, was first ostracised and then transported to the concentration camp of Minsk. Mitterer made his theme the absurd fact 'daß [...] ein bisher beliebter, geachteter und verdienter Bürger plötzlich zum Schurken und Volksschädling gestempelt und zuletzt ermordet wird, weil es sich herausstellt, daß er Jude ist' ('that ... a hitherto popular, respected and deserving citizen is suddenly branded a villain and public enemy and finally murdered, because he turns out to be a Jew').[4]

Die Kinder des Teufels ('The Devil's Children') is based closely on the 'Zauberer-Jackl' trials that took place in Salzburg between 1675 and 1681 and in which 139 persons were accused of witchcraft, tortured and executed. Along with the trials in Calw, Württemberg, in 1673, the Salzburg trials constitute the last great outbreak of mass witch-hunting, in a region in which it had been relatively rare and a quarter of a century after it had finally abated in Southern Germany. Unusually, more than one-third of the victims were under fifteen years of age and more than two-thirds male. The trials were called after one Jakob Koller of Mauterndorf, the son of a knacker and executioner's assistant named Kilian Tischler and of Barbara Kollerin, nicknamed 'Schinterbärberl', a beggar-woman and thief who implicated her son while herself being tried for black magic in Salzburg in 1675. Her accomplice Paul Kaltenpacher, accused of robbing an offertory box, gave evidence that Jackl led a band of young miscreants around with him. After the mother's execution in August of that year, and the rumour that 'Zauberer-Jackl' had been found dead in St Wolfgang on Good Friday, 1677, the search for him was called off, until a twelve-year-old mendicant named Dionysus Feldner, being tried in May 1677, claimed he had last been in the company of Jackl only three weeks previously. Without intending to do so, the historian Heinz Nagl has commented, this young beggar let loose an avalanche of misery that was to remain unique in the history of Salzburg.[5] Feldner became the first victim of the mass trials, being beheaded and burnt in September 1677. Jacob Koller himself, despite a prolonged manhunt that extended far beyond the borders of the archdiocese, was never to be found. In the absence of the main 'male-factor', the pious wrath of the Court Councillor Dr Sebastian Zillner turned all the more upon the children supposedly associated with Jackl. In the month of December 1677 alone, eighteen alleged partners in sorcery were arrested and thrown into the dungeons of Salzburg. In the following year, in which the trials reached a frenzied pitch, 109 persons lost their lives in the most gruesome ways. In some exceptional cases, as for instance where the delinquent demonstrated remorse, the Archbishop of Salzburg exercised 'clemency' by ordaining that he or she should be strangled or, in the case of young children, decapitated before being burnt.

The list of those interrogated, as drawn up by Heinz Nagl and giving the name, age, place of origin, profession, as well as the date, place and means of execution, makes distressing reading.[6] The youngest to be tried was the two-year-old Matthias Kärfues, who was pardoned because of his youth and handed over to adoptive parents. Ten was regarded as the downward age limit for capital punishment, while the oldest victim was the eighty-year-old Margarethe Reinbergerin. In some cases whole families were liquidated. Many victims are simply described as 'young' or 'adult' because neither their date or place of birth were discernible. Ten people were released as simpletons. The vast majority were beggars by trade, while some few carried out the lowliest of agrarian occupations such as shepherd, cowherd, drover, carter, day labourer or farmgirl. Only six out of 198 suspects belonged to the settled or propertied class: one schoolmaster and five peasants. Of these, none was executed. While one farming couple died in prison, the others were released due to lack of evidence or because the allegations of witchcraft made against them were withdrawn.

These statistics bear out Norbert Schindler's thesis that the entire operation, while being rationalised as a holy struggle against Satanic forces, was in fact an elaborate mechanism to stamp out the growing vagrancy problem in the decades following upon the widespread population displacements of the Thirty Years War. The municipal alms lists of the times, Schindler says, convey a vivid picture of the motley crowd of minstrels and conjurers, physically and mentally handicapped, ex-convicts and political refugees, demobilised soldiers and journeymen who streamed along the highways and byways. The begging strategies became more and more aggressive, the gestures of threat more offensive, and the vagrants formed ever larger groups to lend more emphasis to their demands. This, he claims, is the reason why the settled population refused to come to the aid of the Salzburg victims. The gulf between them and the roving mendicants had become deep enough for the state to intervene without incurring the moral indignation of their subjects, even if the authorities did not yet dare to take explicit action against vagrancy as such but preferred to disguise it as witch-hunting.[7]

Not only did the settled population turn a blind eye to the plight of the Salzburg victims, but in theological and intellectual circles too a certain backlash against liberalisation seems to have set in. The critique of witch-hunting led by the Jesuits Adam Tanner and Friedrich Spee had died down with the abatement of the practice itself around 1630, but in the meantime voices, such as that of the Bavarian Court Chaplain Jeremias Drexel in 1637, were to be heard calling anew for the extermination of witches:

> Hier rufe ich so laut ich kann und auf göttliches Geheiß zu den Bischöfen, Herren, Fürsten, Königen: Lasset die Zauberer nicht am Leben. Mit Feuer und Schwert muß diese entsetzliche Pest ausgerottet werden. Ausgerissen muß dieses Unkraut werden, daß es nicht in übergroßer Fruchtbarkeit emporschieße, wie wir es leider sehen und beklagen. Aufgeräumt soll werden mit den Gottlosen, daß die Pest nicht weitergreift, brennen sollen die Aufrührer Gottes, damit sie nicht das Reich des Teufels auf der Erde verbreiten.[8]

> [Here I call as loudly as I can, and at God's command, to the bishops, lords, princes, kings: do not suffer the magicians to live. This terrible plague must be exterminated with fire and sword. These weeds must be torn out, lest they flourish in great fruitfulness, as, alas, we see and lament. An end must be made of the godless, that the plague may not spread; the rebels against God shall burn, lest they extend the empire of the Devil on earth.]

The fact that the Catholic and Protestant denominations could interrupt their mutual sniping and willingly close ranks in the face of this supposed threat is demonstrated by the treatise *Die gebrochene Macht der Finsterniß* ('The Power of Darkness Broken') published in 1687 in Augsburg by the Protestant theologian Theophil Spitzel in unquestioning approval of the 'Zauberer-Jackl' Trials. He reports the bizarre confessions of the 'malefactors' of Salzburg as if they were descriptions of factual occurrences, using the quotative subjunctive only in the last three sentences:

> Wie sie dann ohne vorhergegangene H. Beicht, zu zwey oder mehr mahlen gleich auf oder nach einander, in dieser und jener Kirchen die Hochheil. Hostiam in den Mund empfangen, aber unvermerckt des Priesters und der Umstehenden gleich wieder heraus und in die Schneitz-Tuchl gethan, mit sich in obige Au getragen, daselbst auf Anstifften des Zauber-Jaeggls und Teufels mit dem Messer darein gestochen, bis das Blut haeuffig heraus geflossen, wobei sie dann die allerschaendlichste Gottes-Laesterung heraus gestossen, so ich hier zu wiederholen billig grosse Scheu und Bedencken trage, die H. Hostiam haben sie auch zu Zeiten in denen s.h. Schuhen oder wohl gar in denen *partibus posterioribus* auf die Hexen-Taentze getragen, allwo sie und andere ihres gleichen vorderst dem Satan, so auf einem hohen Thron gesessen, tieffe Reverenz gemacht, ihren Gott und Herrn genennet, die Fuesse und den Hindern gekuesset, angebetet, und darauf die dahin gefuehrte Hostiam mit Messern und zugespitzten Hoeltzlin gestochen, darauf in das Koth eingegraben, und im Unflath liegen lassen. Hernach haben sie nach wiederholten abscheulichen Gottes-Laestrungen ihre Kurtzweilen angefangen, viel Tische seyen mit Speisen von Gesottenem und Gebratenem besetzt, und sie vom besten Wein tractiret worden etc. Nach dem Essen haetten sie mit einander, unde zwar ein jeder mit seiner Liebhaberin getantzet, bald aber auf die Seite gegangen, und mit denen Teufeln als ihren vermeynten Liebhabern die Unzucht *etiam inversa venere* getrieben, in welcher schaendlichen Vermischung sie bald *incubos* bald *succubos* vertreten etc. Zu Belohn- und Vergeltung dieses Gehorsams habe ihnen der Teufel ein graues Pulver zum Wettermachen und ein schwartzes zum Leut und Vieh toedten oder kruemmen verehrt.[9]

> [Without previously making confession, they received the sacred host in their mouths, two or more times in succession, in this or that church, but immediately, unseen by the priest or the other people present, spat it out into a handkerchief, took it to the above-mentioned meadow, and there, at the urging of Zauber-Jackl and the Devil, stabbed it with a knife until the blood streamed out, and uttered the most scandalous blasphemy, which I dare not repeat here. Sometimes they took the host in their shoes or even in their private parts to the witches' dances, where they and others of their kind first bowed down before Satan, who was seated on a high throne, kissed his feet and his bottom, worshipped him, and then stabbed the host with knives and sharpened pieces of wood, buried it in excrement, and left it lying in filth. Thereupon, after repeated abominable blasphemies, they began their pastimes; it is said that many tables were laden with

boiled and roast food, and they were served with the best wine, etc. After the meal it is said that they danced, each with his lover, but soon they went aside and engaged in perverted sexual activities with the devils as their supposed lovers, in which scandalous commingling the devils were sometimes on top as *incubi*, sometimes underneath as *succubi*. As a reward and return for their obedience, it is said that the Devil presented them with grey powder for raising storms and black powder for killing or injuring people and cattle.]

The accusations of perverted sexual acts can be adequately explained by modern psychology in terms of the phenomenon of projection, that is, the transference of one's own unadmitted and unactualised fantasies on to a communally selected scapegoat group. The accusation of magical interference with the weather had more concrete economic connotations and was also used by Jeremias Drexel as perceptible evidence of witchcraft:

> Daß sich im christlichen Staate Zauberer und Hexen, die schlimmsten Teufelsdiener, finden und zwar in nicht geringer Anzahl, ist ein derartiges Uebel, daß es einigen unglaublich erscheint. Aber die Wirklichkeit spricht. Unberechenbarer Schaden an den Saaten, am Vieh, an den Menschen legt Zeugnis dafür ab.[10]

> [That magicians and witches, the worst servants of the Devil, are to be found in a Christian state, and moreover in no small numbers, is such an evil that to some it appears incredible. But the facts speak for themselves. It is attested by the incalculable damage done to crops, cattle, and human beings.]

But just as the medieval ignorance of bacteriology had led people to conclude that the plague resulted from the Jews poisoning the wells, so the lack of knowledge about meteorology during the general climatic deterioration in the late seventeenth century (the 'Little Ice Age'[11]) caused the peasant population to invent witches as the source of crop failure and weather damage so as to be able to canalise and compensate for their own anxieties by taking out their frustrations on the target group. Once the accusation had been formulated, it became institutionalised as a stock response to freak weather or unexpected sicknesses.

Such *a posteriori* interpretations, however, do not explain the curious fact that some of the victims in Salzburg seemed eager to substantiate or even surpass the prosecutors' worst suspicions with regard to magic spells cast upon humans as well as intercourse with demons. Wolfgang Behringer ascribes this to the youthfulness of the accused persons, pointing out that they made every imaginable confession even without being tortured by simply relating their personal superstitions and fancies.[12] Meinrad Pizzinini sees an explanation in the method of interrogation: it was only a question of time, he says, before the accused confessed under pressure of suggestive questions combined with the threat or actual use of torture.[13] Norbert Schindler adds that the reputation of having magical powers was exploited by the vagrants to extort favours from the settled population in an increasingly abrasive confrontation, and that notoriety even became their badge of honour and source of group identity. The witch-hunters, he writes, treated the beggars in a manner that corresponded to their own self-image, which explains the astonishing and seemingly suicidal readiness of many defendants to assume the role offered to them by the authorities or even to outdo it by means of extravagant self-accusations. It was in this spine-chilling process of self-stylisation and self-denigration, he says, that the court found its 'proofs' while the beggars found the very social recognition that they missed in their daily lives.[14]

In *Die Kinder des Teufels* the figural constellation of the dramatis personae underscores from the start the social polarisation which, according to Wolfgang Behringer, had been becoming more and more prevalent in Central Europe since the late sixteenth century.[15] On the one hand there are the Court Councillor and his scribe with their titular apparatus, 'deputierter Almosen- und Hexenkommissar' Dr Sebastian Zillner and 'hochfürstlicher Taxator-Adjunkt' Gregori Finsterwalder, who both use a highly depersonalised and Latinised officialese, and on the other hand the eight young beggars, 'gewiefte Plauderer und freche Rotzlöffel',[16] whose nicknames already signal their social alienation and degradation. 'Fetzen-Leni' is so called because she clothes herself in rags bought from the gypsies, 'Stadtschmeißer' because he has so often been thrown out of town by the beadles. Their outsider role is exacerbated by their various handicaps: 'Dreckstierer' is so named because he is suffering from wryneck, 'der krumme Veitl' has a misshapen foot, Michl is blind, Dofferl is 'deppert' ('daft'), Dionysus is epileptic and has the mange, Andree Mayer has scabies. Few of the 'Malefikanten' know their own age; three of them have no surnames; Dionysus knows nothing of his mother and cannot find his father; Andree's mother died early, his father hanged himself, and he knows nothing of his siblings, except that a brother was shot dead. The torturer and executioner Moritz Ehegartner, as a former knacker and distant relative of 'Zauberer-Jackl', has ironically close ties with the underclass which he is employed to exterminate, a fact which accounts psychologically for his need to set himself apart from the victims through gratuitous brutality. 'Ich bin ein getreulicher Freimann! Ich würde meine eigene Mutter verbrennen! Wenn es sein muß!' (I am a loyal freeman! I would burn my own mother if I had to!) (*Die Kinder des Teufels*, p. 54).

The text of the play is preceded by a note corroborating the documentary nature of the victims' outlandish statements: 'Die Geständnisse der Angeklagten sind authentisch und im Hauptstaatsarchiv München sowie im Salzburger Landesarchiv einsehbar' (The defendants' confessions are authentic and may be inspected in the Main State Archive at Munich and in the local archive at Salzburg) (p. 8). As Caroline Hohmann says, the manipulated and tormented children counter the nightmarish repression with cryptic phantasms which are their ultimate psychic refuge. These outcasts behave as they are expected to, and the most over-zealous confession is nothing other than the mirror image of the system that sets out to eliminate them.[17] The twelve-year-old Dionysus smiles while telling of a meeting with the Devil in the shape of a green huntsman on a black steed, and begins to glow when recounting the blasphemies which the Devil has compelled him to utter, but betrays his waiflike ingenuousness when describing the rewards promised for so doing: 'Essen! Trinken! Ein dickes Federbett! Hunderttausend Taler!' ('Eating! Drinking! A thick feather-bed! A hundred thousand thaler!') (p. 81). And Veit wistfully describes the Witches' Sabbath in terms of a splendid feast: 'Fleisch und Bratwürste und Strauben und, und (*es fällt ihm nichts mehr ein*) Krapfennudeln und Butterzipf und alles, alles!' (Meat and sausage and dumplings and, and [*he runs out of ideas*] doughnuts and butter pastry and absolutely everything!) (p. 81). Both Dionysus' and Veit's alleged acts of magic amount to nothing more than the revenge fantasies of humiliated down-and-outs, Dionysus claiming to be able to create mice to ruin the grain of miserly farmers, and Veit to cripple people who have jeered at his deformity: 'Wer mich einen krummen Hund heißt, der soll selber erkrummen!' (If anyone calls me a crippled dog, he'll be crippled himself!) (p. 40).

The readiness to confess is partially due to the intentionally misleading signals transmitted by the commissioner. While Dionysus advises the other prisoners to reveal what they know, or think they know, of Jackl ('Wenn man ihnen erzählt, was der Jackl kann, dann geben sie Ruh!' (If you tell them what Jackl can do, they'll leave you alone!) (p. 35), Veit comes to the opposite conclusion: 'Wer zugibt, daß er den Jackl kennt, der ist dran!' (If you admit you know Jackl, you've had it!) (p. 56). The commissioner uses the techniques of modern police interrogation by switching abruptly from harmless banter and feigned concern to staccato-like grilling, and tricks the defendants by means of duplicitous promises into denouncing one another. Veit's 'reward' for co-operation by incriminating his fellow-beggars is that he will be garrotted before being burnt at the stake. The commissioner forces confessions of incest and bestiality out of Dionysus and his eight-year-old sister Lisl by threatening them with flogging or the thumb-screw and by putting words into their mouths. After an aroused and unvarnished interrogation ('Und Ihr habt es alle mit der Kuh getrieben, nicht wahr?' [And you've all done it with the cow, haven't you?] p. 48) he reverts to his customary sang-froid in his report, using the rhetorical camouflage of Latin to conceal any personal interest in the alleged acts:

> Schluß für heute! (*Zum Schreiber:*) Gütliches Examen, keine Zwischenfälle! Mitteilung an die Kollegen: Da in progressu examinis sich indicia hervortun ratione sodomiae cum bestiis commissae, sollen sie ihre Fragebögen dahingehend reformieren! (p. 50)
>
> [That's enough for today! (*To the scribe:*) A kindly interrogation with no incidents! Information for colleagues: as the course of the inquiry has revealed signs of sodomy committed with animals, they are to revise their lists of questions accordingly!]

Only the worldly-wise seventeen-year-old 'Fetzen-Leni' seems to see through the commissioner's veneer of self-righteousness, taunting him with lurid descriptions of intercourse with the Devil and causing him to lose his composure completely by recommending cunnilingus with his wife. When he persists in interrogating her, she replies insinuatingly: 'Wollt Ihr Euch das wirklich antun? Mir scheint, es regt Euch zu sehr auf!' (Do you really want to do this to yourself? I think it's getting you too excited!) (p. 81). And when coming to the description of the sex orgies of the witches' sabbath, she pauses and asks probingly: 'Ihr könnt Euch das nicht vorstellen! Oder doch?' (You can't imagine it. Or can you?) (p. 82). She alone turns the tables on the interrogator, if only for a brief moment making him the object of moral scrutiny and implication, and being made to suffer all the more for it. After having her arms pulled out of their sockets on the rack, the commissioner condemns her to such a horrific form of execution that the Archbishop of Salzburg commutes the sentence in the manner described above:

> Magdalena Pichlerin, ich hab für dich (*schaut auf Papier*) Schleifung zur Richtstatt, Schneidung von Riemen aus deinem Leib und lebendige Verbrennung mit Anhängung eines Pulversackes beantragt! Seine hochfürstliche Gnaden, der Erzbischof und Landesherr, hat dir in seiner üblichen Güte die Schleifung und Riemenschneidung erlassen und hat verfügt, daß du nur drei Zwicke mit der glühenden Zange erhältst, und zwar einen in den Oberarm, einen in die Brust, einen in die Wange! (p. 108)

> [Magdalena Pichlerin, I have requested the following punishment for you (*looks at paper*): you shall be dragged to the place of execution, the skin shall be flayed from your body, and you shall be burnt alive with a bag of gunpowder attached to you! His Princely Grace, the Archbishop and ruler of our country, has in his customary kindness let you off the dragging and flaying and has decreed that you shall only be pinched three times with red-hot tongs, once in the upper arm, once in the breast, once in the cheek!]

Leni also demonstrates insight into the true nature of the trials when she says: 'Mein Urteil war schon gesprochen, bevor ich auf die Welt kam!' (My sentence was pronounced even before I was born!) (p. 107). In an exchange between the 'Freimann', the commissioner and the scribe, it takes the intellectually least sophisticated and accordingly least prevaricatory executioner to betray the blunt truth about the purpose of the trials:

FREIMANN:	[...] Alle in eine Grube, und Pech drüber und anzünden! Fertig! – So löst man das Bettlerproblem! So und nicht anders! Jedenfalls nicht mit so einem kostspieligen Prozeß!
KOMMISSAR:	Herr Freimann! Wollt Ihr damit andeuten, der Zweck dieses Prozesses sei die Bettlerausrottung?
FREIMANN:	Was sonst?
KOMMISSAR:	Es geht hier um die Bekämpfung einer Teufelsverschwörung! Habt Ihr das nicht begriffen?
FREIMANN:	Ich begreife mehr als Ihr glaubt, Herr Kommissar!
SCHREIBER:	Also bitte, Freimann! Wenn der Herr Hofrat schon so

vornehm ist und Euch nicht das Maul verbietet, dann tu ich es! (p. 94)

[FREEMAN: Throw them all into a pit, add pitch and set it alight! There you are! That's how to solve the problem of beggars! Just like that! Not by such an expensive trial, at any rate!
COMMISSIONER: Freeman! Are you suggesting that the purpose of this trial is the extermination of beggars?
FREEMAN: What else?
COMMISSIONER: What we're doing here is fighting against a conspiracy with the Devil! Haven't you understood that?
FREEMAN: I understand more than you think, Commissioner!
SCRIBE: Please, freeman! If the Counsellor is too grand to make you hold your tongue, then I'll do it!]

The Salzburg trials marked less the end of the Middle Ages than the beginning of modern times and the 'Big Brother' State. Although the commissioner starts the interrogation by blessing himself, utilises the jargon of demonology and surrounds himself with ecclesiastical paraphernalia, he is really the secular representative of the reasons of state of Early Absolutism in its effort to establish total 'rational' control by registering all its citizens, making sure that they are productive, and keeping the ungovernable at bay.

The parallels with the twentieth century hardly need to be pointed out. The scribe, who in the course of the play becomes more and more concealed behind the growing stacks of files on his desk and is punctilious with regard to the letter of the law, is the prototype of the latter-day 'Schreibtischtäter', doing his finger exercises while the children are being tortured in the chamber next door. But the analogies are not confined to the totalitarian systems of yesteryear. When *Die Kinder des Teufels* was first performed in the Theater der Jugend, Munich, in May 1989, the programme notes drew a parallel between the economic crisis towards the end of the seventeenth century, which sought its scapegoats among the very poor, and the economic stagnation at the beginning of the 1980s with the subsequent repatriation of 'guest workers' and those seeking political asylum.[18] And indeed one can hardly help thinking of recent attempts to exclude 'economic migrants' from Europe when the commissioner has his scribe write to the Inner Austrian government of Graz:

Und sie sollen dafür – wir bitten höflichst – jenes Gesindel zurücktreiben, das aus dem Süden kommt und durch die Steiermark auf Salzburg loszieht! (p. 29)

[And we humbly request them to repel the rabble from the South that is moving through Styria towards Salzburg!]

T. E. Bourke

Notes

1. Magdalena Stöckler of 'Pro Senectute Österreich', whose report appeared in Hilarion Petzold (ed.), *Arbeit mit alten Menschen* (Vienna, 1985).
2. Felix Mitterer, *Stigma, Eine Passion* (Feldafing, 1983), p. 95.
3. See Francis Russell, *A Concise History of Germany* (London, 1973), p. 117.
4. Mitterer, 'Anmerkungen zum Stück', in Mitterer, *Kein schöner Land. Ein Theaterstück und sein historischer Hintergrund* (Innsbruck, 1987), p. 91.
5. Heinz Nagl, 'Der Zauberer-Jackl-Prozeß im Erzstift Salzburg 1675–1690', in Mitterer, *Die Kinder des Teufels. Ein Theaterstück und sein historischer Hintergrund* (Innsbruck, 1989), p. 115.
6. In *Die Kinder des Teufels*, pp. 120–33.
7. Norbert Schindler, 'Die Entstehung der Unbarmherzigkeit. Zur Kultur der Salzburger Bettler am Ende des 17. Jahrhunderts', in *Die Kinder des Teufels*, pp. 137–8.
8. Jeremias Drexel, 'Lasset die Zauberer nicht am Leben!', in Wolfgang Behringer (ed.), *Hexen und Hexenprozesse in Deutschland* (Munich, 1988), p. 422.
9. Theophil Spitzel, 'Die gebrochene Macht der Finsterniß', in Behringer, p. 426.
10. Drexel, in Behringer, p. 422.
11. See Hartmut Lehmann, 'Frömmigkeitsgeschichtliche Auswirkungen der "Kleinen Eiszeit"', in Wolfgang Schneider (ed.), *Volksreligiosität in der modernen Sozialgeschichte* (Göttingen, 1986), pp. 31–51.
12. Behringer, p. 403.
13. Meinrad Pizzinini, 'Der Hexenwahn. Ursachen – Folgen – Hintergründe', in *Die Kinder des Teufels*, p. 152.
14. Schindler, p. 144.
15. Behringer, p. 129.
16. Christine Dössel, 'Der Zauberer-Jackl lebt noch', *Süddeutsche Zeitung*, 11 April 1989.
17. Caroline Hohmann, 'Kreuz aus Eis', *Die Deutsche Bühne* (1989), vol. 6.
18. See Barbara Schmitz-Burckhardt, 'Kinder des Teufels', *Frankfurter Rundschau*, 12 May 1989.

Jelinek's Ibsen: 'Noras' Past and Present

Allyson Fiddler

Critical reaction to Elfriede Jelinek's first play, *Was geschah, nachdem Nora ihren Mann verlassen hatte oder Stützen der Gesellschaften (What Happened After Nora Left Her Husband or The Pillars of Societies)* can in no way be compared to the 'firestorm of critical debate and dissent' which met the world première of Henrik Ibsen's *A Doll's House* (Copenhagen, 1879), the drama which provides the starting-point for Jelinek's 1977 sequel.[1] For a writer whose national and international reputation has largely, and unjustifiably, been the result of extensive controversy – her play *Burgtheater* (1985) assured her the name of 'Nestbeschmutzer' within Austria, and her novel *Lust* (1989) more recently gained her bestseller status with its advertised claim to be 'feminine' pornography – Jelinek's first play is almost notable because of its scandal-free reception.[2] Partly as a result of this and partly because of the mostly negative reviews which greeted its première, it has not received the critical attention it deserves.

Against dismissive claims that *Nora* is merely a programmatic 'Lehrstück', 'ein Lehrstück wie aus dem Lehrbuch, fast leer inzwischen' ('a didactic play, straight out of a textbook and with nothing between the covers'),[3] this essay will argue that Jelinek's theatrical début should be accorded greater importance in Jelinek studies since it presents at an early stage key components of the author's dramatic technique and political preoccupations. Firstly, the use of montage, the definitive characteristic of both Jelinek's dramatic and narrative technique, is prevalent in *Nora* and can be seen to offer interesting interpretive perspectives. Secondly, the 'woman question' is given a powerful new political and arguably also a contemporary dimension as the liberal humanist context of Ibsen's marital drama is exploded and replaced by an examination of material issues such as women's work, solidarity between women and their function as sexual commodities. Thirdly, the setting of Jelinek's play – 1920s Germany – is chosen by the author in order to imply a symbiosis between patriarchal capitalism and fascism, a connection which is established in a somewhat piecemeal and symbolic fashion. Jelinek's greatest achievement in *Nora* is that, in engaging with Ibsen as her intertext, she produces a complex discussion of feminist politics. While clearly serving to show how women are manipulated by the workings of capital, the play also functions as a critical confrontation with certain commonly accepted feminist axioms. To understand these layers of the text, a reading of *Nora* must be sensitive to its historical and political context.

The idea of writing such a sequel is not a new one. Those familiar with the reception of Ibsen's *A Doll's House* will know that virtually as soon as his play had been premièred, all manner of sequels appeared which sought to 'put right' what was seen as the morally unacceptable or psychologically implausible ending of Ibsen's drama. With titles such as *Das Wunderbarste oder Der 4. Akt von 'Ein Puppenheim'* (*The Most Wonderful Thing; or, the Fourth Act of 'A Doll's House'*) and *Nora's Return: A Sequel to 'The Doll's House of Henrik Ibsen'*, these versions had Nora either deciding that she could not bring herself to abandon her children and husband or returning to repent having done so.[4] Jelinek is thus not the first playwright to opt for a cyclical structure for her sequel, neither is she the only one to have placed her protagonist within the framework of Marxist debate: the declared intention of the Danish playwright Ernst Bruun Olsen, with his 1968 treatment of this material *Wohin ging Nora, als sie hinausging?* (*'Where did Nora go when she went out?'*), was to make 'aus dem Protest Noras gegen die bürgerliche Ehe, gegen die verlogenen Moralkategorien der bürgerlichen Gesellschaft eine revolutionäre Tat gegen die Klassengesellschaft' ('to take Nora's protest against the bourgeois institution of marriage and against the deceitful moral categories of bourgeois society, and make of it a revolutionary act against class society'). Angelika Gundlach could not have been more wrong, however, when she said of Olsen's version that it was 'wohl die letzte Überlegung zu diesem Thema' ('probably the last word on this subject').[5] The late 1970s saw two German-language sequels by women playwrights: Jelinek's own, and a 'backlash' alternative by the anti-feminist Esther Vilar, entitled *Helmer oder Ein Puppenheim* (*Helmer; or, a Doll's House*), which shows Helmer as a sensitive and caring 'Aussteiger'[6] who gives up his job to look after his son and refuses to return him to a hysterical and callous mother who now has to provide the alimony. Premièred in Graz as part of the 'Steirischer Herbst' festival of 1979, Jelinek's play was then published in book form in 1980 and again in 1984. It was also published in a much modified and abridged radio play version in 1982.[7]

Having left her bank director husband, Torvald Helmer, Jelinek's Nora sets out into the big wide world to get a job. But with no formal education or references, her idea of embarking on a 'career' is too optimistic and she lands herself a job on the conveyor belt of a factory. Things at the factory do not turn out as Nora had expected; she decides that she is above the mechanical work she is required to do and that she will return to her children: 'Ich halte es hier nicht aus. ich [sic] muß in eine Umgebung gehen, wo meine Kinder auf mich warten. Nur mehr für die Kleinen will ich jetzt leben und so meinen Fehler wieder gutmachen' ('I can't stand it here. I must go to a place where my children are waiting for me. I shall make amends and live only for them from now on') (*Nora*, p. 15). Nora rejects the amorous advances of the lowly foreman: 'Ich liebe dich, Nora. Ich weiß von dem Augenblick an, da ich merkte, daß du das Beste bist, was ich im Moment erreichen kann, daß ich dich liebe' ('I love you, Nora. I know that I love you, I've known from the moment I realised that you're the best thing I can currently hope to achieve') (*Nora*, p. 12), only to succumb to those of the business magnate Konsul Weygang, who is attracted to her during a tour of the factory premises. He is entertained with some songs from the firm's choir – Nora sings the solo – and with a tarantella, which is also performed by Nora. Lured by Weygang's money and by the concomitant prospect of social betterment, Nora does not return home, but instead becomes Weygang's mistress. She is later persuaded to disguise herself and employ her sexual wiles on her ex-husband Helmer, who holds valuable business information of use to the Konsul. Helmer is director of Conti-Bank, the main shareholder of the company Nora had been working for and which the Konsul wishes to purchase. (The 1992 production explained that he wished to build a nuclear power station on the site.) In their sado-masochistic encounter Nora whips Helmer until he divulges the fact that he has been boosting the saleable value of the land by spreading rumours that a railway line is to be built through the area. At this point Nora removes her mask and reveals her identity to Helmer.

Nora then pays a brief visit to the factory but fails to apprise her ex-colleagues of the speculation deals concerning their company which will result in its closure and in the loss of their jobs. She returns to Weygang, who, having no further use for her – she has provided him with the information he needed and has lost her sexual attractiveness for him – leaves her free to return to her husband. She is forced to take this step after an unsuccessful attempt at securing a living by prostitution. Weygang has acted swiftly, buying the piece of land in question, exposing Helmer's role in the scandal and causing him to lose his job at the bank. Nora's feeble threats to bribe him, therefore, are naive: 'Nora: Ich erpresse dich mit der Gewerkschaft, der Presse und nicht zuletzt mit dem Aufsichtsrat der Conti-Bank. [...] Weygang: Hörst du mir überhaupt zu? Ich sage, daß ich die in Frage stehenden Liegenschaften bereits gekauft habe. Helmer ist der Blöde' ('Nora: I'll use the union, the press and, what's more, the board of directors of Conti-Bank to blackmail you. Weygang: Are you listening to me at all? I tell you, I've already bought the property in question. Helmer is the idiot') (*Nora*, p. 56). Weygang provides the Helmers with a small textiles shop and the play closes with the couple listening to the news of a fire which has razed to the ground the factory which Weygang had bought. Weygang will claim on his insurance and is now free to develop the land as he chooses. The curtain falls on Helmer insisting that Nora leave the radio on: the fascist marching music is very much to her husband's liking.

That Ibsen is the key source of Elfriede Jelinek's montage is obvious from her title, which mimics two of Henrik Ibsen's: *Nora oder Ein Puppenheim* and *Die Stützen der Gesellschaft* (*The Pillars of Society*). Jelinek has given societ*ies* in the plural in order to suggest the double meaning of society and company or firm, as implied by the German *Gesellschaft*. Most of Jelinek's characters are taken from the former, but Consul Bernick of *The Pillars of Society* is transmogrified into Consul Weygang. The number of quotations and references which have been 'lifted' from the Ibsen original are too numerous to list in full. They include the tarantella dance and Helmer's reaction to it. Helmer's 'Why, Nora dear, you're dancing as if it were a matter of life or death' (*A Doll's House*, p. 106) becomes Weygang's 'Du tanzest ja, als ginge es um Leben und Tod' ('But you're dancing as if it were a matter of life or death') (*Nora*, p. 20). Even Nora's goal of self-liberation and personal fulfilment, 'I believe that before all else I am a human being, just as much as you are – or at least that I should try to become one' (*A Doll's House*, p. 147), is echoed in Jelinek's version, where Nora proclaims to her prospective employer what is, in Jelinek's new context, a naive and apolitical goal: 'Das Wichtigste ist, daß ich ein Mensch werde' ('The most important thing is that I become a human being') (*Nora*, p. 8).

It is not just textual passages which are 'quoted' by Jelinek but ideas, too, which find their way into her play in a transmuted form. For example, Helmer admits to his wife that he sometimes secretly wishes she were threatened by some danger, so that he could protect her (*A Doll's House*, p. 133). In Jelinek, the women who work in the factory long to have such a man and contemplate the idea of deliberately injuring themselves in the machinery in order to capture the attention of some caring, well-to-do man (*Nora*, pp. 22–3). Such men are not much in evidence on the shop floor, however. It is possible that Jelinek's montage method might have deliberately turned the teasing rebuke of Dr Rank by Nora – she hits him lightly round the head with her silk stockings – into the very 'real' whipping of Helmer in the sado-masochistic scene (scene 13, *Nora*). To cite one last example, the heart of the business intrigue lies in the rumour surrounding the railway line, an idea which comes from Ibsen's *The Pillars of Society*, which is explicitly acknowledged in Jelinek: 'Bei der Spekulation handelt sich's um eine Eisenbahnlinie wie in dem Stück *Stützen der Gesellschaft*, auch von Ibsen' ('The speculation is all about a railway line, like in *The Pillars of Society*') (*Nora*, p. 32).

Such pointers are not merely intended for those who would otherwise be unaware of these quotations. As one of the many variants of the 'alienation technique' employed in order to stress the constructed and fictional nature of the stage action, they constitute a deliberate part of Jelinek's aesthetic strategy. All of Jelinek's plays incorporate material from other sources. Sometimes she provides a list of sources which she has used in her montage, as in *Clara S*; sometimes she acknowledges that she has employed this technique and leaves it to her critics to discover her sources, as is the case with *Burgtheater*.[8] This 'meta-theatrical' element is stressed more in the stage version than in the radio version of *Nora*. Nora's opening lines in the former include: 'Ich bin Nora aus dem gleichnamigen Stück von Ibsen' ('I am Nora, from Ibsen's play of the same name') (*Nora*, p. 7). In the radio play, Nora does not claim to *be* Ibsen's Nora but is merely recognised by Weygang as having the same name as Ibsen's character (*Frauenhörspiele*, p. 178). But it is not only Ibsen who is quoted in this new context: Nora reads out loud from Freud and cites both Hitler and Mussolini on gender-related subjects. Jelinek has also acknowledged the use of management and business magazines in her montage. This provides one of the main sources of humour in the play since she has her characters use the jargon of capitalist economics when they speak about love and use the language of love when describing business plans: 'Das Kapital ist jedoch von allergrößter Schönheit. Nicht einmal Vermehrung beeinträchtigt seinen hervorragenden Wuchs' ('Capital, however, is of the utmost beauty. Not even multiplication detracts from its excellent stature') (*Nora*, p. 26).[9] The growth of capital can only be a 'beautiful' thing, it would seem, but a woman 'growing' can only mean either that she is getting fat, or that she is pregnant, in either case 'amounting' to a decrease in attractiveness.

Although an understanding and enjoyment of *Nora* are fully possible with no prior knowledge of Ibsen's plays, it is clear that these quotations are more than simply 'raisins in the cake' and that a structural analysis of the play cannot ignore them.[10] Such an analysis is beyond the scope of the present essay and has been undertaken elsewhere.[11] Before looking more closely at the political context of Jelinek's play, however, it is useful to expose some aesthetic and political points of comparison regarding these two texts. Ibsen's Naturalist exploration of Nora's situation was concerned to present real people in all their psychological depth: '"Ich schreibe keine Rollen, ich schildere Menschen", hatte Ibsen immer betont und sich geweigert, seine Figuren zu Sprachrohren irgendeiner politischen Richtung erklären zu lassen' ('"I don't write roles, I portray people", Ibsen always stressed, refusing to have his figures proclaimed as mouth pieces for any political orientation').[12] Various lobbies had tried to cast Ibsen's play as a manifestation or proof of their ideas, most persuasively, of course, the women's movement. Both the claim that he was furthering the women's cause and the appropriation of his ideas by the Social Democrats, who saw his play as presenting some of their own criticisms of the bourgeois state, were vehemently repudiated by Ibsen, and successive generations of Ibsen critics have taken him at his word, at least on the first of these counts. Joan Templeton, however, is one critic who endeavours to redress the de-gendering of *A Doll's House* by those who argue that Nora is something of an 'Every*man*': '... to say that Nora Helmer stands for the individual in search of his or her self, besides being a singularly unhelpful and platitudinous generalisation, is wrong, if not absurd. For it means that Nora's conflict has essentially nothing to do with her identity as a nineteenth-century married woman, a married woman, or a woman.'[13]

Remarkably, Elfriede Jelinek's play has been beset by exactly the same misunderstanding. At every opportunity Jelinek has stated her Marxist view of society and has tried to shake off the label of 'women's writing', or, more disparagingly in German, *Frauenliteratur*: 'Daß man mich [...] als Vertreterin von "Frauenliteratur" bezeichnet, kann ich nicht akzeptieren, obwohl ich meine, daß man sich der Frauen schon besonders annehmen muß' ('I cannot accept being described as a representative of "women's literature", although I do think that women deserve special attention'). In this interview with Josef-Hermann Sauter, she goes on to point out that 'wie man weiß, gibt es keinen Mann, der so arm, ausgebeutet und kaputt ist, daß er nicht noch jemanden hätte, der noch ärmer dran ist, nämlich seine Frau' ('as we know, there is no man who is so poor, so exploited and worn out that he doesn't have somebody else who is still worse off – his wife').[14] This is a feminist condition which Jelinek places on her Marxism: certainly she believes that class struggle and the fight against capitalism are prerequisites for women's emancipation and that this will not be an automatic consequence of a socialist society, but she is also aware that women are at present consistently worse off in all classes and societies. Her favourite dictum is in fact reiterated by one of the factory girls in *Nora*, who says: 'Es ist keiner so niedrig, daß er nicht noch etwas Niedrigeres hätte, seine Frau' ('nobody is so low that he doesn't have something even lower than himself – his wife') (*Nora*, p. 22).

In line with these general principles, Jelinek insists that her play is 'nicht so sehr ein ausschließlich feministisches, als vielmehr ein politisches Stück, ein

Stück übers Kapital' ('not so much an exclusively feminist play but rather a political one, a play about capital').[15] The distinction between political, on the one hand, and feminist, on the other, is indeed misleading, but it is not surprising that Jelinek has had to clarify her intentions, since *Nora* presents almost exclusively the oppression of *women*, both in the working and petty-bourgeois classes, using the 'Arbeiterinnen' ('women workers') and Nora respectively to exemplify these. The social situation of the 'Vorarbeiter' ('foreman') is not explored, and his lines focus entirely on Nora as an object of love and as a sexual commodity. But Jelinek does not present her female characters as somehow constituting a 'class' in their own right; the differences between Nora and her co-workers in terms of intellect and class background are made clear. As Evelyn Reed explains: 'to oppose women as a class against men as a class can only result in a diversion of the real class struggle.'[16] The original text was severely cut for both the Graz and Vienna scripts and the passages cut were mainly the longer and more overtly 'political' ones dealing with questions of capital. This produced a leaner play, but one which, despite Jelinek's description of it as a play about capital, now looks to be more about feminism than about class issues. In an interview on the eve of the March 1992 production in Vienna, Wolfgang Herles asked some of the actors whether they did not find Jelinek's critique of capitalism dated and therefore no longer credible. Their response to this indicated that this aspect had been cut severely enough for them not to have to consider it – 'Die Kapitalismuskritik ist weitgehend rausgestrichen' – and they had understood the battle of the sexes in exactly the way Jelinek had intended: 'Irgendwo spielt bei uns auch eine Kritik an der Frau sehr stark mit. Es kommen hier die Männer nicht sehr gut weg, aber die Frauen auch nicht. Nora ist nicht nur ein Opfer' ('The critique of capitalism has largely been cut. We think there's quite a strong criticism of women, too. The men come off pretty badly, but so do the women. Nora isn't only a victim').[17]

To return to Ibsen's aesthetic 'manifesto', 'Ich schreibe keine Rollen, ich schildere Menschen' ('I don't write roles, I portray people'), it may be seen that Jelinek's own is diametrically opposed to this. She openly calls her characters, or rather figures, 'Schablonen, Bedeutungsträger, nur Repräsentanten' ('stencils, conveyors of meaning, mere representatives'), and explains that this is part of her exaggerated, 'black and white' style. Acknowledging her indebtedness to Brecht she explains that this exaggeration is carried out so as to produce a sharper picture of reality and one which is thus easier to understand.[18] This is just one of the characteristics which Jelinek has borrowed from the Brechtian 'Lehrstück', with which her drama has been compared. Many of her characters bear generic names, and the main characters, although given individual names such as Nora, Weygang and Helmer, have a representative function, as do 'die Arbeiterinnen' or 'der Vorarbeiter'. Nora's self-introduction at the opening of the play, too, is reminiscent of the introductions by, for example, the 'Lehrer' ('teacher'), 'Ich bin der Lehrer' ('I am the teacher'), or by 'der junge Genosse' ('the young comrade'), 'Ich bin der Sekretär des Parteihauses' ('I am the secretary of the party headquarters') in *Der Jasager (He Who Said Yes)* and *Die Maßnahme (The Measures Taken)* respectively.[19] As in the original opening to Brecht's *Der*

Jelinek's Ibsen: 'Noras' Past and Present

Ozeanflug (*The Flight over the Ocean*), Jelinek's radio play, *Ballade von drei wichtigen Männern sowie dem Personenkreis um sie herum* (*The Ballad of Three Important Men as well as the Circle of People Around Them*), begins with Lindbergh introducing himself: 'My name is Charles Lindbergh'.[20] As in Brecht this is an 'epic' device, a barrier between the stage and the audience designed to alienate and to promote critical reflection.

In the most recent production of Jelinek's play in Vienna (premièred on 8 March 1992), a Brechtian-style narrator introduced each scene after playing a few discordant bars on her violin. In addition, the Volkstheater producer Emmy Werner used a wide range of songs to punctuate the text; while the desired effect may have been alienation, however, the result was far from being so. The songs were mostly well known – ranging from 'Somewhere over the Rainbow' and 'Maria' (from *West Side Story* but sung to the name Nora), to 'Tomorrow Belongs to Me' (*Cabaret*). Often these were only small snippets, or first phrases, and served less to disrupt the action than to make the audience laugh. It is doubtful whether the Viennese public picked up on the producer's cynical parody of media reality in these songs and it is more likely that they enjoyed them for the brief 'sing-along' opportunity they afforded.[21]

Whereas Brecht conceived the 'Lehrstück' as 'an instrument of political and moral (but also aesthetic) education, designed to help the performers come to terms, in various ways, with the kind of problem represented in the action of the plays', the political and moral education of the actors themselves is not an express part of Jelinek's aesthetic programme.[22] We have already seen that actors in the 1992 production reproduced more or less a Jelinekian understanding of the action. Petra Fahrnländer, however, who played Nora in the world première in Graz, had a very traditional understanding of gender roles and Jelinek's play did not help her to a more enlightened understanding: 'Emanzipiert? Was heißt das eigentlich? Sich gleichstellen mit dem männlichen Geschlecht? Das ist nicht möglich. Die Frau bekommt die Kinder, nicht der Mann' ('Emancipated? What does that actually mean? Being equal with the male sex? That's not possible. The woman has the children, not the man').[23]

Emmy Werner came up with a brilliant strategy to make the part of Nora itself alienating. By dividing it among five actresses, she made it difficult for the audience to identify with Nora as a character and ensured that the stress for both actresses and audience fell instead on the many different roles which she has to play. *Nora* takes on the feel of a 'Stationendrama' as the first actress departs as wife, the next allows herself to be seduced by Weygang, a different one again lives with him, a fourth becomes the 'Domina' torturer, a fifth turns to prostitution and the last 'Station', the return to wife and mother, is played once more by the first actress. For Sibylle Fritsch, this division emphasises the contemporary relevance of Jelinek's play: 'Nora '92: eine multiple Persönlichkeit – die Fließbandarbeiterin, die Geliebte, die Domina in schwarzer Reizwäsche und Lederstiefeln, die Nobelprostituierte, die Heimkehrerin schließlich als Mutter, Hausfrau und Textilhändlerin zugleich, die Schizophrenie der Postmoderne, die allen Frauen Flexibilität und Rollenvielfalt abverlangt' ('Nora 92: a multiple personality – production line worker, mistress, dominatrix in sexy black underwear and leather boots, high class prostitute, homecomer and finally mother, housewife and textiles dealer all in one. Such is the schizophrenia of the postmodern age, which demands flexibility and a variety of roles from all women.') Fritsch finds the 'class war' language of Jelinek's play old-fashioned but feels that the political realities of the 1990s breathe fresh life into the 'scheinbar abgedroschenen Thesen von der Unterdrückung der Frauen durch Kapitalismus und Patriarchat' ('seemingly hackneyed theories of the oppression of women by capitalism and patriarchy').[24]

Inspired by the political atmosphere of the 1970s, set in the 1920s and performed again, after a gap of eleven years, in the 1990s: just what are the temporal references in Jelinek's play and what function do they fulfil? The present-tense allusions to Hitler and Mussolini as men whose ideas were influencing political thought at the time are obvious references, as are the 'Anklänge an den frühen deutschen Faschismus' ('musical reminders of early German fascism') (*Nora*, p. 62). The anti-Socialist laws were in force in the lifetime of Jelinek's workers, it would seem. Eva, the brightest of the working women, and possibly Jelinek's only positive (i.e. politically aware) figure, reminds them of the books that were banned during this time: 'Erinnert ihr euch noch an die Zeit der Sozialistengesetze? Bebels *Frau und der Sozialismus* und das *Kapital* von Karl Marx wurden als staatsfeindlich verboten' ('Do you still recall the days of the anti-Socialist laws? Bebel's *Women and Socialism* and Karl Marx's *Capital* were banned as subversive literature by the government') (*Nora*, p. 53). She also reminds them of comrades who died in the May Day demonstrations (*Nora*, p. 51). But the workers are not to be infected by Eva's cynicism and show a blind faith in the 'social democracy' (of Weimar) when she tries to convince them that there is substance in the rumoured closure of the factory (*Nora*, p. 49). Her prophecies do nevertheless seem a little before their time as she warns her colleagues – in the 1920s – that they will have to provide 'Gold für Eisen, dann Kinder für den Frontkampf' ('Gold for iron and then children for the front line') (*Nora*, p. 11).

In the radio play version, the 'Arbeiterinnen' protest 'Noch haben wir das Recht auf Nichtarbeit nicht errungen' ('We haven't yet won the right not to work') (*Frauenhörspiele*, p. 173), a comment which may seem at first sight to be merely a flippant remark, reversing the familiar feminist preoccupation with women's employment. However, when one considers that 'in 1915 the ADF [Allgemeiner Deutscher Frauenverein] ('General German Women's Association') [...] switched its sixty-year commitment to protective legislation and the right to work to "protection from work"', the workers' bourgeois aspirations seem more plausible.[25]

The above are just some of the allusions which situate the political context of the play. Some of the allusions are common knowledge and will be recognised by the audience. Some specific ones, however, such as the reference to Hugo Stinnes, whom Weygang admires for his 'Zusammenschluß des Elektrizitäts-Trusts von Siemens-Schuckert mit den Kohle- und Eisenzufuhren der Rheinelbe zu diesem Superkartell' ('joining the Siemens-Schuckert electricity trust and the Rheinelbe coal and iron supplies to make that super-cartel')

(*Frauenhörspiele*, p. 176), will be more likely not to be familiar. The point, with all these references, is to recreate a 1920s atmosphere of financial intrigue. Industry in this period was becoming increasingly concentrated in the hands of large state monopolies and it was quite usual for bankers to hold government positions and thus be extremely instrumental in the buying, selling and expansion of such industrial concerns. In addition, they would have played a crucial role in the securing of American loans for allocation to large companies.[26]

Setting the play in modern dress, as happened in the 1979 production, clearly makes a nonsense of such culturally and temporally specific references. Critics have pointed out that some of Jelinek's characters are based on well-known businessmen, a fact which underlines the possible contemporary relevance of her play. Gerald Grassl suggests this is the reason why, initially, no West German theatre was interested in staging Elfriede Jelinek's play: 'Obwohl Elfriede Jelinek das Stück im Auftrag eines BRD-Verlags geschrieben hatte, konnte es bisher in keinem Theater der Bundesrepublik placiert werden, da Wirtschaftsmagnate, die im Stück vorkommen, zu gewissen realen Mächtigen "zu starke Ähnlichkeiten" hätten' ('although Elfriede Jelinek wrote the play for a West German publisher, up until now no West German theatre has come forward to produce it, since the business tycoons in the play bear "such striking similarities" to certain real-life power-brokers').[27] One of the men has been identified as Hanns-Martin Schleyer, the president of the West German Federation of Industries, and of the Employers' Federation, who was taken hostage in September 1977 by the Red Army Faction and brutally murdered two weeks later. Given the tip by the playwright herself in the programme leaflet, Lothar Sträter completes the detective work but is appalled by the conclusion he is forced to draw:

> Vollends ärgerlich wird es aber, wenn die Autorin im Programmheft ihren allmächtigen und bösartigen Konzernherrn, den Konsul Weygang, als eine Mischung zweier existierender Personen bezeichnet mit dem Zusatz 'von denen die eine nicht mehr existiert, sie ist tot'. Solche kaum ver*schleyer*te Denunzierung eines Mannes, der ermordet wurde, führt zu der beklemmenden Frage, ob Frauen wie Elfriede Jelinek, wenn sie mehr Macht hätten, wirklich eine Humanisierung der phallozentrischen Welt erreichen würden.[28] [my emphasis]

> [It gets really annoying, however, when, in the programme, the author describes her all-powerful and malicious big business man, Consul Weygang, as a mixture of two existing people, adding, 'one of whom doesn't exist any more, he is dead'. Such a thinly-veiled denunciation of a man who was murdered leads us to the uneasy question of whether women like Elfriede Jelinek, if they had more power, would really have a humanising effect on the phallocentric world.]

If it is difficult to prove contemporary parallels such as these, the contribution made by the play to debates of the 1970s, '80s and '90s surrounding subjectivity, the individual and feminism is a much more tangible one. Jelinek's Nora labours under the illusion from the very start that the most important thing is to become a 'Mensch' ('human being'), a project which is doomed to failure. For Nora, the petty-bourgeois housewife, sees her emancipation on an individual level and fails to show solidarity with the other factory workers. Only such solidarity could have led Nora to a fuller understanding of her own alienation and to a fight against the ruling class and its system of rule, capitalism. As the play stands, however, Nora's individual rebellion against her own private circumstances is shown to be fruitless. There is only one moment when it appears that Nora might initiate collective action, but her rallying cry 'Ihr müßt verbrennen, was euch unfrei macht!' ('You must destroy whatever robs you of your liberty') (*Nora*, p. 52) belies her participation in the emancipatory struggle. Jelinek's protagonist does not have a Marxist understanding of her situation. She identifies men as her oppressors, and does not direct her criticism at the 'real' enemy: the entrepreneurs, bankers and government ministers, in short, the bourgeoisie. Nora advocates radical means to attain her liberal goal of self-fulfilment, as she implores others of her sex to turn to violence: 'Die Geschichte der Frau war bis heute die Geschichte ihrer Ermordung. Ich sehe nicht, wie man Ermordung wieder ausgleichen kann, wenn nicht durch einen Akt neuerlicher Gewalt!' ('The history of womankind to this day has been the history of her murder. I don't see how you can compensate for murder other than with renewed violence!') (*Nora*, p. 51). But it is not only the radical stance that Jelinek is attacking and her criticism of 'the humanist school' is more pointed still. As Tobe Levin explains, the 'bankruptcy' of liberal humanist conceptions of the free subject is made plain when an 'Arbeiterin' misunderstands the addition of a crèche and library to the factory's facilities as something like the culmination of human progress since the French Revolution. The women are in fact being distracted from taking possible industrial action to prevent the closure of their factory; the crèche is an empty promise and will never have to be built. Levin explains how Nora, too, is duped by the humanist view: 'Claiming, "by working for wages I wanted to transform myself from object to subject. ... And most importantly, ... to become my own person" [*Frauenhörspiele*, p. 171) she echoes the humanist school whose bankruptcy becomes even clearer as both terms, "person" and "woman", are emptied of meaning.'[29]

This attack on liberal humanism and on its understanding of feminism is ultimately what makes Elfriede Jelinek's play so effective. The name 'Nora' has come to epitomise women's attempt to emancipate themselves and go out into a man's world to fight for recognition and equal rights. But Jelinek demystifies Nora's heroic status and shows her attempt at self-liberation to be misguided. It is not enough to simply liberate oneself from husband and family. 'Endlich ein Stück, das mit der Frauenfrage nicht erbaulich umgeht', Sigrid Löffler exclaims, welcoming at long last a play 'das sich traut, den Softi-Männern und Manzi-Mädchen ihr liebstes Gedankenspielzeug wegzunehmen und kaputtzumachen – die aufmüpfige Zwitscher-Nora' ('At last a play that doesn't make something edifying out of the woman question, a play which dares to take the favourite hobby-horse of wimpish men and women's libbers away from them: rebellious, chirpy little Nora').[30] As has been shown by the 'false consciousness' of the 'Arbeiterinnen', however, Jelinek not only deconstructs radical and liberal humanist feminisms, but also cautions against a too simplistic Marxist understanding of women's oppression. Nora's hope of transforming herself from object to subject through waged employment indicates a twofold misconception on her part. She is labouring under the liberal understanding of subjectivity *and* under a misunderstanding of the Marxist promotion of women's waged work. This, as Marx and Engels argued, can only be 'the first condition for the liberation of the wife'.[31] Women's employment, Jelinek's play clearly shows, can only be a first step towards female emancipation and is certainly no automatic solution to their problems.

It can be seen that *Nora* is much more complex than has hitherto been suggested. Parallels between the historical model of 1920s capitalism and its emerging political champion, fascism, and any contemporary economic and political developments are, certainly, difficult to reconstruct. *Was geschah, nachdem Nora ihren Mann verlassen hatte* is important because it helps to establish Elfriede Jelinek's literary-political agenda. In her writing she is concerned throughout to demystify, whether the object of her critique be pornography, her native Austria, the role of the media, or, as is the case here, feminism itself. It is a feminist play, but one which warns against a certain *kind* of feminism, a liberal humanist feminism, which will ultimately force any 'Nora' back into the hands of her patriarchal capitalist husband.

Notes

1. See Frederick J. Marker and Lise-Lone Marker, *Ibsen's Lively Art* (Cambridge, 1989), p. 46. To avoid confusion, I shall refer to Jelinek's play as *Nora* and use the English title *A Doll's House* for Ibsen's play. References to Ibsen are to *The Collected Works of Henrik Ibsen*, edited and translated by W. Archer, 11 vols (London, 1906), vol. vii.
2. For the controversial reception of these works, see my 'Problems with Porn: Situating Elfriede Jelinek's *Lust*', *GLL*, 44 (1991), pp. 405-15; and 'Demythologising the Austrian "Heimat": Elfriede Jelinek as "Nestbeschmutzer"', in M. McGowan and R. Schmidt (eds), *From High Priests to Desecrators: Contemporary Austrian Literature*, forthcoming.
3. Andreas Rossmann, 'Die Domina als mißbrauchter Wirtschaftsspion', *Frankfurter Allgemeine Zeitung*, 2 April 1990, p. 35. The critic is using the homonyms 'Lehr' (from 'lehren', to teach) and 'leer' (empty) to suggest the worthlessness of what he sees as Jelinek's moralising endeavours.
4. See Angelika Gundlach's 'Nachwort' to her own translation, *Henrik Ibsen. Ein Puppenheim* (Frankfurt, 1978), pp. 143-5.
5. Both quotations are from Gundlach, *Henrik Ibsen. Ein Puppenheim*, p. 145. Olsen's play was not received very positively: see, for example, Manfred Rieger, 'Nora und die Hafenarbeiter', *Frankfurter Rundschau*, 14 August 1970, p. 9.
6. In this context, someone who opts out of the 'rat race'. Esther Vilar, *Helmer oder Ein Puppenheim. Variationen über ein Thema von Henrik Ibsen* (Frankfurt, Berlin, Vienna, 1981).
7. *Was geschah, nachdem Nora ihren Mann verlassen hatte oder Stützen der Gesellschaften* was first published in *manuskripte* 17, no. 58 (1977/1978), pp. 98-116, then by Sessler (Vienna and Munich, 1980) and finally in Ute Nyssen (ed.), *Theaterstücke* (Cologne, 1984), pp. 6-62. My quotations are from the latter unless otherwise stated.

Quotations from the radio play version of this material are from a volume of radio plays by women writers published under the title *Was geschah, nachdem Nora ihren Mann verlassen hatte? Acht Hörspiele von Elfriede Jelinek, Ursula Krechel, Friederike Mayröcker, Inge Müller, Erica Pedretti, Ruth Rehmann und Gabriele Wohmann*, edited by Helga Geyer-Ryan (Munich, 1982), pp. 170–205; this will be referred to as *Frauenhörspiele*. English translations are my own.

8. *Clara S.* and *Burgtheater* are also published in Ute Nyssen (ed.), *Theaterstücke* (Cologne, 1984).
9. This is her stated intention. See Sibylle Fritsch, 'Die fünffache Nora', *profil*, 11, 9 March 1992, pp. 92–3.
10. This is indeed the premise of Herman Meyer's *The Poetics of Quotation in the European Novel* (Princeton, 1968); see p. 4.
11. See my Ph.D. thesis 'Rewriting Reality: Elfriede Jelinek and the Politics of Representation' (Southampton, 1990), for a discussion of the important theoretical and political questions governing the use of quotation, borrowing, plagiarism and so on.
12. Angelika Gundlach, *Henrik Ibsen. Ein Puppenheim*, p. 148.
13. Joan Templeton, 'The *Doll House* Backlash: Criticism, Feminism, and Ibsen', *PMLA*, 104 (1989), p. 31.
14. Josef-Hermann Sauter, 'Interviews mit Barbara Frischmuth, Elfriede Jelinek, Michael Scharang', *Weimarer Beiträge*, 27, no. 6 (1981), pp. 99–128.
15. Quoted in Stefan Makk, 'Ein politisches Stück, ein Stück übers Kapital', *Kleine Zeitung*, Graz, 6 December 1979, p. 20.
16. Evelyn Reed, quoted in Alison Jaggar, *Feminist Politics and Human Nature* (Brighton, 1983), p. 102. Josef-Hermann Sauter interviews Jelinek on the subject of her politics in 'Interviews mit österreichischen Autoren'.
17. Wolfgang Herles, 'Fünf Wochen für fünf Noras', *Der Standard*, 7/8 March 1992, p. 12.
18. See münchener literaturarbeitskreis, 'gespräch mit elfriede jelinek', in *mamas pfirsiche*, 9/10 (Münster, 1978), pp. 171–81.
19. See Bertolt Brecht, *Fünf Lehrstücke*, ed. Keith A. Dickson (London, 1969), p. 45 and p. 64.
20. *Ballade von drei wichtigen Männern sowie dem Personenkreis um sie herum*, in Elfriede Jelinek, *Die endlose Unschuldigkeit* (Munich, 1980), p. 17. See Brecht, *Fünf Lehrstücke*, p. xix for the Brecht quotation.
21. 'Tomorrow Belongs to Me' was used more as a realist device. This was the song playing on the radio which Nora is told not to switch off. The fascist associations of this song – known to the audience through the film *Cabaret* – are likely to be more obvious than the 'marching songs' of the original. Far from leaving members of the audience with a bitter taste in their mouths, however, some of them walked out humming this catchy tune to themselves. I was left wondering whether they had completely missed the point.
22. Ronald Speirs, *Brecht's Early Plays* (London/Basingstoke, 1982), p. 175.
23. Quoted in Erna Lackner, 'Grazer *Nora* im Fernsehen: Wie sehr ist Petra F. eine Nora?' *Kleine Zeitung*, 27 November 1979, p. 18.
24. Sibylle Fritsch, 'Die fünffache Nora', p. 92.
25. See Prue Chamberlayne, 'The Mothers' Manifesto and Disputes over Mütterlichkeit', *Feminist Review*, 35 (1990), p. 17. This passage proves that the radio play is not simply a shortened version of the stage play since this idea does not feature in the latter.
26. I draw my information here from Helmut Burg *et al.*, *Der Imperialismus der BRD* (Berlin, 1971), and from extremely helpful discussions with Jill Lewis.
27. Gerald Grassl commenting on a reading of the play, 'Frauen und andere Unterdrückte', n.p., 20 April 1978.
28. Lothar Sträter, 'Die Abenteuer der befreiten Nora', *Mannheimer Morgen*, 16 October

1979. The reviewer is making a pun on the term 'verschleiern', which means 'to hide' or 'to veil'.
29. See Tobe Levin's analysis of the radio version, 'Jelinek's Radical Radio: Deconstructing the Woman in Context', *Women's Studies International Forum*, 14, nos. 1/2 (1991), pp. 85–97 (p. 91).
30. Sigrid Löffler, 'Nora, ganz ohne Puppenheim', *profil*, 42, 15 October 1979, p. 78.
31. Quoted in Paul Chao, *Women Under Communism: Family in Russia and China* (New York, 1977), p. 51.

Havel's Satirical Theatre
J. P. Stern

In what sense are Havel's plays avant-garde theatre? The term, it seems, was first used in Paris in 1845 by Gabriel-Désiré Laverdant, a disciple of Charles Fourier of pre-Marxist fame, and denoted an art – in literature as well as painting – which would have the same revolutionary relation to existing bourgeois art as the Communist revolution would have to bourgeois society. Baudelaire thought the term merely demonstrated the French critics' inveterate attachment to military clichés. Lenin called the CP 'the avant-garde of the proletariat', allowing avant-garde art to figure as an analogy to the revolution but no longer as one of its agents. And yet the fervent belief in art as a means of helping in the overthrow of the ruling class as well as a means by which to enlighten the proletariat – this fervent belief in the double function of avant-garde art persisted in Germany into the early 1930s.

The most important moment in the history of the avant-garde is the suicide of Vladimir Mayakovsky in 1930. It is the point – basely unacknowledged by Brecht, Becher, Seghers and others – when the Revolution's greatest surviving poet acknowledges the reversal of roles: the avant-garde is no longer an agent of the revolution, or even its analogy, but has been declared its enemy and socialist realism (an industrialised form of the old bourgeois realist idyll) has been enthroned as the one and only form tolerated by the regime. The poet Mayakovsky faces the consequences. He had lived just long enough to see the liquidation of every single independent-minded Russian poet who had failed to escape abroad.

It says a good deal for the intellectual and artistic inertia of Russian communism that when Václav Havel comes on the scene in Prague some thirty years later, the situation is apparently unchanged. The heirs of the revolution cultivate the literature of 'reálny socialismus' with its didactic message of factory solidarity, its clichés covering the proletarian fight against 'fascism', its psychology determined by the clichés of the class struggle, and its political content reduced to a few anti-American and anti-German slogans; and the literature of protest – once the literature of the avant-garde – has either emigrated or gone underground.

Václav Havel was born into a bourgeois family in 1936, the year before Tomáš Garrigue Masaryk died, and two years before the death of Masaryk's creation, the First Czechoslovak Republic. Havel's grandfather, an enterprising builder, came to Prague from the Moravian town where Havel's friend Tom Stoppard was born; Havel's father, a civil engineer turned architect and speculative builder, got into debt by putting up one of Prague's prettiest residential suburbs above the river Vltava, and he was popular enough with his workforce to retain a managerial job in the theatre and leisure complex he had built in town, even after the Communist takeover. The cosseted 'master's son' grew up, first in Prague, then in Moravia, with a feeling of undeserved privilege: 'It may seem paradoxical', he writes in one of his letters from prison to his wife Olga, 'but I think that because of those early experiences I have always had a heightened sensitivity and aversion to various manifestations of social inequality, and to privilege in general.' This, together with his chubbiness ('I was just a well-fed piglet'), gave him a feeling of 'being a bit outside the order of things', which in turn made him prey to uncertainties about his place in the world, and to the fear that there might be a fatal flaw in his character which justified his exclusion from the company of his less privileged schoolmates. But at the point where this self-portrait looks like becoming pure Oblomov, the 'Czech' element in his character prevails: his 'oddness' (he adds) is not only the source of his self-doubts, but also 'a lifelong wellspring of energies directed at continually improving my self-definition [...] it is also a decisive force behind everything worthwhile I have managed to accomplish.' After 40 years spent in the shadow of 'isms' – called now 'Communism' or 'Marxism', then again 'socialism with a human face' or 'reálny socialismus' – he acknowledges in himself 'that traditional quality of the bourgeoisie [mest'anstvo], particularly in the era of liberalism, which is the ability to take risks, the courage to start all over again from nothing, the ever vital hope and élan to begin new enterprises'.

Because of his family's 'political profile', the formal schooling of the 'millionaire's son' ended abruptly when he was 15. For the next four years he attended evening classes while working as a technician in a chemistry lab; in 1955 he published his first articles and appeared for the first time as a public speaker at a government-sponsored young writers' club. His applications for a place at the University and on a film course were turned down; called up for military service, he was not allowed to finish an economics degree at the Technical High School, but in the army he, together with a friend, wrote a satirical play which turned out an embarrassing success. In 1959 he was taken on as a stagehand by Jan Werich, by then the Grand Old Man of the Czech theatre. When Werich died in October 1980, 'an isolated, sad, bitter and disaffected man, without faith and hope', Havel wrote to his wife that he owed to him his first practical experience of the theatre as a socially and politically conscious institution; Werich's death 'was the definitive end of an era in Czech intellectual history'.

I spoke of the apparent stagnation on the literary scene as the result of the complete and not merely apparent stagnation on the political scene. In their different way the Moscow-dominated communists continued the work of the German wartime occupation: they too suppressed all signs of an independent Czech cultural life. What this meant in the theatre was that all signs and achievements of the independent avant-garde theatre of the First Republic were now condemned as subversive – and this was above all true of the work of the Liberated Theatre (Osvobozené divadlo) of Voskovec and Werich – its founders and playwrights, actor-managers and owners.

From the early nineteenth century onwards, the small popular theatres in Prague and in the provinces expressed the patriotic aspirations of the Czech people; in these theatres (often with amateur casts) the Czech language was cultivated in defiance of Austrian censorship; national pride and its historic roots were asserted in opposition to Habsburg rule. By 1927, when Werich together with his partner Jan Voskovec took over the Liberated Theatre, the patriotic themes could be guyed and replaced by a mildly left-wing, anarchic form of humour: Voskovec's and Werich's energy and talent created what was probably the most influential and certainly the most popular of the many small theatres of the First Republic. They wrote, directed and staged the musical revues, acting the main parts stereotyped as chalk-faced surrealist pierrots, with Voskovec as the romantic, occasionally melancholy Don Quixote and Werich as Sancho Panza, romping through closely rhymed, topical dialogues and songs. All this came to an end in 1938, by decree not of the Germans but of their own Government. After the war the Voskovec and Werich collaborative enterprise did not have a real comeback, though their lyrics, set to superb jazz music by their own composer, Jaroslav Jezek, are alive in Prague to this day. Through Werich, Havel caught a glimpse of the ribald end of the intellectual life of the First Republic, and a little of this heritage remained alive in his plays throughout the long years of single-party rule.

Apart from getting a job first at the ABC Theatre, later at the Theatre on the Balustrade through Werich, and apart from the osmotic effects of an old man who had spent his entire adult life acting and writing plays, what else did Havel acquire through his contact with Jan Werich? Is there anything Havel's plays – there are thirteen to date – have in common with the twenty-odd 'reviews' and sketches of the Voskovec and Werich theatre?

Above all it is the mode of anti-realist and occasionally surrealist farce with a satirical component – where inevitably the satire, and therefore the political implications, of the plays are stronger, more central in Havel's plays than they ever were in the plays of the Liberated Theatre. The most memorable aspect of Voskovec and Werich were their songs – texts set to the theatre's jazz tunes – and these of course have no equivalent, along with puns and dead clichés and topical allusions which Voskovec and Werich took over from the Commedia dell' Arte and which in suitably modified form are taken up by Havel.

For example, the first act of *The Garden Party* of 1963 opens with the parents of the young man who will be at the centre of the play nervously waiting for a friend who is well in with the authorities and has promised to fix things for the son of the family. And while they are waiting, a sort of dialogue is about to develop between husband and wife, but it never quite does, because every statement that is related to the actual situation of waiting for someone (who never comes) is cut short by some platitude or proverb or party slogan. The platitudes are invariably irrelevant, the proverbs cock-eyed, the party slogans misunderstood and misremembered.

PLUDEK: He's probably a bit delayed.
MRS PLUDEK: What do you mean, delayed?
PLUDEK: Well, he might have met somebody and forgot to watch the time.
MRS PLUDEK: But whom?
PLUDEK: A chum from the army –
MRS PLUDEK: But you said he's never been in the Army.

Havel's Satirical Theatre

PLUDEK: Well – so there you are. He's bound to come.
MRS PLUDEK: Let's hope so!
PLUDEK: Dear son! The middle classes are the backbone of the nation. And why? He who fusses about a mosquito net can never hope to dance with a goat. Jaros used to say – life is a blank page. You mean to tell me you don't know what to write on it?
HUGO: [who has been playing chess against himself, winning at one end of the table and losing at the other]: I don't, Dad.
PLUDEK: Did you hear that, Berta?
MRS PLUDEK: Never mind, Albert. Did somebody ring?
[Peter, the second son, enters.]
PLUDEK: No. [To Hugo] Dear son! Should I?
MRS PLUDEK: What time is it?
PLUDEK: Two.
MRS PLUDEK: Already? Of course, you must!
PLUDEK: Dear son!
HUGO: [makes his move]: Check! [Changes sides]
PLUDEK: Still playing?
HUGO: Yes, Dad.
PLUDEK: And how goes it?
HUGO: Badly, Dad, badly!
PLUDEK: Pig-headed, that's all. [To Hugo] Dear son! Not even the Hussars of Cologne would go to the woods without a clamp. Jaros thought about his future and so he studied, and studied, and studied. Have you thought about yours?
HUGO: No, Dad.
PLUDEK: How's that?
HUGO: I've studied, Dad.
PLUDEK: Did you hear that, Berta?
MRS PLUDEK: Never mind, Albert. Did somebody ring?
PLUDEK: No ... Dear son! He who knows where the bumble bee hides his stinger never rolls back his leggings! When one calls Jaros, Jaros calls back, and that's the whole point. The basis of life is the idea you form of life. You think anybody will form it for you?
HUGO: Yes, Dad. Jaros. [Makes a move] Check. [Changes sides]

Is there any method in this madness? The translation I have used – Vera Blackwell's – does little to preserve the actual images and close literal meanings of these proverbs and saws, and in this way remains faithful to the general meaning of this and many such passages, which is that there is no further meaning; and of course we notice the move in the direction of erudition – often more determined and more elaborate – reminiscent of similar passages in Beckett. Such passages are not intended to characterise the speaker, except incidentally; nor are they philosophical disclosures on a cosmic scale – symbols of nihilism, Heidegger's 'das Nichts, das nichtet' except by way of a modest, private intimation. What they characterise is time – the time of waiting of the powerless who have nothing to fall back on, no defence and no selfhood except what survives in their patter, their 'Gerede', in the Czech vernacular 'Kecy' and 'Kecám'. However, unlike in Heidegger's notion of 'Gerede', there is here no contempt at all (indeed, if I may interject a biographical observation: there is, considering his six years in gaol, of which almost two were spent in solitary confinement, astonishingly little contempt in Havel anywhere) – no contempt, then, and also no heroism, but a way, the least dangerous, the most innocuous, of filling time and killing time while waiting for ... oh, whatever power maniac might come along and relieve this couple, this Mr Pludek, of their and his anxiety.

How could I (you will ask), how could I possibly think it necessary to *deny* that this is a heroic attitude? Because that is what the good soldier Švejk's patter has often been called, wrongly I think, but there is here a connection: many of Havel's characters share this unheroic, self-defensive habit of the good soldier, though their different educational standards and different political situations provide *their* patter with different fillings. But his motto is theirs too: 'I'm not saying one way *or* the other, but you mark my words!'

What happens in *The Garden Party?* 'Co se stalo?' 'What's happened?' Time and again, one of Havel's plays or the peripeteia of a scene is introduced by that question. It marks the moment when the life of an individual or of a family has been disrupted by a sudden ukase from above, an order that is pointless yet unignorable. And even though 'what happens' hardly ever takes the form of what has been expected, and occasionally the answer to the question is 'Nothing, nothing at all', from that moment on everything is senselessly different. There is no obvious cause-and-effect connection between one action or one state and the next; instead there is an uneasy feeling that there might be, only it is not quite clear how one might find out and influence the outcome. Another Prague bourgeois writer expressed the connection in the last sentence of his story 'A Country Doctor': 'Einmal dem Fehlläuten der Nachtglocke gefolgt – es ist niemals gutzumachen.' 'Once you have answered the false ringing of a nightbell, things can never be the same again.' The secret police are expected, and instead friends come, or a couple of political sympathisers, and their importunate arrival, encouraging patter and well-intentioned enquiries, brings with it disruptions which seem worse than any havoc the police may wreak (*Largo Desolato*). In *The Garden Party* a friend who is well in with the authorities and has promised to fix things for the son of the family is expected but does not come, and instead his secretary arrives, reading out a series of telegrams interlarded with her plans for a weekend excursion with friends and the menu for the picnic she has thought up; at last the son, Hugo, turns up after all, as expected, and lo and behold, he has the job his father's friend had been supposed to secure for him; which he got by ousting the family friend from his place in the *nomenklatura*. But now the father, Mr Pludek, is sure Hugo will be too grand to talk to them – and indeed, Hugo is so grand that he is not their son any more but someone quite different, and of course the garden party where the deal was struck was not a garden party at all but an anxious get-together where everybody watches everybody else hoping for preferment or fearing demotion – preferment and demotion being of absolute, existential importance, like the Fates and the stars of old. The job Hugo has secured is in the Inauguration Service – a branch of the government, but then everything is a branch of the government – and his new job involves him in the ceremonial opening of the Department of Liquidation. (Havel has insisted that the meaning of his plays is not to be limited to the bureaucratic lunacy of Communism. I shall come to that: I know of at least one university in the United Kingdom which, in order to be able to stop inviting visiting lecturers, had to set up a department for this purpose.) Now (to return to Hugo) the first job of the Department of Liquidation is to liquidate the Inauguration Service, while its *next* job is to liquidate itself, all under Hugo's direction. You may, once again, be reminded of another of Kafka's scenes, that of the officials – but then most people are officials – at the end of *The Castle*, about to liquidate the case against K: 'How suicidal our happiness can be!' says Kafka's inaugurating liquidator.

To be actively involved in the world of Havel's play – as Hugo is, and as his parents, Mr and Mrs Pludek, are not – is to be involved in play-acting, and in this sense and to this extent Havel's theatre is a self-referential theatre: you *are* the head of the Liquidation Service as long as you behave like that head and are acknowledged by others as that head – that is your identity and you have no other, non-functional one, least of all when, in order to lay his secretary, a director of Department X claims that he is not only a director but is really a human being with all the desires and loneliness of a human being... And when, for whatever reason – for instance by being challenged and defeated by a counter-claim – you *are* displaced and make your way into another department and play another role, you *are* that other function and other identity and *have* no other, non-functional one. And this is demonstrated and verified by the constant, unending repetition with which these plays abound, where phrases, sentences, whole paragraphs are repeated, now by the same characters, now by different ones, sometimes in the same order in which they first occurred, sometimes, like a crab-fugue, in the reverse order. Again this reduction of character identity to function within the bureaucratic structure takes us into Kafka's world – but Havel's depersonalising and functionalising of the characters comes more than half a century after Kafka's and goes that much further: in most of his plays – in fact in all his plays except the last two, the Faust play *Temptation* and *Asanace* (Restoration) – there is nothing or almost nothing in the characters presented that derives from or reflects some private, non-bureaucratic experience. Of the Faust play, at all events, it may, I think be said that it is weakest where private feelings and insights into characters are invoked.

On numerous occasions, in interviews, in his essays, in his letters from prison, Havel has spoken of his interest in and concern for the predicament of human identity in the modern age. Communism (he has claimed) is different from western consumerism above all in bringing *more* pressure to bear on the private self, raising the cost of nonconformism, making the threat more radical: but the threat to an individual self – to what Schopenhauer called the individuation of the will – is there in both systems, both ideologies.

J. P. Stern

The last scene of *The Garden Party* shows how this threat to a coherent individual self is conveyed on stage, how play-acting is enacted. We are back in the Pludeks' family living room-cum-kitchen; once again the three characters of the opening are left, but Hugo, who has been put in charge of liquidating not only the Inauguration Service but also the Liquidation Department, is now a different person from what he was at the beginning, and therefore, in conversation with old Pludek, speaks in his new person, as a stranger, enquiring from old Pludek about the old Hugo that was. At last the old man turns to him:

PLUDEK: [To Hugo] Listen, who are you in fact?
HUGO: Me? You mean who am I? Now look here, I don't like this one-sided way of putting questions, I really don't. You really think one can ask in this simplified way? No matter how one answers this sort of question, one can never get hold of the whole truth, but always only of one of its limited parts. What a rich thing is man [should we, I wonder, recall the irony of Hamlet's 'What a piece of work is a man! How noble in reason! How infinite in faculty!'?] – What a rich thing is man, how complicated, changeable, multiform – there is no word, no sentence, no book that could describe and contain him in his whole extent ... Today the time of static and unchangeable categories is past, the time when A was only A and B always B is gone ... I am sure you yourselves feel that what you feel today you've not felt yesterday, and what you felt yesterday you don't feel today, but might perhaps feel tomorrow... Do you feel that? ... Anyway, we all *are* a little bit all the time and all the time we are *not* a little bit; some of us are more, and some of us are more not; some only *are*, some are only, and some only are not; so that none of us entirely *is* and at the same time each one of us is not entirely; and that point – [this is where the political consideration occurs, the adjustment of the self's identity to what the moment requires] – and the point is just *when* it is better to be more, and to not be less, and when – on the contrary – it is better less to be and more not-be; besides, he who is too much may soon not be at all, and he who – in a certain situation – is able to a certain extent to not-be, may in another situation be all the better for that, etc.

And the tirade ends as did the first scene, with 'Checkmate!'

MRS PLUDEK: Listen, Bertie –
PLUDEK: What is it?
MRS PLUDEK: Not bad what he said, was it?
PLUDEK: It was excellent! And do you know why?
MRS PLUDEK: Why?

PLUDEK: Because clearly he has in his veins the healthy philosophy of the middle classes! You know, without gum-boots not even Jaros can get to Královec! [Sings]
Rule Bohemia!
Bohemia rules the waves
Bohemians
Never, never, never ...

I am sure it has occurred to you before that this invocation of the middle classes is a way of getting round the censor, who would clamp down on any satirical remarks about the working classes. However, what is really funny here is that the complex, multiform and multi-faceted self is of course very much a middle or if you will an upper middle class concept – it is David Hume's self as 'the bundleman', of which he affirms at the end of book I of *A Treatise on Human Nature* that 'the self ... is nothing but a bundle or collection of different perceptions which succeed each other with an inconceivable rapidity, and are in perpetual flux and movement'.

So there seems to be nothing particularly modern about this view. What is modern is that this notion of the self is moralised – as soon as it has left the domain of philosophy this self is felt to be a predicament, the source of inauthenticity, and in the domain of politics especially (this is the meaning of the tirade I have quoted) it becomes a justification of and an apologia for the Vicar of Bray. There is of course no suggestion in Hume or Kant (who accepts the notion of the self as a multi-faceted thing, a mere bundle of experiences) that this diversity in any way justifies perfidy or a change of allegiances, which is precisely the point of Hugo's last speech.

Is there nothing, no single object of a character's identity or experience, that is constant? Surely his or her language remains unaltered, the same? In fact the funniest moments in these plays are the occasions of verbal humour where there is a play on the contrast between the characters' normal, cliché-ridden office or party jargon (the jargon of the functionary) and the folksy, sentimental patter – grandad's saws, grandma's proverbs – which takes over when 'the human concern' is being expressed. You can see that this play with linguistic conventions is difficult to convey from one language to another. One such emotional climax of 'true human concern' occurs in *The Garden Party* where two speakers, overwhelmed by the force of their own phoney sincerity, find themselves slipping from Czech into the (for some reason more earthy) Slovak.

This brings me to *The Memorandum*, first produced in 1965, the play in which the use of language (indeed of three languages) serves to symbolise the self whose identity is divided. Although this is in some ways intellectually Havel's most ambitious play, its action is easily summed up: the cast are two bureaucrats, Josef Gross and Jan Balás, their underlings, temporary bosses and secretaries, all working in three different offices of probably one ministry – what kind of ministry or department we do not know; all except the women secretaries are involved in the mutual back-scratching ideology of a competitive power struggle. A mysterious higher authority (you may, if you like, think of Kafka's Castle) orders, or at least is said by some of the underlings to order, a new bureaucratic procedure; one bureaucrat is blackmailed by the other to adopt this new procedure, and to support a move towards establishing an office where the new procedure can be learned and another, a language lab, where it is practised; then the order from above is countermanded, or at least is said to be countermanded, and a new procedure, diametrically opposed to the first, is to replace the first one, and a new set of courses, designed to help people to unlearn the first procedure and start learning the second, is instituted, and the second bureaucrat, the quicker, more skilful of the two, is once again able to blackmail the first and get the better of him. The struggle here is not so much for power, for the authority needed to decide who runs what and who is in charge of what; the struggle is for the chance to avoid responsibility, to avoid being incriminated, to pass the buck.

Again a biographical digression may be relevant: Havel the man and the politician identifies the chief value of modern ethics with a person's readiness to be responsible for his or her own decisions and in the political context for the decisions of the given group or community of interests; and Havel sees the shunting of responsibility from one party member to the next as the chief ethical procedure of the mutual back-scratching ideology – the ideology which he identifies with the rule of 'real socialism'.

To return to *The Memorandum*. Although we are never told in what ministry all this is happening, we are given a very precise idea of the 'procedures' that are at issue. They are two different artificial languages, the first called Ptydepe, the second Chorukor. If these names have any meaning, it has escaped me, but I think their meaning is that they haven't one. These languages are, as I said, diametrically opposed constructs: both are intended 'to increase the accuracy of official correspondence' and 'the exchange of information between departments'. Ptydepe (we are told by its chief instructor) is designed so as to minimise the number of ambiguities and linguistic mix-ups, and this is achieved by making all words as unlike each other as possible, and having as few letters and combinations of letters in common as possible. This is known as a 'maximum redundancy language' and it is, incidentally, a perfectly logical inference from Saussurian linguistics. Chorukor (which is only about to be introduced at the end of the play) is commended (by the same instructor, lecturing to the same class) for its opposite qualities: whereas the need to avoid verbal confusion by similarities led Ptydepe to ever greater prolixity so that a simple call-up order took thirty-six closely printed pages to formulate, Chorukor is built on the opposite principle, maximum similarities leading to brevity and the purposeful organisation of family likenesses. The instructor who was teaching Ptydepe abandons it in favour of Chorukor with the same absolute conviction that the Party can do no wrong even if it changes the direction of its policy by 180 degrees.

So here is the first and most obvious functional meaning of the two artificial languages, and of the sudden unexplained, dictatorial swop from one to the other: it is an allegorisation of the process whereby, for instance, the members of the British Communist Party in the last week of September 1939 changed their view about the nature of the British declaration of war against Germany because the Soviet Union had just concluded a friendship pact with Hitler and one of its spokesmen said that 'the fact of the matter is that [the Soviet Union] is a socialist state' and 'a socialist state in that position can do no wrong and is doing no wrong, and this is what we have to stick to'. End of message.

This political meaning is what Havel underlined in his introduction to the play's performance at the Vienna Burgtheater, which of course he could not attend because he was not allowed out of the country. But there is another, less narrowly political meaning – in a sense perhaps more fundamental. There is something slightly arbitrary about the allegorisation of an artificial language into ideological politics; I mean that some other kind of object – say one figure of the personality cult being superseded by another – would do just as well. The shadow of arbitrariness is dispelled as soon as we take the idea of an artificial *language* seriously. You will remember that I spoke of three languages. Between the two artificial languages lies the ordinary vernacular, Czech, which of course must be used in order to initiate the learning of either construct. Gross, the clumsier, less skilful of the two bureaucrats, in his reluctance to encourage the introduction of Ptydepe, defends the natural language (his defence is as serious as the defence of the multi-layered self I quoted from *The Garden Party*). But the seriousness of his argument is undermined by being expressed in support of a phoney motive, as it was in *The Garden Party*, so that it sounds like the opposite of the truth. Here is the crucial dialogue between Balás, the with-it innovator, and Gross the conservationist.

> BALÁS: You can't ignore the attitude of the masses. The entire office is in ferment and waiting for you to say the word.
> GROSS: I won't have myself being dictated to by the rabble.
> BALÁS: You call it rabble, we call it the toiling masses.
> GROSS: You call it the masses, but it is a rabble. I am a humanist and my concept of running this office is based on the idea that every official is a human being and must constantly strive to be more of a human being. But if we take his living language away from him – which was created and fashioned by a centuries-old national cultural tradition – we make it impossible for him to be fully that human being and we deliver him directly into the clutches of alienation [this phrase will be used again by another character]. I'm all in favour of exactness in official transactions but only to the extent that exactness humanizes a person. In the spirit of this innermost conviction I can never agree to the introduction of Ptydepe.

I need hardly say that all this is hedged in with heavy irony. This 'innermost conviction' is indeed retracted two scenes later, just as the accused in the Slánsky trials in November 1952 changed their minds and agreed with their erstwhile colleagues before fourteen of them were tortured and put to death.

But let me emphasise again that no perfidious conformism makes Gross's statement about language and the national tradition in any way less true – true,

I mean, especially of the Czech language which was not only (as he says) 'fashioned by a centuries-old national culture' but which also fashioned that culture and with it the nation itself, for we are talking about Central Europe – the one area in Europe (and perhaps in the world) in which – in epochs of subjugation at all events – national consciousness is identical with language consciousness, language is politics. And finally, taking the idea of the two artificial languages seriously, we can see that in imposing now one, now the other, upon a multi-faceted self, the powers that be press their influence into the very last corners of the private self, proving by their replacement of the first language by a second the total determinability and *disponibilité* of the self – but nobody really knows whether 'those above' the authorities, Moscow or Berlin, have really given the order or whether these are rumours by spittle-licking apparatchiks eager to anticipate orders from above. And if, finally, we push the language idea one stage further, seeing the constructs not as constructs but as natural foreign languages – the first as the German of the first occupation, the second the Russian of the second occupation – we can see what a wealth of meaning Havel has succeeded in squeezing into this play; and foreigners may begin to understand a culture in which it has been seen as a virtue *not* to know first one language and then the other.

Part Two
Review Articles

Haydn Studies and the Mozart Bicentenary

Denis McCaldin

Mary Sue Morrow, *Concert Life in Haydn's Vienna: Aspects of a Developing Musical and Social Institution*, Sociology of Music Series, no. 7 (Stuyvesant, NY: Pendragon Press, 1989), xxii + 552 pp., $47.

David P. Schroeder, *Haydn and the Enlightenment: The Late Symphonies and their Audience* (Oxford: Clarendon Press), 232 pp., £25.00.

James Webster, *Haydn's 'Farewell' Symphony and the Idea of Classical Style*, Cambridge Studies in Music Theory and Analysis (Cambridge: Cambridge University Press, 1991), xix + 402 pp., £45.00.

W. Dean Sutcliffe, *Haydn: String Quartets, Op. 50*, Cambridge Music Handbooks (Cambridge: Cambridge University Press, 1992), ix + 114 pp., £19.50.

Nicholas Temperley, *Haydn/ The Creation*, Cambridge Music Handbooks (Cambridge: Cambridge University Press, 1991), vii + 135 pp., £19.50.

In musical circles the past few years have been coloured by the bicentennial celebrations surrounding the death of Mozart in 1791. Indeed it is doubtful whether anyone interested in classical music has not been touched by some aspect of these festivities. The raising of awareness has been through all the major information channels: newspapers, journals, books, as well as broadcasts and recordings. Among the more astonishing projects was that of Philips records, who produced versions of all Mozart's extant compositions on CD, including the incomplete scores and sketches - an encyclopaedic undertaking that was rumoured to occupy more than one-and-a-half metres of shelf space. Against this level of activity, Haydn studies might have been seriously eclipsed. Yet the reverse seems to have happened. Rather as Nigel Kennedy's recording of the Vivaldi 'Four Seasons' brought a new following for Baroque music, so the Mozart celebrations have attracted fresh interest not only in his own work, but also in that of his other great contemporaries.

Although there is no specific event comparable to Mozart's death in 1791, the final decade of the eighteenth century was also a time of great significance for Haydn. His visits to London prompted the last twelve symphonies as well as numerous other works, and it was only after his return to Vienna that the six Hermenegild masses and the two great oratorios, *The Creation* and *The Seasons*, were completed. Five useful monographs have recently appeared on Haydn and his times. The most general, *Concert Life in Haydn's Vienna* by Mary Sue Morrow, appeared in 1989. As its title suggests, the book covers a period in Viennese life from around 1760 to 1810, when the pattern of public concert-going was less established than in contemporary London or Paris. More than half the volume is devoted to archival data concerning private and public concerts and as such is a useful resource. This is preceded by a series of chapters skilfully charting concert provision in Vienna during at that time. Initially, music was performed in private and predominantly in the palaces of the aristocracy. The emergence of public concerts has an interesting parallel with England in that new enterprises were most likely to thrive in Lent and Advent, when the theatres were generally closed and balls were banned. It was during such times that playhouse managers were particularly hospitable to public concerts, since they provided a legitimate opportunity to remain open. Outside these periods, astute entrepreneurs such as Philip Martin, with whom Mozart later collaborated, recognised the importance of responding to the normal patterns of Viennese fashionable society. The Augarten gardens, opened to the public by Emperor Joseph II in 1775, soon became a favourite spot in summer for breakfast and a promenade. Later in the day, the shade of the Prater was more favoured and in the evening the theatre held sway. In such circumstances the early morning public concerts in the Augarten naturally flourished. They normally started at about 7 a.m. and would last for about two hours. Programmes offered the usual range of symphonies, concertos and operatic arias. The orchestra was composed almost entirely of gifted amateurs (dilettantes), since the professionals were mainly employed by the theatres.

Ms Morrow's study of the journals and periodicals of the time reveals many interesting aspects of the imperial capital's musical life. She notes that Vienna, like most German-speaking countries, lagged well behind the rest of eighteenth-century Europe in the production of independent publications. Journalism fell into three main categories. The largest were the official publications where some public concerts were advertised but the reviews, if any, studiously avoided negative criticism. This was in stark contrast to London, where much of Haydn's standing resulted from the spirited debates in the newspapers about the merits or otherwise of his latest composition. Other writing contrasted the seriousness of North German attitudes to the art of music with that of the Viennese and one or two journals, most notably the *Allgemeine Musikalische Zeitung*, provided genuine reviews. As elsewhere, these showed that the public enjoyed variety, with an emphasis on concertos and solo vocal items. Haydn's symphonies were regularly given, though they were rarely seen as the most significant part of the programme. Mozart and Beethoven were also well represented, mainly through their concertos and theatre pieces. Although the quantity of critical writing during this period was not large, Ms Morrow is surely right to conclude that we have been misled in thinking that the concert-going public in Vienna was unduly conservative and that it actively neglected its own composers. Her evidence shows that, on the contrary, the Viennese public clearly recognised the superior talents of its great names while absorbing a great deal of other new music at the same time.

Haydn and the Enlightenment examines the composer's instrumental music. The author, David P. Schroeder, doggedly attempts to portray Haydn as a prophet of Shaftesbury's new philosophy but the evidence remains sparse. The truth is that neither the composer nor his two biographers Griesinger and

Dies made significant comments on the Enlightenment movement, and although it is entirely possible that he occasionally visited Vienna's literary salons, if so, he was remarkably reticent about it. More valuable is Schroeder's analytical work, which is directed towards substantiating the view that one of Haydn's achievements in later life was 'to devise procedures for instrumental music that would allow an intelligibility previously thought possible only when words were present'. He takes one of the Paris symphonies, No. 83, 'La Poule' to demonstrate Haydn's growing mastery in balancing the inherent conflict between stasis and instability in his symphonic first movements before discussing the London symphonies in some detail. The notion that Haydn had an overall strategy for his English concerts, widening his audiences' understanding through a sequence of entertaining and more didactic compositions, is attractively developed.

James Webster's *Haydn's 'Farewell' Symphony and the Idea of Classical Style* continues somewhat along the same lines, though it employs rather more rigorous analytical methodology. The author, one of the United States' most respected younger scholars, is currently collaborating with Christopher Hogwood and the Academy of Ancient Music in a new series of recordings of all the Haydn symphonies. No doubt the invitation to participate in this important initiative stems from Webster's interest in musical analysis. In this book, the author suggests that the Farewell symphony is a through-composed work in which each movement is closely dependent on the music that has gone before. He believes that its form reflects the difficult times surrounding Haydn and his orchestra during their enforced absence from their families in the country during the summer of 1772. Because of the unfamiliar, almost alien environment at Esterhaza, Professor Webster sees the piece not as a 'Farewell' but rather as an 'Absence' symphony, which may account for its unusual form and strange key of F sharp minor. For him, the entire work is a search for tonal resolution. Ambiguous expectations set up in the opening movement are modified but not resolved in the succeeding adagio. Even the minuet and trio, usually accepted by listener and composer alike as less weighty in content, is teasingly irresolute, and in this way, the author believes, Haydn keeps his audience in suspense until the concluding 'farewell' section of his bipartite finale.

Later, Webster challenges the traditional idea that composers such as Haydn and Beethoven were 'evolutionists' – that is to say technically clumsy youngsters who only slowly and painfully came to 'master' the implications of the so-called Classical Style. Haydn in particular was always experimenting, not only technically, as in the contrapuntal finales of the Op. 20 quartets, but with extra-musical associations as well. All his vocal music and most of his instrumental works reveal such connections. The symphonies are influenced by many subjects including nature (the seasons, the hunt and similar pastoral themes), religion, and folk culture. Through-composition and cyclic integration in many of these scores is not accidental or sporadic. One has only to consider the unity of Symphonies 6, 7 and 8 ('Le Matin', 'Le Midi', 'Le Soir') from 1761 and the inter-movement links in No. 104 ('London') to realise that an evolutionary model cannot describe Haydn's creative work adequately. It is a healthy sign for Haydn studies that so many aspects of Professor Webster's book challenge the accepted view of his subject's work. To have in our midst a writer skilful enough to bring his analytical and socio-historical talents into such close symbiosis bodes well for the future.

Evolutionary thinking is also challenged in W. Dean Sutcliffe's recent Cambridge Music Handbook entitled *Haydn: String Quartets Op. 50*. The volume is part of an attractive new series on major works or groups of works and incorporates recent research. It is noteworthy that among the first dozen titles to be announced, Haydn is the only composer to be represented twice. Both this study and Nicholas Temperley's on *The Creation* offer fresh insights about the composer's work in the context of modern analytical and musicological studies. Dr Sutcliffe acknowledges that in getting acquainted with the composer's prolific output of quartets, there has always been a tendency to concentrate on the better known scores, particularly the works of Op. 64, 76 and 77. Earlier sets, such as the amazing Op. 20 and Op. 33, have too often been treated as worthy but slightly uncertain stepping-stones towards these later pieces.

The circumstances surrounding the rediscovery of four of the six autographs of the Op. 50 quartets in Australia during a Haydn Festival at Melbourne in 1982 are astonishing. Purchased by Prince Nicolaus Esterhazy II, the last of Haydn's noble patrons, they resurfaced in London in 1851. Hummel, who succeeded Haydn, probably brought them over when he visited England in 1830, along with several other autographs which are now in the British Library. Here the quartets were sold to an English colonel who was about to emigrate to New Zealand and who may have bought them as some kind of insurance investment against an uncertain future. Settling in Christchurch, he decided to have the documents bound, and in this form they subsequently travelled round Australasia with his descendants before finally coming to rest in Melbourne. Their discovery has revealed more than a thousand misreadings in the extant printed editions. Some are relatively trivial, while others, such as the confusion over tonalities in the trio in No. 5, are fundamental.

Haydn's motives for composing such pieces at a time of considerable activity within the Esterhazy court are unclear. Sutcliffe suggests that since the composer was always aware of the precariousness of life as a courtly employee, he may have hoped to gain a measure of financial independence through the publication of his music. As if to prepare the way, he signed a new contract with his prince in 1779 which specifically omitted a key clause in the earlier document declaring that all his compositions were the exclusive property of his employer. Haydn probably recognised that much of his earlier work, such as the baryton trios, could not be exploited commercially and this would explain his determination henceforth to produce marketable scores, such as the Op. 50 quartets, even though still heavily committed in his prince's service.

A substantial part of the book is concerned with the diversity of Haydn's compositional procedures in these quartets. The author's main ideas are remarkably similar to those expressed by James Webster. Sutcliffe suggests that these scores reveal a consistently challenging attitude to the sonata principle with its strong emphasis on the manipulation of stable and unstable features – motivic and textural as well as harmonic. Significant too is the suggestion that the unity between movements within each quartet was important to Haydn. This means that the intensity of the opening allegros is balanced by more relaxed slow movements and minuets which precede the increasingly significant finales. The author repeatedly cautions the reader against the accepted idea that Haydn's music improved as he grew more experienced, preferring instead to emphasise the master's restless sense of enquiry.

Nicholas Temperley's monograph on *The Creation* draws attention to some of the puzzles that still surround this popular work. As well as discussing differences between the English and Viennese oratorio, he also offers some helpful background on the place of religion in Georgian England and Catholic Austria. He explains some of the difficulties concerning the authorship of the libretto and the translations both into German and then back into extremely crude English. Reporting on recent editions, including his own, he is able to bring first-hand knowledge of these problems and to offer advice to conductors. He wisely avoids commenting on the musical quality of every number and instead devotes space to the oratorio's reception history as well as providing useful guidance on aspects of performance practice.

As 1991 approached I was concerned that the enthusiasm for Mozart generated by the bicentennial celebrations would, in H. C. Robbins Landon's words, 'in the long run, eradicate almost entirely' his great precursor's reputation. Happily this does not seem to be the case. If anything, the new audience for Mozart, some of it no doubt attracted by Landon's enthusiastic writing, has begun listening afresh to the other Viennese masters. In this article I have described some recent publications on Haydn, to which the activities of the record companies should also be added. Four versions of *The Creation* have appeared on CD in the last few years and mention has been made already of one of three new projects in progress involving all the symphonies. The indications are, therefore, that contrary to Landon's expectations, Haydn's reputation has not been overshadowed by the Salzburg genius. Mozart himself explained why:

> There is no one who can do it all – to joke and to terrify, to evoke laughter and profound sentiment – and all equally well: no one except Joseph Haydn.

Recent Nestroy Scholarship

W. E. Yates

This review of advances in Nestroy scholarship since the end of the 1970s aims to construct an outline map, showing the contours of recent work and also providing a guide to the main landmarks by which those wanting to explore any of the areas covered may best take their bearings. Publications mentioned are listed in a separate bibliography at the end of the article, to which reference is made by the Author–Date system. This material is limited to what has been published from 1979 (the year in which the plays began to appear in the new critical edition of Nestroy's works) up to the end of 1991.

Perceptions of an author among non-specialists inevitably lag behind the current state of research; sometimes a long way behind. This very point has been made in relation to Nestroy in a wide-ranging critical assessment of the state of Nestroy scholarship by Friedrich Walla (Walla 1991). It is also clear from passing allusions in essays on other subjects that a very dated image of Nestroy's work survives. What his name still suggests to the general reading public is the rival of Raimund, adored by the rather cosy public of Biedermeier Vienna for a succession of light-hearted if rather cynical farces dashed off with great facility, sometimes spiced in performance with daring extempores – part of an innocent theatrical idyll interrupted only briefly by the revolution of 1848, when Nestroy and his fellow-actor Wenzel Scholz, decked out in theatrical uniforms and arms, paraded in the Leopoldstadt district alongside the National Guard.

What this image strikingly lacks is not only appreciation of the depths underlying the satire but also awareness of Nestroy the working dramatist, operating within the commercial theatre. Far from writing with carefree abandon, he subjected his plays to painstaking revision; and while as a satirist he may have thought in cosmic terms, presenting society as governed by inescapable principles of providential injustice, in practice he was constantly subject to the pressures of reception by a changing theatre public and a largely hostile press, and of an endless struggle to outwit the vigilance of the censor.

Nestroy scholarship has moved rapidly in recent years. This is a result principally of the launching of the new historical and critical edition, which coincided with growing understanding both of the importance of 'Rezeptionsgeschichte' and also of the exigencies of work in the commercial theatre, the realities of Nestroy's working practices and environment. The coming together of these various strands has allowed major advances to be made in our understanding of his work; that these advances have not been appreciated outside specialist circles is due in part, no doubt, to the fact that in the last twelve years – precisely because perceptions have been developing so rapidly – there have actually been very few scholarly monographs on Nestroy published.

It is, by contrast, well known that in the twenty-five years or so after 1950 a rapid expansion of Nestroy studies took place, with a number of scholarly studies appearing. Work on Nestroy at that stage was still mainly influenced by the editorial and historical publications of Otto Rommel and the interpretative essays of Karl Kraus. Rommel treated him essentially within the framework of a local Viennese tradition of 'popular' (that is, dialect) comedy stretching back to the Baroque theatre and forward to the realism of Anzengruber; Kraus presented him essentially as a master of satirical language. The best-known general study that appeared towards the end of this stage of work, Franz H. Mautner's monograph *Nestroy* (Heidelberg, 1974), is characteristically indebted to Kraus in its interpretative approach and to Rommel's editions for its documentation.

The spread of scholarly interest led to the establishment in the 1970s of three forums which have continued to provide central organs of debate: the Internationale Nestroy-Gesellschaft, founded in Vienna in 1973, an annual conference ('Nestroy-Gespräche') held in Schwechat from 1975 onwards, and the journal *Nestroyana*, launched by the Internationale Nestroy-Gesellschaft in 1979. One function of *Nestroyana* has been to record the principal proceedings of the Schwechat conferences, and some numbers have centred on specific themes, reflecting the Schwechat programme: for example, Nestroy's female roles (vol. 4, no. 3/4 [1982]), parody (vol. 5, no. 3/4 [1983–4]), Nestroy in translation (vol. 6, no. 1/2 [1984–5]), Nestroy and his contemporaries (vol. 7, no. 1/2 [1987]).

For bibliographical guides we are especially indebted to Jürgen Hein. His volume in the 'Sammlung Metzler' series (Hein 1990b) is the best factual outline available and entirely supersedes an earlier bibliography (Conrad 1980) which is neither complete nor reliable in detail. The progress of Nestroy scholarship up to the early 1970s has been charted by Hein in two earlier essays, 'Nestroyforschung (1901–66)' and 'Neuere Nestroyforschung (1967–73)', which appeared in 1968 (*Wirkendes Wort*, 18, pp. 232–45) and 1975 (*Wirkendes Wort*, 25, pp. 140–51) respectively, and a further study, first published in 1978 and reissued in an expanded form in 1991, summarising the state of research in the whole field of Viennese dialect theatre (Hein 1991b). These three surveys should form a starting-point for anyone seeking an overview of the pre-1979 material. It is also thoughtfully reviewed in the long chapter on Nestroy in the final volume of Friedrich Sengle's *Biedermeierzeit* (Sengle 1980). Sengle's account is in tune with subsequent developments in two ways: first, in arguing against exclusive concentration, under the influence of Kraus, on Nestroy's language at the expense of practical traditions in the theatre; and secondly, in studying Nestroy within the wider cultural context of his time, without falling into simplistic concentration on his social criticism.

Up to the end of the 1970s, Nestroy studies were basically dependent on the fifteen-volume edition *Sämtliche Werke*, edited by Fritz Brukner and Otto Rommel (Vienna, 1924–30; henceforth referred to as *SW*). Despite the pioneering importance of that edition, however, its deficiencies were clear. Its whole organisation, with plays divided into supposedly separate genres, has long been discredited; neither Nestroy's correspondence nor his early romantic drama *Prinz Friedrich* is included; the documentation both of variants and of contemporary reception is incomplete; the transcription of manuscripts, both in the main text and in the variants, is very inaccurate, as also is that of reviews, though regrettably the apparatus to the edition is still widely cited; and the information on Nestroy's sources is incomplete. Discontent with the picture of Nestroy's work transmitted from the Rommel era came to the fore most notably in an important study of Nestroy's early work by Siegfried Diehl, *Zauberei und Satire im Frühwerk Nestroys* (Bad Homburg, 1969), which advanced substantial evidence of the need for a new edition.

In the mid-1970s the Viennese publishing firm Jugend und Volk Verlag launched a new critical edition, designed to remedy all these failings, in the first instance under the general editorship of Jürgen Hein and Johann Hüttner. The first two volumes to appear (in 1977) were *Briefe*, which superseded a smaller collection of letters edited by Fritz Brukner in 1938, and an illustrated catalogue of portraits of Nestroy both in private life and on stage, *Nestroy im Bild*. Since 1979 the dramatic works have steadily been appearing; by the end of 1991 the following twelve volumes of *Stücke* had been published: 1, 6, 7/i, 7/ii, 12–14, 18/i, 19–21 and 34. Over a quarter of Nestroy's dramatic work is now available in the new edition. A large number of textual emendations have been made; significant divergences in separate manuscripts are clearly shown; contemporary reception is comprehensively documented. Other specific advances have lain in the edition of the early drama *Prinz Friedrich*, which was not included in any of the older collected editions (*Stücke 1*); the separate printing of the complete texts of *Die Verbannung aus dem Zauberreiche* and a quite distinct earlier version, *Dreyßig Jahre aus dem Leben eines Lumpen* (*Stücke 1*); clarification of the relation between *Das Verlobungsfest im Feenreiche* and the revised version, *Die Gleichheit der Jahre*, and the discovery of Nestroy's main source for the material, K. G. Prätzel's story 'Die Schloßmamsell' (*Stücke 7/i*); the reproduction in facsimile of the sources of *Einen Jux will er sich machen* (*Stücke 18/i*), *Liebesgeschichten und Heiratssachen* (*Stücke 19*), *Eisenbahnheiraten* (*Stücke 20*), and *Der Zerrissene* (*Stücke 21*); the edition for the first time of a number of full scenarios for plays of the early 1840s (*Einen Jux will er sich machen, Liebesgeschichten und Heiratssachen, Nur Ruhe!* and *Eisenbahnheiraten*); and in *Stücke 34* the comprehensive tracing of the genesis of '*Nur keck!*', linking its inception to Nestroy's notes on a contemporary version of Molière's *L'Étourdi* as well as treating its relation to its main source (Boucicault's *London Assurance*), which had been identified only some years after Rommel's edition.

It would be idle to pretend that all publications since the end of the 1970s are informed by newly-discovered documentation; but certainly the material being published in the edition has provided the main basis for the advances made in Nestroy scholarship in the last ten years. That the flow of monographs has decreased is directly related to the quantity of new material to be digested and evaluated; this, however, inevitably makes it harder for non-specialists to perceive the shifts in emphasis that have taken place. That is, indeed, the justification for offering the present account. It makes no claim to comprehensiveness; on the contrary, I have excluded material intended for a general readership, articles and editions designed primarily as teaching aids, and work that relies wholly on the older editions and reflects dated critical approaches, and have tried to concentrate on scholarly publications that illustrate the kind of advances being made and the central issues in recent debate. Much, then, has been omitted. Indeed, even most of the authors mentioned have published work on Nestroy other than that listed here. Furthermore, neither unpublished dissertations nor contributions to theatre programmes have been included; and a considerable number of items in *Nestroyana*, in particular shorter articles and those on single plays, have not been listed separately, since the whole run of the journal must be considered a fundamental cumulative record of modern Nestroy scholarship. (Its use was facilitated by the publication in 1991 of an index to volumes 1–10.) On the other hand, I have included three items that appeared in the *Neue Zürcher Zeitung*, as these are more likely to be overlooked in orthodox scholarly bibliographies, and I have tried to give due weight to material in English, which Hein lists but tends not to assess in detail (Hein 1990b; Hein 1991b).

The first and no doubt most important advance lies in the text of the new edition, which establishes an authentic and homogeneous text, based so far as possible on autograph manuscripts. The issues and principles involved have been discussed by each of the editors of the first twelve volumes of plays to appear in the new edition (most recently Hein 1989a). Illustrations of the kind of textual inaccuracy found in *SW* are given by Friedrich Walla (Walla 1980). Other recently discovered examples include a striking one in the first act of *'Nur keck!'*: the white-haired Holzstamm says he looks like an old badger that has been crawling through snow, whereas his friend Graufalter stands before him as dark as a raven – as Rommel's text has it, 'wie ein Rabe in der Trauer, ein Kinn von beschämender Schwärze' ('like a raven in mourning, with a chin of humiliating blackness') (*SW* XIV, 177), but correctly 'wie ein Rabe in der Trauer, in Kienrußbeschämender Schwärze' ('of a black to put pine soot to shame') (*Stücke 34*, p. 13). Where subsequent discoveries, either of manuscripts or of background material, have been made that supplement volumes already published, these have been documented in *Nestroyana*: newly discovered letters have been published by Walter Obermaier (the editor of the *Briefe*), Jürgen Hein and Gerda Baumbach in volumes 2, 6, 9 and 10 of *Nestroyana*, addenda to *Stücke 1* in volumes 5 and 8, to *Stücke 12* in volume 6, to *Stücke 13* in volumes 6 and 8, and to *Stücke 34* in volume 10.

The emphases of the new critical edition – the concern with textual accuracy, detailed accounts of Nestroy's sources, and the placing of his work in its social, political and theatrical context – have also been reflected in other smaller editions. As research tools, two published by Reclam are particularly useful: one of parodies from the Viennese dialect theatre tradition (Hein 1986), which includes Nestroy's *Tannhäuser* in a text based on the first edition of 1857, and one of *Höllenangst* (Hein 1987b), which provides a detailed comparative synopsis of the French source.

It is moreover striking that whereas a decade ago Peter K. Jansen could lament the shortage of interpretative studies of single Nestroy plays (Jansen 1980), there have since then been a growing number of critical and interpretative articles on individual plays. One of the fullest is his own reading of *Der Talisman* as a radical satire deploying the utopian structure of a *Märchen*-like plot. More recently Hauke Stroszeck has published a challenging exploration of biblical motifs in the same play (Stroszeck 1990). Walla, arguing that interpretations of individual works as artistic entities, rather than just as examples of general points about Nestroy, are a prerequisite of serious appreciation of his dramatic work, expresses concern that there are still not enough of them (Walla 1991); but several essays devoted to single texts have arisen out of work on the new edition, either on volumes in preparation (Hüttner 1980b; Aust 1987) or on volumes that have already appeared (Walla 1979a; Walla 1979b; Walla 1981a; Hein 1988a). The last of these, on *Der Zerrissene*, provides a particularly useful synthesis, a concise and informative introduction to Nestroy's technique in mid-career and to the critical cruxes associated with the interpretation and evaluation of a single play (including Nestroy's treatment of his source, the characteristic interplay of linguistic registers, and the significance of the critical reception). *Der Zerrissene* has in fact been the object of much discussion, new interpretations stressing the coherence of the word-play in relation to the central motifs of friendship (Yates 1979) and sexuality (Stroszeck 1988); Nestroy's treatment of the theme of friendship has also been explored in relation to his combination of melodrama and satire in *Mein Freund* (Aust 1988).

Much more central is the attention that has been given to Nestroy's sources. Over and above the publication in *Stücke 7/i* of the source for *Das Verlobungsfest im Feenreiche* and *Die Gleichheit der Jahre*, two other important discoveries had been published by the end of 1991, further reducing the number of plays for which the source is still unknown. The plays concerned are both late ones, *Heimliches Geld, heimliche Liebe*, which has been shown to be based on a popular French novel of the mid-1840s, *Au jour le jour* by Frédéric Soulié (Walter 1986), and *Frühere Verhältnisse*, which is now known to be an adaptation of a one-act farce by Emil Pohl, *Ein melancholischer Hausknecht oder Alte Bekanntschaften* (Hein 1990a; Tutschka 1990). Pohl's play is the first Nestroy source to be identified that was not available to Nestroy as a printed text: a work that had flopped in the Wallner-Theater in Berlin (it had only three performances there) and which must have been supplied to him in manuscript by a theatrical agency. As well as these finds, advances have been made – again, over and above work on the new edition – in close discussion of Nestroy's procedures in adapting his (predominantly French) sources (Wimmer 1986; Doering 1988; Aust 1991; Schneilin 1991). In particular, *Häuptling Abendwind*, which is based on a one-act Offenbach operetta, has been a subject of recurrent interest (Obermaier 1984; Spohr 1985; Spohr 1989). Attention has also continued to be paid to his use of English sources, especially in *Einen Jux will er sich machen* (most recently Yates 1991). Earlier essays on this subject (Walla 1981c; Mitchell and Murdoch 1983) antedate the appearance of the volumes tracing Nestroy's detailed work on the sources in question (*Stücke 18/i, 19, 34*).

The interest in Nestroy's sources is part and parcel of the intensification of investigation, stimulated largely by editorial work, into the mechanics of his working methods, the whole organic process of the genesis of a play (Yates 1985b; Hein 1991a). This extends from practicalities such as his re-use of material from his own earlier plays (Walla 1981b) into wider questions of style and dramatic technique, for example the parodistic and satiric function of the characteristic 'epic' quality in his dramatic technique (Münz 1988); the strategic 'conjoining of farce and political satire' exemplified in his depiction of the 1848 Revolution in *Freiheit in Krähwinkel* (McKenzie 1980); the function of money as the driving force in the dramatic action (Aust 1989); and his use not only of rhetorical devices that were taught as part of the school curriculum of his time (Neuber 1987) but also (parodistically) of stylistic devices derived from the Baroque sermon (Kastl 1991), of quotation (Hein 1987a), of type-names (Walla 1986), of theatrical imagery and the metaphor of theatre (Hein 1983), or of the traditional happy ending of comedy (Yates 1988b). The happy endings fit in with the utopian idealism implicit in much satire (see Hein 1985; Münz 1988), even if Nestroy's analysis of the materialism of human relations has more radical implications (Aust 1989). In sum, Nestroy's style and technique are now attracting the kind of wide-ranging analysis, grounded in literary and aesthetic theory, that has long been applied to contemporaries such as Heine or Büchner.

A further dimension in Nestroy scholarship is supplied by the need to take into account at every step the practical constraints of the commercial theatre. Nestroy's plays not only had to be planned round the specific actors at his disposal; they also involved close collaboration with his composer Adolf Müller, and under the regime of the impressario Karl Carl he had to avoid the need for expensive scenery (Hüttner 1981; Yates 1985b). The most irksome source of constant pressure was the supervision of texts by the official censor. Though censorship was a crucial part of Viennese theatrical life, its workings have hitherto been only patchily documented (see Hüttner 1980a, a valuable survey). Details of words and phrases expunged by the censor in plays by Nestroy are given in volumes *Stücke 1, 6, 7/i, 7/ii,* and *13* of the new edition. Work on the edition has also provided significant documentation of the provisional pre-censorship practised in the dialect theatre as a way of preparing in advance for the (predictable) objections of the official censor, which required eleventh-hour alterations. Nestroy usually entered these precautionary variants himself in his autograph manuscript, but there are also examples in a copy manuscript of *Der Kobold*, which are set out in *Stücke 14*. His practice has been lucidly expounded by Hüttner (Hüttner 1980c), and Walla has also analysed the whole process and effects of censorship and pre-censorship as evidenced in the plays already covered in the new edition (Walla 1989; see also the apparatus to *Müller, Kohlenbrenner und Sesseltrager* in *Stücke 7/ii*).

This documentation of the practical side of work in the theatre is complemented by two other areas of advance. The first is essentially biographical, in relation both to Nestroy's early years and to aspects of his work in mid-career: discussion of his educational background (Berghaus 1982; Neuber 1987), information in the diary for 1835 of his friend Ernst Stainhauser, later financial controller of the Carltheater under his direction (Obermaier 1982; Obermaier 1985b), and the expansion of our knowledge of his appearances outside Vienna both in the 1820s in Amsterdam (Hein 1988c) and later in his many guest appearances in Prague, Berlin, Graz and other cities (Obermaier 1985a; Neuber 1987). The second area of advance is the comprehensive documentation in the new edition of the critical reception of his plays, which has prompted enquiry into the effect of that reception in determining the subsequent development of his writing and in influencing the evolution in the late 1830s – the decisive turning-point may be seen in *Glück, Mißbrauch und Rückkehr* (1838) – of the form of 'Posse mit Gesang' characteristic of his mature work (Yates 1988a). The special importance of the critical climate for Nestroy's works was established in the 1970s in an East German monograph, *Wiener Volkskomödie und Vormärz* by Erich Joachim May (Berlin, 1975), and the findings of this influential study have been both extended and modified as detailed attention has been paid to the contemporary Viennese press (Obermaier 1991), to the criteria adopted by the reviewers (Neuber 1987; Yates 1987), and particularly to the debate about the notion of an idealising 'Volksstück', championed by critics of conservative persuasion both in matters of aesthetics (notably critics in the *Wiener Zeitschrift für Kunst, Literatur, Theater und Mode*) and in politics (the most vocal being M. G. Saphir, from 1837 onwards the editor of *Der Humorist*) (Hein 1979; Yates 1985a; Hein 1989b). A start has also been made on documenting the reception of Nestroy's plays outside Vienna (Theobald 1990).

At the same time, growing recognition of the commercial factors bearing on Nestroy's work, which have been explored in particular by Johann Hüttner (e.g. Hüttner 1979), has stimulated critical approaches to the Viennese dialect theatre unheard-of in earlier scholarship. First, attention is being directed less exclusively to Nestroy's farces, and the case has been argued for allowing more fully for the popularity in his own time of pieces of essentially melodramatic character (Hüttner 1980b; Hüttner 1985). Secondly, no longer is the emphasis on '*popular* theatre', with its rather sentimental overtones of folksiness; increasingly the theatrical life of mid-nineteenth-century Vienna is treated not just as a unique example of cosy local continuity but in a wider international context, with links and parallels between the Viennese suburban theatres and comparable theatres of entertainment in other European capitals of the time, in particular London and Paris (Hüttner 1986), so that increasingly Nestroy's work is being seen in the context of the international theatre of his time (Bauer 1990; Valentin 1991). The Paris theatre, Nestroy's source of a series of plots in the 1830s and 1840s, again exercised direct influence on the repertory of the Viennese dialect theatres from the early 1850s through the operetta (Obermaier 1988).

This widening of critical horizons is reflected also in the appearance of comparative studies. These have not only pursued the tempting comparison between the conventions of the Viennese theatre in Nestroy's time and those of Elizabethan London (Draudt 1980); Nestroy's work has also been compared with that of contemporaries such as Labiche (Koppen 1982), Boucicault (Yates 1988a) and Heine (Haida 1987), and there have been discussions of his affinities with Horváth (Adey 1989), of possible 'echoes' of *Der Schützling* in Wittgenstein (Barker 1986) and of his influence on Karl Kraus (Rössler 1981). More fundamentally, whereas once Nestroy was seen almost exclusively in terms of a narrowly autochthonic stage tradition, he is now increasingly discussed in relation to the whole intellectual and cultural climate of his time, either in Austria (Baur 1981; Doering 1987) or more widely in German-speaking Europe (Sengle 1980; Haida 1987; Mills 1990). In the older theatre histories the roots of Viennese dialect comedy used to be placed firmly in Baroque theatre; now Nestroy – who after all satirised the old *Zauberspiel* in his early comedies and abandoned it from the mid 1830s – is perceived to be essentially an anti-Romantic (Münz 1988).

Inevitably, this shift of emphasis has prompted reassessments of his satirical range, its relation to social and political reality. Again, this has in part been related to texts in the new edition (Yates 1981; see also the apparatus to *Stücke 18/i* and *Stücke 19*) but has also extended to questions such as his un-idealising depiction of family life (Schmidt-Dengler 1982), his treatment of women against the background of the contemporary debate on emancipation (Yates 1985c), his satire of trends within the theatre of his time (Münz 1988), and the politically 'subversive' implications of his use of language (Decker 1987). The closeness of his work to the realities of popular life and work in the late Biedermeier period has been documented in two substantial essays by the social historian Wolfgang Häusler (Häusler 1989; Häusler 1991) and is reflected in a reinterpretation of *Lumpazivagabundus* as an exposé, against the background of rising alcoholism, of the materialist morality of the bourgeoisie in which the uncritically conformist Leim is integrated (Mills 1990).

In the political sphere Nestroy's scepticism towards the rising tide of nationalism is undisputed (Obermaier 1984), but on the vexed question of anti-Semitism there has been an extended debate. This was prompted by a well-documented article by Colin Walker which reached conclusions critical of Nestroy's presentation of Jews (Walker 1981) and which led to further review of that issue (Walla 1985; Hein 1988b). It is in the nature of the satirist that he is critical of social groups he treats and, in Nestroy's case, of distinctive ways of speaking. Just how innocent Nestroy is of any specifically anti-Semitic intention beyond such satire is still an unresolved question, complicated both by shifts in perception between the mid-nineteenth century and today and by the element of parody in the main text at issue, *Judith und Holofernes*, and related also to the wider difficulty of defining the political thrust of Nestroy's plays. As an actor-dramatist, he would appear on stage and deliver lines – often memorably pithy lines – which he himself had written but which, whether within the plot proper or in the solo-scenes, are spoken by fictional characters; anyone seeking to extrapolate political implications enters a methodological minefield, to be approached with great caution. This whole problem has been expounded by John McKenzie in a wide-ranging paper (McKenzie 1985). The most substantial subsequent essay on Nestroy's use of political material is Walker's detailed exposition of his satirical treatment of the Redemptorists in *Freiheit in Krähwinkel* against the background of the history of the Congregation, the hostility to it in Vienna, and its expulsion in 1848 (Walker 1990). The essay concludes with a reassessment of the ambivalent ending of the play, in which,

Walker argues, 'by endorsing the expulsion [...] Nestroy was undermining the message of his own play – that the Viennese were playing at revolution'.

The complexities now perceived in interpreting Nestroy are symptomatic of the advances surveyed in this article. Nestroy scholarship has developed its own history; indeed the very history of his critical reputation has also been charted anew, starting with mid-nineteenth-century literary historians schooled by expectations of 'realism' (Neuber 1987) and also covering changes in taste down to the cultivation and performance of Nestroy in Austria up to the end of the Nazi period (Obermaier 1987). It is in the period since 1979 that Nestroy scholarship has come of age, in particular informed by our increasing insight into the working environment of the mid-nineteenth-century commercial theatre. Hüttner rightly points out that Nestroy's greatness lies precisely in his capacity to overcome such constraints (Hüttner 1981); but this implies that appreciation of his achievement involves detailed understanding of the whole complex of strategies he adopted in order to attain his satiric ends – his very deliberate construction of his plays, his careful revision of his manuscripts at various stages, his deployment of a wide range of dramatic devices. It is this perception, now fully integrated into modern Nestroy scholarship, that makes the naive and often rather dismissive oversimplifications characteristic of some older criticism utterly outdated.

At the same time Nestroy has begun to be better known internationally outside academic circles. This is largely a consequence of the success of *On the Razzle*, Tom Stoppard's very free adaptation of *Einen Jux will er sich machen*, which was first published by Faber and Faber in London in 1981, and reprinted 'with corrections' – that is, reflecting the changes made to the text for performance – in 1982. Other translations that have appeared in the 1980s, though much more run-of-the-mill in quality, furnish further evidence of growing international awareness: an American volume, *Three Viennese Comedies* translated by Robert Harrison and Katharina Wilson (Columbia, SC, 1986), contains, as well as a version of *Der Talisman* (one of four plays that were already available in American translations), versions of *Das Haus der Temperamente* and the parody *Judith und Holofernes*. That takes the number of plays available in some kind of English version beyond the six translated into Italian by Alighiero Chiusano (Nestroy, *Teatro* [Milan, 1973]). In 1988 the University of Rouen published a volume containing French versions of two plays, *Der Zerrissene* (*L'Homme déchiré*, translated by Jean-Louis Besson and Heinz Schwarzinger) and *Einen Jux will er sich machen* (*Une Pinte de bon sang aux dépens d'autrui*, translated by Félix Kreissler). It is, indeed, only realistic to acknowledge that the publication that will prove most effective in advancing international recognition of Nestroy's standing will probably not be a piece of academic scholarship at all but a translation, less free than Stoppard's adaptation, by a dramatist of equal genius. To report that this is something we still lack is meant not as defeatism but as a challenge.

W. E. Yates

Select Bibliography 1979–91

Adey, Louise (1989), '"By indirections find directions out": Horváth, Nestroy and the Art of Obliquity', *Sprachkunst*, 19, no. 2 (Ödön von Horváth zum 50. Todestag), pp. 107–21.
Aust, Hugo (1987), 'Nestroys *Kampl*. Aspekte der klassischen Form', *Wirkendes Wort*, 37, pp. 181–92.
Aust, Hugo (1988), 'Possendramaturgie des Paares. Zu Nestroys *Mein Freund*', *Nestroyana*, 8, pp. 29–38.
Aust, Hugo (1989), 'Sprachspiele des Geldes. Ein Nestroysches Thema im Lichte Wittgensteins', *Wirkendes Wort*, 39, pp. 357–71.
Aust, Hugo (1991), 'Einige Überlegungen zum Problem der Literaturnutzung am Beispiel von Eugène Sues *L'Orgueil* und Johann Nestroys *Kampl*', in Stieg and Valentin 1991, pp. 9–22.
Barker, Andrew W. (1986), 'Nestroy and Wittgenstein: Some Thoughts on the Motto to the *Philosophical Investigations*', *German Life and Letters*, 39, pp. 161–7.
Bauer, Roger (1990), 'Wienerisches und Europäisches in den Komödien Johann Nepomuk Nestroys', in Herbert Mainusch (ed.), *Europäische Komödien*, Darmstadt, pp. 379–88.
Baur, Uwe (1981), 'Nestroy und die oppositionelle Literatur seiner Zeit. Zum Verhältnis von "Volk" und Literatur in der Restaurationsepoche', in Johann Holzner, Michael Klein and Wolfgang Wiesmüller (eds), *Studien zur Literatur des 19. und 20. Jahrhunderts in Österreich (Festschrift für Alfred Doppler)*, Innsbruck, pp. 25–34.
Berghaus, Günter (1982), 'Quellen zu Nestroys Weltanschauung und Lebensphilosophie', *Nestroyana*, 4, pp. 3–24.
Conrad, Günter (1980), *Johann Nepomuk Nestroy 1801–1862. Bibliographie zur Nestroyforschung und -rezeption*, Berlin.
Decker, Craig (1987), 'Towards a Critical *Volksstück*: Nestroy and the Politics of Language', *Monatshefte*, 79, pp. 44–61.
Doering, Susan (1987), 'Nestroy und die Zeitgenossen', *Nestroyana*, 7, pp. 6–14.
Doering, Susan (1988), 'Schnipfer oder Dichter? Zur Frage der Vorlagenbearbeitung bei Johann Nestroy', in Valentin, 1988, pp. 55–70.
Draudt, Manfred (1980), '"Der unzusammenhängende Zusammenhang": Johann Nestroy und William Shakespeare. Dramatische Konventionen im Wiener Volkstheater und im elisabethanischen Public Theatre', *Maske und Kothurn*, 26, pp. 16–58.
Haida, Peter (1987), 'Nestroy und Heinrich Heine', *Nestroyana*, 7, pp. 15–27.
Häusler, Wolfgang (1989), '"Überhaupt hat der Fortschritt das an sich, daß er viel größer ausschaut, als er wirklich ist." Stichworte für den Historiker aus Johann N. Nestroys vorrevolutionärer Posse *Der Schützling* (1847)', in *Römische historische Mitteilungen*, 31, pp. 419–51.
Häusler, Wolfgang (1991), '"Wart's, Gourmanninen!" Vom Essen und Trinken in Nestroys Possen und in Nestroys Zeit', *Österreich in Geschichte und Literatur*, 35, pp. 217–41.
Hein, Jürgen (1979), 'Possen- und Volksstück-Dramaturgie im Vormärz-Volkstheater. Zu Johann Nestroys *Zu ebener Erde und erster Stock* und *Der Unbedeutende*', *Der Deutschunterricht*, 31, pp. 122–37.
Hein, Jürgen (1983), 'Die Bühne als Welt. Bild und Rolle des Theaters im Werk Johann Nestroys', *Neue Zürcher Zeitung*, 9–10 April 1983 (no. 82, pp. 67–8).
Hein, Jürgen (1985), 'Der utopische Nestroy', *Nestroyana*, 6, pp. 13–23.
Hein, Jürgen (1986), (ed.) *Parodien des Wiener Volkstheaters*, Stuttgart.

Hein, Jürgen (1987a), 'Nestroys Verhältnis zu den "Klassikern"', *Neue Zürcher Zeitung*, 17–18 January 1987 (no. 13, p. 69).
Hein, Jürgen (1987b), (ed.) Johann Nestroy, *Höllenangst*, Stuttgart.
Hein, Jürgen (1988a), 'Johann Nestroy: *Der Zerrissene*', in Helmut Arntzen (ed.), *Komödiensprache. Beiträge zum deutschen Lustspiel zwischen dem 17. und dem 20. Jahrhundert*, Münster, pp. 83–97.
Hein, Jürgen (1988b), 'Judenthematik im Wiener Volkstheater', in Hans Otto Horch and Horst Denkler (eds), *Conditio Judaica. Judentum, Antisemitismus und deutschsprachige Literatur vom 18. Jahrhundert bis zum Ersten Weltkrieg*, 2 vols, Tübingen, I, pp. 164–86.
Hein, Jürgen (1988c), 'Nestroy in Amsterdam', *Nestroyana*, 8, pp. 53–70.
Hein, Jürgen (1989a), 'Aspekte der Nestroy-Edition', *Editio*, 3, pp. 114–24.
Hein, Jürgen (1989b), 'Johann Nestroy', in Hugo Aust, Peter Haida and Jürgen Hein, *Volksstück. Vom Hanswurstspiel zum sozialen Drama der Gegenwart*, Munich, pp. 143–9.
Hein, Jürgen (1990a), 'Frühere Verhältnisse und Alte Bekanntschaften', *Nestroyana*, 9, pp. 51–9.
Hein, Jürgen (1990b), *Johann Nestroy* (Sammlung Metzler, 258), Stuttgart.
Hein, Jürgen (1991a), 'Aspekte der Textkonstitution von Nestroys Possen-Szenarien', in Martin Stern (ed.), *Textkonstitution bei mündlicher und bei schriftlicher Überlieferung*, Tübingen, pp. 100–8.
Hein, Jürgen (1991b), *Das Wiener Volkstheater. Raimund und Nestroy*, 2nd edn, Darmstadt (Erträge der Forschung, 100).
Hüttner, Johann (1979), 'Machte sich Nestroy bezahlt?', *Nestroyana*, 1, pp. 2–15.
Hüttner, Johann (1980a), 'Theatre Censorship in Metternich's Vienna', *Theatre Quarterly*, 10, no. 37, pp. 61–9.
Hüttner, Johann (1980b), '*Der Treulose* – ein Fall für die Nestroyforschung', *Nestroyana*, 2, pp. 61–71.
Hüttner, Johann (1980c), 'Vor- und Selbstzensur bei Johann Nestroy', *Maske und Kothurn*, 26, pp. 234–48.
Hüttner, Johann (1981), 'Das theatrale Umfeld Nestroys', *Nestroyana*, 3, pp. 140–55.
Hüttner, Johann (1985), 'Der ernste Nestroy', in Yates and McKenzie 1985, pp. 67–80 (notes p. 157).
Hüttner, Johann (1986), 'Volkstheater als Geschäft: Theaterbetrieb und Publikum im 19. Jahrhundert', in Valentin 1986, pp. 127–49.
Jansen, Peter K. (1980), 'Johann Nepomuk Nestroys skeptische Utopie: Märchen und Wirklichkeit in *Der Talisman*', *Jahrbuch der deutschen Schillergesellschaft*, 24, pp. 247–82.
Kastl, Maria (1991), 'Beobachtungen zur barocken Predigttradition bei Nestroy', *Jahrbuch der Grillparzer-Gesellschaft* (3. Folge), 17, pp. 71–83.
Keith-Smith, Brian (ed.) (1990), *Bristol Austrian Studies*, Bristol.
Koppen, Erwin (1982), 'Die Zeitgenossen Nestroy und Labiche', in Herbert Zeman (ed.), *Die österreichische Literatur: Ihr Profil im 19. Jahrhundert (1830–1880)*, Graz, pp. 615–32.
McKenzie, John R. P. (1980), 'Political Satire in Nestroy's *Freiheit in Krähwinkel*', *Modern Language Review*, 75, pp. 322–32.
McKenzie, John R. P. (1985), 'Nestroy's Political Plays', in Yates and McKenzie 1985, pp. 123–38 (notes pp. 160–2).
Mills, Ken (1990), 'Alcoholism and the Apocalypse? Reflections on a Norm in Nineteenth-Century Literature', in Keith-Smith 1990, pp. 117–37.
Mitchell, Michael and Murdoch, Brian (1983), '"Wer kennt heute noch John Oxenford?": The Fortunes of a Farce from Nestroy to Stoppard', in B. O. Murdoch

and M. G. Ward (eds), *Studies in Nineteenth Century Austrian Literature. Six Papers*, Glasgow, pp. 59–76.

Münz, Rudolf (1988), 'Nestroy und die Tradition des Volkstheaters', *Impulse*, 11, pp. 192–254.

Neuber, Wolfgang (1987), *Nestroys Rhetorik. Wirkungspoetik und Altwiener Volkskomödie im 19. Jahrhundert*, Bonn.

Obermaier, Walter (1982), 'Nestroy und seine Freunde', *Nestroyana*, 4, pp. 92–7.

Obermaier, Walter (1984), 'Johann Nestroys *Häuptling Abendwind* – Offenbachrezeption und satirisches Element', *Nestroyana*, 5, pp. 49–58.

Obermaier, Walter (1985a), 'Neue Einblicke in Nestroys Biographie. I. Die Gastspielreisen 1834 bis 1836', *Nestroyana*, 6, pp. 42–50.

Obermaier, Walter (1985b), 'Nestroy und Ernst Stainhauser', in Yates and McKenzie 1985, pp. 41–54 (notes pp. 154–6).

Obermaier, Walter (1987), 'Nestroyaufführungen in Wien 1938–1945', *Nestroyana*, 7, pp. 52–64.

Obermaier, Walter (1988), 'Der Einfluß des französischen Theaters auf den Spielplan der Wiener Vorstadtbühnen in den 50er Jahren des 19. Jahrhunderts, insbesondere die Offenbachrezeption Nestroys', in Valentin 1988, pp. 133–53.

Obermaier, Walter (1991), 'Nestroy und die Presse', in Stieg and Valentin 1991, pp. 109–18.

Rössler, Helmut (1981), *Karl Kraus und Nestroy. Kritik und Verarbeitung*, Stuttgart.

Schmidt-Dengler, Wendelin (1982), 'Familienfassaden. Zur Funktion der Familie bei Johann Nestroy', *Nestroyana*, 4, pp. 83–91.

Schneilin, Gérard (1991), 'De *L'homme blasé* (Duvert et Lauzanne) à *Der Zerrissene* (Nestroy)', in Stieg and Valentin 1991, pp. 143–56.

Sengle, Friedrich (1980), *Biedermeierzeit. Deutsche Literatur im Spannungsfeld zwischen Restauration und Revolution 1815–1848*, 3 vols, Stuttgart 1971–80, III, pp. 191–264, 'Johann Nestroy (1801–1862)'.

Spohr, Mathias (1985), '"Man lachte und frug nicht viel, woher und warum": Offenbachs Operette *Vent du soir* und Nestroys *Häuptling Abendwind*', *Neue Zürcher Zeitung*, 9 November 1985 (no. 261, p. 68).

Spohr, Mathias (1989), '*Häuptling Abendwind*. Nestroys Entgegnung auf das kulturelle Umfeld der Pariser Operette', *Nestroyana*, 9, pp. 17–21.

Stieg, Gerald and Valentin, Jean-Marie (eds) (1991), *Johann Nestroy 1801–1862: Vision du monde et écriture dramatique*, Asnières.

Stroszeck, Hauke (1988), 'Der Millionist und die Milich. Zur Motivik in Johann Nestroys *Der Zerrissene*', *Nestroyana*, 8, pp. 74–85.

Stroszeck, Hauke (1990), *Heilsthematik in der Posse. Über Johann Nestroys 'Der Talisman'*, Aachen.

Theobald, Rainer (1990), 'Nestroy am Alexanderplatz', *Nestroyana*, 10, pp. 55–67.

Tutschka, Irene T. (1990), 'Synoptischer Abdruck: *Ein melancholischer Hausknecht – Frühere Verhältnisse*', *Nestroyana*, 9, pp. 61–110.

Valentin, Jean-Marie (ed.) (1986), *Volk – Volksstück – Volkstheater im deutschen Sprachraum des 18.–20. Jahrhunderts*, Berne.

Valentin, Jean-Marie (ed.) (1988), *Das österreichische Volkstheater im europäischen Zusammenhang 1830–1880*, Berne.

Valentin, Jean-Marie (1991), 'Nestroy sur la scène française: *Du haut en bas ou Banquiers et fripiers* (Mélesville et Carmouche) et *Zu ebener Erde und erster Stock* (Nestroy)', in Stieg and Valentin 1991, pp. 177–92.

Walker, Colin (1981), 'Nestroy's *Judith und Holofernes* and Antisemitism in Vienna', *Oxford German Studies*, 12, pp. 85–110.

Walker, Colin (1990), 'Nestroy and the Redemptorists', in Keith-Smith 1990, pp. 73–115.

Walla, Friedrich (1979a), 'Nestroys Spiel mit der Biographie: *Der Tod am Hochzeitstage oder Mann, Frau, Kind*', *Seminar*, 15, pp. 97–113.

Walla, Friedrich (1979b), 'Die menschliche Tragödie: Johann Nestroys *Der Tod am Hochzeitstage oder Mann, Frau, Kind*', *Nestroyana*, 1, pp. 41–61.

Walla, Friedrich (1980), 'Prolegomena zur neuen Nestroy-Ausgabe', *Jahrbuch für Internationale Germanistik*, 12, no. 1, pp. 196–201.

Walla, Friedrich (1981a), 'Über *Prinz Friedrich* von Johann Nestroy: Noch nicht, aber doch schon', *Études Germaniques*, 36, pp. 1–14.

Walla, Friedrich (1981b), 'Der Dichter als Handwerker: Selbstzitate bei Nestroy', *Nestroyana*, 3, pp. 3–13.

Walla, Friedrich (1981c), 'Von *Einen Jux will er sich machen* bis *Nur keck!*': Johann Nestroy und seine englischen Quellen', *Nestroyana*, 3, pp. 33–52.

Walla, Friedrich (1985), 'Johann Nestroy und der Antisemitismus. Eine Bestandaufnahme', *Österreich in Geschichte und Literatur*, 29, pp. 37–51.

Walla, Friedrich (1986), 'Weinberl, Knieriem und Konsorten: Namen kein Schall und Rauch', *Nestroyana*, 6, pp. 79–89.

Walla, Friedrich (1989), 'Johann Nestroy und die Zensur', *Nestroyana*, 9, pp. 22–34.

Walla, Friedrich (1991), 'Johann Nestroy im Urteil und Vorurteil der Kritik', *Österreich in Geschichte und Literatur*, 35, pp. 242–62.

Walter, Klaus-Peter (1986), 'Peter Dickkopf und Mademoiselle de Prosny. Der französische Zeitungsroman *Au Jour le jour* als Vorlage zu *Heimliches Geld, heimliche Liebe*', *Nestroyana*, 6, pp. 90–3.

Wimmer, Ruprecht (1986), 'Der Teufel als Mißverständnis. Gedanken zu Johann Nestroys Posse *Höllenangst* und ihrer französischen Vorlage', in E. Heftrich and J.-M. Valentin (eds), *Gallo-Germanica. Wechselwirkungen und Parallelen deutscher und französischer Literatur (18.-20. Jahrhundert)*, Nancy, pp. 187–205.

Yates, W. Edgar (1979), 'Nestroys Komödie der Freundschaft: *Der Zerrissene*', *Österreich in Geschichte und Literatur*, 23, pp. 43–8.

Yates, W. Edgar (1981), 'Zur Wirklichkeitsbezogenheit der Satire in Nestroys Posse *Eine Wohnung ist zu vermiethen*', *Maske und Kothurn*, 27, pp. 147–54.

Yates, W. Edgar (1985a), 'The Idea of the "Volksstück" in Nestroy's Vienna', *German Life and Letters* (New Series), 38, pp. 462–73.

Yates, W. Edgar (1985b), 'Das Werden eines Nestroystücks', in Yates and McKenzie 1985, pp. 55–66 (notes pp. 156–7).

Yates, W. Edgar (1985c), 'Nestroy, Grillparzer, and the Feminist Cause', in Yates and McKenzie 1985, pp. 93–107 (notes pp. 158–9).

Yates, W. Edgar (1987), 'Nestroy und die Rezensenten', *Nestroyana*, 7, pp. 28–40.

Yates, W. Edgar (1988a), 'Nestroys Weg zur klassischen Posse', *Nestroyana*, 7, pp. 93–109.

Yates, W. Edgar (1988b), '"Die Sache hat bereits ein fröhliches Ende erreicht!": Nestroy und das Happy-End', in Valentin 1988, pp. 71–86.

Yates, W. Edgar (1991), 'Aus der Werkstatt eines "schreibelustigen" Genies: Zu Nestroys Bearbeitung englischer Vorlagen', in Stieg and Valentin 1991, pp. 165–76.

Yates, W. E. and McKenzie, John R. P. (eds) (1985), *Viennese Popular Theatre: A Symposium*, Exeter.

The Ideology of the Salzburg Festival

Wendelin Schmidt-Dengler

Michael P. Steinberg, *The Meaning of the Salzburg Festival: Austria as Theater and Ideology, 1890–1938* (Ithaca and London: Cornell University Press, 1990), 253 pp., $24.95.

It is surprising that the ideological background of the Salzburg Festival has received so little critical attention from scholarship in the context of cultural history. The discussion has hitherto been conducted in the sphere of literary journalism. In 1973 (the year which saw the centenary of Max Reinhardt's birth) Hans Mayer delivered a polemic against Giorgio Strehler's production of the Shakespeare collage *Das Spiel der Mächtigen* ('The Play of the Powerful'), charging Strehler with betraying his own principles by putting on reactionary theatre. It seems accepted as an established fact that Salzburg is an affair of the conservative cultural and (in particular) literary scene, and accordingly this phenomenon has been left on one side – the right-hand side. A study by Walter Weiss[1] tried to situate both Hofmannsthal's programmatic statements and the latent message of his festival dramas (*Jedermann* and, particularly, *Das Salzburger große Welttheater*) in two contexts: one was the 'conservative revolution' (the slogan which Hofmannsthal propagated so successfully in his 1927 Munich lecture, 'Das Schrifttum als geistiger Raum der Nation' [Literature as the Nation's Spiritual Space]), and the other was the social theory of Othmar Spann, whose lecture on the 'True State' was held precisely in 1920, the year in which the Salzburg Festival was founded. Weiss concluded that the Festival could not be discussed in mere party-political terms, and that the disjunction between literature (or culture in general) and politics could no longer be sustained. This made it necessary to interrogate the source afresh, to go back to the origins of the Salzburg Festival, re-examine the starting-points and revise the diverse judgments.

That is what Michael P. Steinberg, a historian at Cornell University, has done in this book with great thoroughness. And in the blurb William McGrath has provided the work with a kind of certificate of quality: 'I have rarely seen a work which so effectively sets its subject in such long-range perspective as this one does [...]' Indeed: Steinberg does not simply stick to his material, but tries above all to situate the history of the Salzburg Festival within the ideological controversies of our century. The work, however, is primarily oriented towards the writings of Hugo von Hofmannsthal, and so it effectively becomes a book about this author; comparatively little is to be found in it about Max Reinhardt or even Richard Strauss. The theme is approached in the first chapter (pp. 1–36) via the ideology of the Baroque, to which Steinberg also returns at the end of the book, where he tries to establish a series of connections with the concept of

The Ideology of the Salzburg Festival

allegory put forward in Walter Benjamin's *Origins of German Tragic Drama*. Thus the history of ideas supplies a wide-angle lens with which to focus the theme: the renewal of the theatre from the spirit of Baroque allegory. But in attempting to trace Hofmannsthal's concept of the Festival back into cultural and intellectual history, Steinberg performs a veritable slalom, weaving his way among the ideologies of the Baroque, anti-Semitism, Protestantism and Catholicism. Richard Wagner is described as a 'megalomaniacal Saxon Protestant' and Hofmannsthal as a 'delicate Viennese Catholic' (p. 29). Steinberg's method turns out to be determined by oppositions of this kind, even though he cannot maintain this confrontational mentality and reaches a synthesising conclusion. Thus the Catholic character of Wagner's *Parsifal* (censured sarcastically by Nietzsche) is emphasised, and so the Catholic background shared by the ideology of the Bayreuth Festival is made manifest (p. 30).

The book's documentary basis is to be found primarily in the second chapter, entitled 'Festival Planning and Cultural Planning' (pp. 37–83). The value of this section, which in my judgment is central to the entire book, lies above all in its exact account of Hofmannsthal's actual efforts to establish the financial basis of the Festival. Hofmannsthal is here presented, for the first time, as a cultural manager who could teach many people nowadays a thing or two about adroit fund-raising. His ability to produce a working amalgam of ideas from the rich storehouses of Western culture is pointedly summed up by Steinberg in the words 'Hofmannsthal was a great synthesizer' (p. 76). The blunders Hofmannsthal could sometimes commit in choosing his comrades are illustrated by his short-lived enthusiasm for Rudolf Pannwitz. When the latter condemned the concept of the Festival as too profane, Hofmannsthal must have felt as though he had stepped under a cold shower (p. 82).

With the paradoxical title 'Nationalist Cosmopolitanism' (pp. 84–115) Steinberg tries to juxtapose Hofmannsthal's political activities during the war with the Festival's supra-national programme. Nationalism and cosmopolitanism appear as 'branches of the same tree' (p. 101). To take this leap, Steinberg has to go back a long way: to Kant, Justus Möser and, in particular, to Thomas Mann's *Betrachtungen eines Unpolitischen*. Thus what Hofmannsthal called supra-nationalism turns out to be a German-centred affair. What appeared to be an achieved consensus with marginal groups was in reality the absorption of all groups into the centre. This formulation is borrowed from Stuart Hall's study of the ideological function of the American media in the 1950s and 1960s; Steinberg thinks it can be transferred to the Austrian situation, especially to the liberal ideology which survived the collapse of the monarchy (p. 89). The demystification of Hofmannsthal as a consistent upholder of a distinctive and supra-national Austrian culture is continued in the next chapter, 'German Culture and Austrian *Kulturpolitik*' (pp. 116–41). 'Austria during this period [i.e. between 1914 and 1933] continuously approached the intellectual and political problem of national self-definition, always in a general German context' (p. 116). Rudolf Pannwitz's confused ideas once more flit through the book, but for Bahr, Redlich and Hofmannsthal himself they probably functioned as a kind of litmus test. Pan-Germanism and opposition to union with Germany were not incompatible, at least for such a versatile character as Bahr (p. 134).

The links between Hofmannsthal's literary work and the ideological programme of the Festival are set out in the fifth chapter, entitled 'Allegory and Authority in the Work of Hugo von Hofmannsthal' (pp. 142–63), where Hofmannsthal's revaluation of allegory is related to similar tendencies in Benjamin and Lukács (p. 143). In his discussion of Hofmannsthal's plays Steinberg relies mainly on Hermann Broch's essay *Hofmannsthal and his Time* and the relevant works of Carl Schorske.[2] Thus Hofmannsthal's dramas and libretti are decoded as ideological messages; his early, pre-ideological phase of linguistic crisis is said to have been brought to an end by the texts written for Strauss, in which music had the function of an antidote to mythical and ideologising tendencies. And Steinberg concludes: 'Where there was no music, as in the Catholic morality plays, the path toward allegory and ideology was cleared' (p. 163). The next section is called 'The Catholic Culture of the Austrian Jews' (pp. 164–95), and sets out to unravel the extremely intricate question of Hofmannsthal's origins in the Jewish bourgeoisie and his socialisation as a Catholic. Freud, Mahler and Schoenberg serve as contrasting examples, to demonstrate the highly diverse attitudes of Jewish intellectuals to Catholicism. At all events it is virtually impossible to reach an unqualified conclusion. It might have been appropriate to refer to writings like Fritz Wittels's *Der Taufjude* or to cite, by way of comparison, the efforts of Franz Werfel and Joseph Roth to come to terms with Catholicism.

A late section deals with 'The Festival Repertory and its Context, 1920–1943' (pp. 196–222), giving particular attention to Max Reinhardt's legendary production of Goethe's *Faust* in 1933. According to newspaper reports, this made Salzburg an international city, despite the thousand-mark tax imposed by Hitler on all Germans crossing the Austrian border. A short section also deals with the changing image of Mozart and the various ways in which the National Socialists staged *The Magic Flute* in order to press it into their service. Both the militarist interpretation by Clemens Krauss and Gustaf Gründgens and the non-ideological one by Karl Böhm and Ludwig Sievert (here Steinberg speaks of 'Burgtheater innocence') suited the Nazis' book.

In his conclusion ('Transformations of the Baroque', pp. 223–31) Steinberg returns to his starting-point, arguing that Hofmannsthal and Benjamin converged in their uses of allegory, the one as 'conservative ideologue', the other as 'modernist historical critic' (p. 231). This rounds off the study neatly, linking the ideological analysis with discussions of aesthetic theory. There follows a list of the plays performed in the Festival from 1920 to 1943, an extensive bibliography, and an index of names.

The analyses are persuasive in their own terms, and the material used is extraordinarily extensive. Steinberg has examined a great deal of unpublished material in Marbach, the Vienna Theatersammlung, Hofmannsthal's *Nachlaß*, and elsewhere. My misgivings begin when he approaches the texts themselves. His desire to assign every text and every author a definite place in ideological history, and to treat Catholicism, Protestantism, and Judaism as fixed quantities which can be used in argument, proves somewhat unpropitious, especially when he deals with works of literature in the narrow sense. When discussing Hofmannsthal's often self-contradictory essays one should pay more attention to the often embarrassing extent to which they are adjusted to the expectations of their readership; and the reduction of his dramatic work to its ideological message is sometimes rather unfortunate. This is especially blatant in the discussion of *Der Schwierige* ('The Difficult Man'), whose central character, Hans Karl, is made into a simple 'war hero' and who, contrary to the text, delivers a speech in Parliament 'during' (!) the play. Anyone who knew *Der Schwierige* only from Steinberg's reference would acquire an extremely odd notion of this sublime comedy. Of course this play could also be subjected to a political reading, but Steinberg stops at the point where many previous interpreters have stopped, describing this play as a late document of Hofmannsthal's linguistic crisis (pp. 158ff.).

In Hofmannsthal's letters and essays his political legacy takes decidedly coarse-grained forms; in his dramas and libretti it is expressed much more subtly through his art of indirection. The best example of how the political message (entirely in the service of the 'conservative revolution') can vanish into the form is the post-war comedy *Der Unbestechliche* ('The Incorruptible Man'), where Hofmannsthal has implanted the political theme so subtly that it escapes most critics' attention. The very title contains a marked allusion to Robespierre, who was nicknamed 'l'Incorruptible', and the servant Theodor illustrates very nicely how order can be restored if servants remain servants but subject their masters to a kind of moral reformation. Unfortunately Steinberg never mentions this play, which is so often dismissed as a trifling farce. It would also have been wise to look more closely at Max Mell's *Apostelspiel* ('Apostle Play'), in which the anti-Bolshevist message is even more vigorously proclaimed.

Steinberg is anxious to read the Salzburg Festival from the viewpoint of *German* intellectual history, and for this he no doubt has good reasons. He unmasks Hofmannsthal's Austrian idea as – to put it bluntly – a very German business. However, he also illuminates the political and ideological setting of the Festival extremely well. In particular, the figure of Franz Rehrl, the *Landeshauptmann* of Salzburg, receives due consideration. His conservative and anti-Semitic but also anti-Nazi standpoint exemplifies the indistinct attitude common to many Austrians in various political camps. I venture to doubt whether Steinberg's observations always do justice to the specifically Austrian tensions at work. He is certainly well informed about the ideological disputes that tore the First Republic apart, and deals with the development of the Corporate State and its ideology, but he does not distinguish clear stages of historical development. It should have been mentioned that the various political groupings in the First Republic sought to assert or preserve their identity precisely through a culture of festivals which they built up through intensive effort. The festivals of the Social Democrats (misleadingly abbreviated as SPÖ on p. 119) would have provided a foil to Hofmannsthal's programme and at the same time supplied many surprising parallels. Alfred Pfoser's *Literatur und Austromarxismus* (Vienna, 1980) would have provided useful information on this score. The collection of essays edited by Franz Kadrnoska, *Aufbruch und Untergang*.

Österreichische Kultur zwischen 1918 und 1938 (Vienna, 1981), and Friedbert Aspetsberger's book *Literarisches Leben im Austrofaschismus* (Königstein/Ts., 1980) supply an indispensable basis for the study of cultural politics in the First Republic. Although Hermann Rudolph's work on the conservative revolution does figure in the bibliography, its findings are not discussed. Three volumes of Thomas Bernhard's autobiography are listed (under the wrong dates) in the bibliography, but their implications, which are very closely related to Salzburg, have obviously been suppressed.

How little importance Steinberg attaches to the criticisms originally levelled at the Salzburg Festival is apparent from the marginal treatment meted out to Karl Kraus. And Alfred Polgar, whose sharp-witted journalism sheds harsh light on the conjunction of conservative ideology and theatrical practice, is never mentioned at all.

One must certainly agree with Steinberg's thesis that the Salzburg Festival was central to the self-understanding of Austria between the two world wars. Yet he falls prey to Hofmannsthal's wiles in interpreting the latter's programme as uniquely representative of Austrian cultural life. Although he deals very minutely with Hofmannsthal's actual political work and thus extends our knowledge of the Festival's material underpinning, his study remains more indebted to a superstructure of ideas, as shown by his excursions into German intellectual history and his excursuses on Freud, Mahler and Schoenberg. To combine the social-historical basis of literature with the analysis of complex texts is one of the most difficult tasks of literary scholarship, and one that remains largely unsolved. In the last twenty years German literary scholarship has done important spadework in this area. The debate on the Austrian ideology and the ideology of Austrian authors, initiated twenty-five years ago by Claudio Magris, has been the subject of numerous works which make some of Steinberg's observations seem not particularly novel. Some questions are still awaiting answers. What were the consequences of Hofmannsthal's death for the Festival? How did assessments of the Festival change between the 1920s and the 1930s? Can any gaps in continuity be perceived, for example in 1933 or 1934? How is political rhetoric related to the Festival? A further-reaching task would be that of establishing which conception of the Festival survived after 1945 to make continuity possible.

At any rate, this book differs gratifyingly from most celebratory publications; although Steinberg's attitude to Hofmannsthal is not uncritical (especially as regards the Festival plays *Jedermann* and *Das Salzburger große Welttheater*), he treats the author's artistic achievement and sensibility with respect. The number of errors in the bibliography and the text is within the limits of tolerance. It is slightly odd to see the Trabrennplatz, where Dollfuss delivered his programmatic speech in September 1933, transformed into the 'Trabenplatz' (p. 127).

Any treatment of this thorny material must provoke objections. On the one hand, Steinberg deserves credit for attempting to describe the Festival ideology in a broad context, extracting it from those Austrian debates that seem so petty at a distance, and avoiding the mere party-political terms deplored by Weiss. On the other hand, the history of the Salzburg Festival in the context of the Austrian ideology has still to be written.

Notes

1. 'Salzburger Mythos? Hofmannsthals und Reinhardts Welttheater', originally a lecture given at the 1974 conference of the Institut für Österreichkunde; published in Friedbert Aspetsberger (ed.), *Staat und Gesellschaft in der modernen österreichischen Literatur* (Vienna, 1977), pp. 5–19.
2. Hermann Broch, *Hugo von Hofmannsthal and his Time*, tr. Michael P. Steinberg (Chicago, 1984); Carl E. Schorske, *Fin-de-Siècle Vienna: Politics and Culture* (New York, 1980).

Part Three
Reviews

Anton Schindling and Walter Ziegler (eds), *Die Kaiser der Neuzeit 1519–1918: Heiliges Römisches Reich, Österreich, Deutschland* (Munich: Beck, 1990), 506 pp., DM 48.

Prospective readers should not be misled by this book's seemingly conventional title and organisation. Seventeen different historians have contributed individual chapters on the twenty-one Austrian and German emperors who have reigned since Charles V. Yet their principal goal is not to present biographical sketches or summary narratives of their reigns. Rather, it is to discuss and analyse their individual contributions as the imperial heads of state of German-speaking central Europe during modern times. It is this mission that brings together what would otherwise be an eccentric mixture of fifteen Holy Roman Emperors with the rulers of the two 'successor states', the Austrian Empire and the Second German Reich.

The volume builds confidently on the trends of recent scholarship that have stressed the effectiveness of imperial institutions, by pointing to the major contributions made by most of the rulers themselves. Although it sometimes overstates their importance, it seems justified in assuming this generally positive vein, just as the last (and only Anglo-American) contributor, John Röhl, is on target in writing one of the volume's most critical evaluations, concerning the hapless William II.

The book's German focus encourages at best a partial coverage of its Habsburg rulers. The emphasis throughout is on foreign policy, diplomacy, and political relationships with the institutions and estates of the Holy Roman Empire. When the authors touch on the Habsburgs' domestic policies, they limit themselves to the Austrian and Bohemian *Erblande*. Hence, individual chapters overlook the Spanish world of Charles V, the innumerable Hungarian crises of Leopold I, and Charles VI's contributions to the Austrian Baroque; although Harm-Hinrich Brandt's forty-page contribution on Francis Joseph is twice the length of the typical essay, it concentrates on Schwarzenberg's German policy, the end of the German Confederation, and Austria's expulsion from Germany – and ends in 1867. All of which suggests that one of the volume's most important strengths for Austrian scholars is the attention that it focuses on the German dimension of Habsburg policy.

Another noteworthy characteristic is the volume's pitch. Rather than give the reader a brief and, at best, pedestrian overview, each chapter attempts to bring the reader abreast of the current state of research on his or her subject. While this might frustrate lay readers, it should afford scholars a convenient vehicle for refreshing their knowledge, especially about lesser-known Habsburg monarchs like Ferdinand III, Francis Ferdinand and Charles I, or the ill-fated Hohenzollern Frederick III. Each essay concludes with handy biographical data, the volume itself with a lengthy appendix that includes a chronology, annotated bibliography, and lists of key ministerial figures.

CHARLES INGRAO

Waltraud Heindl, *Gehorsame Rebellen: Bürokratie und Beamte in Österreich, 1780 bis 1848* (Vienna: Böhlau, 1990), 375 pp., DM 36.

It has long been recognised, in a general way, that bureaucracy represented a crucial element in Austrian state power during the last century and more of Habsburg rule. Influential analyses, such as Joseph Redlich's, were markedly coloured by that insight. But historians have been slow to subject Habsburg officialdom to detailed enquiry. Now, in the wake of two important volumes about the later nineteenth-century administration (the collective work on *Verwaltung* in the *Habsburgermonarchie, 1848–1918* series and a monograph by Karl Megner) we have Dr Heindl's pioneering contribution on the formative period of the bureaucracy, from Josephinism to the *Vormärz*.

The author seeks a broad view of the life and work of officials in the central departments of state. We learn a good deal, from archival and literary sources, about their background, ethos and culture. Heindl stresses the advance of commoner bureaucrats at the expense of nobles: even the notorious principle of promotion by seniority (*Anciennität*) was conceived as a way of countering the advantages of the latter. By 1848 the character of the service was essentially middle-class, even though aristocrats maintained a strong hold on the highest offices (the author might have been more explicit here about the implications of ennoblement and she perhaps exaggerates the exclusiveness of the Staatsrat). The status of *Beamte* became more clearly defined and their *esprit de corps* enhanced; in a variety of ways, from uniforms to pension schemes, their values and interests were protected. Yet the regime ploughed resources into expanding officialdom rather than paying it properly: in fifty years the number of positions roughly doubled, while salaries failed to keep pace with inflation, especially during the years of devastating price rises after 1800 and again in the 1830s and 1840s.

These considerations supply a framework for Heindl's principal theme: the three-cornered relationship between bureaucracy, absolutism and reform. Joseph II called a new *Beamtentum* into being in order to implement his thoroughly autocratic vision of a modernised, rationalised and coherent Austrian state. Within twenty years that reform programme had been disowned by his successors, and the administration suffered a crisis of confidence. On the whole, it drifted back towards the old conservative dynastic loyalties, yet sufficient innovative purpose remained (especially in the sphere of economic policy, about which this book has curiously little to say) to prevent total reaction. The outcome was a debilitating stagnation, which in the end condemned the whole system.

There is more in this book about 'obedience' than about 'rebellion', and the author might profitably have discussed the political activities of (ex-) bureaucrats during 1848. Yet the balance is surely just, for the year of revolution soon gave way to a further, and more intensive, instalment of administrative absolutism, which set its stamp on subsequent developments. If more had also been said here about the antecedent growth of officialdom under Maria Theresia, the longer-term congruence between state authority and civil service would have appeared still closer. The slower, but parallel evolution in Habsburg Hungary, which patriots wrongly believed to be essentially unbureaucratic, could further confirm that conclusion. Heindl's consistently lucid and stimulating volume represents a major step towards better understanding of the processes of state-building in nineteenth-century Central Europe.

R. J. W. EVANS

Edith Saurer, *Straße, Schmuggel, Lottospiel: Materielle Kultur und Staat in Niederösterreich, Böhmen und Lombardo-Venetien im frühen 19. Jahrhundert*, Veröffentlichungen des Max-Planck-Instituts für Geschichte, vol. 90 (Göttingen: Vandenhoeck & Ruprecht, 1989), 532 pp., DM 108.

Odd books with simple titles are not uncommon, nor are simple books with odd titles, but this is an odd book with an odd title. Potential readers may well wonder what roads, smuggling and lotteries have in common – and by the end of this substantial volume they will still be wondering. Indeed, their perplexity will have grown rather than have diminished, for they will have encountered *en route*, among many other things, long sections on such diverse topics as bread riots, snuff-taking, smoking and public finance. It might be thought that the missing link is supplied by the subtitle – 'material culture and the state' – but this proves not to be the case. The brief introduction is more like a preface and does not begin to provide a coherent framework for the disparate information which follows. Instead, it offers a number of gnomic epigrams about space and time, drawn mainly from the work of Fernand Braudel. These may mean a great deal, or they may mean very little; they certainly sound more persuasive in the original French. For all his gifts, Braudel is not the best guide to what 'material culture' might or might not mean. Dr Saurer does not seem to have got to grips with this difficult but important concept. Her own bibliography lists one work by Geertz and one by Foucault, but she does not actually cite the former and there are only two brief references to the latter. There is no reference anywhere to Gadamer, Ricoeur, Barthes, Derrida or any other appropriate theorists. It is very unusual to have to complain about a lack of theoretical underpinning in a German work, but such is the case here. The situation could have been rescued by a proper conclusion, which would have pulled all the threads together and would have told us where we had gone and why, but once again the opportunity is spurned. What we get instead is a ten-page collection of observations on national character drawn from travellers' tales. The book just fizzles out.

This is all a great shame, for Dr Saurer shows that she has done a great deal of research in a wide range of archives (in Milan, Venice and Vienna) and can present her discoveries lucidly and cogently. Particularly important is her discussion of communications in the *Vormärz*. She shows convincingly that the improvements made to Austrian roads accelerated and increased traffic appreciably during the first half of the nineteenth century, even to the extent of calling into question the revolutionary nature of the coming of the railways. This quickening and thickening of communications also casts doubt on the conventional picture of the *Vormärz* as a period of stagnation. She is also very interesting on the interdependence of material and ideological developments.

The Austrian customs system, for example, still based on the prohibitive tariff of 1784, was seen by contemporaries as a symbol of intellectual oppression. In the same vein was a comment by an Austrian official that the building of railways was incompatible with continued denial of freedom of expression. As these two examples show, there is much of interest here for all historians of the Habsburg Empire in the *Vormärz*, but the book's impact would have been greatly enhanced if it had been provided with an adequate introduction and conclusion.

T. C. W. BLANNING

Peter Branscombe, *W. A. Mozart: 'Die Zauberflöte'*, Cambridge Opera Handbooks (Cambridge: Cambridge University Press, 1991), xv + 247 pp., £30.00/£9.95.

John A. Rice, *W. A. Mozart: 'La clemenza di Tito'*, Cambridge Opera Handbooks (Cambridge: Cambridge University Press, 1991), xii + 181 pp., £27.50/£9.95.

Mozart's last two operas were a remarkable feat, not least for being composed at a feverish pace and amid the periods of illness affecting the last six months or so of his all-too-brief life. *Die Zauberflöte (The Magic Flute)*, which received its première at Vienna's Theater auf der Wieden on 30 September 1791, is a comic German 'Singspiel', interleaving music and spoken dialogue in what now seem strikingly innovative ways. Less than one month before – on 6 September – *La clemenza di Tito* was staged in Prague to celebrate the coronation of Emperor Leopold II as King of Bohemia: here we have a conventional Italian *opera seria*, with arias, ensembles and sung recitative in the traditional mould. That Mozart could switch from one to the other – as he evidently did in the course of their composition – and produce such different music bears witness not only to his extraordinary facility but also to his remarkable sensitivity to questions of genre and style.

La clemenza di Tito has tended to remain on the fringes of the mainstream operatic repertory; *Die Zauberflöte*, on the other hand, lies at its heart. Its fairytale fantasy – dragons and flying machines, bird-catcher and wicked queens – its story of goodies and baddies (although which characters are which takes a while to come clear) and its heart-warming morality are no less attractive now than they were in the late eighteenth and nineteenth centuries. So too, for that matter, is Mozart's wonderful music. Peter Branscombe, it seems, cannot lose in having picked so rich a work for his contribution to the splendid Cambridge Opera Handbooks series.

Nor does he. Branscombe takes us efficiently through the sources, the intellectual background, the action, the compositional process, the text, the music (a chapter by Erik Smith) and the first performance and the work's reception through to the 1980s. Anthony Besch then provides a chapter on 'A director's approach', and the book rounds off with a discussion of 'problems' and a conclusion. For all its popularity, *Die Zauberflöte* is by no means an easy work to handle – witness its somewhat confusing plot and the evidently multilayered symbolism (not least the elements drawn from Mozart's experiences as a Freemason) – and it has attracted a wealth of critical attention. Branscombe takes the sensible path, seeking 'to concentrate on the essentials ... questioning traditional assumptions whilst as far as possible avoiding new speculation' (p. 3). But inevitably he does come up with some new ideas, including the addition (made in collaboration with Roy Owen) of Chrétien de Troyes's *Yvain*, or *Le Chevalier au Lion* (c. 1177) to the list of literary and other sources for the opera. Branscombe's careful approach is also useful in sweeping away some old myths: for example, that the opera was directly affected by competition with another magic opera, *Kaspar der Fagottist, oder Die Zauberzither*; and that the libretto was in fact by Carl Ludwig Gieseke, and not the theatre impresario Emanuel Schikaneder (also the first Papageno). And Branscombe is admirably sanguine about the contradictions and inconsistencies in the plot, which are surely less problematic than some critics would have us believe.

Much as I admire Erik Smith, his chapter on the music is a little disappointing. It roves widely without focusing on specific issues in enough detail, and it seems strange to use Mozart's *Le nozze di Figaro* (1786) as the paradigmatic Italian *opera buffa* when the composer had so significantly modified the paradigms in his most recent *opera buffa*, *Così fan tutti* (1790). The rather sweeping generalisations, too - in terms of structure, *Die Zauberflöte* 'broke free from the bonds of the eighteenth century' (p. 111) – are a little worrying. Smith is certainly on to something with his notion of 'vestigial recapitulations', referring to Mozart's loose use of sonata-form structures (with returns to the home key but not to the opening thematic material). But when is a recapitulation not a recapitulation? Similarly, he starts to make some useful motivic connections between different sections of the opera but scarcely penetrates the complex web of references and relations in what is arguably Mozart's most allusive score. Also, it is curious to find no words in the music examples.

Besch's chapter is a personal account of his extensive professional experience with the opera. That the singers 'will have been required to learn the music of their rôles before rehearsals begin' (p. 194) seems to state the obvious, while 'The soprano studying the rôle of Pamina will consider her mother's influence and what characteristics she may have inherited from her' (p. 201) betrays a particular view of how singers should work through their parts. The discussion of the staging problems, and Besch's various solutions to them, is interesting enough, but one wonders whether some form of symposium, with input from a few more directors, might not have been more effective.

Besch is emphatic on the Masonic elements in *Die Zauberflöte*: in contrast, Branscombe repeatedly plays down the issue, more out of (understandable) ignorance than from conviction, it seems. Their differences – while healthy enough – are perhaps symptomatic of a book not quite under firm editorial control: Besch keeps to the traditional view that the Schaffer engravings of sets for the opera (some are reproduced here) 'may well derive from the stage-plan of the original production' (p. 187), whereas Branscombe has already said that they are 'more likely to be depictions of a provincial staging' (p. 175); Branscombe himself duplicates his material (compare pp. 77 and 216); and sometimes the text becomes slightly repetitious. Two omissions from the bibliography would profitably have helped matters here: Malcolm S. Cole, '*The Magic Flute* and the Quatrain', *Journal of Musicology* (1984), pp. 157–76 (for the libretto); and James Webster, 'To Understand Verdi and Wagner We Must Understand Mozart', *19th-Century Music* (1987–8), pp. 175–93 (with a provocative discussion of the Act I finale). And on the whole, the reader is left with the feeling of things not quite gelling. But perhaps that is Branscombe again being admirably faithful to his source.

John Rice has a somewhat easier time of it. Writing on his own, and on an opera that even seasoned Mozartians often treat as a none too successful *pièce d'occasion*, he can focus on a straightforward account of the opera and (for no less than a third of the book) its chequered history since the première. He is good on the context requiring a work so specifically tied to imperial propaganda (the new emperor was facing political and social crisis) and to the operatic tastes of a patron who, as Grand Duke of Tuscany since 1765, had well-established preferences for Italian opera in serious, rather than comic, vein. Mozart had to work hard to meet these demands, and he encountered the prejudices against a non-Italian composer that had dogged his career: Empress Maria Luisa's comment that *La clemenza di Tito* was 'una porcheria tedesca' ('German pigswill' comes close) is almost certainly apocryphal, but it reflects a typical view of Mozart's seemingly too complicated music.

Rice has new material on the commission for the opera (the imperial Kapellmeister Antonio Salieri was the impresario Domenico Guardasoni's first choice) but fudges the fraught question of chronology: the piece that became Vitellia's rondò 'Non più di fiori' seems to have been performed in April 1791, whereas the commission for the opera could only have reached Mozart in mid-July (another curious piece of evidence – that Mozart began composing the part of Sesto for a tenor voice, despite the clear intention of using a castrato in Guardasoni's contract – is not brought into play here). He also has some useful things to say about the performers in the first production: Mozart knew that the part of Tito was to be sung by the tenor Antonio Baglioni and so produced palpably similar vocal writing to that of Baglioni's other main Mozart role, Don Ottavio in *Don Giovanni* (Prague, 1787); and he could also count on the talents of the clarinettist Anton Stadler (for whom the composer wrote his clarinet quintet and clarinet concerto), who is given much chance to shine in the opera. And Rice's admirable plea for the merits of *opera seria*, hinging in large part on the notion that we should treat the recitative as a serious element of the drama, is only slightly weakened by the fact that Mozart seemingly delegated the composition of the recitative to his pupil, Franz Xaver Süssmayr.

The libretto for *La clemenza di Tito* was by that great early eighteenth-century librettist, Pietro Metastasio (it was revised for Mozart – turned into a 'true opera', he said – by the imperial theatre-poet, Caterino Mazzolà). Given the number of settings of Metastasio's libretto – by Caldara, Leo, Hasse (the young Mozart saw this version in Cremona in January 1770), Veracini, Wagenseil, Pampani, Gluck, Jommelli, G. Scarlatti, Holzbauer, Galuppi, Bernasconi, Naumann, Anfossi, Sarti and Ottani – it seems curious that they receive scant discussion here (a brief quotation from Gluck apart). Instead, Rice's gaze is fixed firmly on events after the first performance. *La clemenza di Tito* was hawked around by Mozart's widow, Constanze, as almost his last work – the sympathy vote, as it were, worked to her considerable financial benefit – and it also achieved some popularity in more conservative centres (including London) into the first decades of the nineteenth century: here we perhaps need more on how particular singers treated it specifically as a show-piece (it clearly is, for all its problems) at their own benefit performances. But as the times fell out of sympathy with the old-fashioned aesthetic of the *opera seria*, *La clemenza di Tito* was left to languish on the library shelves, unperformed and unloved even by the most avid Mozartians (and despite the composer's own clear liking for the piece). For its recent revival, we owe a clear debt to Jean-Pierre Ponnelle, whose productions (and a film) did a great deal to show the opera in a new light: the latest Glyndebourne production has continued the process in the United Kingdom.

The circumstances surrounding the first performance of *La clemenza di Tito* made it a striking testimony of a threatened political and ideological regime: Mozart's resonant echoes of Handel in the penultimate chorus are eloquent reminders of times past. One might say precisely the same of *Die Zauberflöte*. Here, Mozart scarcely 'broke free from the bonds of the eighteenth century': the debt, instead, is to Bach (from the echoes of the E flat fugue from Book II of *The Well Tempered Clavier* in the overture to the stern chorale prelude in the Act II finale). Both operas, for all their rich differences, are intimately linked (something neither Branscombe nor Rice covers properly here) as eloquent statements betraying a world in crisis as political events threatened to overturn the social order and the elaborately constructed edifice of Enlightenment reason. The Romantics vilified *La clemenza di Tito* and exalted *Die Zauberflöte:* many of us do the same today. But either way, this reflects a fundamental misunderstanding of the essence of Mozart as a composer of and for his time. Both operas are powerful witnesses to a dying age, whose successes and failures resound through to modern times. If these Cambridge Opera Handbooks maintain this resonance, they will have fulfilled their task.

TIM CARTER

Erich Wolfgang Partsch (ed.), *Franz Schubert – Der Fortschrittliche? Analysen – Perspektiven – Fakten*, Veröffentlichungen des Internationalen Franz Schubert Institutes 4 (Tutzing: Hans Schneider, 1989), 256 pp., DM 80.

Elizabeth Norman McKay, *Schubert's Music for the Theatre*, Veröffentlichungen des Internationalen Franz Schubert Institutes 5 (Tutzing: Hans Schneider, 1991), 412 pp., DM 125.

The Internationales Franz Schubert Institut, under the direction of the indefatigable Ernst Hilmar and with the valuable assistance of the publishing house of Hans Schneider, has been responsible for bringing to wider attention some of the most exciting Schubert research of the past few years. These two volumes, representing the most recent fruits of their endeavours, highlight the importance of the Institut as an international focus for Schubert studies and reflect the enormous amount of research into all aspects of his life and œuvre presently being conducted.

Franz Schubert – Der Fortschrittliche?, a collection of fifteen short essays with an introductory note by Claudio Abbado, provides examples of some of the most stimulating research to have emerged recently, both in Europe and in America. Despite the general focus on the 'progressive' tendencies of Schubert's music, it is inevitable that such a volume will, by its very nature, be somewhat amorphous. Perhaps most noticeable is the inordinately wide range of analytical techniques and other approaches which are brought to bear on a variety of topics. Invidious as it is to single out individual essays, mention must be made of some of the most impressive contributions. Walter Dürr, on aspects of Schubert's use of tonality and modulation, is characteristically sensitive in his judgment, while Tom Denny deals in similarly shrewd fashion with the phenomenon of 'directional tonality' in the songs. Despite its somewhat laconic style, Kurt von Fischer's metrical analysis of the *Moment Musical* in C major D 780/1 is convincing in its own right, while also suggesting new lines of enquiry for other such familiar works. Particularly touching is the lapidary summation of 'Schubert the Progressive' by that doyen of Austrian composers, now sadly deceased, Ernst Krenek, who, as the only composer to contribute to this volume, writes from a perspective otherwise unrepresented.

Although the work of no British scholar is included in *Franz Schubert – der Fortschrittliche?*, this deficiency is amply remedied in the next volume published by the Internationales Franz Schubert Institut, the study of Schubert's theatrical music by Elizabeth Norman McKay. She began her work on Schubert thirty years ago, producing an Oxford doctoral thesis which until the present publication constituted practically the only large-scale work devoted to the subject. While the passage of time has seen a veritable flood of writings on Schubert's life and *œuvre*, his operas and other stage works have remained comparatively neglected. During this period the cultural, and more especially the musical, history of Biedermeier Vienna has been the subject of extensive research, and the need for a re-evaluation of Schubert's theatrical works has become ever more pressing.

In his preface Claudio Abbado refers to Schubert's operas and Singspiels as 'unexplored treasures'. Many would dispute the use of such effusive praise, though few who have acquaintance with the best of Schubert's dramatic writing (represented above all by *Fierrabras*, now available in a recording made by Abbado himself, and *Alfonso und Estrella*) could deny that it contains passages of great charm and lyrical beauty. The criticism most frequently levelled at Schubert, and a point that has been advanced passionately by respected commentators down the years, is that he possessed no dramatic gift and no real feeling for the theatre. This may or may not be true, depending on whether one compares Schubert merely to the greatest operatic composers, against whom the defects of his scores are glaringly apparent, or, more realistically, to the mainstream of his day, against which he appears in a far more favourable light. But the essential point is that so much of Schubert's time and energy was devoted to a fruitless attempt to conquer the Viennese stage that it is impossible to appreciate any other facet of his activities without giving due acknowledgement to the central role which opera and quasi-operatic music played in his creative life. In producing this magnificently detailed account of Schubert's theatrical music Elizabeth Norman McKay has thus performed a great service for all those interested in his *œuvre* in general, as well as providing a detailed and cogent examination of the works in their own right.

In the introductory chapters she paints a broad picture of the Vienna in which Schubert lived, paying particular attention to the organisation and repertoire of the various theatres, as well as to the operatic heritage which he absorbed and to which he responded. The main body of the text is a detailed examination of each of his stage works, commencing with the earliest Singspiels (e.g. *Der Spiegelritter* and *Der vierjährige Posten*) and leading through to his most significant achievements, *Alfonso und Estrella*, *Fierrabras* and *Der Graf von Gleichen*. In each case the genesis of the work is sketched, the dramatis personae fully catalogued, and an exhaustive synopsis provided; this is followed by a sensitive discussion of the music and the reception of the work. A helpful list of recent performances and recordings of Schubert's stage works is provided by Father Reinhard van Hoorickx.

Working through Elizabeth Norman McKay's book, one cannot but be impressed by the sheer scale of her undertaking and the apparent ease with which she has mastered such a mass of material. Doubtless, as these works come to be examined yet more thoroughly during the preparation of modern critical editions for the Neue Schubert-Ausgabe, the picture both of individual works and of Schubert's overall contribution to the repertory will be amplified and enhanced. However, there can be no doubt that this will be the standard work on Schubert's stage music for many years to come; it was thus highly appropriate that its launch coincided with the festive inauguration of the Schubert Institute (UK), an organisation which has as one of its central aims the supporting of research into Schubert's music.

EWAN WEST

Hugo Aust, Peter Haida and Jürgen Hein, *Volksstück: Vom Hanswurstspiel zum sozialen Drama der Gegenwart*, Arbeitsbücher zur Literaturgeschichte (Munich: Beck, 1989), 370 pp., DM 48.

Alfred Ziltener, *Hanswursts lachende Erben: Zum Weiterleben der Lustigen Person im Wiener Vorstadt-Theater von La Roche bis Raimund*, Europäische Hochschulschriften, Reihe 1, Deutsche Sprache und Literatur, 1241 (Berne, Frankfurt, New York, Paris: Peter Lang, 1989), 207 pp., SF18.

These books could hardly provide a greater contrast – the one wide-ranging, elegantly written and produced, a major scholarly achievement, and the other deliberately restricted, rather casually presented and, for all the interest aroused by its subject-matter, distinctly disappointing.

Volksstück is a splendid example of felicitous teamwork. So swiftly and thoroughly has it established its worth that it is already difficult to recall how one managed without it. It covers an unusually broad and extended field and combines with admirable clarity theoretical considerations, historical developments and pertinently chosen examples. The book is divided into seven 'Arbeitsbereiche'. The first is concerned with definitions and introduces conceptual and practical considerations, such as mime, *commedia dell'arte* and kinds of improvisatory playing. The second, 'Volkstheater-Praxis und Textpoetik im 18. Jahrhundert', includes the 'Haupt- und Staatsaktionen', extempore theatre (Kurz-Bernardon), 'regularised' theatre (Hafner), the 'Singspiel', and the 'Zauberstück'; these first two chapters are by Hugo Aust. With the third section we reach the heartland, Viennese popular theatre of the first half of the nineteenth century, with Raimund, Nestroy and their predecessors. Jürgen Hein is responsible for the Viennese material, and also for an informative study of the 'Posse' in Frankfurt and Darmstadt; Professor Aust performs a similar service for Berlin, before providing in the book's fourth section an expert consensus on the Viennese scene in the age of Realism (with subsections on 'Volksdrama', Anzengruber and the Berlin of Kalisch, L'Arronge and Voss). 'Arbeitsbereich' V, written by Peter Haida, covers the period from the turn of the century to World War I and embraces 'Volksstück und Naturalismus', 'Volksstück und Heimatkunst', and the more marginal areas of popular entertainment and workers' theatre, as well as the 'Volksstück' of social criticism. The sixth main section, written by all three authors, covers the inter-war period (Kaiser, Zuckmayer, Fleisser, Horváth, Brecht, and the 'völkische Volksstück'); and the last, again the work of the troika, is devoted to tradition and renewal since 1945.

A feature is the ease of reference, thanks to the twelve-page-long table of contents; there is also a good if not quite complete index. Especially valuable is the bibliographical detail contained both in the annotated 'Gesamtbibliographie' and in the individual brief notes that precede each subsection and give the essential information on primary texts and secondary literature.

An individual user might wish for coverage of different plays – Raimund is represented by *Die unheilbringende Zauberkrone* and *Der Verschwender*, Nestroy by *Der Unbedeutende*; reasons of space had to preclude areas like melodrama, festival plays, and the relationship between 'Volksstück' and literary drama. Hofmannsthal thus hardly figures, and the index does not even contain the name of Max Reinhardt. But there is logic behind each decision taken, nowhere more apparent than in the decision to write not so much a history of the 'Volksstück' as a study that would, while incidentally providing essential material for such a history, have its emphasis firmly on '"Volksstück" als einen Begriff der Aufführungsgeschichte'. Theoretical considerations are certainly not overlooked, especially in the expository section, but the book will above all be read for its lively, challenging exegesis of a wealth of dramatic material.

Occasionally one would have welcomed the source for a particular quotation (documentation is generally excellent); Bäuerle is generously evaluated as dramatist, but his *Theaterzeitung* seems not to be mentioned (there is no index of subjects; that would be a welcome addendum to a second edition); Gerhart Hauptmann perhaps gets more attention than he deserves in the present context, but special pleading is generally absent from a book that can be as illuminatingly dipped into as profitably read from cover to cover.

Alfred Ziltener's study traces the comic figure from Stranitzky to Raimund, with a brief concluding survey of Nestroy's place in the Viennese tradition. Exemplary plays by the main dramatists are discussed, the emphasis constantly placed upon 'der Derisor'. There are generally helpful though hardly original comments on Stranitzky, Kurz and Hafner in the first section; and in the second, which deals with the period following the 'Spektakel-Freiheit' of 1776 (which is not identified or explained), the principal authors are Hensler, Schikaneder, Bäuerle, Gleich and Meisl, followed by a separate section on Raimund, four of whose plays are analysed: *Die unheilbringende Zauberkrone, Der Barometermacher auf der Zauberinsel, Der Alpenkönig und der Menschenfeind* (with which Gleich's *Der Berggeist* is compared), and *Moisasurs Zauberfluch*.

A somewhat artificial series of twelve 'models' of the comic character forms the backbone to the book – the 'lustige Person' as his master's companion, as critical observer, benefactor, wire-puller or wire-puller's victim, social climber, conférencier, etc. This works quite well, though sometimes at the expense of subtleties in the characterisation.

Worrying aspects of the book include the generally rather dated feel of its assumptions and sources, and the large number of errors. Misprints abound, but there are also many errors of fact, over-simplifications, and unjustified sweeping assertions. Was the *commedia dell'arte* an important formative element in the Viennese Volkstheater, or was it not? Ziltener is casual with dates – Stranitzky took over the Kärntnertor-Theater in 1712 and died in 1726; the Freihaus-Theater opened in 1787. Karl Meisl is given the Christian name Kurt. And there is confusion over Maria Theresia's attitude towards the German theatre company. Johann La Roche is described as fat, whereas surviving pictures suggest a thin, gangling man. And quotations need to be checked – I found eleven errors in one ten-line-long citation.

It is a great pity that much more care was not taken by both author and publisher (the book is rather scruffily reproduced from typescript), for there is valuable material lurking here.

PETER BRANSCOMBE

Steven Beller, *Herzl*, Jewish Thinkers (London: Peter Halban, 1991), 161 pp., £6.95 (paper).

This synoptic study of the life, the *œuvre* and the historical role of the leader of the Zionist movement, is impressive for its clarity and its objectivity, even if it does not present any new results in research. Throughout, Theodor Herzl appears as an ambivalent figure, both fascinating as a political *démiurge* and disquieting as the sorcerer's apprentice of a cause that, by all the evidence, overtook him. Beller quotes in the introduction a witty remark by a Zionist historian: 'A book on Herzl as a Jewish thinker should be very short, because Herzl was neither a thinker, nor really Jewish.' In fact, one is struck by the instability of the young Herzl's identity, torn between his Hungarian connection and his desire to assimilate into the Austro-German *Kulturbürgertum*. His Jewishness (Beller describes him justly as 'a near-pathological, self-hating version' of the Central European Jew) was the least complicated aspect of his identity. Though his vocation was uncertain (writer, journalist, or politician?) he was possessed by an unquenchable thirst for social success. From this perspective the contradictions in Herzl's 'Zionist thought' appear as a logical consequence of an identity crisis which had never been completely resolved.

Although Beller says that 'without *Der Judenstaat* there might never have been a state of Israel' (p. 36), the outcome of his analysis of the 'Herzl case' appears rather negative. Above all, one is alarmed by his judgments on anti-Semitism, which at times he seems to consider an objective ally of the Zionist cause, and which Herzl is said to rival in ferocity: 'Indeed his general description of the Viennese Jewish bourgeoisie could be mistaken for anti-Semitic propaganda' (p. 91). In general terms, Herzl was too influenced by the hostile image of the East European Jew which was being propagated by the anti-Semites, and he was too blind to face the possibility of Jewish assimilation in democratic societies. Is Zionism incompatible with Jewish culture in the Diaspora? And what should be said about Herzl's theories on the Jewish state, of which the cultural Zionists, starting with Ahad Ha'am, were justifiably suspicious? On the one hand, a naive liberal modernism and a 'welfare system organized like the Austro-Hungarian army' (p. 99); on the other, 'an essentially colonialist approach to the Holy Land' (p. 80), incapable of taking into account the Palestinian and Muslim problem.

What remains indisputable, but alas quite utopian, in Herzl's theories is his vision of the Jewish state as 'inclusivist and non-racial' (p. 101). As Beller emphasises: 'The incursion of religion into Israeli politics and the central place of the army in national life are a travesty of Herzl's intentions. Recent events in Jerusalem have exacerbated the troubled status of the city, which Herzl's idea of extra-territoriality might have solved' (p. 134). Beller concludes that 'one can hardly blame Herzl for present-day Israel; in one crucial respect, the need for legality and international guarantees, Zionism after Herzl largely departed from his policies' (p. 139). This is true. Yet it is no less true that Herzl's personal contradictions put Zionism on the dangerous slope of *Realpolitik*.

JACQUES LE RIDER

Burkhard Spinnen, *Schriftbilder: Studien zu einer Geschichte emblematischer Kurzprosa*, Literatur als Sprache: Literaturtheorie – Interpretation – Sprachkritik, vol. 9 (Münster: Aschendorff, 1991), VI + 337 pp., DM 98.

Despite periodic admonitions about the historical problems involved in interpreting modern literature in emblematic terms, such studies continue to proliferate; and this book, a Münster dissertation, is not exactly calculated to dispel lingering methodological qualms. Spinnen in fact dashes through the controversies surrounding emblematics research and arrives rather abruptly at a partial agreement with the late Dieter Sulzer's revision of Schöne's pioneering explications. Like Sulzer, Spinnen insists that emblematic meaning derives from the interdependence of textual and pictorial elements; unlike him, he asserts that emblematic prose can and does substitute verbal descriptions for what had traditionally been considered the indispensable visual image.

Although the book contains an engaging comparison of Lichtenberg and Lavater and two sets of excursuses, Spinnen focuses on the 'Impressionist

Emblematics', the 'Satirical Emblematics' and the 'Philosophical Emblematics' that he perceives operating in a narrow band of texts by Peter Altenberg, Karl Kraus and Walter Benjamin, respectively.

The interpretation of Benjamin's *One-Way Street* as a modern emblem book is not entirely without precedent; and, given his attention to the cultural history of the Baroque in the *Trauerspiel* book, the adaptation of emblematic structures even acquires a plausible source. Since this is not so obviously the case either for Karl Kraus or, especially, for Peter Altenberg, it makes sense to concentrate on the strengths and weaknesses of Spinnen's innovative and challenging readings of their works.

Although Spinnen does not discount recent attempts to understand Altenberg's unconventional short texts conventionally as impressionistic sketches or prose poems, he considers emblematics a more useful hermeneutic device for explaining the stylistic and structural anomalies that are particularly evident in the earliest works. Altenberg's sketches, like emblems, depict the concrete and the everyday with the intention of creating meaning but without concealing the resulting process of transformation and the subjectivity it entails. His texts thus thrive on the emblematic tension between representation and interpretation.

Understandably concerned to demonstrate more than such general analogies, Spinnen purports to find adaptations in Altenberg's sketches of the standard triadic structure of *inscriptio/pictura/subscriptio*. That this interpretive expedition should turn up a 'literary double emblem' (p. 115) is one thing; but when Spinnen divides another sketch into several 'sub-emblems' (p. 139) in which at least one subscriptio is quite arbitrarily determined (p. 143), doubts are bound to arise. Nevertheless, the readings of individual texts are both subtle and sophisticated. They show how carefully Altenberg calculated his stylistic effects, how he consciously manipulated registers of diction, and how he designed the best series of sketches both to undermine narrative conventions and to coalesce into emblematic 'macro-structures' (p. 130).

Considering the overall visual orientation of Altenberg's work and especially his interest in photography, it is curious that Spinnen is so reluctant to investigate the inscribed photographs and postcards that constitute a sizeable part of the poet's *œuvre*. To his credit, Spinnen does briefly treat the photographic reproductions in *Kunst*, Altenberg's short-lived art magazine, as 'photographic emblems' (pp. 169ff.) that do not conform to the conventional practices of the illustrated press of his time. Yet this cursory discussion both slights the experimental character of these word-image combinations and reveals considerable ignorance of the context in which they appeared.

To begin with the latter, the first supplement to *Kunst*, *Das Andere*, was edited of course by Adolf, not 'Alfred', Loos (p. 169); and only the first of the two issues of this famous counter-cultural journal actually appeared together with Altenberg's magazine. It is grossly inaccurate to speak of photography being a 'new medium' in 1903 (p. 170), and the addition of another supplement, *Der Gummidruck* (The Gum-Bichromate Print), beginning with the sixth issue of *Kunst* did not mean that the photographs reproduced there were exemplars of that process (p. 195). In fact, two of the most striking images in *Kunst*, views of a woman's hand, were reproduced from photographs with extremely sharp focus, the very antithesis of the impressionistic effects for which the gumbichromate process was favoured. In general, Spinnen seems quite ill-informed about the medium that he calls the 'pre-eminent interpretive strategy of the epoch' (p. 31). This is hardly surprising, however, in light of the handful of secondary titles he cites, which includes Marianne Kesting's rather crude polemic, *Die Diktatur der Photographie*.

Spinnen's cavalier treatment of the history and discourses of photography also seems to have caused him to misinterpret and overlook basic visual evidence concerning the emblematic texts to which he restricts himself. In one case, he sees a photograph that is not there. The picture of a missing girl that catches the eye of the narrator in 'Locale Chronik', Altenberg's first published sketch, was a drawing – not a 'photograph' (p. 165) – that both allows Altenberg's 'exemplary reader' (p. 164) to construct his fantasy more actively and implicates him in the journalistic exploitation of the girl's disappearance. In the case of what might have been a central text for his purposes, 'Picture Postcards', Spinnen assumes that the published text which contains only the written messages, has properly elided the postcard view. Yet Altenberg actually produced revised versions of these messages inscribed on postcards featuring visual motifs that alter the emblematic equation (one of these cards is to be found in the Vienna Stadtbibliothek). Spinnen's failure to consult archival materials allows him to dismiss Altenberg's inscribed photographs and postcards as private amusements (p. 171), whereas the evidence indicates that the poet consciously produced them for sale and considered them an alternative form of publication.

In the case of Karl Kraus, Spinnen pursues the more modest goal of elucidating the satirical glosses as modern emblems, and indeed many of these underrated texts exhibit the classic structure. The title functions as an inscription that often parodies newspaper headlines; a quotation from a journalistic source corresponds to the documentary aspect of the pictura; and a commentary acts as a critical subscriptio. Again Spinnen delivers a brilliant analysis of the linguistic complexities in individual texts as well as demonstrating how carefully Kraus constructed the series of glosses published in the *Fackel*. Yet Kraus also incorporated actual photographic images into his works, creating word-image combinations that do not function as straightforwardly as the textual picturae in the glosses. Although Spinnen provides a rather forced interpretation of one of these photographs in emblematic terms (pp. 205f.), he clearly senses that most of them resist the paradigm he has constructed and therefore gives them a wide berth.

Spinnen's aversion to coming to terms with the visual meaning of photography, which amounts to a kind of iconophobia, goes hand in hand with his neglect of the ideological distortions present in the texts of both Altenberg and Kraus. As important as their attempts were to create prose forms that would offer a critical alternative to the insidious clichés of the print media, the problematic treatment of issues of race and gender that crops up even in their most progressive texts should not be ignored. One does not have to be 'politically correct' to expect more attention to be paid to these crucial matters in a study that places such value on theoretical and methodological concerns.

LEO A. LENSING

Samuel Fischer and Hedwig Fischer, *Briefwechsel mit Autoren*, ed. Dierk Rodewald and Corinna Fiedler, with an introduction by Bernhard Zeller (Frankfurt: Fischer, 1989), 1,201 pp., DM 148.

The S. Fischer Verlag exemplifies the fundamental importance of literary institutions for modern writing. According to Siegfried Unseld of Suhrkamp, Samuel Fischer ran his publishing house in such a way that 'the history of the Verlag corresponds to the history of German literature in this period'.[1] Besides its extensive influence on developments associated with naturalism, the Verlag also made an indisputable contribution to Viennese modernism. The Viennese critic Raoul Auernheimer, himself a Fischer author, is credited with the observation that members of the 'Viennese School' had nothing in common, apart from their publisher. The publication prospects for Austrian writers at the end of the nineteenth century were scarcely different from today. They were faced with the difficult but necessary task of making an impact on the German market, while at home they had to contend with the notorious Austrian lack of interest in home-grown talent. To make a reputation in Austria, they first had to make a detour through Germany.

In the final decade of the nineteenth century it was above all the Fischer Verlag that made this detour possible. First came Hermann Bahr, who in 1890 was for a few months the controversial editor of Fischer's journal *Freie Bühne* and whose first book, *Die gute Schule*, was published by the Verlag that same year. He was followed as a Fischer author by Arthur Schnitzler (*Sterben* and *Anatol*, 1895), Hugo von Hofmannsthal (*Theater in Versen*, 1899) and Richard Beer-Hofmann (*Der Tod Georgs*, 1900). Thus Fischer had gathered under his imprint the most significant representatives of Viennese modernism. And the list of Austrian authors was soon to include Leopold von Andrian, Peter Altenberg, Felix Salten and Jakob Wassermann (a German author who settled in Vienna), and later Robert Musil and Stefan Zweig.

The history of their relations with their publisher is richly documented. Publications to mark the S. Fischer centenary in 1986 included a bibliography, a condensed history of the Verlag (by Reiner Stach), a meticulous exhibition catalogue from Marbach, and an appreciative study of the graphic design of Fischer book jackets.[2] The standard work, however, remains Peter de Mendelssohn's monograph *S. Fischer und sein Verlag* (1970). Twenty years later, we are now able to welcome the long-promised edition of the correspondence between Samuel Fischer, his wife Hedwig and their authors.

The difficulties besetting such a project are already familiar from Mendelssohn's book. In 1936 the National Socialists suppressed the Verlag and divided its operations in two. The Fischer archives remained in practical (but not in legal) terms with Peter Suhrkamp, who was director of the section of the Verlag that continued to exist in Berlin. At the end of the war those archives were destroyed.

What survived was the private correspondence with authors (which was preserved by Hedwig Fischer), together with some other files and some of the unpublished papers of individual authors. The problems with which the editors of this volume have had to contend reflect the disastrous break in continuity suffered by the Verlag and hence also by German literature. Schnitzler and Beer-Hofmann were among the authors banned by the Nazis, though Hofmannsthal, who had only one Jewish grandparent, was an exception. The preliminary work that had to be done for this edition, the search for documents and the preservation of what could be found, thus itself deserves great credit; for in effect this meant reconstituting the fractured literary tradition. Where, as with Schnitzler, an extensive correspondence between author and publisher survives, there was conversely the problem of making a representative selection of letters from several decades. This task was made all the more difficult by the fact that no fewer than forty-two authors are included in this volume. In addition to the Austrian authors, they include the leading German writers Gerhart Hauptmann, Thomas Mann and Hermann Hesse, the Scandinavians led by Ibsen, and other outstanding figures like Zola, d'Annunzio and Bernard Shaw.

In consequence, the reader is left uneasily aware that much has been omitted. But this is a price that must be paid, given the historical break in continuity. For the editors have done everything possible to bridge the gaps, an immense scholarly achievement given the size of the book. The commentary, a treasury of biographical and bibliographical information, establishes connections by detailed cross-reference, without detracting from the text itself. Thus this exemplary edition can be read in several different ways. Occasionally, we may regret the failure to identify letters which had already appeared in print, but they too have been carefully re-edited on the basis of surviving sources. In addition, the volume has a detailed general index and index of book titles. The division of the correspondence into sections relating to individual authors is complemented by a chronology of all surviving letters.

This chronology makes it possible to construct a cross-section through a single month, for example February–March 1922. On 25 February we find Hofmannsthal writing to Fischer about difficulties arising from the planned collected edition of his works. He adds that he understands Fischer's situation, 'because for you too the peculiar and never easy task of publisher and mediator has been made a thousand times more difficult in ways that no one could have anticipated'. 'But', he continues, 'you must also understand my position: you are concerned with many intellectual existences, competing with each other, balancing each other out – I am an individual, on my own in more than one respect.' Then Fischer writes to Schnitzler in connection with the author's sixtieth birthday, requesting a contribution for the May number of the *Neue Rundschau* which is to be dedicated to him. On 3 March Hermann Bahr comments on Fischer's delayed reaction to manuscripts he has sent in: 'It would be foolish of me to expect you to make any great efforts on my behalf, since you have lost confidence in my work. But it is your duty to allow me access to publishers who have not lost confidence in my work.' On 10 March Schnitzler declines the invitation to send in a contribution (ten days later Fischer replies expressing his regret).

On 11 March, mollified by a letter from Fischer, Bahr writes again in a different mood: 'The basic element underlying all my laments about "publishers" was only the increasing bitterness of my feeling over the years that you were becoming more and more remote from me [...] You seemed to be loosening those ties which derive from a common starting point and which unite people so wonderfully.' The following day a further letter arrives from Hofmannsthal, who has also received a reassuring letter from Fischer. Hofmannsthal writes that 'as an Austrian' he is naturally 'predisposed towards the reconciliation of conflicts of interest'. He is nevertheless not prepared to renounce those links with other publishers which Fischer dislikes, least of all those with the Insel Verlag, whose traditionalism is congenial to his creativity: 'That is what it means to be Austrian – in a sense I am perhaps the only Austrian – I would call Schnitzler Viennese, not Austrian – and furthermore [for an Austrian] the connections with the epoch are in a sense *detached* – as if one's position were halfway to somewhere else, not gratuitously, but by destiny.' (' ... ein halb wo anders–Stehen, nicht aus Willkür, sondern als Schicksal').

Through such interactions we discern the profile of a publisher torn between the claims of art and profitability, between authors who need his friendship and recognition on the one hand, and paper shortages on the other. Fischer's task was to mediate between aesthetic considerations and the pressure of literary politics and the market. By putting on record his responses to such pressures, these letters make the nature of his achievement clear. This collection serves as a impressive monument to a committed publisher who was able to counteract the purely 'capitalist' dimensions of his enterprise by means of the well-documented patriarchal structure of his 'publishing family' and through a liberalism of outlook which in business terms was anachronistic. Rebellions against this father figure were commonplace. On the question of royalties the Austrian authors certainly did not create any greater difficulties than those from elsewhere (the most outrageous financial demands were made by Hauptmann). What was more problematic was that sense expressed by Hofmannsthal of being 'halfway to somewhere else'. It was from outside that this group of Austrian authors (who certainly did not perceive themselves as such) acquired a profile which distinguished them from other Fischer authors. Sometimes this took the form of an undercurrent of resentment, expressed by Fischer himself on one occasion, after the outbreak of the First World War. Fischer had given his backing to Richard Dehmel, the patriotic German poet who had volunteered for front-line service. By contrast, Fischer commented to Schnitzler 'that even now the Austrians are apparently not coming up to scratch' ('nicht auf der Höhe der Situation', 25 September 1914). This was an impression which Schnitzler repudiated.

Even in the 1890s the poetic programme of 'Young Vienna' had, for the Verlag, originally been half-way to somewhere else, at least so far as Bahr's essays 'Overcoming Naturalism' were concerned (Fischer did not publish that volume!). It was, according to Reiner Stach, a shrewd move on Fischer's part to maintain his contacts with Bahr, despite these disagreements. By this means he was able to add the authors of Viennese modernism to his list.[3] But naturalism nevertheless remained the home ground for the Verlag. As late as 1906 the Verlag catalogue contained a preface by Fischer and his editor Moritz Heimann describing naturalism as the 'source of rejuvenation' ('Verjüngungsquell') for subsequent literary developments.[4] The policy of giving German naturalism precedence over so-called Austrian impressionism resulted in certain tensions, sometimes reinforced by the forceful judgments of Moritz Heimann: 'These Austrian poets! They ought [...] to learn how to prune', 20 July 1901).[5] Even more significant are criticisms of style which also relate to matters of substance, as in the case of Heimann's comments on Schnitzler. He accuses him of 'mangling the language' ('Sprachverhunzung', summer 1901), and condemns *Der Weg ins Freie* as 'this indiscreet, feuilletonistic, highly embarrassing novel which reveals on every page that its author is only at home in shorter forms and in larger ones loses his way, waffling on superficially', 31 January 1908).

Clearly, Heimann's judgments were not infallible. Nevertheless, his letters form the secret heart of the book, perhaps indeed of the publishing house. We can only guess what Heimann achieved as editor for the Fischer Verlag and what he contributed to the success of specific authors, Wassermann in particular. His contribution can hardly be overestimated. In this particular case the unavoidable one-sidedness of the correspondence is not necessarily a cause for lament (the replies of Fischer and his wife are lost as a result of the brutal events which disrupted their dialogue). Even without the replies, Heimann's letters are on target. They carry beyond the sphere of the Verlag, forming a record of editorial activity which has enduring value. For including these letters the editors deserve special gratitude.[6] Even in a period of economic crisis Heimann, in a letter of 3 January 1922, propounds the following guiding principle for the Verlag: 'The moment you think "Don't people have more serious problems than buying books?" you are on the defensive. You must think: "Even if they're starving, they'll be reading all the same, without books they cannot survive." Everything depends on this inner conviction.' This uncompromising stance explains his scepticism towards the Austrians. But over and above this there is an example of his sense of justice. Heimann's review of *Elektra* (1903), which expresses grave reservations about Hofmannsthal's aestheticism, concludes as follows:

> Is a reviewer allowed to confess that he is not infallible? During the process of writing (and as everyone knows of thinking and feeling) there is a tendency to drift gently away from the line that was envisaged. You wanted circuitously to reach the white rock; but you find you've landed on the grey one. So you jump back into the water and make for your original goal. I admire Hofmannsthal; I know he has a voice that will enunciate great things.[7]

A disarming and conciliatory judgment: what more could an author ask for? The publishing house which Heimann represented was, after all, a rewarding detour for Austrian authors.

Notes

1. Siegfried Unseld, *Der Autor und sein Verleger: Vorlesungen in Mainz und Austin* (Frankfurt, 1978), p. 28.
2. *100 Jahre S. Fischer Verlag 1886–1986: Eine Bibliographie*, ed. Knut Beck (Frankfurt, 1986); Reiner Stach, *100 Jahre S. Fischer Verlag 1886–1986: Kleine Verlagsgeschichte* (Frankfurt, 1986); *S. Fischer Verlag: Von der Gründung bis zur Rückkehr aus dem Exil* (Marbach Exhibition Catalogue), ed. Friedrich Pfäfflin and Ingrid Kussmaul (Marbach. 1985); Friedrich Pfäfflin, *100 Jahre S. Fischer Verlag 1886–1986: Buchumschläge* (Frankfurt, 1986).
3. Stach, *Verlagsgeschichte*, p. 30.
4. Pfäfflin, *Katalog*, p. 198.
5. It should be added that Heimann's comments related to a rather second-rate work, the novella *Genesung* by Siegfried Trebitsch.
6. Dierk Rodewald is also preparing an edition of Heimann's literary-critical essays.
7. Moritz Heimann, *Was ist das: ein Gedanke? Essays*, ed. Gert Mattenklott (Frankfurt, 1986), pp. 22–3.

KONSTANZE FLIEDL

Robert Musil, *Precision and Soul: Essays and Addresses*, ed. and tr. Burton Pike and David S. Luft (Chicago: University of Chicago Press, 1990), xxviii + 301 pp., $29.95.

Hannah Hickman (ed.), *Robert Musil and the Literary Landscape of his Time* (University of Salford: Department of Modern Languages, 1991).

Claus Erhart, *Der ästhetische Mensch bei Robert Musil. Vom Ästhetizismus zur schöpferischen Moral*, Innsbrucker Beiträge zur Kulturwissenschaft, Germanistische Reihe, Band 43 (Innsbruck: Institut für Germanistik, 1991), 334 pp., 564 Sch.

The year 1992 marked the fiftieth anniversary of the death of Robert Musil: *Precision and Soul* and *Robert Musil and the Literary Landscape of his Time* are thus timely reminders to his English-speaking readership of the breadth and quality of his work. The first is a generous selection of Musil's essays and addresses translated into English for the first time, from volumes 8 and 9 of Adolf Frisé's 1978 *Gesammelte Werke*; the second is the proceedings of a conference held at Salford University in July 1990, a collection of thirteen papers by British and continental Musil specialists with an opening address by Marie-Louise Roth. In their different but complementary ways both publications are highly valuable. The one is a much-needed addition to the translated canon which seeks to proselytise for Musil's credentials as thinker in 'Anglo-Saxony', where he is still known primarily for his unfinished masterpiece *Der Mann ohne Eigenschaften (The Man Without Qualities)*; the other takes those credentials as read. *Precision and Soul* deliberately lifts Musil out of his narrower context to project him onto the larger European stage, and the *Literary Landscape* volume sets him firmly back in it.

The title of the essay collection derives from one of the many different formulations of Musil's dualistic outlook when Ulrich, the hero of *Der Mann ohne Eigenschaften*, posits a 'secretariat of precision and soul' as a bridge between the two poles of existence which Musil elsewhere repeatedly calls the 'ratioid' and 'nonratioid' ('Sketch of What the Writer Knows'). The search for a synthesis of these two preoccupies him throughout his career, and in 'The German as Symptom' (1923), for example, he writes: 'The smallest fact from the connection between the soul and hormonal balance gives me more perspectives than an idealistic system.' This concern to proliferate perspectives is encapsulated in Ulrich's 'utopia of essayism', his project to lead a life 'rather as an essay in the sequence of its sections takes a thing from many sides without comprehending it fully'. However, Musil's application of the term to an existential option is only made possible by the profound understanding of the form that he gained over an essay-writing career that spanned more than twenty years.

The differences in style and scope between Musil's essays before and after the First World War (the latter as a rule treating larger problems with greater assurance) are reflected in the main divisions within the collection into 'Essays 1911–1914', 'Essays 1918–1933' and 'Addresses', with the larger corpus of post-war essays being subdivided: 'On Literature', 'On Politics and Society' and 'On Culture and Theory'. There are no major exclusions and some important pieces which mark undoubted high points in Musil's output: 'Helpless Europe', 'The German as Symptom' and 'Toward a New Aesthetic', as well as the addresses on Rilke and stupidity and a good selection of the political essays from the immediate post-war period. The editors give a representative selection, however, and the more heavyweight contributions are interspersed with unfinished, unpublished fragments such as the positively quirky 'Literary Chronicle'. This volume provides a fine overview: the translations are on the whole sensitive, and the critical apparatus makes for accessibility; each piece is given a paragraph's introduction to set it in context, and there are sparing but judicious notes. Because the practice of the 1978 German edition has been followed, in the unfinished pieces the text has been kept scrupulously fitful, although one could question the wisdom of countering Frisé's policy and deliberately omitting an index.

The general aim of *Precision and Soul*, as Luft makes clear in his Introduction, is to instate Musil as 'a full participant in the intellectual exchange of our culture', and therefore the editors leave out his more context-specific articles. In *Robert Musil and the Literary Landscape of His Time*, however, the balance is restored through contributions by Anne Servranckx on Robert Müller, Annette Daigger on Musil and contemporary criticism (especially Fontana and Csokor), and Rosmarie Zeller on Musil and contemporary theatre. The only previous Musil conference in Britain, held at the Institute of Germanic Studies in the centenary year of 1980, resulted in *Musil in Focus* (London, 1982): here the focus is deliberately more blurred, even if the underlying brief – of encouraging the acknowledgement that Musil was more than a one-book author – remains the same.

Hickman's collection gives itself a varied palette with which to paint the literary landscape, and a fair cross-section of Musil's work is also covered. The greatest number of contributions still touch on *Der Mann ohne Eigenschaften*, and Carmen Lavin's is devoted to it entirely, but there are two papers each on *Törleß* (Andrew Webber, Renate Schröder-Werle), *Vereinigungen* (Lothar Huber, David Midgley) and the plays (Dietmar Goltschnigg, Rosmarie Zeller), while Philip Payne continues his discussion of the diaries begun in *Musil in Focus*. There are familiar contexts like Nietzsche, and also the less familiar: Ritchie Robertson on 'Musil and the "primitive mentality"' in the light of Lévy-Bruhl's anthropology, for example. Even the range of theoretical approaches is broad:

of particular interest are Schröder-Werle's ambitious typology of the literary narrative, and two psychoanalytical pieces from Midgley and Webber. The volume also contains contributions on Robert Müller (Anne Servranckx) and on Schnitzler's *Frau Berta Garlan* (Michael Levene), and a comparative piece on Musil and Canetti (Noel Thomas).

Der ästhetische Mensch bei Robert Musil addresses Musil's development from *Törleß* to *Der Mann ohne Eigenschaften* via *Die Vollendung der Liebe* and *Die Schwärmer*. The territory it covers is largely familiar, for Erhart's terms of reference – particularly the possibility–reality tension and the notion of creative indeterminacy – are uncontroversial, despite the impression he gives with his title, which proves to be singularly inappropriate. The figure of the 'ästhetischer Mensch' ('aesthetic person') is created from the fusion of a number of characteristic turn-of-the-century features which Erhart successfully analyses in Törless. In his introduction, however, he admits that the rest of the characters whom he is going to bring under this umbrella term differ from Törless 'quite fundamentally', but that he is nevertheless still going to apply it to them. As a result it proves a conceptual tool by turns irrelevant and confusing: in his treatment of *Die Vollendung der Liebe* he in any case drops it in favour of the rather more fruitful 'paradox of the possible', which allows him to consider Musil's narrative technique; by the time he reaches *Der Mann ohne Eigenschaften* the few references still made to the notion are but gestural.

The merit of this book lies less in its overall argument than in the stagingposts along the way, for there are many perceptive formulations and genuinely illuminating sections – a discussion of *Die Schwärmer* in the light of Siegfried Kracauer's essay 'Die Wartenden', for example. As one would expect from a doctoral thesis there is ample consideration given to the existing secondary literature, around which Erhart moves with considerable facility; his command of the primary texts, including Musil's letters, diaries and essays, is impressive, and his range of reference is extensive. Rather than giving the false impression that he intends to synthesise Musil's characters into some sort of pervasive archetype, however, he would have been better advised to take his 'developmental' subtitle as his title.

DUNCAN LARGE

Phillip H. Rhein, *The Verbal and Visual Art of Alfred Kubin*, Studies in Austrian Literature, Culture and Thought (Riverside, CA: Ariadne Press, 1989), 179 pp., $24.95.

Kubin once observed: 'Ich habe kein maßgebendes Urteil in literarischen Dingen, habe vorher nie etwas zur Veröffentlichung Bestimmtes geschrieben, ja, mir ist das Schreiben selbst eine unsympathische Tätigkeit [...]' ('I have no competence in judging literary matters: I have never written anything for publication before; indeed, I never find writing a particularly agreeable occupation'). Modesty, perhaps, or whimsy, or provocation – nevertheless, we are drawn to him not only as a very skilled graphic artist but also as the author of that strange novel *Die andere Seite (The Other Side)*. Professor Rhein attempts a discussion of Kubin as a *Doppelbegabung*, an artist at home in two media:

whether or not, as he claims, Kubin 'produced some of the most exciting art known to the West' and whether he could really be called 'double gifted' are contentious claims, but his short book (only eighty-odd pages of text, the remainder being reproductions of plates, a chronology, a description of sequences of pictures by Kubin and a list of major exhibitions) goes some way to bringing this figure closer to the English-speaking reader.

The chapter 'Kubin on Kubin' is straightforward: Kubin left many an autobiographical account of his life, and this self-advertisement eases the curiosity of the inquisitive. Professor Rhein is on safe ground here, but might have been more scathing of Kubin's 'philosophy', which is surely little more than a farrago of half-baked lucubrations. More might have been made of Max Klinger, particularly the sequence *Fund eines Handschuhs (Finding a Glove)* which still has the power to disturb and bewilder. The Hans von Weber Mappe is also described – that famous warrior-figure may well have entered German literature via Georg Heym (the intermediary being Paul Cassirer). The next chapter, 'The Turning Point', takes us into the realms of Patera (but why no speculation about the name and its meaning? Patera as bowl or receptacle does surely mean something here, and Richard Schroeder has said much that is pertinent). *Die andere Seite* is certainly an interesting read, but cannot be called a successful piece of prose – it is prolix, shapeless and episodic. But the illustrations are perhaps some of the best that Kubin ever did, and the apocalyptic ending does have a gruesome power of its own. Professor Rhein rightly sees that it is a dream journey, but fails to get to grip with the mysterious Elders; it is a journey of self-exploration, and any attempt to find a political allegory must fail. We know that Kubin had begun to provide Meyrink with illustrations for his *Golem*, but had struck off on his own after Meyrink had entered a sterile period; another impetus to writing may have been the reading of Marco Polo's account of his travels through Central Asia, a topography which, like Kafka's China, stood for a mysterious psychic landscape.

Professor Rhein does not talk about Kubin's later prose utterances, admittedly peripheral, but indicative of a need to write as well as draw. Some of the plates are badly reproduced (*Der Todessprung (The Dive of Death)* for example, on p. 118 – an amusing example of Kubin's pornography). Professor Rhein does not convince us of a genuinely twofold talent, but at least makes us think about Kubin, particularly if we live in the land of Mervyn Peake.

R. S. FURNESS

Jura Soyfer, *Sturmzeit: Briefe 1931–1939*, ed. Horst Jarka, Antifaschistische Literatur und Exilliteratur 5 (Vienna: Verlag für Gesellschaftskritik, 1991), 255 pp., 228 Sch.

Gerhard Scheit, *Theater und revolutionärer Humanismus: Eine Studie zu Jura Soyfer*, Antifaschistische Literatur und Exilliteratur 1 (Vienna: Verlag für Gesellschaftskritik, 1988), 169 pp., 188 Sch.

These two volumes come as a welcome addition to the secondary literature on Soyfer, a writer whose work has been largely neglected by critics. It is principally thanks to the efforts of one man, Horst Jarka, that Soyfer's works have been collected, edited and published over the past ten years; Jarka has also undertaken the even more daunting task of translating a selection of the plays, poems and prose pieces. Ironically the massive tome that was published by the Europa Verlag in 1980 put the young communist's work well beyond the reach of those for whom he had been writing; the three-volume edition of Soyfer that came out in paperback in 1988 happily made the collected works accessible to a much larger audience.

Unfortunately the letters had to be omitted from that edition for reasons of economy; Jarka has, however, more than compensated for this with his most recent contribution to Soyfer scholarship.

Jarka has once again made an excellent job of editing, supplying not only a useful glossary, covering terms used by Soyfer and contemporary events and publications, but also giving a succinct introductory commentary on each batch of letters, which includes historical and political as well as biographical background material. An incidental benefit from the delay in bringing out the correspondence has been that Jarka has unearthed thirty-one previously unpublished letters that give further insight into Soyfer's early life and work. In these, and most notably in the twenty-five letters to Marika Szecsi, both Soyfer's irrepressible political optimism and his journalistic voyeurism are to be found combined with his personal passions and uncertainties. These letters speak of youth and to youth with a rare clarity and directness.

Gerhard Scheit's essays speak with a good deal less clarity and with an unwelcome degree of political and sociological jargon that rather detracts from their appreciation of such a lucid writer as Soyfer. This brief study is made up of seven essays, four in the main body of the text and three as an appendix, these three having previously been published elsewhere. Scheit's unnecessarily titled 'Statt eines Vorworts' rightly points out that Soyfer has remained for too long *ante portas* in the world of theatrical criticism. In his opening essay Scheit illustrates how Soyfer's writings are only apparently left-wing party pieces: his humanity, his understanding of the small man caught up in the capitalist machine and his compassionate yet humorous portrayal of couples in love mingle with a delightful sense of the absurd and the surreal to create 'Mittelstücke' that are both ahead of their time and dramatically powerful. Scheit then attempts, in an essay comparing Soyfer with Horváth (unemployment as a theme in *Kasimir und Karoline* and *Der Lechner Edi schaut ins Paradies*) and Canetti (he points out an interesting parallel between *Die Hochzeit* and *Der Weltuntergang* where a parrot is used to echo and illuminate the words of lonely people), to establish the place where these 'Mittelstücke' might belong. As others have done before him, Scheit places Soyfer firmly in the same mould as Horváth. In both authors he sees the 'Demaskierung des Bewußtseins', to use Horváth's phrase, as central to the dramatic process. This essay is by far the most satisfying in a collection whose anti-Fascist spirit and credentials are faultless but whose direction is too often obfuscated by ideological diatribe. This is especially true of the piece on Richard Billinger, 'Die Zerstörung des Volksstücks'. That such a play as *Der Gigant* should have been performed in Vienna to rapturous applause in 1983 is alarming, but Scheit fails to justify including this in a study of Jura

Soyfer, however much one might share the aggrieved tone of this essay's final sentence: 'Wie oft wird eigentlich Jura Soyfer am Wiener Volkstheater gespielt?'

Other chapters in this volume look at what the author terms the false continuity in Austrian drama; the difficulties, encountered by many before him, in formulating any adequate definition of the genre 'Volksstück'; a specifically Marxist epilogue to *Der Lechner Edi schaut ins Paradies*, clearly one of Scheit's favourite Soyfer plays; a final word on the creative skills of writers in the anti-Fascist Resistance, suggesting that Soyfer's Mittelstücke 'drängen die übrigen Nummern und Szenen des Abends an den Rand und stehen heute für sich selbst' (put the evening's other numbers and scenes in the shade and now stand on their own).

More careful editing would have avoided many of the infelicities in the text: on p. 18 an entire paragraph is repeated and yet the last word in that paragraph has been corrected from 'werden' to 'werfen'. The notes to each essay are comprehensive but there is regrettably no bibliography. In fact the overall impression is one of an over-hasty lumping together of material that would have benefited from careful sifting and rearranging. As Heinz Primus Kucher says in his equally unnecessarily titled 'Statt eines Nachworts', it would also be desirable to give Soyfer a place in the school curriculum.

Sadly, Gerhard Scheit's jargon-logged essays will do little to endear Soyfer to schoolchildren or their teachers; whereas the publication of Soyfer's letters with the apparatus provided by Horst Jarka will undoubtedly serve to promote his place in Austrian literature as well as in the classroom.

IAN HUISH

Gerald Stieg, *Frucht des Feuers: Canetti, Doderer, Kraus und der Justizpalastbrand* (Vienna: Österreichischer Bundesverlag, 1990), 237 pp., 248 Sch./DM 35.

The poetic title is apt for several reasons. This is a brilliant study of Canetti and an introduction for Germanists to the history of Austria between the wars. In addition, it is an entertaining book for all lovers of literature, and one that is accessible to historians who are less fond of literary criticism. It is much more as well. It represents a polite and respectful farewell to the vastly overrated Heimito von Doderer. It provides a survey of the wedding theme in literature, including an essay on *The Marriage of Figaro* and *Fidelio*. It provides information about Freud's unfortunate 'Eros–Thanatos' theory and his break with Wilhelm Reich over the latter's mass psychology. And finally it traces the image of fire through literature in a way that leaves Gaston Bachelard's *The Phenomenology of Fire* far behind.

For some students of literature the significance of the burning of the Palace of Justice in Vienna may require explanation. Reactionary jurisdictions in Germany and Austria were placing a heavy strain on the popular sense of justice. In 1927 two Fascists in Austria ambushed and murdered a disabled ex-soldier and a child who were taking part in a demonstration. On 14 July a star National Socialist lawyer obtained an acquittal for the murderers. On 15 July the Social Democrats of Vienna poured into the city centre, brought traffic to a standstill, knocked threateningly at the doors of the university where the Fascists were hatching their plans, demonstrated in front of Parliament, spontaneously set fire to the Palace of Justice, and ransacked a few newspaper offices and police stations. The Chancellor, Seipel, ordered shots to be fired into the crowd of demonstrators and bystanders. Women and 'Jewish'-looking people were favourite targets for the police. Ninety people were killed and one thousand injured.

Stieg sketches an impressive picture of reactions to these events in the media, in Parliament, party conferences, and literature. He analyses forty examples of this 'July literature' which, with Canetti, he calls 'fruits of fire'. By stringently avoiding Hegelian and Freudian theories, Stieg develops his 'complementary interpretation' with a specific focus on poetic and historical perspectives.

The symbolism of fire is central to Stieg's considerations. He takes it from Canetti's *Crowds and Power*, which has unjustifiably come to be considered in the same realm as Goethe's theory of colour. Canetti's substitution of the metaphor of fire for the indefinable metaphor of 'the mass', a term applied to a range of phenomena from the working masses to the 'lonely crowd', may be regrettable, but Stieg shows that at bottom this inherently ambivalent fire symbolism has immense value. This is important both for the construction of sociological-historical theory and for the interpretation of Canetti. Stieg demonstrates once and for all that Canetti's Vienna writings cannot be interpreted in Freudian terms. Canetti may be writing against Freud, but, because of this attitude, knowledge of Freud should be the premise rather than the substance of any analysis.

Looking at the poetic use of fire symbolism in ideological terms, Stieg tackles, among others, the Weininger virus, and exposes hostility to Jews and women even in Kraus and Doderer. Just as Schiller discriminates against women in his fear of revolutionary fire in 'Das Lied von der Glocke' ('Women become hyenas'), reactionary Austria treats the masses in revolt as feminine.

Another of the many surprises in Stieg's book is his impressive analysis of Freud's reaction to the events of 15 July, a reaction which has not previously received comment.

It need hardly be said that this reviewer does not share Stieg's sympathetic view of the glib and opportunistic Doderer. Reference may be made, in this connection, not only to the excellent analyses of Doderer in this book but to the article 'At Random in Vienna' (*Times Literary Supplement*, 20 April 1973) and to Doderer's own sketch of his life, cheerfully encouraging the Fascists in Berlin, which Stieg has procured from the Berlin Document Centre and reproduces on pages 216–27.

We have been waiting for a long time for an Austrian Germanist to write such a book. In France, where Stieg teaches, the local tradition of German studies tended until recently to treat psychoanalytic and sociological approaches with perhaps undue caution. By combining both, this book represents a landmark, not only in the study of Austrian literature, but also in German studies as practised in France.

JÜRGEN THÖMING

Jill Lewis, *Fascism and the Working Class in Austria 1918–1934* (Providence, RI and Oxford: Berg, 1991), x + 236 pp., £32.50.

The history of Austria between the collapse of the Habsburg monarchy and the German invasion has long been dominated by a consensus, which has depicted a largely helpless new state, dogged by intractable political and economic problems, before finally succumbing to Nazi aggression. Discussion of the First Republic's internal political conflicts has been limited (primarily, one feels, in order to avoid reopening old wounds). This book challenges a number of received ideas about the period. The main focus is on Styria, and this in itself is something of a corrective to the preoccupation with 'Red Vienna' in histories of this period. Dr Lewis confronts a number of thorny issues. Historians, like contemporary Viennese socialists, have chosen to overlook the apparently high level of support for fascism in industrial Upper Styria, a phenomenon which requires some explanation. Of course, high levels of unemployment enabled employers to discriminate in favour of members of the so-called 'independent' unions, sponsored by the Heimwehr, effectively coercing them into a fascist organisation. But that is only a part of the explanation. If the leadership of the Social Democratic Party (SDAP) had been less preoccupied with Vienna, the erosion of the provincial party organisations might have been avoided, and fascism more effectively opposed.

The achievements of the SDAP in Red Vienna appear in a more critical light than has hitherto been the case. If the party initially sought to turn the city into 'living propaganda' which would win over the national electorate, then this was a strategy that failed. Instead, employers and landlords, the Viennese bourgeoisie and the Catholic peasantry outside the capital were all antagonised by what they perceived to be reckless Socialist experimentation and the threat of Bolshevik dictatorship. The common political agenda they shared scarcely needed to be articulated as such by the parties of the right: the Christian Social party was prepared to co-operate with anybody to keep the SDAP out of power nationally, and when the SDAP threatened to win a parliamentary majority even so, parliament was suspended. Developments in Austria are sufficiently close to those elsewhere to justify Dr Lewis's characterisation of the indigenous dictatorship which destroyed Austrian democracy four years before the Anschluss as a 'distinct form of Austro-fascism'. This book not only makes a contribution to our understanding of Austria between the wars; it also contributes to our understanding of the emergence and development of fascism as a generic phenomenon.

TIM KIRK

Edith Prost (ed.), *'Die Partei hat mich nie enttäuscht...': Österreichische Sozialdemokratinnen*, Österreichische Texte zur Sozialkritik 41 (Vienna: Verlag für Gesellschaftskritik, 1989), vi + 343 pp., 298 Sch./DM 43.

This book is a collection of biographical essays exploring the lives of eight women socialists, all of whom became members of the National Assembly in the Austrian

Republic(s). The first six, Adelheid Popp, Anna Boschek, Emmy Freundlich, Therese Schlesinger, Gabriele Proft and Amalie Seidel, pioneered the campaign for women's rights in the final years of the Habsburg Monarchy. In the First Republic their energies were channelled into social reform. Maria Emhart was a defendant in the 1936 trial of Revolutionary Socialists and Hilda Krones belonged to the radical wing of the Social Democratic Party after the Second World War. According to the editor, the purpose of the book is to examine the role which women played in the Social Democratic Party and so plug a gap in SDAP/SPÖ historiography, which has been an exclusively male terrain. In addition to this, each contributor provides both a private and a political biography of her subject. The aim is laudable, but the task is too great for this format. Many of the articles are packed with details, but the private histories are romanticised and the political analysis is often naive. The result is an uneven and unfocused set of articles, some of which fail to address common issues and some of which overlap confusingly.

The first four articles concentrate on the years before the First World War, when women socialists fought a battle on two fronts. On the one hand there was the law. Article 30 of the Association Law (Vereinsgesetz) barred women from membership of political parties. Those women who rose to powerful positions within the labour movement did so through the trade unions (Boschek), the Party press (Popp) or the co-operative movement (Freundlich). Even here they met resistance. Trade union leaders blocked the establishment of women's organisations and Party leaders concurred, warning of the dangers of 'separatism'. The campaign to extend the franchise to workers, which succeeded in 1907, did not include the call for votes for women. The class struggle was the dominant struggle and all other struggles were deviations. Nor was there consensus among the women. When the Party Fathers finally submitted and sanctioned the Conference of Socialist Women (Frauenreichskonferenz) in 1898 (responding to an initiative by the Christian Social Party rather than the campaign mounted by Socialist women), Boschek supported the official line that membership should be limited to women trade unionists. The dissenters responded by setting up the Union of Seamstresses (Gewerkschaft der Näherinnen), open to all women who could use a needle.

The story of the fight for recognition of women's rights within the Party is fascinating, but difficult to untangle in the context of these individual biographies. The book lacks an introduction outlining the birth and demise of the women's organisations and the internal arguments. Details can be found in the articles by Regina Köpl and Marina Tichy, but even these cover only part of the story and the reader is left to fit the pieces together. Few explanations are given. This may be a consequence of the source material favoured by the contributors, who rely heavily on memoirs and Party publications. The strength and the weakness of the SDAP/SPÖ lay in unity. Public criticism, even years after the event, was severely discouraged.

The later articles provide less information on the position of women within the Party and less personal information, with the exception of Doris Ingrisch's study of Hilde Krones. But by this time the point of the book has been lost. This reader finished the book still asking why these women were not more disappointed by the Party.

JILL LEWIS

Johann Holzner, Sigurd Paul Scheichl and Wolfgang Wiesmüller (eds), *Eine schwierige Heimkehr: Österreichische Literatur im Exil 1938–1945*, Innsbrucker Beiträge zur Kulturwissenschaft, Germanistische Reihe 40 (Innsbruck: Institut für Germanistik, 1991), 406 pp., 654 Sch.

Peter Muhr, Paul Feyerabend and Cornelia Wegeler (eds), *Philosophie, Psychoanalyse, Emigration: Festschrift für Kurt Rudolf Fischer zum 70. Geburtstag* (Vienna: WUV-Universitätsverlag, 1992), 488 pp.

Eine schwierige Heimkehr brings together, with the now almost customary delay, the papers presented at an international symposium in the University of Innsbruck in 1988. Only two of the talks given have not been included, that by Alfred Doppler on the exile situation in Horváth's late plays, focusing on 'Ein Dorf ohne Männer', which has been published separately in the author's *Geschichte im Spiegel der Literatur* (Innsbruck, 1990), and Konstantin Kaiser's critical comments on literary theory in the post-war period, which is being developed into a full-scale study. Those already familiar with Exile Studies will be pleased to see papers from the leading scholars in the field: Ernst Loewy, Michael Winkler, Peter Eppel, Guy Stern, and many more. While attempting to give a comprehensive picture of research since the Vienna Conference of 1975, the Innsbruck Conference concentrates, as the title suggests, on problems which faced not only individual authors in exile deciding whether or not to return to Austria after 1945, but the general problem of the integration of exile literature into the accepted canon. Many authors in exile were either socialists or left-wing radicals; many were Jewish; all seem to have encountered similar difficulties, even such outstanding figures as Stefan Zweig, who, as Klaus Zelewitz shows, remained *persona non grata* in Austria after 1945.

In his keynote address Ernst Loewy takes the famous Brecht poem 'Gedanken über die Dauer des Exils' as his point of departure to question conventional time-limits, as the year 1945 was the end of forced emigration for many but not the end of exile. In addition, he argues that particular focus on the limited period 1933–45 has directed attention almost exclusively towards anti-Fascist literature and obscured the significance of Holocaust literature. Michael Winkler, by contrast, examines Hermann Broch, Manès Sperber and Elias Canetti, who did not return to Austria, but who did try indirectly to influence its cultural and political revival. Despite great international recognition their works failed completely to establish a new tradition. Richard Thieberger presents Oskar Jellinek, Hermann Broch, Johann Urzidil and Fritz Hochwälder as examples of 'the impossible return'. In his paper Felix Kreissler attempts to establish a typology of 'non-return': writers murdered by the Nazis (Adolf Unger, Heinrich Steinitz, Leo Grünstein, Emil Alphons Rheinhardt); writers who died early in exile (Joseph Roth, Guido Zernatto); writers unwilling to return to a country still unaware of the injustice done to them (Fritz Brainin, Ernst Waldinger, Erich Fried, Joseph Kalmer).

In the second section of this volume the focus shifts from general problems of integration or return to exile organisations and their activities. Of particular interest to British readers will be the paper by the Nestor of Exile Studies in Great Britain, Herbert Steiner, who from his own personal experience is able to report on the cultural activities of the Free Austrian Movement in Great Britain and support his comments with documentary material (the only illustrations in this book). This is a useful reminder of the sheer size and scope of the group, which had its own printing and publishing facilities. Erich Fried, an active participator, was first published in this way. Herbert Exenberger's paper deals with organisations coping with socialist authors in exile in Czechoslovakia, America and Britain. Fritz Brügel, Marianne Pollak and other socialists have not, so far, attracted the attention of British researchers, but Theodor Kramer, a long-term resident in London and one of the few to return to Austria, is now increasingly recognised as a major poet. In general, organisations in the United States like the 'American Guild for German Cultural Freedom' and the 'Deutsche Akademie' in exile, or the *Austro-American Tribune* (as Helmut F. Pfanner shows, 'the voice of a free democratic Austria'), have enjoyed a higher profile than similar or even more significant British exile associations and newspapers. There is still no extensive study of the Austrian newspaper *Der Zeitspiegel* and its circulation in Great Britain.

The final section of this symposium volume is devoted to individual authors of both sexes and it has to be said that, for all the desirability of rescuing authors like Csokor, Ernst Lothar and Ludwig Ullmann from oblivion, the life and works of Lili Körber, Lotte Lenya and Hermynia zur Mühlen are really more deserving of rediscovery. In recent years the case-history of Hermynia zur Mühlen and the transformation from her original persona as Gräfin Folliot de Crenneville-Pontet into one of the most outstanding left-wing radicals of her generation has been variously chronicled. Of particular interest to British readers once again is the fact that for her latter years till her death in 1951, she lived and wrote in English in England. While Hermynia zur Mühlen has been remembered, Anna Gmeyner remained completely forgotten until rediscovered recently, still alive and still writing, although she has since died. Heide Klapdor-Kops, in a magnificent essay with the title 'Eine Heimkehr, die noch stattzufinden hat', reminds her readers of this authoress, who was brilliantly successful in the Weimar Republic with her play *Heer ohne Helden* based on the 1926 miners' strikes in Scotland, which she had personally observed. Anna Gmeyner, otherwise Anna Reiner or Anna Morduch, became a prolific writer in exile in Great Britain, where she worked on films with Berthold Viertel, changed from dramatic to narrative forms, and, most importantly, changed language from German to English.

Essays of this quality make *Eine schwierige Heimkehr* essential reading, not only for those already interested in the problems of exile, but for all those seriously interested in Austria and its literature.

A distinguished Austrian exile has just been honoured by a Festschrift on his seventieth birthday. Kurt Rudolf Fischer was born in Vienna in 1922. By 1938 he found himself forced to flee from Austria and like many others made his way to Shanghai. He survived this experience of exile and managed to get to the United States where he was able to enrol as a student at Berkeley at the age of 27. At St John's University, Shanghai, he had already started to study philosophy, psychology and German. He completed his BA at Berkeley and successfully proceeded to an MA in German in 1952. His doctorate on Franz Brentano's philosophy of evidence was not to be completed till twelve years later. Fischer taught philosophy at the University of California in Davis, in Berkeley, at Mills College (Oakland, California), at Harvard, at City University of New York, and at the Millersville University of Pennsylvania, where he was Head of Department for ten years. He also taught at Franklin and Marshall College (Lancaster, Pa.). In 1979 he returned to Vienna as Fulbright Research Scholar and as Fulbright Professor, and later became guest professor and honorary professor at the University of Vienna.

One result of Fischer's unusual career becomes evident to even the most casual reader dipping into this volume of essays, for his combination of the Anglo-American approach to philosophy and the quite different Austrian tradition is clearly reflected in the sheer scale of the essays for him from friends and colleagues, young and old, from both sides of the Atlantic. Professor Fischer was from the start of his academic career deeply involved not only in philosophical but also in psychological issues, a passion reflected in his work with the ÖAGG, the Österreichischer Arbeitskreis für Gruppentherapie und Gruppendynamik. This psychoanalytic area too is strongly reflected in the themes of the essays collected in this volume. By contrast, some readers may be disappointed to find comparatively little reflection of Fischer's interests as a Germanist; in fact only one essay, 'Eros und Apperception in Heimito von Doderers *Tangenten*', by David Luft, is directly related to Austro-German literature. But, apart from this, the range is broad, extending from sociology (football games in Vienna) to matters associated with National Socialism and exile, from Nietzsche and Neurath to Heidegger and Wittgenstein, and from there to an essay by Ruth Wodak: 'Die Sprache derer, die keine Antisemiten sein wollen'. This volume can be warmly recommended both as a fitting tribute to a great survivor of exile and re-migration and as a stimulating collection of essays in its own right.

J. M. RITCHIE

Malcolm Pines and Roy Wisbey (eds), 'Translation in Transition: the Question of the Standard Edition', *The International Review of Psycho-Analysis*, 1991, vol. 18, part 3, pp. 321–461 (London: Routledge), $44.00.

This journal is not a book: it will be difficult reading for a person who is not already informed about the kinds of problems that come up when one tries to translate Freud because it is a miscellaneous collection of observations and ongoing arguments about the British *Standard Edition* of Freud's psychoanalytic works. Some of this material has been published before, and several of these articles grew out of papers read at a 1989 conference in London.

The publishers of the *Standard Edition* (1953–66) have relatively few sets of these books left in stock. In this issue, they describe their present plans. Instead of beginning the enormous task of actually revising, they have decided to reprint Strachey's edition with minor corrections while inserting a few of the works missing from their edition. Because they feel that Strachey's text 'cannot be tampered with' and, perhaps more reasonably, because they contend that his page numbers must be preserved for reference and teaching, they will restrict themselves to putting a few of Freud's original German words in wider margins. However, they will do that only when what they regard as 'Strachey's equivalent' term strikes them as technical and problematical or controversial (pp. 459–60) and worthy of discussion in their German–English glossary. Thus they will perpetuate Strachey's strategy, that is, singling out and setting apart certain German words in selected contexts as designated technical terms. The same words in other contexts will again be translated variously.

Many serious students of the work Strachey's team produced regard Freud's discourse (the formal expression of his ideas) as more than fine scientific writing. We have begun to comprehend many rather intricate compositions including an engaging personal prosody (the rhythmic qualities of language), plays on those patterns of sound, ingenious nets of word stems, evocative imagery that vividly pictures his conceptions, turns on catch phrases, subtle allusions, and so on. We believe that Freud's meaning is often ambiguous or explicitly contradictory because he is simultaneously describing his own conceptions of several levels of simultaneous psychic activity and experience. Obviously these creations will cause a word-for-word translator some difficulty.

In this issue the editors claim once again that their *Standard Edition* is 'authorised' and 'complete' (neither of which is true), and now they will also call it 'revised'. Riccardo Steiner's characteristically combative contribution is much longer than any of the others and is mostly about British psychoanalytic politics with opinions on the translation of a few disputed terms. He argues, once again, that had Freud lived long enough he would have approved of the *Standard Edition*. Steiner further documents, but does not explain, the near-absolute power accorded by the British to Ernest Jones and his bewildering control over Strachey's scientific lexicon. Help is on the way: editions of Freud's correspondence with Jones, Joan Riviere, Sandor Ferenczi (a French edition) and Ludwig Binswanger may all be published before the end of 1993.

Strachey believed he could roughly match the schooling and scholarship of his own, and now famous, imaginary English author to the education and reading Freud obtained. Harald Leupold-Löwenthal and Sander Gilman show why this is impossible. Gilman clarifies some turn-of-the-century Austrian Jewish traditions, and traditional Austrian anti-Semitism, that may have influenced Freud's style in ways which would be inaccessible to Strachey. Agreeing that a new English Freud is absolutely necessary and that this must be based on a new German Freud, Gilman favors a programme much like that of the French team now producing the first ever *Œuvres complètes*. He believes a working German edition could be produced within a decade.

Jean Laplanche sketches the way his heterogeneous team is now producing the first ever *Œuvres complètes* and gives examples that will enlighten any person who has a working knowledge of French, German and English. Applying Walter

Benjamin's classic study of translation, he shows how through this very process one may gain a singular understanding of the linguistic resources and complexities Freud exploited, and then may stretch and enrich the target language in order to bring over more of what Freud had to say. Instead of imagining Freud as a French author and scientist, these translators have conceived what they describe as 'Freudian French'. Laplanche's team is translating for a reader who wants to reach into the murky, personally disturbing, unconscious life of Freud's own conception.

Laplanche suggests that Freud's *Nachträglichkeit* is crucial for an understanding of Freud's frequent simile between psychoanalysis and translation. In the elegant last paragraph of his early paper on 'Screen Memories' or 'Cover Memories' (*Deckerinnerungen*, 1899), Freud said that although it is easier to talk about memories *from* childhood, it is much more probable that we can do no more than consciously remember *about* childhood and that what we loosely call 'memories' are really developed as they become conscious. Actual memories may appear to 'turn up', but it is more accurate to say that a whole series of modern motives which have little use for historical truth influence both their selection and their development.

Martin Stanton gives a choice example from Freud's typical self-analysis of a day-dream which he had mistaken for a memory. Because nothing is postponed at the time of a present and then subsequently remembered event, 'subsequent supplementary response' (Patrick Mahony), 'retrospective attribution' (Arnold Modell) or something like 'reconstrual after the event' (Thomä and Cheshire) would carry more of Freud's '*Nachträglichkeit*' over into English. Helmut Thomä and Neil Cheshire go into exquisite detail about this idea, which Strachey so often (and mistakenly) translated into 'deferred action'.

In a second essay, the same authors argue that Freud really was a positivist in Bernfeld's (1944) sense, that therefore Strachey could not have imbued Freud with a *false* 'air of positivism' (p. 434), that Freud's admitted flexibility of language was unintentional (p. 449), and indeed, that Strachey 'explicitly set his face against the idea of the translator trying to tidy up the original ...' (p. 446). All of this is debatable and will not be settled for a long time. Thomä and Cheshire do recognise that Bernfeld's famous paper, 'Freud's Earliest Theories and the School of Helmholtz', is a simplifying artefact of the metapsychological era in psychoanalysis (pp. 434–6) and that Freud was a master of descriptive language – 'The characteristic of real science is *variety*' – and that Strachey made one of his rare, outright, and portentous mistakes in asserting that he had not tidied up, had withheld his own theoretical opinions, and had steadfastly square-bracketed or footnoted all of his own modifications in order to deliver 'Freud, the whole of Freud, and nothing but Freud'. Strachey made that uncharacteristic and bewildering boast after having finished his entire *Standard Edition*. Surely he knew better.

Cheshire and Thomä are among those who would defend Strachey from supposed detractors whom they accuse of proposing that 'what we accept as the Structural Theory is more Strachey's invention than Freud's', or sarcastically, that Strachey even 'invented Freud'. They put it that 'Strachey has been charged with a major felony', that is, betraying Freud. Such straw men are silly. They may serve polemically but most of those who have studied Strachey's work have nothing but respect for the man and awe at his undeniable accomplishments (Laplanche, Cotet, Bourguignon, Mahony, Holder, Villarreal, Junker, Gilman, and others). Even the arrogant and sentimental Bruno Bettelheim did not go quite that far. For example, Freud would never have claimed originality for what he preferred to call a tripartite 'topographical conception', because he was quite aware of precedent conceptual trinities like the demonic, mundane and sacred, or affect, reason and conscience.

Stanton shows how standards for scholarly translation have improved since Strachey's time and that Strachey's unfamiliarity with the scientific contexts of Janet, Grasset and Charcot distorted his understanding. Strachey tried to get on with the job in hand by not translating certain French expressions used by Freud, but this tidy tactic left both Strachey and his reader with no way to comprehend distinctions drawn in the original. Gilman says that Freud usually avoided foreign words when he wrote in German because a cosmopolitan Jew of his time would feel that one who lapses into a second language reveals an inadequate command of German. This makes Stanton's observation that, when Freud translated, he chose not to translate certain technical phrases from French into German, all the more meaningful.

DARIUS GRAY ORNSTON

Günther Feuerstein, *Visionäre Architektur: Wien 1958/1988* (Berlin: Ernst & Sohn, 1988), 296 pp., DM 96.

Peter Noever (ed.), *Tradition und Experiment: Das Österreichische Museum für Angewandte Kunst* (Salzburg: Residenz, 1988), 311 pp., 980 Sch./DM 140.

John Zukowsky and Ian Wardropper, *Austrian Architecture in the Nineties* (Berlin: Ernst & Sohn, 1991), 160 pp., DM 86.

It has long been recognised in Vienna that the driving force behind architectural progress is not reason, but fantasy. In his inaugural lecture, delivered to the Akademie der bildenden Künste in 1894, Otto Wagner challenged his final year students to transcend the restraints of cost and function:

> Den Schülern des 3. Jahrgangs empfehle ich die Lösung einer Aufgabe, welche im Leben wohl nie an Sie herantreten wird, deren Durchbildung aber dazu beitragen wird, den gottlichen Funken der Phantasie, der in Ihnen glimmen soll, zur leuchtenden Flamme anzufachen.

> [To the third-year students I recommend a task that will never confront them in real life, a task whose solution will serve to fan into bright flames the divine spark of fantasy that should be glowing within them.]

Taking the master at his word, the radical design partnership Coop Himmelblau suspended a tubular frame construction above the courtyard of the Technische Universitat, Graz, in 1988, turned on the gas that ran through the tubes, and lit a match. The blazing result – symbolising the group's motto 'Architektur muß brennen', 'Architecture must burn' – glows on the front cover of Günther Feuerstein's survey of architectural radicalism in Vienna over the thirty years 1958–88. As the author admits on the very first page: 'Diese Arbeit ist subjektiv. Diese Arbeit ist nicht vollständig – noch fehlt die historische Distanz.' [This work is subjective. This work is not comprehensive – the historical distance is still lacking.] It was, however, the historical distance from the flowering of architectural modernism in the 1920s that promoted the radical gestures of the early 1960s. While the modernist masters - Le Corbusier, Gropius, Mies van der Rohe – had offered inflexible, pseudo-rationalist strategies in a bid to improve the world through design, the generation of their grandchildren allowed themselves to doubt these functionalist certainties. As Fritz Hundertwasser's 'Verschimmelungsmanifest gegen den Rationalismus in der Architektur' [Mildew-manifesto against rationalism in architecture] proclaimed in 1958: 'Die funktionelle Architektur hat sich als Irrweg erwiesen, genauso wie die Malerei mit dem Lineal. Wir nähern uns mit Riesenschritten der unpraktischen, der unnutzbaren und schließlich der unbewohnbaren Architektur.' [Functionalist architecture has shown itself to be a mistake, just like painting with a ruler. With giant steps we are approaching an architecture that is impractical, unusable, even uninhabitable.] Reason was to be replaced by emotion, the tyranny of the set-square by the freedom of the curvaceous and capricious.

The epicentre of the architectural revolution was the Technische Hochschule in Vienna, where the leading non-conformist lights on the faculty were Karl Schwanzer and his assistant, Günther Feuerstein, with a student focus in the so-called 'Klubseminar', set up in 1963. Remarkably, the new, iconoclastic freedom of the 1960s expressed itself in a comparatively small range of motifs, which reappeared again and again in the radical projects of the 1960s. A list would include pneumatic structures, sphere-clusters reminiscent of DNA models, geodesic spaceframes, and mega-city structures into which the appropriate living and transportation elements could be inserted as desired. The little historical imagery that was admitted came not from the static Euclidean forms of 'Neues Bauen', but rather from the dynamic geometries of Italian Futurism and Soviet Constructivism. Running through all the various schemes was an insistence on impermanence and flexibility, on flux and movement. The house was equated with the motor car, the city – in Hans Hollein's most celebrated image – with the aircraft carrier. The language of impermanence was American English, the language of Kerouac, Ginsberg and Ferlinghetti. Flipping through Feuerstein's copious illustrations we find titles in a strange meta-language that hints, seductively, at a fully-automated life under the Californian sun: 'Pneumo-City', 'Mind Expander', 'Relaxing Room 68', 'Great Auto-Expander', 'Recreation Environment'.

The city of the future was the recurring context, and one given formal acknowledgement in the exhibition 'Urban Fiction', held in the Galerie nächst Sankt Stephan in Vienna in 1966, an exhibition that united all the radical forces then active in Austria: Feuerstein, Laurids Ortner, Hans Hollein, and Wolf-Dieter Prix, who together with Helmut Swiczinsky and Michael Holzer founded Coop Himmelblau in 1968. That an exhibition of avant-garde design, with edible exhibits, loud rock music and a riotous *vernissage*, could have been held in a gallery belonging to the Catholic Church says much about the liberalism of the Austrian church at that time. It is also, however, a measure of the social conservatism of the architectural radicals. While their contemporaries in late 1960s and early 1970s Berlin were on the streets fighting the police and the Springer Press, the radical Viennese groups like Haus-Rucker-Co and Coop Himmelblau were creating ingenious street furniture and giant inflatable footballs to celebrate the transformation of the Graben into a pedestrian zone. As the critic Friedrich Achleitner commented at the time: 'Das Reformerische, Neutönende ist weder aggressiv noch anklagend, auch nicht provozierend oder ironisch. Hier sind keine Weltverbesserer am Werk, sondern, wenn man will, Weltverschönerer.' [The reforming, new-sounding spirit is neither aggressive nor accusatory. There is no ambition to improve the world, but rather to make it more beautiful.] The ability to realise their projects, even if on a small scale, does, however, distinguish the Viennese groups of this period from their Anglo-American counterparts, whose projects remained on paper. One thinks of Haus-Rucker-Co's Oase Nr. 7 at the 1972 Kassel Documenta 5 – a giant transparent balloon housing a geodesic oasis – a theme picked up again by Hans Hollein in his interior for the offices of the Österreichisches Verkehrsbüro in Vienna, completed in 1978 and demolished ten years later. Writing in 1968, Hans Hollein proposed: 'Die Erweiterung des menschlichen Bereiches und der Mittel der Bestimmung der Um-"Welt" geht weit uber eine bauliche Feststellung hinaus. Heute wird gewissermaßen alles Architektur.' [The expansion of the human sphere and the means of determining the environment go far beyond built solutions. Everything today is, in a certain way, architecture.] Radical though this position may have seemed at the time in the more sedate groves of academe, this non-structural view of architecture actually had very respectable historical precedents, and ones which had found a particular resonance in Vienna in the nineteenth century.

Gottfried Semper penned his report on the 1851 Great Exhibition, held in the Crystal Palace in London, under the title *Wissenschaft, Industrie und Kunst*, and saw in the symbiosis of these three disciplines the way forward for architecture in particular and wider society in general. Implicit in this even-handed approach was the obliteration of the division between high and low culture, between the products of the academy and those necessary for the pursuit of daily life. In his subsequent writings, most notably *Die vier Elemente der Baukunst* (1851), Semper located the origins of architecture in the the ornamental 'Bekleidung' [cladding, dressing] of a simple wooden frame, elevated above a hearth. This theory implied not only that all the arts had a shared starting-point, but also that the 'art' of architecture had its origins not in structural science, but rather in ornamentation. This elevation of the decorative arts to a position of primacy found a direct echo in the establishment of national collections of applied art in the 1850s and 1860s, in the wake of the Great Exhibition. Keen to build a permanent institution on the success of the Great Exhibition, Prince Albert and Henry Cole established a Museum of Science and Art in Kensington, intended as a collection of exemplary works of applied art, which would then inform the educational programmes pursued in the school of design that was attached to the Museum. The Museum itself was initially housed in a glass and iron shed, the 'Brompton Boiler'. The example of the London museum led directly to the establishment in 1864 of the Museum für Kunst und Industrie in Vienna, with Rudolf von Eitelberger as its founding director. Eitelberger saw the Museum not only as a repository of admirable models and as a catalyst for future design, but also as a means of broadening local perceptions and horizons. He subsequently noted:

> Es gibt in Österreich eine Art von Lokalpatriotismus, der über die engsten Kreise der Beteiligten nicht hinausreicht und statt zu fördern, der Kunstbildung hemmend in den Weg tritt. Nirgendwo gibt es so viele Pessimisten, nirgendwo so viele Fremdenhasser und Selbstbewunderer als in Österreich.
>
> [There exists in Austria a sort of local patriotism that extends no further than the narrowest circle of protagonists, and instead of promoting artistic education stands inhibitingly in its way. Nowhere else are there so many pessimists, nowhere else so many xenophobes and self-admirers as in Austria.]

To mark the 125th anniversary of its foundation, Peter Noever – Director of the Museum since 1986 – has published a series of essays, under the title *Tradition und Experiment*. As the title suggests, the texts are devoted not only to the historical evolution of the institution, as housed after 1871 in Ludwig Ferstel's Italianate palace on the Stubenring, but also to a discussion of what relevance such a collection might possibly have in the age of computer graphics and virtual realities. This beautifully produced book acts, therefore, not only as a record of an institution that peaked in the golden days of the Wiener Werkstätte and had become moribund in more recent years, but also as a forum for discussion on the role of the Museum, and even as a manifesto for future action. By a happy coincidence, Noever appears as an artist in Feuerstein's book, where he is represented by an earth-art work called 'Die Grube'. Combining as its principal elements a circular enclosure surround by an earth mound, approached by a long, white, ritual walkway, 'Die Grube' is praised by Feuerstein as 'eine exemplare Verwirklichung einer zweckfreien Architektur, die gleichwohl die 'archetypischen' Aspekte bis an den Rand der erotischen Symbolik überzeugend vorträgt' [an exemplary realisation of a functionless architecture, which nevertheless manages to convey convincingly the 'archetypical' quality almost to the point of erotic symbolism]. This ability of architecture to support intellectual discourses that go far beyond the mere provision of shelter was used further by Noever in his strategy for the revival of the Museum. Indeed, architecture provided the dominant theme for the exhibitions and symposia arranged in the early years of the new administration, beginning in 1986 with an exhibition on the work of the early modernist Rudolf Schindler, who built in Los Angeles after training in Vienna. The Schindler exhibition was followed in the same year by 'Wiener Bauplätze', an exhibition in which thirteen building sites in the city were documented in their historical and current states, with the work of the crassest commercial designers given the same prominence as the projects of the avant-garde. The Semperian theory of cladding resurfaced in a third exhibition of the same year, 'The Heavy Dress – Die Oberflächlichkeit als Manifest', which proposed, among other things, new clothes for old skyscrapers. The most striking of the architectural exhibitions, however, and that which offered a completely fresh strategy for the display of architectural production, was held in 1988 and devoted to Günther Domenig's 'Steinhaus'. As the leading figure in the architectural revival centred on Graz, Domenig produced the first sketches for his own house, the 'Steinhaus', in 1986.

Still under construction, the house has become the concrete realisation of Domenig's theoretical engagement with such antipodal notions as 'Natürlichkeit' and 'Künstlichkeit', 'Natur' and 'Kopf', 'Innenwelt' and 'Außenwelt'. The exhibition in the Museum für angewandte Kunst included not only the conventional sketches, models, plans and photographs of the building, but also elements of the structure later to be incorporated into the 'Steinhaus' itself, and a live TV link documenting the construction process. These various elements combined, in Noever's words, to give 'die authentische Darstellung eines Prozesses, dessen Anspruch und Kraft auch noch in der Präsentation vehement spurbar bleibt' [the authentic depiction of a process, whose demands and power still remain vehemently perceptible even in the presentation]. A model of the 'Steinhaus', whose external circulation scheme carries distinct echoes of Noever's 'Grube', is included among the 125 objects from the Museum's collection that are reproduced in lavish full-page colour photographs.

The dynamic relationship between Viennese tradition and current practice was the theme of an exhibition held at the Art Institute of Chicago in 1991. Although the subtitle of the catalogue points to a world *Beyond Tradition in the 1990s*, the great majority of the high-quality illustrations are devoted to architectural and design production in the 1980s. It thus provides 'das Happy-End' to the experimental phase of the 1960s and '70s, as documented by Feuerstein. Instead of pathos-laden manifestos and wildly unrealisable fantasies we find the same architects and designers producing buildable, inhabitable space. Yet the twin theoretical piers of architectural delight unconstrained by function, and dynamic structure frozen – as it were – at a single moment in space, still survive in many of the recent schemes: in Domenig's extension to the Funder factory in St Veit, for example; in Coop Himmelblau's intervention on Melrose Avenue in Los Angeles; or in Szyszkowitz/Kowalski's Biotechnical Institute at the University of Graz. In breaking free from static and monumental expectations, architecture invests itself with a precious, hand-crafted, almost jewel-like quality, while revealing the possibility, for example, of monumental jewellery. This particularly Viennese quality, characterised by Feuerstein as a 'coincidentia oppositorum', is well illustrated on the back cover of the Chicago catalogue: a Bösendorfer grand piano designed by Hans Hollein in the manner reminiscent of the retro interiors in the Haas-Haus on Stock-im-Eisen Platz.

IAIN BOYD WHYTE

Notes on Contributors

T. C. W. BLANNING is Professor of European History at Cambridge University. His books include *Reform and Revolution in Mainz, 1743–1803* (Cambridge University Press, 1974) and *The French Revolution in Germany* (Oxford University Press, 1983).

SRDAN BOGOSAVLJEVIĆ is a Lecturer in German at the University of Belgrade. His *Robert Musil: Duh i utopija* (Mind and Utopia) is in press.

T. E. BOURKE is Senior Lecturer in German at University College Galway. His publications include *Stilbruch als Stilmittel: Studien zur Literatur der Spät- und Nachromantik* (1980) and articles on many topics including contemporary Austrian and German poetry.

PETER BRANSCOMBE is Professor of Austrian Studies at St Andrews University. His most recent book is *Mozart: 'Die Zauberflöte'* in the Cambridge Opera Handbooks series (1991).

TIM CARTER is Reader in Music at Royal Holloway and New Bedford College London. His books include a study of Mozart's *Le nozze di Figaro* in the Cambridge Opera Handbooks series (1987).

R. J. W. EVANS is Professor of European History at Oxford University, and the author of *Rudolf II and his World: A Study in Intellectual History, 1576–1612* (Oxford University Press, 1973) and *The Making of the Habsburg Monarchy, 1550–1770* (Oxford University Press, 1979).

ALLYSON FIDDLER is a Lecturer in German at University College of Swansea. Her doctoral thesis, 'Rewriting Reality: Elfriede Jelinek and the Politics of Representation' (Southampton, 1990), is to be published by Berg.

KONSTANZE FLIEDL is Assistant in the German Department at Vienna University. Her edition of the correspondence between Arthur Schnitzler and Richard Beer-Hofmann has recently been published by Europa-Verlag.

IAN FOSTER is a Lecturer in German at Salford University, and author of *The Image of the Habsburg Army in Austrian Prose Fiction 1888 to 1914* (Peter Lang, 1992).

R. S. FURNESS is Professor of German at the University of St Andrews. His publications include *Wagner and Literature* (Manchester University Press, 1982) and (with Malcolm Humble) *A Companion to Twentieth-Century German Literature* (Routledge, 1991).

KLAUS-PETER HINZE is Professor of German and Comparative Literature at Cleveland State University.

IAN HUISH teaches German part-time at Westminster School, London. He has published a study of Ödön von Horváth, editions of several Horváth plays, and articles on Soyfer, Mann and Härtling.

Notes on Contributors

LOUISE ADEY HUISH teaches German at Lincoln College, Oxford. She has published numerous articles on nineteenth-century German and Austrian literature, and is preparing two plays for publication in the new historical-critical edition of Nestroy.

CHARLES INGRAO is Professor of History at Purdue University. His books include *In Quest and Crisis: Emperor Joseph I and the Habsburg Monarchy* (Purdue University Press, 1979) and *The Hessian Mercenary State* (Cambridge University Press, 1987).

TIMOTHY KIRK is a Lecturer in History at the University of Northumbria. He is currently working on urban popular culture in the Habsburg Empire.

DUNCAN LARGE is a Lecturer in German at University College of Swansea. He recently completed an Oxford D. Phil. thesis on Musil, Proust and Nietzsche.

LEO A. LENSING is Professor of German at Wesleyan University, Middletown, Connecticut, and author of a study of Wilhelm Raabe. He is at work on a biography of Karl Kraus.

JACQUES LE RIDER (University of Paris V – Saint-Denis) is the author of *Modernité viennoise et crises de l'identité* (Presses Universitaires de France, 1990), an English translation of which is due from Polity Press.

JILL LEWIS is a Lecturer in History at University College of Swansea and the author of *Fascism and the Working Class in Austria* (Berg, 1991).

DENIS MCCALDIN is a conductor and musicologist. He is Director of Music at Lancaster University and President of the Haydn Society of Great Britain.

RALPH MANHEIM, who died in 1992 aged eighty-five, was the outstanding translator of his generation, particularly noted for his translations of Brecht, Grass and Handke. With characteristic generosity he refused to accept any fee for the articles which he translated for *Austrian Studies*.

JOHN MILFULL is Professor of German and Dean of the Faculty of Arts and Social Sciences at the University of New South Wales. He has recently edited *The Attractions of Fascism: Social Psychology and Aesthetics of the 'Triumph of the Right'* (Berg, 1990) and *Why Germany? National Socialist Anti-Semitism and the European Context* (Berg, 1992).

DARIUS GRAY ORNSTON, Jr, is the editor of *Translating Freud* (Yale University Press, 1992). He is Chairman of the Department of Psychiatry at the Marshall I. Pickens Hospital and the Greenville Hospital System, and teaches at both the Medical University of South Carolina and the University of South Carolina School of Medicine in Columbia, South Carolina.

J. M. RITCHIE is Emeritus Professor of German at Aberdeen University. He has published numerous studies and translations, mostly of twentieth-century German literature, including *German Literature under National Socialism* (Croom Helm, 1983). He is now working on a study of German and Austrian exiles in Great Britain.

SIMON RYAN is Lecturer in German at the University of Otago, New Zealand. His Cambridge Ph. D. thesis on 'Gerhard Roth and the Graz Literary Revival' is about to be published.

Notes on Contributors

WENDELIN SCHMIDT-DENGLER is Professor of German at Vienna University. His many studies of Austrian literature range from Raimund and Nestroy to Doderer and Bernhard.

J. P. STERN, who died in 1991, was Emeritus Professor of German at University College London. His many books include *Re-interpretations: Seven Studies in Nineteenth-Century German Literature* (1964; reissued by Cambridge University Press, 1981), *Hitler: The Führer and the People* (Fontana, 1975), and *The Heart of Europe: Essays on Literature and Ideology* (Blackwell, 1992).

JÜRGEN THÖMING is Professor at the University of Osnabrück (Abteilung Vechta) and has published numerous studies of Musil and his contemporaries.

JOHN WARREN teaches German at Oxford Brookes University. He is co-editor, with Kenneth Segar, of *Austria in the Thirties: Culture and Politics* (Ariadne Press, 1990).

EWAN WEST is Research Fellow in Music at Mansfield College, Oxford. He has recently completed a study of the Viennese *Lied*.

IAIN BOYD WHYTE is Director of the Centre for Architectural History and Theory at Edinburgh University.

W. E. YATES is Professor of German at Exeter University. His books include *Grillparzer* and *Nestroy* (both published by Cambridge University Press in 1972) and *Schnitzler and Hofmannsthal* (Yale University Press, 1992), and he is one of the editors of the new edition of Nestroy.

Austrian Studies

Acknowledgements: The Editors gratefully acknowledge the support of the Austrian Institute in London. Thanks are also due to the colleagues listed below for their willingness to serve on the Advisory Board.

Advisory Board; Andrew Barker (Edinburgh), Peter Branscombe (St Andrews), Amy D. Colin (Pittsburgh), R. J. W. Evans (Oxford), Sander L. Gilman (Cornell), Murray G. Hall (Vienna), Leo A. Lensing (Wesleyan), Eda Sagarra (Dublin), W. G. Sebald (East Anglia), Joseph Peter Strelka (New York), Robert Wistrich (Jerusalem), W. E. Yates (Exeter).

Books for review should be sent to Ritchie Robertson, St John's College, Oxford OX1 3JP, England.

Manuscipts for publication should be submitted in duplicate to Edward Timms, Arts Building, University of Sussex, Brighton BN1 9QN, England.

Guidelines: Articles should be written in English and should not exceed 7,500 words. They should be typed double-spaced, using endnotes (not a numbered bibliography) to identify the source of quotations. Quotations should normally be given in the original language, followed by an English translation. A detailed style sheet is available from either of the Editors, on request.

Austrian Studies may be ordered through any bookshop. Since it is designed as an annual publication, it may also be obtained by subscription direct from the publishers, Edinburgh University Press, 22 George Square, Edinburgh EH8 9LF, Scotland.